Sport and the Military

On battleships, behind the trenches of the Western Front and in the midst of the Desert War, British servicemen and -women have played sport in the least promising circumstances. When 400 soldiers were asked in Burma in 1946 what they liked about the army, 108 put sport in first place – well ahead of comradeship and leave – and this book explores the fascinating history of organised sport in the life of officers and other ranks in all three British services from 1880 to 1960. Drawing on a wide range of sources, the book examines how organised sport developed in the Victorian army and navy, became the focus of criticism for Edwardian army reformers and was officially adopted during the Great War to boost morale and *esprit de corps*. It shows how the services adapted to the influx of professional sportsmen, especially footballers, during the Second World War and the National Service years, and how sport helped to bridge the gap between civilians and the military.

TONY MASON is Professor Emeritus at the International Centre for Sport History and Culture at De Montfort University, Leicester.

ELIZA RIEDI is Lecturer in Imperial History at the University of Leicester.

'Athletes' – the sportsmen of the 1st Battalion King's Own Royal Regiment pose in the local photographer's studio, Aldershot 1901.

SPORT AND THE MILITARY

The British Armed Forces 1880–1960

Tony Mason and Eliza Riedi

CAMBRIDGE UNIVERSITY PRESS

CAMBRIDGE UNIVERSITY PRESS
Cambridge, New York, Melbourne, Madrid, Cape Town, Singapore,
São Paulo, Delhi, Dubai, Tokyo, Mexico City

Cambridge University Press
The Edinburgh Building, Cambridge CB2 8RU, UK

Published in the United States of America by Cambridge University Press, New York

www.cambridge.org
Information on this title: www.cambridge.org/9780521700740

© Tony Mason and Eliza Riedi 2010

This publication is in copyright. Subject to statutory exception
and to the provisions of relevant collective licensing agreements,
no reproduction of any part may take place without the written
permission of Cambridge University Press.

First published 2010

Printed in the United Kingdom at the University Press, Cambridge

A catalogue record for this publication is available from the British Library

Library of Congress Cataloguing in Publication data
Mason, Tony.
  Sport and the military : the British armed forces 1880–1960 /
Tony Mason, Eliza Riedi.
    p. cm.
  Includes index.
  ISBN 978-0-521-87714-5 (hardback) – ISBN 978-0-521-70074-0 (pbk.)
  1. Great Britain–Armed Forces–Sports–History–19th century.
  2. Great Britain–Armed Forces–Sports–History–20th century.
  3. Military sports–Great Britain–History–19th century. 4. Military sports–Great Britain–History–19th century. I. Riedi, Eliza. II. Title.
  U328.G7M37 2010
  355.1'2–dc22
                                                    2010033571

ISBN 978-0-521-87714-5 Hardback
ISBN 978-0-521-70074-0 Paperback

Cambridge University Press has no responsibility for the persistence or accuracy of URLs for external or third-party internet websites referred to in this publication, and does not guarantee that any content on such websites is, or will remain, accurate or appropriate.

Contents

	List of illustrations	*page* vi
	Acknowledgements	viii
	Introduction	1
1	The growth of service sport, 1880–1914	15
2	Officer sports and their critics, 1880–1914	50
3	Sport in the Great War	80
4	The amateur era, 1919–39	112
5	Soldiers, sailors and civilians	144
6	A different kind of war	178
7	The national service years: the summit of military sport?	217
	Conclusion	253
	Select bibliography	264
	Index	283

List of illustrations

'Athletes. 1st Battalion King's Own Royal Regiment, Aldershot 1901'. Courtesy of the King's Own Royal Regiment Museum, Lancaster. *page* ii

1. 'Brigade of Guards boxing at Chelsea', *Illustrated Sporting and Dramatic News*, 5 March 1898. Courtesy of Cambridge University Library. 20
2. 'Leicestershire Regiment Rugby XV, winners of the 1910–11 Army Rugby Cup', ref. DE5834/36. Courtesy of The Record Office for Leicestershire, Leicester and Rutland. 24
3. 'An inter-regimental football match at Murree, 1896', National Army Museum, Negative Number 27756. Courtesy of the Council of the National Army Museum, London. 36
4. 'Royal Irish Fusiliers football team (1906–7) including Captain R. J. Kentish', *Faugh-a-Ballagh* 6 (1907). Courtesy of the Royal Irish Fusiliers Museum. 45
5. 'The Staff of a Kadir Cup' from Major A. E. Wardrop, *Modern Pig-sticking* (1914). 58
6. 'Polo: The Irish Subalterns' Cup', *Navy and Army Illustrated* 2 (1896), 254. 64
7. 'Boxing tournament organised by the Grand Fleet, July 1918', IWM Q 19867. Courtesy of The Trustees of the Imperial War Museum, London. 92
8. 'Football Final of the 48th Divisional (Fanshawe) Cup, Trissino, Italy, 1918', IWM Q 26357. Courtesy of The Trustees of the Imperial War Museum, London. 95
9. 'Physical and Bayonet Training Headquarters Staff, St Pol, 1917'. Reproduced by kind permission of the Army Physical Training Corps Museum. 105
10. 'The Army Isn't ALL Work', IWM PST 7686. Courtesy of The Trustees of the Imperial War Museum, London. 126

List of illustrations

11. 'Sergeant J. Hart', *The Oak Tree* 31 (1946). Courtesy of The Mercian Regiment (Cheshire). 137
12. 'Two gunner football champions', *Navy and Army Illustrated* 7 (1898–9), 605. 165
13. Stan Cullis leads out a British Forces team, Yugoslavia, 1945. Reproduced by kind permission of the Army Physical Training Corps Museum. 181
14. BAOR plays a Polish XI, Warsaw, November 1945. Reproduced by kind permission of Andrew Ward. 194
15. RAF hockey players, Aden, 1944. Reproduced by kind permission of the Royal Air Force Sports Board. 202
16. Andrew Hawarden, Stalag 383. Reproduced by kind permission of Sandra Hawarden-Lord. 211
17. 2nd Battalion, The Durham Light Infantry, winners of the 1955 Army Cup, Aldershot, D/DLI 2/2/148(274). Reproduced by permission of the Durham County Record Office. 235
18. 'WAF triumphs in Inter-Service Games', 1919. Reproduced by kind permission of the Royal Air Force Sports Board. 248
19. RAF personnel watch the 1943 Tripoli Cup final. Reproduced by kind permission of the Royal Air Force Sports Board. 262

Acknowledgements

All writing is essentially a solitary business, but writing history depends on a lot of other people who offer help and support in important ways. It is doubtful if this study would have been begun, let alone completed, without a substantial grant from the Arts and Humanities Research Council. Another essential factor is the provision of sources and we are particularly grateful to the Sports Boards of the army, navy and the Royal Air Force for allowing us access to their records, for making us so welcome when we turned up to look at them and, in the case of Steve Parlor of the RAF Sports Board, for being so helpful about pictures. We would also like to thank particularly Major Billy Thomson of the Army Football Association and Major Bob Kelly, the curator of the Army Physical Training Corps Museum at Aldershot.

We are grateful for the help of the staff of the Imperial War Museum, the National Army Museum, the Museum of the Royal Engineers of Chatham, the Royal Navy Museum at Portsmouth, the National Archives, and the Special Collections department of University of Birmingham Library. Several visits were made to the archives of a number of civilian sporting organisations including the Football Association and the MCC.

Many other people have kept us going by their encouragement and insights, in particular the members of the International Centre for Sport History and Culture at De Montfort University. Neil Carter, Jeffrey Hill, Richard Holt, Pierre Lanfranchi, James Panter, Dilwyn Porter, Matthew Taylor and Jean Williams have all learned more about military sport than they ever needed to know. We would also like to acknowledge the help particularly in the early part of the project provided by Chris Brader, Tony Collins, Mike Cronin and John Roberts. Neal Garnham told us several things we didn't know about Ireland, and John Bale did the same for Roy Fowler. At an important stage of the enterprise Paul Dietschy spurred us on by inviting us to read papers at a seminar in Paris, and Dave Russell did the same in Preston. Roderick Suddaby and Neil Young of the Imperial War Museum were kind enough to read the manuscript, as was Jeffrey Hill. They not only corrected errors of fact and made helpful suggestions but provided us with the impetus to accelerate down the finishing straight. Any remaining errors are of course ours. We are grateful to all those who shared memories of service sport with us, notably Robin Harland and Geoffrey Yates and in particular to Andrew Ward for the photograph of his father playing football in BAOR at the end of the Second World War. Ros Lucas typed several of the chapters.

A version of chapter 2 was published as 'Brains or Polo? Equestrian Sport, Army Reform and the Gentlemanly Officer Tradition, 1900–1914' in the *Journal of the Society for Army Historical Research* 84 (2006), 236–53. A version of chapter 3 was published as '"Leather" and the Fighting Spirit: Sport in the British Army in World War I' in the *Canadian Journal of History* 41 (2006), 485–516. We are grateful to these journals for allowing us to republish material.

Finally we would like to thank Clare Wightman and James Bothwell for their forbearance and support for a project that took longer than any of us had anticipated.

Introduction

[In the autumn of 1885 the 2nd Battalion moved to Pembroke Dock] a very pleasant station, with lots of hunting, fishing and shooting and enjoyable weekends in Tenby. But it was a dreary spot for the men. During the winter of 1885–86 I was the Acting Adjutant of the Battalion and, with a view to providing recreation for the men, I managed to hire a fairly level field near the Barracks – an amenity not easily come by in that hilly country. Further I purchased all the essential requirements of football, really nothing but goalposts and some balls ... Now it is hardly believable, but it is an absolute fact that only some 47 years ago hardly a man in the Battalion could be persuaded to come down even to kick a ball about, still less to take part in a game.
'Reminiscences of Lt. Gen. Sir Gerald Ellison KCB, KCMG',
The Lancashire Lad. The Journal of the Loyal Regiment (North Lancashire)
(April 1933), p. 10

In a recent study of British military medicine, Mark Harrison found it hard to think of any other aspect of military life that had been so poorly served in histories of the British armed forces.[1] If there is another it might be sport, which over the last century and a half and particularly during the years with which this study deals, 1880–1960, took up a good proportion of the time and energies of many serving sailors, soldiers and later airmen. It has certainly been left out of the accounts of most writers on military history who have, perhaps unsurprisingly, had more warlike themes on their minds. Edward Spiers, in a number of authoritative studies of the Victorian and Edwardian army, only occasionally alludes to the role of sport, usually as a part of that package of reforms designed to improve the lot of the ordinary soldier in part to provide a stimulus to recruiting in the last decades of the nineteenth century, or as one of the activities that soldiers could enjoy in rear areas and garrisons even on active service in the imperial

---

[1] M. Harrison, *Medicine and Victory: British Military Medicine in the Second World War* (Oxford University Press, 2004), p. 1.

'small wars' of that period.² A. R. Skelley, similarly, only devotes a few pages to physical training and a paragraph to sport, as an example of other ranks recreations, in his exploration of the lives of British regular soldiers in the later years of Victoria's reign.³ There have been some recent signs that a more serious look at the role of sport in the services may not be too far off. Anthony Clayton had emphasised its role in the training and recreation of West African recruits during the years preceding and the decade or so after the Second World War and he has returned to the subject of sport in his latest history of the British army officer.⁴ Historians of the Victorian navy have also made some recognition of the role which sport played in the lives of sailors in the later nineteenth century. Henry Baynham, Peter Kemp and Eugene L. Rasor all mention the development of naval sport briefly, again in the context of improvements in the conditions of service for ordinary seamen over the latter half of the nineteenth century.⁵ The sailors whose reminiscences contributed to Baynham's *Men from the Dreadnoughts* remembered sport as a fairly significant part of their naval life.⁶ A more sustained analysis was recently offered by Oliver Walton, suggesting that sport provided one of the key ways through which the late Victorian navy rendered alien landscapes familiar, affirmed the bonds of empire through matches against colonial settlers and 'natives' and fostered productive competition between ships.⁷

---

[2] E. M. Spiers, *The Army and Society* (London: Longman, 1980), p. 63; *The Late Victorian Army 1868–1902* (Manchester University Press, 1992), pp. 96–7; *The Scottish Soldier and Empire, 1854–1902* (Edinburgh University Press, 2006), p. 195.

[3] A.R. Skelley, *The Victorian Army at Home: The Recruitment and Terms and Conditions of the British Regular 1859–1989* (London: Croom Helm, 1977), pp. 58–60, 162–5. J. M. Brereton, *The British Soldier. A Social History from 1661 to the Present Day* (London: The Bodley Head, 1986) thought sport an important part of army life but again provided only a few descriptive paragraphs about it.

[4] A. Clayton, 'Sport and African Soldiers: The Military Diffusion of Western Sport throughout Sub-Saharan Africa', in W.J. Baker and J.A. Mangan (eds.), *Sport in Africa. Essays in Social History* (London: Frank Cass, 1987), pp. 114–37; *The British Officer. Leading the Army from 1660 to the Present* (London: Longman, 2005).

[5] H. Baynham, *Before the Mast: Naval Ratings of the Nineteenth Century* (London: Hutchinson, 1971), p. 117; P. Kemp, *The British Sailor: A Social History of the Lower Deck* (London: Dent, 1970), pp. 210–11; E.L. Rasor, *Reform in the Royal Navy: A Social History of the Lower Deck 1850 to 1880* (Hamden, Conn.: Archon Books, 1976), p. 106.

[6] H. Baynham, *Men from the Dreadnoughts* (London: Hutchinson, 1976). Christopher McKee's more recent *Sober Men and True: Sailor Lives in the Royal Navy 1900–1945* (Cambridge, Mass.: Harvard University Press, 2002) explicitly excluded consideration of 'organized competitive sport', along with a number of other topics which he nevertheless recognised as 'important in themselves' (p. 5).

[7] O. Walton, 'A Social History of the Royal Navy, 1856–1900: Corporation and Community', unpublished PhD thesis, University of Exeter, 2004, pp. 198–203.

Introduction

The study of the roles played by sport in the United States military is somewhat more developed – surprisingly, perhaps, since it seems clear that the growth of American military sport lagged some way behind that of the British, and at times was strongly influenced by its example. (It also appears to have been much more of a top-down development.) Although Charlston has noted some earlier examples of sporting enthusiasm, sport in the American military was not actively promoted until the Spanish-American War of 1898, when a younger generation of officers with a commitment to the welfare of the other ranks used sport in attempts to combat alcohol, desertion and the lure of prostitution. It was only during the First World War, however, that sport really took off in the American forces, encouraged by the authorities – themselves influenced by the success of the British army sports programme behind the lines on the Western Front – both as a form of social control and as a means of military training.[8]

It was a retired US army officer, J. D. Campbell, who was the first to undertake a serious study of the development of physical training and sport in the British army between the end of the Crimean War and the end of the First World War. His doctoral thesis was an ambitious attempt to describe the processes by which sport and games became 'the most popular and frequent activities for all ranks throughout the entire Army'. That sport was training for war seemed to him an obvious conclusion; it is one that will be tested in the chapters that follow.[9] The belief that sport and war were in some sense the same, that sport was 'mimic war' and war only the 'greater game', was certainly firmly held in the late Victorian and Edwardian public schools. In the ideology of athleticism, expressed in school sermons and schoolboy verses, games produced not only the physical but the moral qualities required in a good soldier – courage and stoicism, quick-wittedness and quick decision, leadership qualities and loyalty to the team.[10] As

---

[8] S. W. Pope, 'An Army of Athletes: Playing Fields, Battlefields, and the American Military Sporting Experience, 1890–1920', *Journal of Military History* 59 (1995), 435–56; W. E. Wakefield, *Playing to Win: Sports and the American Military, 1898–1945* (Albany, N.Y.: SUNY, 1997); J. A. Charlston, 'Disorganised and Quasi-official but Eventually Successful: Sport in the US Military, 1814–1914', *International Journal of the History of Sport* 19 (2002), 70–87.

[9] J. D. Campbell, 'The Army Isn't All Work: Physical Culture in the Evolution of the British Army, 1860–1920', unpublished PhD thesis, University of Maine, 2003. See also his article '"Training for Sport Is Training for War": Sport and the Transformation of the British Army, 1860–1914', *International Journal of the History of Sport* 17 (December 2000), 21–58.

[10] J. A. Mangan, *Athleticism in the Victorian and Edwardian Public School* (Cambridge University Press, 1981), pp. 191–6. See also G. Best, 'Militarism and the Victorian

the headmaster of Harrow School put it in 1906, 'the spirit of subordination and co-operation, the complete authority, the ready obedience, the self-respect and self-sacrifice of the playing field enter largely into life ... There is no cricketer worthy of the name ... who would not be glad to sacrifice himself if he could so win the victory for his side'.[11] Most officers had been educated at the public schools and most seem to have absorbed these ideas without any serious consideration of them. Since war was their profession and sport one of their main pleasures it was natural to call on the sport–war analogy to justify the amount of time devoted to sporting activity. Yet the relationship between sport and war was asserted rather than demonstrated; nor was the ideology entirely coherent. The public-school emphasis on playing the game for its own sake sat uneasily with the insistence that sport was training for war; war, after all, is a 'game' that can only be played to win.[12] Within the army itself, and especially after 1900, the idea that sport fostered 'officer qualities' was challenged by military reformers anxious to create a more professional officer corps.[13]

The benefits of sport to the military may well have been less direct. David French includes in his fine study of the rise and fall of the regimental system the most thoughtful consideration to date of the place of sport in the history of the British army. French is clear about the ways in which sport contributed to the construction of regimental identities and concludes that, although interest in sport was widespread, it was not all-consuming. Though field sports were said to accustom men to taking physical risks, they did not necessarily make officers less apprehensive of battlefield dangers. Sport did facilitate the growth of *esprit de corps* and inter-rank relations and was often an interest shared by officers and men, but it rarely undermined rank and status. As for the inculcation of sporting ideologies, French suggests that, so far as other ranks were concerned, sportsmanship, fairness and good manners were less important than winning, leading him to conclude that their attitudes to sport were probably much like those of working-class males outside the army. French also suggests that sport was one way in which units

Public School', in B. Simon and I. Bradley (eds.), *The Victorian Public School* (Dublin: Gill & Macmillan, 1975), pp. 141–3.

[11] Quoted in W.J. Reader, *'At Duty's Call': A Study in Obsolete Patriotism* (Manchester University Press, 1988) p. 97.

[12] P. Parker, *The Old Lie: The Great War and the Public School Ethos* (London: Constable, 1987), p. 84.

[13] J. Lowerson, *Sport and the English Middle Classes 1870–1914* (Manchester University Press, 1993), pp. 285–9. For a recent restatement of the link between sport, specifically rugby, and leadership skills, see Wing Commander Pat Carter, 'Who Needs Officer Qualities?', *Journal of the Royal Air Force College, Cranwell* (March 2002), 14.

could 'commend themselves' to the civilian communities in which they were embedded.[14]

The issues raised by French will be discussed in greater detail throughout this work. First, however, we must establish the sporting context, both military and civilian, in which service sport developed in the later nineteenth century. Sport was never entirely absent from the mid-Victorian army and navy. Certainly by mid-century military schools such as Addiscombe, Sandhurst and Woolwich were beginning to use sport rather as the public schools had been doing to bring a sense of discipline and purpose to the recreation of their students. A kind of football was certainly played at the East India Company's College at Addiscombe in the 1850s, for example, though it seems mainly to have provided an additional opportunity for the older boys to rough up the younger ones.[15] There was also a twice-yearly athletic meeting which became a popular event attracting crowds made up of parents and local residents. Instruction in 'physical education' was provided by a former corporal in the Life Guards. There were similar activities at Sandhurst and Woolwich. Sandhurst had separate grounds for sports including cricket and racquets. At Woolwich a professional bowler was engaged for two or three days during the cricket season to coach the cadets; racquets and football were increasingly encouraged; and under the reforming Cadet Company officer Captain Frederick Eardley Wilmot an athletics meeting was held as early as 1849. However, such initiatives do not seem to have put down very deep roots. When Eardley Wilmot left Woolwich in 1854 the athletics meeting lapsed. It was the cadet 'mutinies' at both colleges in the early 1860s that led the authorities to endorse sport as a permanent part of college life. General Burgoyne's 1864 report into the Sandhurst 'outbreaks' prescribed 'all outdoor manly exercise', including cricket, football, racquets, boating, swimming, quoits, rifle practice and gymnastics, as the best antidote to youthful unruliness. This certainly reflects what was happening in civilian circles, and it seems that it was from this time, the 1860s, that records of sporting activities

---

[14] D. French, *Military Identities: The Regimental System, the British Army and the British People, c. 1870–2000* (Oxford University Press, 2005), pp. 115–21, 143, 238–9, 305.

[15] This paragraph is based on J.M. Bourne, 'The East India Company's Military Seminary, Addiscombe 1809–1858', *Journal of the Society for Army Historical Research* 57 (1979), 206–22; T. Hearl, 'Fighting Fit: Some Military Initiatives in Physical Education in Britain, 1800–1860', in N. Parry and D. McNair (eds.), *The Fitness of the Nation: Physical and Health Education in the Nineteenth and Twentieth Centuries* (History of Education Society, 1983), pp. 46–69; Col. H.M. Vibart, *Addiscombe: Its Heroes and Men of Note* (London: Constable & Co., 1894), pp. 249–54; A. Shepperd, *Sandhurst: The Royal Military Academy Sandhurst and Its Predecessors* (London: Country Life Books, 1980), pp. 54–5, 70–4.

and performances began to be kept at the colleges, with inter-college competitions providing the main sporting rivalries.

It was also in this period that the first connections between sport and recruiting were made, initially by one of the more thoughtful soldiers, Captain Henry Brackenbury, who in an article in *Fraser's Magazine* on military reform noted that

> We have a race of hardy villagers and stalwart country lads fond of sport, of all games that require pluck and skill, a quick eye, a strong hand, and a fleet foot, to whom the spice of danger enhances the pleasure of such games as football and cricket, and who are ready to join in anything promising a chance of adventure. It would seem that a soldier's life is exactly the career suited to such as these; but the fact stares us in the face that these men will not come in any numbers to the army.[16]

In 1878 (reflecting both the upper-middle-class enthusiasm for organised sport and concerns that the new emphasis on intellectual ability since the abolition of purchase was undermining the physique of army officers) the Civil Service Commissioners proposed setting candidates for first commissions in the army an 'athletic examination' with marks for proficiency in walking, running, leaping, riding, swimming and shot-putting. A debate in the House of Lords, disapproval in the newspapers and opposition from the staff at Woolwich seem to have combined to undermine the idea.[17] By this time sport was also being suggested as 'very beneficial for boys entering the Navy'.[18]

As for the young men already serving in the military, cost seems to have inhibited the development of sporting facilities. As early as 1836 Her Majesty's Commissioners inquiring into the system of military punishments in the army had suggested the provision of games such as fives, racquets, cricket and football might help keep young soldiers out of trouble. Cricket pitches were laid down from 1841 but gymnasia would have to wait until much later, and the Treasury reduced the number of fives courts to be built from 146 to twenty-nine.[19]

In fact there is some evidence that admiration of physical prowess and sport were both already common elements in the framework of service life, if still awaiting organisation, rationalisation and system. The

---

[16] H. Brackenbury, 'Military Reform', Part I, *Fraser's Magazine* 74 (1866), 692.
[17] Hearl, 'Fighting Fit', p. 66. For support for the idea of 'physical competition for the army' see *Field* 56 (1880), 42.
[18] Report of the Committee on the Regulations for the Entry and Training of Boys in Her Majesty's Navy, 15 Dec. 1879, Paragraph 24, ADM 116/704, National Archives, quoted in Walton, 'A Social History of the Royal Navy', p. 200.
[19] H. Strachan, *Wellington's Legacy: The Reform of the British Army 1830–54* (Manchester University Press, 1984), p. 85.

Guards regiments, for example, had a reputation for producing boxers and wrestlers. Feats of strength were widely performed and admired, as on the occasion when James English of the King's Company, Grenadier Guards, carried three of the heaviest privates of the regiment on his shoulders the length of Pall Mall. It is not altogether surprising to learn that a good deal of money was riding on the result.[20] T. H. Kirby was already a well-known pedestrian when he joined the Yorkshire Regiment in 1859, and there were large wagers between the officers' mess and neighbouring ones at Aldershot on whether he could run a mile on the Farnborough Road in less than four and a half minutes. Sentries were placed next to the milestones presumably to inhibit anyone who might have been tempted to move them. A large crowd saw Kirby succeed in the attempt.[21] Prize fights were not uncommon in the areas around Aldershot and in garrisons such as the Curragh. Army officers had been part of the 'Fancy' in the early nineteenth century and would often be seen at the Covent Garden headquarters of the National Sporting Club when evenings of boxing were put on there in the 1890s.[22]

Sporting challenges were another regular feature of military life especially in those far-flung parts of the Empire where soldiers had a lot of time which was hard to fill. A Captain Brigstock of the King's Own Yorkshire Light Infantry once put out a challenge to any other officer to compete against him in six more or less athletic activities: single-wicket cricket, quoits, throwing the cricket ball, putting the stone, billiards and racquets. Colonel W. S. Jervis of the Royal Munster Fusiliers took him on and won by four events to two. 1/King's Royal Rifle Corps, the Greenjackets, provide two other interesting examples. In Malta in 1866 they challenged the rest of the garrison to swim, run, play racquets and cricket and won both the latter two and the one-mile road race. More expansively their officers challenged the rest of the officers in the Jubbalpore Garrison in India in 1908 to polo, cricket, a three-mile road race, a two-mile walking race, billiards, golf, rifle shooting, revolver shooting, racquets, tennis, the racing and jumping of polo ponies and tug of war. This was an event of Olympic proportions which the Greenjacket officers won even though their strength was a

---

[20] *Lloyd's Weekly News*, 30 March 1913.
[21] His time was reported as 4 minutes 26 seconds, which seems suspiciously fast and would not be beaten in the army championships until 1937. *Lloyd's Weekly News*, 3 August 1913.
[22] G. Deghy, *Noble and Manly: The History of the National Sporting Club* (London: Hutchinson, 1956); J. Harding, *Lonsdale's Belt: The Story of Boxing's Greatest Prize* (London: Robson Books, 1994).

mere fifteen compared to fifty in the other regiments. The whole event took six weeks to complete.[23]

Sport in the army and navy would eventually also receive some encouragement from the physical trainers. The Army Gymnastic Staff was established in 1860 and was part of the critical reappraisal of the force which took place after the disappointments of the Crimean War. Twelve NCOs drawn from a variety of units under the charge of a Major Hammersley were sent to Oxford for a six-month course at the Gymnastic School run by Archibald MacLaren. A School of Army Gymnastics was then set up at Aldershot with Hammersley as superintendent.[24] Gymnasia were erected in most garrisons during the 1860s, and in 1865 the first regulations governing physical training in the army were published. It was to Aldershot that NCOs selected from every regiment were sent on courses of physical training lasting six months, from which they returned to their regiments as qualified instructors. By 1890 a staff of fifteen sergeants and twelve assistant instructors were systematically preparing 150 NCOs together with a smaller number of officers whose ambition was to become gymnasium superintendents.[25] There might have been a serious division between these men and those who preferred sport to gymnastics as there was in some European armies. But it is clear that the military PTIs believed that sport and physical training could not only co-exist but that each could benefit the other. Hammersley, for example, was Vice-President of the Aldershot Divisional Cricket Club, and later the Assistant-Inspector of Gymnasia would be Captain W. Edgeworth Johnstone, Royal Irish Regiment, winner of the first officers heavyweight boxing championship and an active promoter of that sport. Moreover PTIs on many camps would play an important part in the growth and development of service sport, as we shall see.[26]

Regular soldiers were also part of the pre-history of football, the game that would become the most popular among the other ranks of

---

[23] *Lloyd's Weekly News*, 20 April, 25 May 1913. John D. Astley was said to have carried off four cups in one day at Aldershot in 1856: 100, 150 and 440 yards races and 200 yards running in heavy marching order. *British Sports and Sportsmen Past and Present*, 13 vols. (London, 1908–), vol. II, p. 183.

[24] His father was not impressed. 'I hope you will not be tempted by the prospect of an easy birth [*sic*] to accept a situation which seems hardly fit for a gentleman, much less an officer, who aspires to military distinction.' Quoted in E. A. L. Oldfield, *History of the Army Physical Training Corps* (Aldershot: Gale and Polden, 1955), p. 2. In 1870 Hammersley was appointed Inspector of Gymnasia with the rank of lieutenant-colonel.

[25] Oldfield, *History*, ch. 1.

[26] The annual assault at arms presented by the PTIs of Aldershot and local regiments included both boxing and gymnastic displays as well as more obviously military exhibitions, *Sheldrake Military Gazette*, 6 September 1871.

Introduction 9

all three services. By the 1850s several regiments were reported as having played a form of football that seems to have combined some of the features that would, by the 1880s, have matured into the separate sports of association and rugby football. The London sporting newspaper *Bell's Life* reported one such occasion at Parkhurst barracks on the Isle of Wight in 1856 when thirty-eight of the 30th, 55th and 96th played against thirty-eight of the 15th and the 34th in a match which consisted of 'two goals out of three' – in other words, the first team to score twice.[27] The same paper also reported a match at Lord's Cricket Ground between two teams of ten players a side drawn from the 3rd Battalion Grenadier Guards and selected on the basis of hair colour – dark or light. Perhaps this had been partly in preparation for a challenge between teams of fifteen a side representing the 2nd and 3rd Battalions which several gentlemen watched and which ended in a tie after nearly four hours.[28] In the same year a match with sixteen players a side was reported from Corfu between the garrison and the 2nd Battalion of the 9th Regiment. The teams were made up of officers including Lieutenant-Colonel Sankey of the 9th Regiment, and the 9th won by 'three goals out of four'.[29] Meanwhile in Sheffield, a town which already had a reputation for being a centre of footballing activity, late in 1860 the 58th Regiment from the local Hillsborough Barracks took on a team of civilians from the Sheffield club and lost by one goal and ten rouges to one goal and five. Not long after, in Aldershot, five officers and fifteen men of the 8th Regiment took on an equal number of the 53rd in what was labelled the 'first match of the season' in November 1861. The correspondent who had submitted the report, presumably a serving officer, added that he hoped 'to see many such matches played at Aldershott [sic] for the amusement of the soldiers, who appear greatly to enjoy the game'.[30]

Football seems to be in the process of becoming a frequent if not necessarily a regular activity in the army during the 1860s. By 1868, what was described as the 'first match between the sister corps' took place between the Royal Artillery and the Royal Engineers. The former had 'not got a club at present' but managed to get ten men together and were given two more by the Engineers to make twelve a side. At least the Gunners were said to have had a splendid goalkeeper,

---

[27] *Bell's Life*, 23 November 1856.
[28] It was to be 'played out another day'. Five officers took part. *Bell's Life*, 13 March 1859.
[29] *Bell's Life*, 17 April 1859.
[30] *Bell's Life*, 23 December 1860, 1 December 1861. A rouge was an outer goal scored when the ball passed between posts four yards either side of the inner goal.

which suggests that this was a match played under similar rules to those drawn up by the five-year-old Football Association.[31] In fact the Royal Engineers joined the Football Association in 1869 and in the ensuing decade became not only an example to all military footballers but important innovators in this rapidly developing sport. The School of Military Engineering on the Great Lines at Chatham in Kent may well have been the first unit in which officers took modern sports seriously. Chatham in the early 1860s may have had no golf or lawn tennis but it did have cricket and croquet, fives and racquets, and rowing and sailing on the Thames and Medway, all these mainly in the summer. At first, football was only played occasionally in the winter[32] but it quickly became established among a group of young officers who had almost certainly played some form of the game at their public schools.[33]

Two officers at Chatham, Major Francis Marindin and Captain William Merriman, seem to have been most responsible for the rise of the RE footballers. Both were players, Marindin mainly at fullback and Merriman in goal, but both were also enthusiasts and leaders, and Merriman in particular was a real sporting virtuoso, being a sprinter, oarsman and cricketer as well as a footballer. Marindin was an Old Etonian who became Brigade Major at the School of Military Engineering from 1867 to 1874. He was also an early member of the committee of the young Football Association and would be its President from 1874 to 1890.[34] Both Marindin and Merriman played for the Royal Engineers when the team reached the first ever FA Cup final in 1872 and again in the final of 1874. Both of these were lost, but Merriman played in the team which beat the Old Etonians to win the Cup in

---

[31] *Bell's Life*, 12 December 1868. There was talk of a return match in the following week.
[32] See Sir B. Blood, *Four Score Years and Ten* (London, G. Bell & Sons, 1933), p. 30. Eight cricket matches were played in the first part of the summer of 1870 including one in which thirteen officers beat twenty-two sappers and NCOs by an innings. *Royal Engineers Journal* 1 (1 July 1870), 20–1.
[33] It seems clear that other army units were less familiar with this new game than the Chatham aficionados. When a team of Royal Welch Fusiliers were beaten 3–0 by the Engineers in March 1870 the chronicler in the *Royal Engineers Journal* (1 August 1870) thought it fair to say that the Welch 'had not played for two or three years and consequently were not in good training'. By 1874 soldiers in the 2nd Battalion the King's Own Yorkshire Light Infantry stationed in Sheffield were sending out challenges to local clubs and playing two or three matches a week although, as they failed to win any of them, it seems they had not quite got the hang of modern football yet. *Bell's Life*, 19 December 1874.
[34] Sir Francis Marindin 1839–1902. On leaving the Engineers he became Chief Inspector of Railways at the Board of Trade and was knighted in 1889. He also refereed eight FA Cup finals between 1880 and 1890.

1875.³⁵ This was the culmination of half a decade in which the Royal Engineers were the most successful football team in England. Between 1871–2 and 1874–5, eighty-six matches were played of which seventy-four were won, nine drawn and only three lost.³⁶ More significantly they were one of the pioneers of a new way of playing the game which would quickly be adopted by all.

Association football in 1870 was a vigorous game of heavy charging and individual dribbling of the ball with teams attempting to rush the opposition into defeat. So far as there was a division of labour for the players it was limited to a goalkeeper, one 'three-quarter' back, two half backs and seven forwards. Some clubs soon withdrew a forward to play as a second three-quarter back. What the Engineers began to do, no doubt based on afternoons of thoughtful practice on the Chatham Lines, was to add passing the ball, short and long, to the skill of individual dribbling. The Queen's Park team were developing a similar method in Glasgow in the same period. A contemporary report describes a match in which the Engineers defeated the Wanderers, probably the leading London team of the day, in 1871. 'The organisation (so urgently required in the army) and concentration of the Engineers' play was universally admired by a large number of spectators; some of the individual play of the Wanderers was very superior, but as a team they failed to work together so well as their opponents.'³⁷ It was this emphasis on teamwork which was so new and effective and which was to be demonstrated to footballers further north at Christmas 1873, when the Engineers went on a four-day tour during which they played against civilian teams including one representative of the Sheffield FA, one of the Derbyshire FA and Nottingham Forest.³⁸

---

[35] Merriman later was posted to India, where he was Chief Engineer to the Commander-in-Chief in Bombay. He retired from the army in 1892. See *The Sapper*, September 1896, 28.
[36] G. Williams, *The Code War* (Harefield: Yore Publications, 1994), p. 46.
[37] *Royal Engineers Journal* 5 (April 1871).
[38] On the tour, see T. Mason, *Association Football and English Society 1863–1915* (Brighton: Harvester, 1980), p. 145, Williams, *The Code War*, pp. 44–6, and R.M. Ruck, 'R.E. Football in the Early Seventies', *Royal Engineers Journal* n.s. 42 (1928). The officers' football team had largely ceased to function by the 1930s. Football in the Royal Engineers was kept going by the various Corps Battalions. The Service Battalion stationed at Aldershot won the Army Cup in 1903, and the Depot and District Base team at Aldershot repeated the feat in 1906 and 1907. The FA Amateur Cup was won in 1908. Even in 1998 the President of the RE Football Club believed that Royal Engineers' football had 'got a great story to tell which confirms and enhances the army's image as a prestigious and innovative sports oriented employer of the highest standing. The FA Cup is an instantly recognisable symbol of sporting achievement amongst young people in this country, and I regard football as a major factor in recruiting and retention of high calibre soldiers' (25 June 1998).

12   Sport and the Military

The football team produced by the School of Military Engineering at Chatham in the 1870s was clearly an exceptional one. Its successes in the FA Cup and general play doubtless influenced other teams both in and out of uniform. There were even a few military teams who joined the Engineers in the FA Cup (including 2/King's Own Yorkshire Light Infantry and the Volunteer regiment the 1st Surrey Rifles), but they rarely got past the first round. Of course, when the Engineers reached the final of the Cup in 1874 there had been only twenty-eight entries for the competition, and there was only one more in the following year, when the team carried the trophy back to Chatham. By 1880 fifty-four clubs were entering, and in the 1883–4 season there were 100 entries. This reflected the remarkable growth of the game in Britain in the 1880s which would soon produce an elite of professional players performing before crowds the size of which astonished contemporaries. No military team had the resources to keep pace with these developments.

In British civil society in the second half of the nineteenth century and particularly after about 1870 the number of sports, the numbers playing them and the numbers watching them play increased dramatically. Moreover the social composition of participants and their geographical range widened. Sport was increasingly part of the curriculum not only of the public and grammar schools but also of the elementary schools as well as the small number of military educational establishments. Rules were written down, more and more clubs and associations formed, and commercialisation and the employment of professionals became widespread for the first time. The timing of sporting activity and performance was radically altered by the spread of the five-and-a-half-day week and the focus on Saturday afternoons. The pace of these changes was unprecedented.[39] Older sports such as angling, athletics, bowls, boxing (the successor to prize fighting), cricket, fox-hunting, horse racing, rowing and swimming increased in popularity, and a range of new sports were developed, such as badminton, croquet, cycling, hockey and lawn tennis. Large crowds would gather to see the big matches and the top teams especially on bank holidays. But it was association and rugby football which produced the most spectacular crowds, especially from the 1880s. Between 1875 and 1884 the average attendance at FA Cup finals in England was 4,900; by 1905–14, it had risen to 79,300.[40] By 1909 it has been estimated that one million people

---

[39] The best summary of these changes is N. Tranter, *Sport, Economy and Society in Britain 1750–1914* (Cambridge University Press, 1998), which argues persuasively that sport in its modern, organised and commercialised form was a revolutionary invention of the late Victorians.

[40] The figures for the same years in Scotland were 8,550 and 51,000.

Introduction 13

watched football on English Saturday afternoons.[41] Most sports had been transformed by this time from essentially local to national activities with their own national championships. Well before 1900 many sports had already developed an international dimension, and it was in London that what was effectively the first modern Olympics took place in 1908. Sport and the associated idea of fair play was part of the social and ideological make-up of the British and increasingly one of the things that foreigners thought of when they tried to sum up what the rulers of the British Empire were like. Awareness of this new sporting sub-culture must have been instantaneously available not only to most parts of the country but also to most sections of the population given the coverage of sport in books, specialist magazines and newspapers and increasingly in the daily and weekly national press. It is this context in which the growth of sport in the British military has to be understood.

We have known for some time that the Duke of Wellington did not claim that the Battle of Waterloo was won on the playing fields of Eton.[42] It is almost impossible to undermine such often repeated and powerful myths. What we hope to achieve in the pages which follow is not to exaggerate the role of sport in the military but to explore how and why organised sport developed as a significant part of service life, both in peace and in war, during the eighty years after 1880, and what it meant for the generations of servicemen (and eventually smaller numbers of servicewomen) who were touched by it. We will examine how the importance and meanings of sport changed over time, explore how far the public-school ideology that saw sport and war as being in some sense versions of each other was echoed within the military and attempt to assess what impact organised sport had on military efficiency. We will pay particular attention to its role in the two world wars of the twentieth century and to its place in the lives of those British military personnel whose primary responsibility was to protect the British Empire. We will also examine the part played by sporting activity in the shifting relations between civilians and the military. This book is both unusual and ambitious in that it aims to analyse the place of sport in all three arms, navy, army and air force, but the authors accept that it is the army which receives the most extensive and detailed coverage in the pages which follow, in part reflecting its size and importance across eight decades but also because the records of its sporting organisations

[41] W. Vamplew, *Pay Up and Play the Game. Professional Sports in Britain, 1875–1914* (Cambridge University Press, 1988), pp. 323–4.
[42] See B. Haley, *The Healthy Body in Victorian Culture* (Cambridge, Mass.: Harvard University Press, 1978), pp. 170–1.

have better survived the vicissitudes of time than those of the other two arms. Again, although we have been conscious of the need to include some analysis of all the many sports promoted and played by service personnel, more space has been given to football partly because the records of the Army Football Association have been so well preserved and partly because football was, without doubt, the most popular game to play and to watch among the other ranks of all three services throughout the years on which this study has concentrated.

1 The growth of service sport, 1880–1914

> What a change in a few years! Football has emptied the barrack rooms (shall it be said the canteens also?).
> Captain E. G. Curtis, 'Football in the Army: Its History and Records', in *The Book of Football* (London: Amalgamated Press, 1906), p. 100

The later nineteenth and early twentieth centuries saw marked improvements in the conditions of service of both ordinary soldiers and the lower deck of the navy. Problems of recruitment and retention (most marked in the army but also experienced by the navy as the service expanded dramatically at the turn of the century); rising expectations in civil society of the services as an employer; the need for better-educated servicemen as naval and military life became increasingly technological; and, in the navy, an increasingly assertive lower-deck movement all combined to create a slow but definite impetus for reform in both arms. In the army the introduction of short service (six years followed by six years in the reserve) made soldiering a more attractive option. Flogging was abolished in 1881; military prisons were reformed; progressive improvements were made in the conditions of barrack accommodation; married quarters and separation allowances were granted for those few soldiers' wives who were 'on the strength'; diet and messing arrangements were improved; even the basic rate of pay was raised, marginally, in 1898, with further improvements in 1902. From the later nineteenth century and especially after 1900 sailors too benefited from more generous leave, better food, better barracks ashore, less brutal punishment and improved prospects of promotion; in 1912 they were granted the first rise in their basic pay in sixty years.[1]

---

[1] For the army see Spiers, *The Late Victorian Army* ch. 5; Spiers, *The Army and Society* ch. 2; Skelley, *The Victorian Army at Home* esp. pp. 160–4. For a detailed discussion of the lower-deck movement and early twentieth-century naval reforms see A. Carew, *The Lower Deck of the British Navy 1900–39: The Invergordon Mutiny in Perspective* (Manchester University Press, 1981), chs. 1–3.

Alongside these developments ran efforts to provide 'rational recreation' for soldiers and sailors. Educational provision was expanded, libraries and reading rooms provided, and Sailors' Rests and Soldiers' Homes set up (initially by philanthropic civilians) to offer alcohol-free accommodation and alternative destinations to the public house. The expansion of organised sport in the army and navy can be seen as part of this movement to elevate the 'moral and intellectual standard' of Britain's servicemen, and as we have seen it is primarily in this context that historians of the armed forces have mentioned it. But although service sport attracted some official approval in the late Victorian and Edwardian period, and the Army Gymnastic Staff provided valuable support, before 1914 it was promoted primarily by sporting enthusiasts found mostly among the junior officer class and the rank and file; for this reason it developed unevenly between ships and regiments, and between ports and garrisons. Dovetailing neatly with the sporting preoccupations of young men in civil society, service sport soon acquired a momentum of its own. Its phenomenal growth before 1914 cannot be understood without acknowledging the variety and interest it brought to the everyday lives of soldiers and sailors. As 'a footballer at headquarters' put it in 1896, 'the fine healthy recreation which the game affords, both in practice and in the matches, the pleasurable excitement to be derived from watching the contests in which the regimental team takes part, and the keen discussions of the doings of the players, fill up pleasantly and profitably much time that would otherwise hang heavily'.[2] This chapter traces the process by which sport became an integral part of life in the late Victorian and Edwardian services, focusing first on the army and then on the navy, and discusses the ways in which sport contributed to military efficiency, as well as some of the problems raised by sporting activity in a military context.

It was the army that led the way in developing both sporting organisations and competitive structures for sport. The first sporting competition involving the entire army at home was the Army Athletic Meeting, held annually from 1876 under the auspices of the Army Gymnastic Staff. Already army athletics were being 'brought much more prominently before the public than previously' through the 'annual sports held by many regiments on the barrack ground' and the inclusion of soldiers' races in amateur meetings in garrison towns, as well as bigger military events like the Aldershot Camp Athletic Sports and Foot Races held in 1870.[3] The origins of the Athletic Meeting may also lie partly

---

[2] 'Football in the Army', *Navy and Army Illustrated*, 11 December 1896.
[3] *Times*, 12 June 1876; Programme, 15 July 1870 (four pages, marked 'For Officers and Civilians Only').

with the civilian press. In early 1876 the *Field* published two articles under the title 'Army Athletics'. The first deplored the lack of fitness in the 'modern soldier'. The second, while acknowledging the work of Colonel Hammersley's staff, suggested the best remedy was to encourage soldiers to undertake 'voluntary permanent training'. An annual military sports meeting would stimulate inter-regimental rivalry, and the victorious sportsmen, returning to their regiments, would 'create a wholesome spirit of emulation'. The following week Captain Moston of the Army Gymnastic Staff announced in the *Field* that there would indeed be a 'grand military athletic meeting' that June. It would be held, as the *Field* had suggested, at Lillie Bridge, the headquarters of the Amateur Athletic Club, under royal patronage and for the benefit of military charities, with 'upwards of £100' in cups and prizes. Only one man per regiment was to compete in each race to encourage regimental events to select competitors.[4]

The first, two-day, 'Grand Military Meeting' of June 1876 combined track and field events, gymnastics and military competitions such as tent-pegging and a 'marching order race'. Over 7,000 spectators including the Duke of Connaught attended the second day. Reporting it, the *Field* hailed the benefits of military sport in terms that would change little as the years passed:

> To become proficient in any branch of athletics a man must exercise a good deal of self-control, great perseverance, and go through a fair amount of hard work in addition to his usual duties. It creates a friendly rivalry among the men, and often brings the private soldier and his superiors in command together in competitions, when for the nonce they meet on equal terms; a fact that cannot help but promote the good feeling which generally prevails between the British soldier and those in authority over him.[5]

From 1877 the meeting was held at Aldershot, the major centre both of British troops and of the Army Gymnastic Staff. By 1911 *The Times* thought it had grown 'from a mere fête to a properly organized meeting' as important as those of the London Athletic Club and the Amateur Athletic Association.[6] As the Black Watch's journal ruefully reflected a couple of years later, competitors now had to be 'in the front rank' of athletics to have any hope of success. The Edwardian army produced some impressive athletes: two men from 1/Royal Irish Fusiliers alone were selected for the 1908 British Olympic team.[7]

---

[4] *Field* 47 (1876), 335, 365–6, 412.
[5] *Ibid.* 692; *Times*, 12 June 1876.
[6] *Times* 27 July 1877, 28 July 1911.
[7] *Black Watch Chronicle* 1 (1914), 134–5; *Faugh-a-Ballagh* 7 (July 1908), 17–18. For reasons discussed in chapter 5 only one, the hurdler Captain Kinahan, competed.

Despite the hopeful comments of the *Field* on the role of sport in bringing officers and men together, most athletic events were highly segregated, with separate races for other ranks, for officers and (in the early years) for NCOs. Other ranks typically received cash prizes: under Amateur Athletic Association rules this made them professionals against whom amateurs could not compete. The half-mile scratch race for the Championship of the Army (a feature of the army athletic meeting in which, after 1895, all ranks could compete) was 'the only one in which, under the laws of the Amateur Athletic Association, amateur and professional runners are allowed to compete together'. In 1908 five further championship events were introduced, including two for regimental teams – perhaps an attempt to circumnavigate AAA rules and encourage more mingling of ranks on the athletics field.[8] Yet separation by rank was not simply the result of civilian interference but also related to concerns about discipline and the preservation of the army hierarchy. The same concerns were seen in boxing, for which parallel competitions were run for officers and other ranks until well after the Second World War.

The army first introduced boxing as a form of military training and (unlike the navy) was initially doubtful about boxing as a sport. There were not only concerns that it might create bad feeling within or between regiments – as the Kaiser asked Sir Evelyn Wood in 1889, 'How do you manage to prevent the men of a defeated boxer's regiment quarrelling in the canteens?' – but an unexpected squeamishness about boxing. Reporting a tournament in 1893, the *Brigade of Guards Magazine* felt bound to assure its readers that 'not a single case even approaching to brutality occurred ... It was a scientific exhibition pure and simple'.[9] J. H. W. Knight-Bruce, a writer on boxing and officer in the Royal Warwickshire Regiment, dated the beginning of organised army boxing, by which he meant officer-run contests under fixed rules within or between regiments, to the mid-1880s. It was only in 1894 that military boxing was officially approved by the Commander-in-Chief, Lord Wolseley, though the Army Gymnastic Staff (particularly Colonel Malcolm Fox and Captain Edgeworth Johnstone, a heavyweight amateur champion) strongly encouraged it.[10] The Brigade of Guards were

---

[8] Amateur Athletic Association minutes, 29 June 1883, 20 October 1883, 28 March 1884, 26 November 1887, 14 December 1889, 6 April 1895, 13 December 1902, 18 April 1903, Birmingham University Library Special Collections; *Times*, 20 April 1903, 6 August 1903, 12 August 1908, 13 August 1908.
[9] General Sir E. Wood, *From Midshipman to Field Marshal* (London: Methuen, 1912), p. 378; *Brigade of Guards Magazine* 6 (1893), 209.
[10] J. H. W. Knight-Bruce, 'Military Boxing: Its Origin and Growth', in J. G. Bohun Lynch, *The Complete Amateur Boxer* (London: Methuen, 1913), p. 198; Col. Sir

early boxing enthusiasts. Boxing was included in the Household Brigade sports from 1889, and in 1892 the Brigade of Guards opened a boxing club at Chelsea Barracks with two well-known professional boxers providing instruction three evenings a week. In 1893 the newly founded National Sporting Club offered to host the finals of the Brigade boxing tournament, donating the cups and medals.[11] But even in units that encouraged boxing participation rates were often low. Many soldiers joined the Brigade of Guards club only to watch others boxing. The Leicestershire Regiment possessed a middleweight champion in Private Palmer and hired professionals to coach its top boxers, but still had to urge its soldiers to 'make the most of the available instruction' (adding, less than reassuringly, that 'deaths from boxing occur but seldom').[12] Regimental boxing meetings, which were supposed to be mainly for novice boxers to gain experience, sometimes became major spectacles with gate money providing big prizes to attract well-known army boxers and perhaps even civilian fighters.[13]

Boxing was introduced into the annual army athletic meeting only in 1892. Two years later it became a separate event (Frank Starr, an Aldershot-based civilian who wrote a weekly column called 'Service Gossip' in the *Athletic News*, suggested it was because interest in boxing was beginning to overshadow the track and field events) which in 1895 became the Royal Navy and Army Championships, with three weights for officers and four for other ranks. Gradually further weights were added, and the meeting expanded from two days to four. Additional championships were introduced for the navy in 1903 and for the army in 1912.[14] By 1912 there were also competitions in each of the army's Home Commands plus India, while the navy had a number of Fleet, Squadron and Port championships at home and overseas.[15] Until 1911 there was no overall body to control service boxing: the Royal Navy and

---

Malcolm Fox, 'Army and Navy Boxing', *Household Brigade Magazine* 16 (1913), 111–12.

[11] *Brigade of Guards Magazine* 2 (1889), 365–7; 5 (1892), 196–7, 571; 6 (1893), 107. See also *Lloyd's Weekly News*, 30 March 1913.

[12] *Brigade of Guards Magazine* 5 (1892), 196; Frank Starr, 'Army Boxing History V', *Aldershot Command News*, 7 February 1928, 13; *Green Tiger*, November 1908, 135, March 1911, 34.

[13] Knight-Bruce, 'Military Boxing', p. 201; Frank Starr, 'Army Boxing History III', *Aldershot Command News*, 24 January 1928, 3.

[14] Knight-Bruce, 'Military Boxing', pp. 198–200; Frank Starr, 'Army Boxing History II', *Aldershot Command News*, 17 January 1928, 4; 'The Army Boxing Championships', *Field* 84 (1894), 295; 'Army and Navy Boxing Championship', *Field* 85 (1895), 882.

[15] Knight-Bruce, 'Military Boxing', p. 200; Minutes of the Royal Navy and Army Boxing Association, 29 August 1912, Royal Navy School of Physical Training, Portsmouth (RNSPT).

Figure 1. Brigade of Guards boxing at Chelsea, 1898.

Army Championships were simply organised by the Army Gymnastic Service on an annual basis. Since money prizes were given at service meetings all other ranks boxers were technically professionals. Many fought regularly as such in civilian meetings in London and other big centres, both at home and in India. Some – most notably Bombardier Billy Wells, twice all-India army heavyweight champion – left the army to make successful boxing careers.[16]

---

[16] S. Shipley, *Bombardier Billy Wells: The Life and Times of a Boxing Hero* (Whitley Bay: Bewick Press, 1993).

The growth of service sport

Major-General Bengough wrote in 1896 that football was 'the only game into which the soldier throws himself with any real zest. At cricket he is a 'dilettante', at football an enthusiast; and this passion is only of very recent development, being indeed synchronous with the keen public interest that has of late been evinced in this game'.[17] We have seen already that some military clubs, most notably the officers of the Royal Engineers at Chatham, had been among the pioneers of this newly organised game as it began to grow so impressively in the 1870s and 1880s. But it was the formation of the Army Football Association in 1888 which gave the process real organisational impetus, while reflecting grass-roots developments already in progress. It was very much an initiative of the infantry, with the Guards regiments heavily involved from the beginning while the cavalry showed less enthusiasm.[18]

The first and most important army sports organisation, the Army Football Association was run by a relatively small group of enthusiastic young officers. Like so many voluntary bodies it was a case of a few activists bearing the administrative burden. In the context of the army it was democratic in structure although few member clubs sent representatives to the annual general meetings.[19] Full responsibility for the operation of this new sports body was to be taken by the officers and a series of quite strict regulations was introduced to ensure that properly constituted authority was respected. An officer from each regiment was to play in every match;[20] correspondence and arrangements for matches were to be carried out by officers; officers were to be the umpires in all matches and referees should be either an officer not a member of the competing units or a civilian.[21] This was an ideal which could not be maintained. Relatively few officers had played association football at school and fewer still were good enough to be included in their unit teams on merit. Most regimental teams were soon like that of 1/Wiltshire Regiment in 1894 with the club having Lieutenant-Colonel

---

[17] Major General H. M. Bengough, 'The Soldier as He Is', *Navy and Army Illustrated*, 17 January 1896.
[18] The amount of time troopers spent on stable duties which extended their working hours may have been partly responsible for this, although a Cavalry Cup was inaugurated in 1896 followed by a Household Brigade League and, in 1906, a Household Brigade Football Association to run it.
[19] See Army Football Association Com. Mins, 20 February 1908, Army Football Association, Aldershot (AFA), at which the hope was expressed that more would attend the general meetings than in former years. There probably was some improvement. At the 1910 AGM, for example, twenty units were represented and nine committee members; in 1911 it was twenty-four units and four committee members.
[20] Army FA rules 1890. New Rule 17.
[21] Umpires were replaced by linesmen in 1891 with the referee becoming the sole judge of fair and unfair play.

Haynes as president, a sergeant-major as vice-president, a lieutenant as treasurer, a corporal as secretary – with two other corporals as assistants – and a committee consisting of two drummers, two bandsmen, two privates, another corporal and a lance-corporal.[22]

There can be no doubt that seriously competitive football in the army was stimulated by the establishment of the Army Cup in 1888. This was a knock-out competition for representative unit teams on the same lines as the FA Cup.[23] Forty-four teams entered the first competition, and these had more than doubled to ninety-three by 1913–14, by which time, as the regimental journal of the Leicestershire Regiment put it, it was 'the only thing that one particularly wishes to win'.[24] The first Army Cup final was played at the Oval in London, venue for all the FA Cup finals between 1874 and 1892. On 27 March 1889, a Wednesday afternoon, 2/Argyll and Sutherland Highlanders beat 2/South Staffordshire Regiment 2–0. A big crowd, mostly of soldiers admitted free, looked on, and the match was refereed by Major Francis Marindin, former Royal Engineer, President of the FA, and probably the foremost referee in England at that time. The umpires were also two undoubted members of the officer class, A.T.B. Dunn, an Old Etonian, and A. Hetherington of the Casuals club. The Duke of Cambridge arrived at half-time, which was soon enough to present the cup and medals.[25] In 1893 the final moved to Aldershot, where it soon became a feature of Easter Monday and regularly attracted crowds estimated at between 10,000 and 20,000, almost all of them soldiers. Frequently attended by senior officers and royalty, it was not only a prestigious sporting event but a social occasion.

By the 1890s many regimental clubs had impressive fixture lists not only with other army teams but with civilian ones. 1/Queen's Own (Royal West Kent Regiment) serve as a good example. In 1891–2 the team, based at Shorncliffe near Folkestone, played thirty-five matches, only fourteen of which were against military opposition. Their civilian opponents included the touring team from Canada and a visit to Royal Arsenal at Plumstead.[26] A notable coup for the representative army team was to gain a match with the leading amateur eleven of the day, and sometime scourge of the professionals, the Corinthians. The first of what would become an annual match was played at the Oval on

[22] *Aldershot News*, 8 September 1894.
[23] In order to minimise travelling the matches were drawn in districts until the quarter-finals, and up to the semi-finals from 1902.
[24] *Green Tiger*, May 1909, 73.
[25] Army FA Minutes, 10 May 1889, AFA.
[26] *The Country Gentleman*, 28 May 1892.

24 December 1892 when an army team containing only one officer lost 4–3 after having led 3–0 at one point.[27]

In contrast with the early development of football, it was not until 1906 that the Army Rugby Union was founded – in a railway carriage, by a group of officers returning to Aldershot after playing for Blackheath against the West of Scotland. The Rugby Football Union made an Army Cup competition possible by agreeing (by a large majority at a special general meeting) to grant dispensation to army players 'who had been associated with the Northern Union professional body'. It also presented the trophy, which was first played for in 1907. Since the main aim was to introduce rugby to other ranks Army Cup rules limited the number of officers per team to eight. But, as Major Rainsford-Hannay remembered, most other ranks 'had never seen any other football than Association, and at the start many difficulties were encountered'.[28] Indeed, the major difficulty facing the ARU was the overwhelming popularity of football in the services. Most regiments simply ignored rugby; others refused to compromise their success at football by taking up rugby as well. In the eight seasons before the First World War the Army Cup was dominated by four regiments: the Welch Regiment, the Leicestershire Regiment, the Duke of Wellington's West Riding Regiment, and the Gloucestershire Regiment. When the Leicestershire Regiment started playing rugby in 1907 its captain was an England international, Lieutenant W. C. Wilson, but 'at least half of the XV had never handled a rugby football before'. As became obvious when Wilson was 'laid out' during a trouncing by Leicester Tigers, 'the team without their Skipper is like a Bar without a Barmaid – I mean of course not so attractive'. They still won the Army Cup in 1908 – a triumph celebrated in song at the local music hall – in 1911 and again in 1912. The rugby cup was a comparatively easy trophy to win: only twelve teams entered in 1907 and twenty-four by 1913. But standards improved fast. By 1913 teams needed to be 'up to the level of a first-class club' to have any hope of winning.[29] Rugby nevertheless remained largely an officer sport. It was not until 1913 that the Devonport Services club included other ranks, and the annual Army

---

[27] *Times*, 23 December, 26 December 1892.
[28] J. McLaren, *The History of Army Rugby* (Aldershot: Army Rugby Union, 1986), pp. 5–7; *Times*, 24 October 1906; *Cavalry Journal* 2 (1907), 262; Major J. Rainsford-Hannay, 'The Army Rugby Union, Its Inception and History', *BEF Sports Journal* 1 (8 February 1919), 5.
[29] *Green Tiger*, December 1907, 137; November 1908, 136; June 1908, 66–7; McLaren, *Army Rugby*, pp. 178–81; Rainsford-Hannay, 'The Army Rugby Union', 5; *Times*, 31 March 1913.

Figure 2. Rugby team of the 1st Battalion, Leicestershire Regiment, winners of the 1910–11 Army Rugby Cup; Lieutenant W. C. Wilson in middle row, to left of cup.

v. Navy game, first played in 1878 but not revived until 1905, remained officers-only until 1919.[30]

Even more than rugby, cricket was an officers' game. An ex-NCO commented on the discomfort of private soldiers included in officer-dominated teams, and Captain Henry Baird spent much of an essay on 'Cricket in the Army' in ridiculing other ranks players. Top players found it difficult to establish a first-class career in civilian cricket because of the barriers of summer training, foreign service and difficulties in securing leave; those born overseas also had problems in obtaining a county qualification. Hampshire, incorporating both Aldershot and Portsmouth, benefited most from service cricketers: in fact its fortunes often depended on the availability of military players. Captain Wynyard (the only serving soldier to play in a test match in England before 1914) captained the side 1896–9 and in 1896 scored 268 runs against Yorkshire; Major Poore scored 1,399 runs for Hampshire in 1899; Captain J.G. Greig, on leave from India, made 249 not out against Lancashire in 1901. But there was little serious cricket within

---

[30] *Athletic News*, 20 January 1913; McLaren, *Army Rugby*, pp. 78–9. Between 1871 and 1939 officers in the military provided more England rugby union internationals than any other occupation (T. Collins, *A Social History of English Rugby Union* (London: Routlege, 2009), appendix 2, pp. 216–19).

the army: there was no inter-regimental cup and before 1919 no Army Cricket Association.[31]

Cross-country running, occupying an ambiguous place somewhere between sport and military training, had been popular with some units at least from the 1890s. In 1899, 19th Field Battery and a civilian club held a joint 'seven-mile paperchase across country' from Topsham Barracks, Exeter. But the first unit to practise cross-country running systematically was 1/Royal Irish Fusiliers, who introduced it to Aldershot Command in 1908. In 1906 and 1907 they had won both the team and individual prizes (with their star runner Private Cook) at the All-Ireland Regimental Championships. An Aldershot championship, instituted in 1909, was won by the Fusiliers every year until 1911, after which they left for Shorncliffe to monopolise the Eastern Command championships. Their successors as Aldershot champions, 1/Hampshire Regiment, had deliberately copied their training methods. In April 1913, to rebut a suggestion that 'their ability was confined to a score or so of specialists', the Hampshires ran a race against the Royal Munster Fusiliers in which some 1,200 soldiers took part. The Munsters won with 297 men home within the set time against the Hampshires' 194. By 1913–14 military teams were winning civilian cross-country competitions across the south of England. The Irish Fusiliers had long used cross-country running as an alternative to route marching, and in this respect too their example was followed. A 1913 memorandum on army training reported that 'cross-country running is practised in most battalions … undoubtedly the men are far more active and alert than they were a few years ago'.[32] In the same year a group of officers, led by Captain Reginald Kentish of the Irish Fusiliers and including Captain R. B. Campbell and Colonel Couper of the Army Gymnastic Staff, established an Army Athletic Association to encourage and control cross-country running and athletics. One of its main aims was to improve facilities to 'enable Commanding Officers

---

[31] 'Ex-Non-Com', 'The Soldier in Relation to Regimental Sport', *United Service Magazine* 40 (1909–10), 32–6; Captain Henry H. C. Baird, 'Cricket in the Army', in P. Warner (ed.), *Imperial Cricket* (London: London and Counties Press Association, 1912), pp. 475–86; 'Captain E. G. Wynyard', *Baily's Magazine* 68 (1897), 435–7; J. Lonsdale, *The Army's Grace: The Life of Brigadier-General R. M. Poore* (Tunbridge Wells: Spellmount, 1992), pp. 3, 60–79; *Athletic News*, 29 June 1914, 5 October 1914; *Games and Sports in the Army* (1932–3), pp. 262–73.

[32] *Broad Arrow*, 1 April 1899; *Lloyd's Weekly News*, 6 April 1913, 27 April 1913; Colonel G. W. W. Hill, 'Fifty Years of Sport in the Royal Irish Fusiliers', unpublished typescript, 7707-45, National Army Museum (NAM); C. E. K. (Captain Kinahan), 'The Need of Games in the Army', *Faugh-a-Ballagh* 4 (January 1907), 11–13, at 13; *Athletic News*, 28 April 1913, 23 February 1914; WO 279/553, quoted in Campbell, 'The Army Isn't All Work', p. 121.

to give effect to the principles laid down in the Training Manuals of all branches of the Army [that] ... "MANLY Games are of value provided ALL the men and not a few selected teams take their part"'.[33]

Kentish in fact was the prime mover in transforming the provision of sports grounds for troops in Britain. Arriving at Aldershot in 1908, he found that, while amenities for officer sport were excellent, those for other ranks were poor. Though there were 20,000 troops in the Aldershot Command, only those corps with a permanent base there, such as the Royal Engineers, the Royal Army Medical Corps and the Royal Army Service Corps, had grounds of their own. Kentish's battalion had access to a football ground only six days a month, since they shared it with three other battalions. With the approval of General Sir Horace Smith-Dorrien, commanding Aldershot, and assisted by the Royal Engineers, Kentish began building playing fields with soldier labour, an operation of 'vast proportions, entailing ... the clearance of big areas of trees, much excavation ... and the deviation of existing roads, water courses and telegraph poles' and involving 'a permanent party of 500 men – and a further 2,000 men on route marching days'. Within a few years Aldershot had sixty-two sports grounds, and in 1913 the Army Council approved the scheme's extension under Kentish's supervision to all Commands. He had time only to begin with Tidworth and Plymouth before work was interrupted by the outbreak of war, the troops 'then having to go and dig elsewhere'.[34] As honorary secretary of the Army Football Association Kentish also enclosed Aldershot Athletic Ground, which included three football pitches, and built a covered stand. The £1,000 required was partially recouped by (unprecedentedly) charging soldiers for admission.[35]

As Kentish demonstrates, initiatives for sport in the services often came from individual soldiers or sailors with a sporting agenda. Sometimes such initiatives came from the top. As Commander-in-Chief of the Mediterranean Fleet (1899–1902) Admiral Fisher increased the number of playing fields at Malta, promoted inter-ship

---

[33] 'Army Athletic Association – Proposed Formation, 1913–14', WO32/5492, The National Archives (TNA); *Athletic News*, 13 November 1916.
[34] Brigadier-General R.J. Kentish papers, 'RJK 2 Accounts of Early Life', 98/12/1, Imperial War Museum (IWM); B. Kentish, *This Foul Thing Called War* (Lewes: Book Guild, 1997), pp. 41–3; *Aldershot Command News*, 3 April 1928.
[35] *Athletic News*, 22 September 1913, 13 October 1913, 8 December 1913. Though Kentish felt that he had been given insufficient credit for his original idea (both Smith-Dorrien and General Harington claiming it for themselves), after his death in 1956 a plaque was unveiled in front of the Aldershot grandstand commemorating 'his services to the Army Football Association and his work in providing recreation grounds for the soldier' (Kentish, *Foul Thing*, p. 46).

and inter-squadron competitions and 'never failed to be present himself whenever important matches were played'.[36] Of the officer commanding Pontefract Garrison in the 1890s the military newspaper *Broad Arrow* reported:

Colonel Clark does everything to encourage sport among the men ... Since his arrival the Modified Gymnasium has been fixed, and sports on the gymkhana principle take place each month from spring to autumn. A cricket pitch at a cost of £50 has been laid down, and in addition Colonel Clark has presented a handsome silver football shield.[37]

More often the moving spirit was a sports-obsessed junior officer. 'Tim' Harington, the King's Regiment, remembered his time at Colchester in the mid-1890s 'chiefly for the amount of games I both played and ran there. Cricket, rugby, association, tennis, racquets, hockey etc. I think I must have done very little soldiering'.[38] 1/Royal Irish Fusiliers, said to be 'the first unit to apply the science of organisation to regimental athletics', boasted a whole group of sporting officers: not only Kentish but Lieutenant H.W.M. Yates (captain of the army football team), Captain C.E. Kinahan (an Olympic and Irish International hurdler), and Lieutenant G.W.W. Hill, a cross-country champion who later compiled a record of the battalion's sporting achievements.[39] Such enthusiasm created a sporting atmosphere. In 1909 Colonel Sherer assured Leicestershire Regiment's sportsmen that their fortunes were 'closely followed by all the Officers who knew the result of the event the same night, whether it be athletics, boxing, football, or cricket'.[40]

Equally crucial to the organisation of both army and navy sport were non-commissioned officers, to whom the training and organising of service sportsmen offered an area where they could exercise skill and authority. The United Services Football League at Portsmouth was managed by NCOs from both services – though when problems arose with the allocation of sports grounds the Superintendent of Gymnasia was only prepared to discuss the matter with a committee of officers.[41] The Portsmouth Royal Artillery football team, spectacularly though briefly successful in the 1890s, was run by two NCOs, Sergeant Major

[36] Kemp, *The British Sailor*, p. 210.
[37] *Broad Arrow*, 25 March 1899, 335–6.
[38] General Sir Charles Harington, *Tim Harington Looks Back* (London: Murray, 1940), p. 12. Harington subsequently became the first president of the Army Sport Control Board.
[39] Lieutenant G.W.W. Hill, 'Fifty Years of Sport in the Royal Irish Fusiliers'; *Lloyd's Weekly News*, 6 April 1913.
[40] *Green Tiger*, August 1909, 123.
[41] Minutes of the United Services (Football) League Committee, 14 October 1913, 4 November 1913, 27 November 1913, RNSPT.

F. Windrum and Sergeant R. Bonney.[42] Sergeant-Major Fowles was the leading spirit of boxing in 1/Grenadier Guards.[43] No wonder that, discussing the shortage of officers in 1910, General Sir Ian Hamilton 'looked to the ranks of sports-playing, charismatic junior NCOs to supply additional officers for the army in wartime'. (Both Windrum and Fowles were subsequently commissioned.)[44] Even private soldiers could be influential in regimental sport. In 1894 the *Bugle*, the journal of 2/Durham Light Infantry at Mhow, commented favourably on the attempts of Private Walsh, already prominent in battalion football, to start a rugby club. Knight-Bruce thought it essential for regimental boxing clubs to include 'privates picked for their intelligence, tact, and keenness' to encourage wide participation through 'the personal appeal and homely persuasions that no one else can give'.[45]

Funding for regimental sports equipment and prizes came mainly from canteen profits. In addition, privates typically paid about 3d. monthly as football or cricket club subscriptions and sergeants '2s. 6d. for the cricket, football and shooting clubs, &c., to which they are practically compelled to belong'.[46] Sometimes officers, especially those who died young, left bequests to encourage regimental sport, like Captain the Hon. Lonsdale R. D. Gray of the 6th Dragoon Guards (Carabiniers) who left £300 as 'The Gray Fund for the promotion of sport, including only shooting, fishing, cricket, football and polo' at his death aged thirty during the Boer War.[47] As army sport grew so did its organisation at regimental level. In 1895 3/Rifle Brigade, stationed in India, was persuaded by Major Frank Raikes, a keen cricketer, to start a sporting club with monthly subscriptions on a sliding scale from one anna for riflemen to one rupee for officers. The club funded entry fees and expenses for football teams in inter-regimental tournaments and men representing the regiment at station sports and provided prizes for regimental

---

[42] A. Gibson and W. Pickford, *Association Football and the Men Who Made It*, 4 vols. (London: Caxton, 1906), vol. IV, pp. 68–9. The Portsmouth RA team is discussed in detail in chapter 5.

[43] *Brigade of Guards Magazine* 6 (1893), 210.

[44] G. Sheffield, *Leadership in the Trenches* (Basingstoke: Macmillan, 2000), pp. 56–7. The percentage of officers commissioned from the ranks was extremely low: 2.0% for 1896–1900, 3.2% for 1901–5 (presumably due to the Boer War), and 2.2% for 1906–10 (Spiers, *The Army and Society* p. 4).

[45] *Bugle*, 14 June 1894; J. H. W. Knight-Bruce, 'Regimental Boxing Clubs and Military Boxing Tournaments', in Bohun Lynch, *The Complete Amateur Boxer*, pp. 211–12.

[46] H. Wyndham, *The Queen's Service* (London: Heinemann, 1899), pp. 103, 256, 259.

[47] *Times*, 6 November 1900. See also, e.g., *Broad Arrow*, 2 October 1897, 362 (Lieutenant B. W. Holman); *Rifle Brigade Chronicle* 1895, 287–9 and B. Farwell, *Mr Kipling's Army* (New York: Norton, 1981), p. 27 (Captain Frederick Eyre Lawrence).

sports.[48] By the Edwardian period this kind of sports administration was common. The replacement in 1913 of the system of dividing battalions into eight companies 'with all their traditions of rivalry in work and in sport' with a four-company system brought further reorganisation. 1/Black Watch, disturbed by the implications for participation rates, responded by introducing an 'all-round' inter-company championship in which marks were given for cross-country running, four separate football competitions, swimming, boxing, cricket and hockey, as well as musketry and bayonet fighting.[49] The growth of sport within regiments thus both encouraged and reflected sporting developments across the army as a whole.

Sport in the navy faced different challenges. Even at sea there was 'scarcely a game that is not played in a more or less modified form on board Her Majesty's war-ships'. Boxing, hockey and cricket were most common. A reporter for the *Navy and Army Illustrated* 'at sea with the Channel Squadron' explained the workings of shipboard cricket:

> The seine (with which every ship is supplied) makes a most efficient cricket net, and stretches completely around the deck. Buckets form the wickets, and the cricket balls are made of spun yarn wound upon a basis of cork ... a penalty is generally exacted from the batsman for a ball hit overboard. A good scoring hit is down a hatchway, or ventilator, in fact there is a good deal of excitement about this sort of cricket.

In 1899 the Reserve Squadron organised inter-ship cricket matches on board during manoeuvres, the officers' team of HMS *Trafalgar* challenging a combined team of officers from HMS *Nile* and HMS *San Pareil* and beating them by fifty runs.[50]

But of course most navy sport took place while ships were in port. Football was the sailor's game as it was the soldier's. By 1896 there were 'few ships serving on stations where the climate allows of violent exercise ... that has not its football team'.[51] The Mediterranean Fleet Cup, presented by the officers and men of HMS *Empress of India*, was first played for in 1898–9. Run between October and March, it reflected

---

[48] *Rifle Brigade Chronicle* 1896, 265–9; 1897, 334. The idea of a sports club had been considered earlier but dropped, it proving 'a difficult matter to arrive at the real opinion of the men on the subject'. There were sixteen annas to the rupee. In 1899 the value of the rupee was fixed at fifteen rupees to the pound (thus 1 anna = 1 d.) but earlier in the 1890s it had fluctuated, reaching twenty rupees to the pound at times.
[49] *Black Watch Chronicle* 1 (1914), 122–6.
[50] *Navy and Army Illustrated*, 26 November 1897, 22 April 1899, 9 September 1899, 2 December 1899.
[51] *Navy and Army Illustrated*, 27 November 1896.

the enthusiasm for the game within the fleet but also the special organisational problems which being at sea entailed. It was not possible for every ship's team to play every other ship's team. To qualify a ship had to play at least two-thirds of all those entered in the league: the team with the greatest percentage of points per number of matches played won. The rules even provided a list of legitimate excuses to cancel fixtures: ships going through the range, except on Saturdays; the match having been scheduled less than forty-eight hours after arrival in harbour or after coaling; and if the ship was preparing for inspection. In the first year twenty-two ships entered, though not all managed to play the qualifying number of matches, and the cup was won by HMS *Anson*'s team (a surgeon, four seamen, a petty officer, four stokers and a Marine corporal) after playing seventeen matches and winning twelve.[52]

It was these kinds of logistical problems which contributed to the delay in forming a Royal Navy Football Association until 1904, sixteen years after the Army FA had been established. A United Services League, containing several naval teams, had flourished in Portsmouth from 1897, and this must also have provided some impetus, but the immediate spur was the influence of the journalist and Hampshire FA member William Pickford, who was concerned by the difficulties caused by the fact that most ships' clubs were not affiliated to any football organisation.[53] With the success of the Army Cup obviously in view, the RNFA quickly set up a knock-out tournament, the Navy Cup, open to naval shore establishments and ships stationed in Home waters or the Channel Fleet. A cup was presented by the *Southern Daily Mail*, and the Portsmouth Royal Naval Barracks team were the first winners. Shore establishments would win every year up to 1914.[54] Organising the Navy Cup proved much more difficult than running the Army one. Ships were often either at sea or abroad in the early part of the year at just the time when the competition was played. 'Exigencies of service' made it hard to fix dates in advance and forced teams to scratch at short notice. This provoked a good deal of structural tinkering with the Cup which was reflected in the relative lack of interest taken in it

---

[52] *Royal Naval Football Association Handbook* (1906–7), pp. 54–7; *Navy and Army Illustrated*, 29 July 1899.

[53] W. Pickford, 'Veteran's Views. A Navy Association' and 'Veteran's Views. The Proposed Navy FA' (1903), William Pickford Papers, Hampshire Football Association, Southampton (HFA).

[54] And beyond. It was not until 1932 that a team representing the 2nd Battle Squadron, Home Fleet won, and the single ship's team to win before 1945 was that of HMS *Ark Royal* in 1939, eighteen months before she was torpedoed and sunk in 1941. *RNFA Handbook* (1954–5), pp. 74–5.

The growth of service sport

by the Fleet.[55] The Navy FA also faced some unique problems in sports organisation, in 1905 losing its register of referees when HMS *Syren* ran aground on the Irish coast.[56] Yet football in the Navy prospered in spite of the difficulties, both contributing to and benefiting from a close relationship with the football sub-cultures in the ports of Chatham, Plymouth and Portsmouth. Fixtures were arranged against civilian teams and the army. In 1908 a new football ground reclaimed from the Mere at Portland opened with a match between Dorset County and the Channel Fleet kicked off by Admiral Beresford.[57] The Army was beaten for the first time in the same year after the Navy players had been kept together for ten days before the match for practice and training.[58]

As in the army there was a strong class basis to navy sport, football being played overwhelmingly by the lower deck and rugby and cricket by officers. Rugby was taken seriously at the Royal Naval Engineering College, Keyham and the Edwardian navy side contained such Internationals as W. J. A. Davies and E. W. Roberts, both former students at Keyham. A Naval Rugby Union was formed in 1906, at the same time as the Army Rugby Union.[59] Cricket was played with 'great keenness' at Osborne and Dartmouth and by cadets in training cruisers, but the navy almost invariably lost its annual match against the army (which replaced a previous navy fixture against the Gentlemen of the MCC in 1908) because officers on the home station found their summers largely occupied by firing, manoeuvres and battle practice. Overseas, however, the situation was different. At Gibraltar there was 'any amount of cricket to be had' on a matting wicket, mostly against regimental teams. At Port Said, 'it is seldom a ship goes through … without playing a match against the local eleven', and cricket could also be found at Singapore, Hong Kong, Amoy, Shanghai, Wei-hai-wei, where it was played 'continuously every day when the Fleet are up there for the summer', and most ports on the Cape Station. As Lieutenant G. C. Harrison concluded, 'wherever there is an English community one can invariably get a game played in a good sporting spirit'.[60]

---

[55] Royal Navy and Royal Marines FA Minutes, Annual Meeting, 31 May 1921, RNSPT. In 1906 the Football Association recorded 180 naval football teams, compared with 578 teams from the army (T. Collins, 'English Rugby Union and the First World War', *Historical Journal* 45 (2002), 797–817, at 799).
[56] Royal Navy Football Association Minutes, 11 July 1905, RNSPT.
[57] *Times*, 4 September 1908.
[58] Royal Navy FA Minutes, General Council, 3 March 1908, RNSPT.
[59] W. J. A. Davies, *Rugby Football and How to Play It* (London: Webster's, 1923), p. 15, p. 44.
[60] Lieutenant G. C. Harrison, 'Cricket in the Navy', in Warner (ed.), *Imperial Cricket*, pp. 465–74.

Indeed, the services, together with traders, missionaries and educationalists, were important agents in the diffusion of British sport across the Empire. In cricket Major R. M. Poore, 'the Army's Grace', first made his mark in India in the 1890s playing for the 7th Hussars and a variety of civilian teams including Secunderabad Gymnasium, Lord Harris's team Ganeshkhind and Bengal and Bombay Presidencies. Captain John Dunn was the star of the Hong Kong team, most of whose members were drowned returning in the *Bokhara* from an inter-port match against Shanghai in 1892.[61] Hockey was introduced to Australia by the navy and to India, where it was quickly adopted by the indigenous population and the Indian army, by army officers. It has been suggested that the prisoner-of-war camps of the Boer War were significant in spreading rugby and cricket among the Afrikaner population. Held captive in St Helena, Ceylon and India, Boer POWs hitherto unfamiliar with these sports learnt them not only from sporting fellow prisoners but from the British soldiers guarding them, the British military authorities providing encouragement and equipment.[62] Meanwhile in South Africa men from the Coloured community of the Western Cape were discovering football while serving as mule-drivers and scouts for the British army, and regimental games in Cape Town and other ports brought the game to the notice of the black population.[63] The founding legend of Indian football tells of ten-year-old Nagendraprasad Sarbadhikary 'kicking the ball back' to a group of British soldiers on the Calcutta Maidan in the late 1870s, subsequently introducing the game to his friends at Hare School.[64] As Frank Richards of the Royal Welch Fusiliers put it, 'if we are ever so unfortunate as to lose our Empire it is a safe bet that soccer will continue to be played all over the world … in eternal memory of the British soldiers who accidentally brought the game along in their kit-bags'.[65]

To the 75,000 British soldiers serving in India sport provided very necessary diversion. As chapter 2 discusses, India was considered a sporting paradise for officers, but even they found that 'the great

---

[61] Lonsdale, *The Army's Grace*, ch. 3; *Athletic News*, 29 June 1914.
[62] F. J. G. Van der Merwe, 'Sport and Games in Boer Prisoner-of-war Camps during the Anglo-Boer War, 1899–1902', *International Journal of the History of Sport* 9 (1992), 439–540; D. Allen, 'Bats and Bayonets: Cricket and the Anglo-Boer War, 1899–1902', *Sport in History* 25 (2005), 17–40, at 32–5.
[63] Clayton, 'Sport and African Soldiers', 117–18.
[64] B. Majumdar, 'From Recreation to Competition: Early History of Indian Football', *Soccer and Society* 6 (2005), 123–41, at 130–1; P. Dimeo, 'Football and Politics in Bengal: Colonialism, Nationalism, Communalism', *Soccer and Society* 2 (2001), 57–74, at 65.
[65] F. Richards, *Old-Soldier Sahib* (London: Faber and Faber, 1936), p. 297.

difficulty in India is to dispose of one's leisure time', especially as no work took place on Thursday or Sunday. For other ranks, India was less attractive. Even ordinary soldiers could go out on shooting parties in search of small game – John Fraser's colonel granted shooting leave 'to all who applied for it, from Wednesday afternoon to Saturday night' – though the civil administration discouraged this after a number of Indian cultivators had been killed or wounded.[66] But, as one old soldier recalled, the 'one great weapon against boredom ... was sport, sport, sport'. Ernest Humphries, an NCO in the Royal Scots at Allahabad, remembered that soldiers were 'married to the regiment' because of the lack of social contact with civilians: 'your whole interest was wrapped up in the company or the battalion in their football and their hockey and their athletics'. Indeed, the monotony of peacetime soldiering in India was such that sport was often the major interest. 1/Sherwood Foresters' report from Bangalore in 1910 – 'the battalion has passed a very uneventful year so far as soldiering is concerned, but it has distinguished itself in several branches of athletics' – could have been echoed by many other regiments.[67]

The Indian climate certainly posed problems for sport. In the hot season soldiers spent most of the day lying on their beds out of the sun and the grounds, hacked out by hard labour and dynamite, were baked rock-hard. In 1909 Sherwood Foresters had 'about forty men attending hospital on account of abrasions, sprains, etc., caused by football'.[68] Nevertheless sport was particularly valued in India as an aid to health. As early as 1863 the Royal Commission on the Sanitary State of the Army in India, heavily influenced by Florence Nightingale, deplored the lack of recreation provided for soldiers and the consequent 'weary idleness of their lives', and linked their 'want of exercise' to the 'high rate of sickness and mortality'.[69] By the 1880s sport, along with other

[66] *Bugle*, 16 August 1894; J. Fraser, *Sixty Years in Uniform* (London: Stanley, Paul & Co., 1939), p. 94; J.M. MacKenzie, *The Empire of Nature* (Manchester University Press, 1988), p. 190.
[67] C. Allen, *Plain Tales from the Raj* (Newton Abbot: Readers Union, 1976), p. 156; Ernest Humphries interviewed in 1972, quoted in P.H. Liddle and M.J. Richardson, 'Voices from the Past: An Evaluation of Oral History as a Source for Research into the Western Front Experience of the British Soldier, 1914–18', *Journal of Contemporary History* 31 (1996), 651–74, at 655; *Sherwood Foresters Regimental Annual* 2 (1910), 43.
[68] *Sherwood Foresters Regimental Annual* 1 (1909), 63.
[69] Rob Hess, 'A Healing Hegemony: Florence Nightingale, the British Army in India and "a want of ... exercise"', *International Journal of the History of Sport* 15 (1998), 1–17; *Report of the Royal Commission on the Sanitary State of the Army in India* [3184] 1863, p. lxiv. The Commission suggested that gymnasia and gymnastics might be the 'best thing ever introduced into the service in India'. Quoits, fives, cricket and sometimes football were already played and 'almost every station' had a ball-court and skittle-alley.

amusements, was being used to 'keep up the men's cheerfulness ... fighting against the ennui that is the breeding ground of sickness'.[70]

All the main sports played by the army in Britain reappeared in India, though not quite in the same order of significance. Hockey, which the army had begun playing in Ireland in the late nineteenth century, had some popularity in Britain (there was an Army Hockey Association and an Army Cup) but was far more prevalent in India, where the hard, dry grounds made it a faster and more skilful game.[71] Boxing was a major interest in the winter months. The 'All-India Championships' were held annually in rotation at the main troop centres. In 1911, at Delhi, they ran for sixteen evenings in an open-air arena which could hold 8,000 spectators. In the 1900s several regiments clubbed together to bring to India as a trainer the professional Jim Maloney. Maloney trained 'Bombardier' Billy Wells, flagged up his talents in the British boxing press and became his manager once Wells, on his advice, had bought himself out of the army for £21.[72] Some suggested that rugby was more popular in India than at home, but it was still a minority sport, and serious rugby-playing units like the Leicestershire Regiment had difficulty finding opponents. There was no army championship in India, though regimental teams were prominent in rugby in Madras, Calcutta and Bombay. From 1894 2/Welch Regiment won the Bombay Cup eight years running.[73]

But football was again the major other-ranks sport, though it took time to become universal. In 1886 a new draft from Britain brought out to the Northumberland Fusiliers, who had only been in India since 1880, 'a new game ... Association Football'.[74] But a few years later 2/Durham Light Infantry's newspaper was complaining of a 'perfect mania' for the game. By the 1890s Calcutta had become a place 'where everything is set aside in certain months of the year to encourage football, where an unlimited supply of first-rate grounds are at the disposal of football players, and where ... the public ... c[o]me in their hundreds to witness the different matches and to cheer on their favourites'.[75]

[70] Lieutenant-General Sir Robert Baden-Powell, *Indian Memories* (London: Herbert Jenkins, 1915), pp. 92, 96.
[71] *Times*, 12 June 1908, 5 September 1908, 26 January 1909, 18 February 1909, 24 April 1909, 27 November 1909; David Morgan, 'Stick and Ball Games', unpublished typescript, 9205–276, NAM; F. G. Aflalo (ed.), *The Sportsman's Book for India* (London: H. Marshall & Son, 1904), pp. 512–15.
[72] Shipley, *Bombardier Billy Wells*, ch. 3.
[73] *Athletic News*, 18 October 1915; *Green Tiger*, October 1908, 123, December 1908, 155–8; McLaren, *Army Rugby*, pp. 21–2; *Navy and Army Illustrated*, 3 February 1900.
[74] Fraser, *Sixty Years*, p. 154.
[75] *Bugle*, 14 June 1894; *Rifle Brigade Chronicle*, 1895, 246.

By 1905 the biggest army football competition outside the UK was the Punjab-Bengal Cup, started ten years before by Lieutenant E. G. Curtis of the Bedfordshire Regiment and now the 'blue-ribbon' army event of Northern India. Most open competitions were also dominated by the military. The Durand Cup at Simla, established by Sir Mortimer Durand in 1888, and the Rovers Cup at Bombay, first played for in 1891, were won by British regimental teams every year until 1940 and 1937 respectively. Military teams won the Calcutta Football League 'on all but nine occasions between its foundation in 1898 and 1933'. When in 1911 Mohun Bagan became the first Indian team to win the Indian Football Association Shield they had to beat three British regimental teams in the process.[76] At local level military and civilian competition proliferated. 1/Sherwood Foresters' fixtures included the Madras Gymkhana Cup, the South India Athletic Association Cup, the Local Gymkhana Cup at Secunderabad, the Gentle Cup, the British Soldiers' Club Cup, and the Bangalore Brewery Cup.[77]

Given the normal attitude of British other ranks in India that 'what had been conquered by the sword must be kept by the sword' – an attitude that translated into habitual bullying and sometimes brutality towards the Indians with whom they came into contact – the regularity of inter-racial football matches is striking. Although barriers were often imposed to restrict Indian participation in football tournaments, sport provided a rare opportunity for friendly contact between Indians and British troops – and not just in formal competitions. The Royal Welch Fusiliers often played matches against a team of 'native students' from Roorkee college. When in 1913 2/Black Watch marched to Dhaka from Calcutta, where they had developed a strong local football reputation, they were 'met at every halting place by Indian teams who were more than anxious to play the Black Watch Football Club'.[78] Sport was introduced to Indian troops in the 1890s, in the hope of shaping them into British models of 'manliness' and the 'martial spirit'. Segregation of competitions preserved imperial hierarchies: British and Indian troops were formally banned from competing against each other in military (though not civilian) sporting contests. Nevertheless, in casual and unofficial games sport and especially football provided a link between

---

[76] Dimeo, 'Football and Politics in Bengal', 58; T. Mason, 'Football on the Maidan: Cultural Imperialism in Calcutta', *International Journal of the History of Sport* 7 (1990), 85–96. The teams beaten by Mohun Bagan in 1911 were 2/Rifle Brigade (1–0), 1/Middlesex Regiment (1–1 and 3–0 in the replay), and 2/East Yorkshire Regiment (2–1 in the final).
[77] *Sherwood Foresters Regimental Annual* 1 (1909), 60–3; 2 (1910), 55.
[78] Richards, *Old-Soldier Sahib*, pp. 142–3, 296–7; *Black Watch Chronicle* 1 (1914), 219. No matches resulted, however, as 'no suitable playing grounds could be found'.

Figure 3. Empire Games. An inter-regimental football match at Murree, a hill station in Rawalpindi, 1896.

the men of India's two armies. Ernest Humphries recalled that 'in the evening we used to go along and have a chat with the Gurkha boys. We would invariably find them playing football and they would immediately split up and demand that we should join them ... forty Gurkhas on each side, each having two or three British ranks playing with them and with the ball being passed to the British ranks by every Gurkha on their side'.[79]

Even during the numerous 'small wars' of the late Victorian period soldiers managed a surprising amount of sport. As W. E. Cairns put it,

> should active operations be stopped for a time, every endeavour is at once made to keep up the health and spirits of the men by organising all sorts of sports and games for their benefit ... anyone suddenly dropping in on the camp ... would hardly believe that he was in the midst of a force engaged on an arduous campaign.

During the Second Afghan War the 59th (the Queen's Own) Regiment of Foot got up two teams – topically christened 'Ghilzais'

[79] Campbell, 'The Army Isn't All Work', ch. 6; *The ASCB Handbook India* (1936–7), p. 16; Allen, *Plain Tales*, pp. 109–10.

and 'Invaders' – to play a rugby match at Kalat-i-Ghilzai. Suitably the Invaders won, though the Ghilzais were said to have put up a better fight than their namesakes. Immediately before the disastrous battle of Majuba Hill in the First Boer War the 58th Regiment and the 60th Rifles played two games of cricket 'with pick handles for bats, and ammunition boxes for wickets'. Captain Curtis and the 1/Bedfordshires seized a moment in the Swat Valley en route to relieve Chitral in 1895 to play a football match, 'the touch and the goal lines [being] marked with string unwound from a native bedstead'. In the 1896 Sudan campaign British soldiers and the soldiers of the 13th Sudanese battalion at Akasheh organised games to relieve the monotony of waiting for the Dervishes to attack, 'tent-pegging, rounders and hockey being the most popular'.[80] During active service in the Boer War, the 5th Imperial Yeomanry managed a cricket match against the Honourable Artillery Company; athletic sports at Mafeking; and at Lichtenburg not only sports, boxing, and inter-squadron bareback wrestling on horses, but a 'Test Match' against the Australian Bushmen which 'England' narrowly won. Their commanding officer, Colonel Meyrick, fitted in a little shooting and some polo.[81]

How far did sport contribute to the efficiency of the Victorian and Edwardian army and navy? There was certainly an element of social control about service sport. Soldiers in peacetime typically had too much time on their hands and too little occupation to fill it. Encouraging healthy recreation would, it was hoped, keep soldiers and sailors away from pubs, brothels and other diversions likely to be prejudicial to military efficiency. Nor did this apply only to other ranks, especially on overseas postings. In 2/Durham Light Infantry at Mhow the adjutant's duties included encouraging young officers 'to go in for all manly games, such as cricket, football, polo etc., on the principle that if they don't go in for healthy amusements they will for others that are not healthy'.[82] Writing of India in the 1880s, John Fraser asked, 'what else was there for the soldier to do but drink? … Drunkenness was rather the fault of the authorities, who provided no alternative recreation for the Tommy in those days'. Drunkenness in the army did decline significantly from

---

[80] [W.E. Cairns], *Social Life in the British Army* (London: J. Long, 1900), p. 223; 'Football in Afghanistan', *Field* 53 (1879), 401; Colonel Sir P. Marling, *Rifleman and Hussar* (London: John Murray, 1931), pp. 52–3; Gibson and Pickford, *Association Football*, vol. III, p. 198; *Times*, 18 May 1896.
[81] R.F. Walker, 'The Boer War Diaries of Lt. Col. F.C. Meyrick', *Journal of the Society for Army Historical Research* 73 (1995), 155–80, at 177. Troops playing cricket while Boer fighters were in the vicinity apparently shocked the *Stirling Observer*: see Spiers, *The Scottish Soldier and Empire*, p. 195. See also Allen, 'Bats and Bayonets'.
[82] *Bugle*, 7 June 1894.

the late nineteenth century onwards, and sport probably played a part in this (that the Royal Army Temperance Association sponsored sporting competitions suggests they thought so).[83] In India sport was enlisted in the army's constant battle against venereal disease in the hope that 'men who take a pleasure in games and are proud of excelling in them will be less liable to risk themselves with prostitutes where disease is known to be so rife'. Kitchener, as Commander-in-Chief of the army in India 1902–9, rejected the traditional approach of providing regulated brothels in favour of encouraging abstinence. 'Drink and idleness' he thought the 'primary causes leading to impurity and disease': commanding officers should 'foster a love for games and outdoor exercises of all sorts' amongst their men. To the soldiers themselves he recommended 'all healthy outdoor sports and games' as a bulwark against the temptations of Indian life. For Kitchener, in fact, sport was of interest only as a route to military efficiency: one commanding officer complained that he had 'spoken of cricket as though it were a medicine to be taken twice weekly by the troops in summer'.[84]

Some hoped that, like other reforms in army life, better recreation would improve recruitment, that perennial problem of the British army, and persuade 'respectable' working-class men to enlist. 'Recruiting for the new [3rd] battalion of the Coldstreamers is being carried on briskly,' reported the *Navy and Army Illustrated*, a periodical both reflecting and promoting the improved status of the military, in 1898. 'Athletics of every description are encouraged in the regiment, and there should be no lack of men to swell its ranks.' The article was illustrated by a photograph of the Coldstreamers' football team. In early 1914 Frank Starr complained that the army authorities failed to appreciate 'the lure which military athletics offer to the hesitating recruit ... it is the attraction of the games and sports which tip the balance in 99 cases out of a hundred'.[85] Some at the War Office did value sport as a recruiting tool. In 1913 the Assistant Adjutant General, R.J. Strachey, remarked that 'the more complete the organisation of army sports the better for recruiting as a whole'. Sir Edward Ward, the Permanent Undersecretary, suggested that 'the advantages gained in Recruiting alone from a proper conduct of athletics' would justify a proposed new

---

[83] Fraser, *Sixty Years*, p. 84. For the decline of drunkenness, see French, *Military Identities*, pp. 182–3.
[84] *General Order by Commander-in-Chief in India, July 1897, regarding Means of Checking Venereal Disease among British Troops in India* [C. 9025], 1898; Sir George Arthur, *Life of Lord Kitchener*, 3 vols. (London: Macmillan, 1920), vol. II, pp. 271–6; P. Magnus, *Kitchener: Portrait of an Imperialist* (London: John Murray, 1958), p. 238.
[85] *Navy and Army Illustrated*, 4 June 1898; *Athletic News*, 23 February 1914.

post of director of army sport.[86] But others were sceptical. Before the First World War sport was systematically used for recruitment only by the auxiliary forces. Sport was one of the attractions of the nineteenth-century Volunteers, and when the Territorial Force was established in 1908 Joseph Lyons (of Lyons Corner House fame) introduced sports programmes organised by a 'General Council of Territorial Sports' in the hope of attracting 'a ready-made army of athletes'.[87]

If the case for sport as a recruiting draw was not clear before 1914, however, sport did contribute to the effective running of the services, and in a number of ways. As David French has recently argued, the adoption in 1881 of the Cardwell-Childers system of doubling and renaming regiments meant that these new regiments had rapidly to create new identities to foster discipline and *esprit de corps*. The problem was made more difficult by the fact that some of the twinned regiments disliked each other; in any case they rarely met since one was normally stationed at home and the other overseas. Army sport, expanding concurrently with these developments, undoubtedly contributed to forging these regimental 'imagined communities'. Sports kit featured regimental colours and emblems. Regimental journals – which for the same reasons became widespread from the late nineteenth century – covered regimental sport in loving detail (those published at intervals of months rather than years had often little else to report) and battalions congratulated each other on sporting victories through their pages. When the 1st and 2nd battalions of the Leicestershire Regiment met in 1906 for the first time since 1882, at Belgaum in India, they marked the occasion with a football match.[88]

Sports teams provided soldiers with a focus for expressions of loyalty to the regiment. Hundreds of supporters might escort teams to away matches, often by special train. At the 1913 Army Rugby Cup final 2/Welch Regiment's supporters came equipped with daffodils, leeks and the Welch regimental goat, which 'studiously ignored the game from a central position'.[89] Successful teams could expect a triumphant homecoming. When the Lancashire Fusiliers team returned

---

[86] 'Army Athletic Association', WO32/5492, TNA.
[87] H. Cunningham, *The Volunteer Force* (London: Croom Helm, 1975), ch. 6; L. Jackson, 'Patriotism or Pleasure? The Nineteenth Century Volunteer Force as a Vehicle for Rural Working-Class Male Sport', *Sports Historian* 19:1 (1999), 125–39; J. Lyons, 'Sports and Territorials: How to Popularise the Force', *National Defence* 3 (August 1909), 137–9. For Territorial sporting programmes see also, e.g., *Times*, 5 July 1910; *Cavalry Journal* 5 (1910), 554, 6 (1911), 261; *Sporting Life*, 10 October 1912; *Athletic News*, 17 March 1913, 2 March 1914.
[88] French, *Military Identities*, esp. ch. 1; *Green Tiger*, December 1906, 4.
[89] *Times*, 31 March 1913.

to Athlone barracks as 1897 army football champions of Ireland, they were escorted through the streets with the drums of the battalion playing and a flaming torch in the shape of their old regimental number (XX), 'a large number of townspeople turning out to give them a hearty cheer'.[90] Arriving home with the 1908 Army Rugby Cup, the Leicesters' team were invited by the colonel into the officers' mess, where the cup was filled with champagne; in the following days it passed to the sergeants' mess, then to the corporals', before going on general show in the gymnasium.[91] Such victories were rare, but 1/Leicestershire Regiment marked the place of sport in its corporate identity every year with a dinner – generally known as the 'sports dinner' – given by the officers to those other ranks who had 'specially contributed to the welfare and reputation of the Battalion'. With cups and trophies on display the Colonel congratulated the sportsmen on their achievements, urged them to further triumphs, and hoped, to cheers, that 'win or lose they would be known as a battalion who loves a clean game and loved sport for sport's sake alone'.[92]

Military and civilian sporting competitions enlivened military life by giving men the opportunity to leave barracks, both as players and supporters. In 1909 360 men of 1/Leicestershire Regiment travelled from Shorncliffe to Dulwich to see their team play Dulwich Hamlet in the FA Amateur Cup. They lost but still enjoyed the day out: 'by midnight – the time at which we left Victoria, nearly all were "A la Falstaffe", full of humour, gaiety and good sense. It quite surprised me to see what a number of female relatives our fellows have in town'.[93] Especially in India officers too were grateful for the chance sport offered to see new places and people. Lieutenant Donald Weir was delighted to leave behind Belgaum station for a rugby tour to Bombay and Madras, 'the meeting of old friends' and the 'big football dinner at the Madras Club'.[94] There was a strong social side to inter-regimental sport. When the teams of the 7th Dragoon Guards and the Northumberland Fusiliers visited Shorncliffe to play 1/Leicestershire Regiment in the first rounds of the army rugby and football cups respectively they were entertained

---

[90] *Broad Arrow*, 27 March 1897, 376.
[91] *Green Tiger*, June 1908, 66–7. On 25 April 1908 350 supporters had travelled to Aldershot from Shorncliffe by special train, only to find the final snowed off. The colonel covered the cost of the train (over £50) so that they could afford to go to the rescheduled match on the 29th.
[92] *Green Tiger*, May 1909, 75–7; June 1910, 84–5.
[93] *Green Tiger*, February 1909, 21. Cf. Kentish, *Foul Thing*, pp. 46–7.
[94] Donald Weir to his parents, 20 August 1909 and 8 October 1909, Donald Weir papers, DE2913/1/2 and DE2913/1/4, Leicestershire Record Office.

by the regimental sports club to lunch and tea: 'we are certainly looking forward to their next visit, the games were so pleasant and clean'.[95]

Sport afforded a safe arena for interaction on almost equal terms between officers and men. W. E. Cairns commented (perhaps a little optimistically) that:

> officers and men take part together in all kinds of sports and manly games ... meeting in the most friendly manner ... without any ill-effect on discipline. It is no unusual thing for an officer to be playing most energetically in a game of football with men whom he may only a few hours before have sentenced to some minor punishment for a military offence, yet, though retaliation would be no difficult matter in the excitement of so rough a game, I never heard of a case where such a thing was attempted.

Opportunities for such encounters between officers and other ranks were extremely rare: in providing them sport performed a useful function in the smooth running of the army. From the ranks Frank Richards described the relationship as 'mutual trust in military matters and matters of sport, but no social contact'. Cairns recalled the case of two brothers serving in the same battalion, one as an officer, one in the ranks – 'practically as much separated as if living in two different continents. On the cricket ground, in the football field, they could meet more or less on a footing of equality as players in the game, but a few minutes of friendly private conversation was quite out of the question'.[96] Officer involvement was thought to 'improve the style of play ... stop grumbling, and raise the general tone', as well as supplying 'brains' for the team.[97]

Sport obviously provided a way of keeping servicemen fit. The development of naval sport can be seen partly as a response to two new problems faced by the Navy at the turn of the century: firstly, the transition from sail to steam, and the consequent search for activities to promote the nerve and agility sail-training had encouraged; secondly, the 'accumulation of men in barracks on shore' and the need to engage them in healthy activity. (It was these developments that led the navy belatedly to establish a Physical Training Branch in 1902.)[98] But in both navy and army there was always 'a pretty considerable number of men' whose enthusiasm was limited to *watching* sport 'with a sort of languid interest'. Hence compulsion was sometimes introduced, as in 1/Leicestershire Regiment, where 'every man Jack under fifteen years

---

[95] *Green Tiger*, December 1907, 138.
[96] Cairns, *Social Life*, pp. 152–4; Richards, *Old-Soldier Sahib*, p. 155.
[97] 'Football in the Army', *Navy and Army Illustrated*, 11 December 1896.
[98] N. Fox, 'The Royal Navy Physical Training Branch: A Study of Innovation', unpublished PhD thesis, University of Liverpool (1982), pp. 109–14.

service … has to turn out and play one game of football a week, Rugger or Soccer just as he chooses'.[99] 1/Sherwood Foresters, at Bangalore, systematically developed a programme of full participation over a three-year period. In 1909 the Adjutant introduced novice boxing instruction and competitions, Major Rigby presented an inter-company swimming cup, and the commanding officer offered 100 rupees for a company five-mile cross-country race. Company sports were held, 830 of the battalion's 983 officers, NCOs and men competing, 'the balance being on command, in hospital, or employed in billets which prevented their attendance'. An Athletic Shield was presented for the best overall company. 'Every man in the battalion has to do something for his company. No longer do twenty-two men play football with five times that number criticising and saying how it *should* be done'. By 1911 sports competitions occupied two days a month and the battalion standard of 'all-round athleticism' was gratifyingly high.[100]

By this time it was officially accepted that sport could act as a form of physical training (though not replace it). The army's first *Physical Training Manual*, produced in 1908, insisted that 'the value of active games and sports as adjuncts to physical training cannot be over-estimated. Games and physical training should be looked upon as complementary to one another.' A wide variety of 'athletic amusements' should be provided to encourage as many men as possible 'to develop habits of activity by employing their leisure time in healthy recreation'. *Cavalry Training* of 1912 instructed officers to 'encourage and arrange active games amongst their men', asserting that 'manly games have a great effect on the military spirit, especially if they are arranged so that all ranks generally, and not only selected teams, take part'.[101]

Sport, it was hoped, could help form the new kind of soldier that technological developments required. The introduction of breech-loading rifles meant that soldiers now needed to fight in more dispersed order, which made top-down control of fighting men more difficult. As David French puts it, 'what was required was not the rigid discipline of the barrack square, but discipline based on intelligence and self-reliance'. It was this intelligence and self-reliance, and the ability to work as a team without having to follow rigid orders, that army sport aimed to produce. 'Football, hockey and kindred games make a man independent, quick eyed and quick witted.'[102] Presumably profiting by the British example,

---

[99] *Bugle*, 19 July 1894; *Green Tiger*, November 1908, 136.
[100] *Sherwood Foresters Regimental Annual* 1 (1909), 63–71; 2 (1910), 52–64; 3 (1911), 64–8.
[101] *Manual of Physical Training*, 1908, pp. 8, 188–9; *Cavalry Training*, 1912, pp. 16, 18.
[102] French, *Military Identities*, pp. 23–4, 115; Kinahan, 'The Need of Games in the Army', 12.

the German army, similarly grappling with open-order tactics, added sport to its training programme in the early 1900s to encourage agility and teamwork.[103]

Some argued that sport had more abstract military benefits. Public-school-educated officers certainly took into the services the belief that war was only another form of sport, the 'greater game'. Major General E. A. H. Alderson told 2/Leicestershire Regiment in 1911 that 'a regiment that is good at games is also good at fighting. I only need to look at you now and at your games to know that you would be good at the real game, which is the game of fighting.'[104] Some sports claimed particular military value. Cross-country running, like hunting, was said to foster 'an eye for the country'. Knight-Bruce argued that boxing, not hunting, was the image of war, promoting qualities 'essential to the soldier': 'courage, fitness, the capacity for keeping one's head, when that said head is dazed and reeling from murderous blows; good temper under reverses, instant obedience to the command of the referee, the knowledge that one still has a chance of winning however terrible a gruelling one may be getting at the moment, lightning quickness to seize an opportunity only presented for an instant'.[105] Often the very different experiences of field sports and team games were elided. 'War becomes easier because of the lessons learnt at boxing, in the hunting or football field, or big-game shooting ... The perfect sportsman should make the perfect soldier'.[106] Such comments have convinced J. D. Campbell that sport contributed unambiguously to military efficiency in the Edwardian army – that 'training for sport' was indeed the same as 'training for war'.[107]

Yet this was not a view universally held by contemporaries. While sport for other ranks before the First World War generally escaped the criticism officer sport attracted in this period (and which is discussed

[103] *Green Tiger*, September 1909, 152; Dennis E. Showalter, 'Army and Society in Imperial Germany: The Pains of Modernization', *Journal of Contemporary History* 18 (1983), 583–618, at 594. The German Navy, too, made 'striking progress' in sport. Just before the First World War a British squadron visiting Kiel found itself 'entirely outclassed' at athletics and only managed to win one out of two football matches (Captain Henderson to Sir H. Rumbold, Berlin, 3 July 1914, Confidential, enclosed in Sir H. Rumbold to Sir Edward Grey, Berlin, 3 July 1914, Gooch papers, at http://www.lib.byu.edu/estu/wwi/1914m/gooch/1–12.htm, accessed 20 March 2009).
[104] *Green Tiger*, March 1911, 39. For Alderson's views on 'hunting as a school for soldiering' see chapter 2.
[105] Kinahan, 'The Need of Games in the Army', 11; Knight-Bruce, 'Military Boxing', p. 194.
[106] 'Ex-Non-Com', 'The Soldier in Relation to Regimental Sport', 32.
[107] J. D. Campbell, '"Training for Sport Is Training for War": Sport and the Transformation of the British Army, 1860–1914', *International Journal of the History of Sport* 17 (December 2000), 21–58.

in chapter 2), there were always dissenting voices. In 1906 Admiral Sir Archibald Douglas, a man of the old school, deplored the softening influence of 'Canteens, Sailors' Homes and Football matches, by the aid of which the men under my command at Portsmouth are fast deteriorating in all that makes for a fighting man'. In February 1914 an unnamed general, believing that there was 'too much sport in the Army', was said to have made the regiments in his command drop boxing and cross-country training.[108] Military sport, in fact, was rarely simple. If it distracted men from drinking, it also encouraged it. Captain William Simpson, refereeing the 1902 Army Cup final, found the drunkenness 'perfectly disgraceful … when it was over I saw men being carried away to their barracks'. As the 'gentleman ranker' Horace Wyndham pointed out, it was an irony that sports were funded from canteen profits, so that the more a regiment drank the more sport it could support.[109] If sport could create good relations between regiments it could also be a focus for hostility. In 1910 General Smith-Dorrien issued an Aldershot Command Order warning that spectators 'shouting out opprobrious remarks to the players' would result in 'foul and unsporting play … bad blood between teams, and even possibly in lasting enmity between corps'. The Royal Welch Fusiliers and the Highland Light Infantry remained 'bitter enemies' for years because of a football incident in India in the 1890s. As in civil society sporting conflict could lead to mass disorder. In 1912 a New Year's Day football match between Scottish and English soldiers undergoing mounted infantry training at Longmore camp led to a 'serious military riot' when 'some chaff on the result of the match led to a general quarrel, which developed into a free fight'.[110]

The most difficult problems of military sport were those relating to officer–men relations, discipline and military efficiency. An anonymous 'ex-non-com' provided a thoughtful analysis of the sporting relations of officers and other ranks – 'an interesting disciplinary problem' that required mutual 'good-natured toleration'. Regimental football, especially, controlled and financed by other ranks, was the private soldier's 'one little democratic delight': the intrusion of his military superiors was not necessarily welcome. The sharp class differences of army life inevitably affected the theoretical equality of the sports field.

---

[108] Minute of 16 April 1906, ADM 1/7796, TNA; *Athletic News*, 23 February 1914.
[109] *Minutes of Evidence Taken before the Committee Appointed to Consider the Existing Conditions under which Canteens and Regimental Institutes Are Conducted* [Cd. 1494] 1903, p. 113; Wyndham, *The Queen's Service*, p. 103.
[110] *Times*, 4 February 1910, 4 January 1912; Richards, *Old-Soldier Sahib*, p. 41.

The growth of service sport 45

Figure 4. Royal Irish Fusiliers football team (1906–7). Captain R.J. Kentish, pioneer of army sports organisation, is second from left in middle row. Note that the team captain (centre) is not Kentish but an NCO, Lance-Corporal Fincham.

If the timorous private fears to show too pronounced a superiority over the officer, so the officer fears to lose his dignity ... if there is the private's temptation to score off an unpopular superior, there is also the superior's temptation to trade on his power, to accentuate his superiority at duty to cover his inferiority at football ... I have known a stripling subaltern march a player off the field into the guardroom; I remember a series of football matches in which no one yearned to play, because of the questionable tactics and unbearable assertion of authority of a youthful staff officer player. [111]

When other ranks captained teams including officers, tact on both sides was essential.[112]

Since sporting success brought prestige to the regiment there was always a temptation to bend the rules, to the detriment of military efficiency. As the 'ex-non-com' put it, 'favouritism – or the suspicion of

---

[111] 'Ex-Non-Com', 'The Soldier in Relation to Regimental Sport', 34–6.
[112] 1/Royal Irish Fusiliers' successful Edwardian football team, for example, included Captain Kentish, but the team captain was Lance-Corporal Fincham (*Faugh-a-Ballagh* 6 (July 1907), 9).

it – is a thing that can scarcely be excluded from regimental sport'. Its 'most malignant forms' included

> awarding the soldier who is a skilful sportsman a less punishment than that awarded to a non-sporting soldier for a like offence; releasing him from cells or defaulters' drill to take part in a momentous game; exempting him from heavy courses of instruction and fatigue work; keeping him with the home battalion when it is his turn to go abroad![113]

Unquestionably sportsmen did often receive more favourable treatment, lighter work, better food and a more indulgent attitude towards military crimes. In 1894, with the Bombay football competitions in view, the officer commanding 2/Durham Light Infantry permitted the battalion team to 'live together, mess together, and be excused as far as possible from duties that will interfere with their training'.[114] The Army FA, keen to clamp down on anything reeking of professionalism, and perhaps anxious about the effects of privileged treatment on *esprit de corps*, introduced a new rule in 1890 forbidding teams in Army Cup ties, on threat of disqualification, from including any man 'who shall have been kept off duty for more than seven days' prior to the match.[115] But, as Simpson explained five years later, if a regiment had a good player

> an arrangement is generally made by which his duties in respect of drills are somewhat lightened. Of course a footballer has to do his ordinary number of guards ... In the early morning, however, he can be let off one of the drills and allowed to go on a training run with the team ...

In the Brigade of Guards, Simpson suggested, a good footballer might be put on 'staff duties' as an officer's servant or even a billiard marker in the officers' mess: this, he said, was 'the only way to do any real good with a man for football'.[116]

That army sport was supposed to be voluntary, 'not a parade', an area of military life in which other ranks could exercise free choice, made it not only extremely unusual but also an area of possible conflict with military discipline. In early 1914 a soldier was sentenced by his commanding officer to twenty-eight days imprisonment for refusing to play football for the regiment one Saturday – though theoretically he had every right to do this.[117] Disciplinary issues were constantly recurring problems, especially for the Army FA. Reginald Kentish feelingly

[113] 'Ex-Non-Com', 'The Soldier in Relation to Regimental Sport', 34–6.
[114] *Bugle*, 19 July 1894.
[115] Army FA Mins, 29 May, 5 November 1890, AFA.
[116] *Chums*, 18 December 1895, 263.
[117] *Athletic News*, 16 February 1914.

recalled the 'many hours' he had spent as its honorary secretary dealing with disciplinary cases involving 'deliberate fouling and unsporting play', 'unsportsmanlike conduct of the spectators' and 'the vilest abuse possible' of the referee.[118] A tricky question arose of whether these were military crimes – and therefore the responsibility of the commanding officer – or merely football crimes, which could be dealt with by the Army FA. The Army FA's punishments for foul play could be severe. The team of 2/Royal Scots was suspended for a month in 1890 for foul language and rough play. An amendment to suspend only the particular players who had offended was defeated.[119] There were also occasions – notably the 1910 Army Cup final – when the behaviour of some members of the football crowd caused concern to both the AFA and the army hierarchy. The Army FA subsequently established three-man sub-committees in all large garrisons to deal with disciplinary cases.[120] Concerns about the sporting behaviour of other ranks were highlighted by the Army Council's decision to allow only officers to play in the army's match against the Dutch army at Aldershot in January 1914. So few officers played football seriously that collecting a team proved difficult, though they ultimately won 3–1.[121]

The last years before the Great War saw an officer-led campaign to remake service sport in the image of amateurism and public-school games. This was often an uphill struggle. The amateur spirit and the desire to win were often incompatible. Both gambling and money prizes were endemic in army sport. Early sports promoters had deliberately used prize money to encourage greater participation. Military athletic meetings and boxing tournaments always carried money prizes – so, though less commonly, did football competitions.[122] Gambling was common even in intra-regimental sport.[123] The service sports organisations founded in the late Edwardian period explicitly sought to clean up military sport. The Army Athletic Association aimed at 'clean running and true sportsmanship'.[124] Service boxing reformers worried that 'the arrival of the big purse' had brought 'evil influences' into professional

---

[118] Brigadier-General R.J. Kentish, 'Army Association Football', *BEF Sports Journal* 1 (8 February 1919), 1.
[119] Army FA Com. Mins 8 February 1890, AFA.
[120] Army FA, AGM, 30 May 1910, AFA.
[121] *Athletic News*, 8 December 1913, 29 December 1913, 2 February 1914; *Times*, 29 January 1914.
[122] For money prizes for football see *Bugle*, 7 June 1894; *Broad Arrow*, 7 March 1896, 278.
[123] See, e.g., Donald Weir to his parents, 20 August 1909, Donald Weir papers, DE2913/1/2, Leicestershire Record Office.
[124] 'Army Athletic Association', WO32/5492, TNA.

boxing, that soldiers and sailors were being exploited by 'scoundrel' promoters, picking up dirty tricks, and coming to regard boxing as a money-making exercise rather than a sport, even refusing to fight at service meetings without substantial financial incentives. After the 1910 RNA Championship a group of officers including Commander Percy Royds, Captain R. B. Campbell and Lieutenant Giffard Martel agreed that a controlling organisation was needed. The Royal Navy and Army Boxing Association, which first met in September 1911, encouraged mass participation, specified six-round competitions, abolished clinching, punished fouls and breaches of boxing etiquette and kept a blacklist of offenders. The reformers hoped thus to introduce the high moral tone they associated with public-school boxing, enabling 'all the great qualities of self-sacrifice, pluck and chivalry' to be brought out in service boxers. They also stipulated that judges and referees, hitherto often civilians, should always be officers (a decision condemned by the sporting press – sometimes, Starr suggested, by journalists who had themselves been 'accustomed to receive kudos and cash for arbitrating at Service meetings'). Within a year the entire army and navy had signed up, and the major service tournaments in Britain, Ireland and India were being held under RNABA rules. Though the RNABA limited prize money, however, it did not abolish it.[125] Amateurism in service sport had to wait for the Great War to be officially approved.

So did the idea of a central controlling body for army sport – 'all forms of Army games and recreation being under one committee and having one common fund with an Officer detailed to look after it who had no other work' – proposed to the War Office in 1913 but turned down on cost grounds. If the army hierarchy was still loath to spend public money on military sport, however, it was already convinced of its utility. The Adjutant General, Lieutenant General Sir J. S. Ewart, was 'quite clear as to [sport's] value to the physical training and fitness of the Army generally'. The Chief of the Imperial General Staff, Sir John French, thought 'the proper organisation and supervision of Games ... most important'.[126] The newly formed Royal Flying Corps

---

[125] Sir Giffard Martel, *An Outspoken Soldier* (London: Sifton, Praed & Co., 1949), pp. 40–1; Knight-Bruce, 'Military Boxing', pp. 200–8; Frank Starr, 'Army Boxing History', *Aldershot Command News*, 17 January 1928, 4–5, 24 January 1928, 3, 14 February 1928, 14, 21 February 1928, 13; 'Boxing in India: Influence of RN&ABA Spreading', *Sporting Life*, 7 October 1912; 'Navarm' [Knight-Bruce], 'Service Boxing: The Success of the RN&ABA', *Sporting Life*, 18 October 1912; 'Services Boxing', *Sporting Life*, 30 October 1912; *Times*, 23 September 1911, 6 March 1914. For disciplinary proceedings, see, e.g., Minutes of the RNABA, 21 October 1911.

[126] 'Army Athletic Association', WO32/5492, TNA; see also WO32/5493 'Army Athletic Association: Suggestion that Officer If Appointed as Above Be Paid out of South African Field Force Canteen Funds'.

believed 'the promotion of all forms of sport and recreation' to be of 'paramount importance in the creation and maintenance of the *esprit de corps* and good fellowship essential for officers in the fighting forces'.[127] But before the First World War service sport was essentially a grassroots movement, driven largely by enthusiasts among junior officers and other ranks. By 1914 it was outgrowing the existing organisation. Early that year Colonel Couper of the Army Gymnastic Staff complained that sports administration took up so much of his officers' time 'and thereby so materially interferes with their Physical Training duties that I shall be compelled to tell them to resign their various honorary Games appointments'; he added that Kentish would be resigning as the Army FA's secretary at the end of the 1913–14 season 'since he also cannot afford to spend some 2 hours a day during 8 months of the year in running Army Football'.[128] It would take the experience of total war to transform the way that service sport was controlled and funded.

---

[127] Royal Air Force Officers' Sports Fund [leaflet], n.d. [1918], AIR 2/71 F8465, TNA.
[128] 'Army Athletic Association', WO32/5492, TNA.

2 Officer sports and their critics, 1880–1914

> The Duke of Wellington said that Waterloo was won on the playing-fields of Eton. Of … the South African War it has been said that the guns at Sannah's Post were captured on the polo-ground at Hurlingham; that Magersfontein was lost at Lords; that Spion Kop was evacuated at Sandown Park; and that the war dragged on for 32 months in the Quorn and Pytchley coverts – because the British officer was accustomed to look upon war as a branch of sport.
>
> 'W. T.' to the Editor, *The Times*, 2 June 1916

Before 1914 criticism of sport in the army focused overwhelmingly on officer sports. In the aftermath of the Boer War officer recruitment and education were among the key topics addressed by army reformers. Officer sport – and especially polo – was attacked as a major contributing factor in the 'extravagance' that restricted commissioned ranks in the cavalry to those with substantial private incomes, and defended on the grounds that it promoted officer-like qualities and acted as a form of military training. Tim Travers has suggested that the Edwardian period saw the 'convergence and frequent conflict' of two ideals of war – the new 'technical, functionally competent, professional ideal' and the 'traditional, gentlemanly, amateur ideal'.[1] For the cavalry, Brian Bond, Edward Spiers, Gerald DeGroot and the Marquis of Anglesey have charted how the movement towards reform of cavalry doctrine in the first years of the twentieth century was rapidly thwarted by the 'forces of reaction'.[2] A key aspect of this reaction was what Spiers

---

[1] T. Travers, 'The Hidden Army: Structural Problems in the British Officer Corps, 1900–1918', *Journal of Contemporary History* 17 (1982), 523–44, at 525 and 537.

[2] B. Bond, 'Doctrine and Training in the British Cavalry 1870–1914', in M. Howard (ed.), *The Theory and Practice of War: Essays Presented to Captain B. H. Liddell Hart* (London: Cassell, 1965); E. M. Spiers, 'The British Cavalry, 1902–1914', *Journal of the Society of Army Historical Research* 57 (1979), 71–9; G. DeGroot, 'Educated Soldier or Cavalry Officer? Contradictions in the Pre-1914 Career of Douglas Haig', *War and Society* 4 (1986), 51–69; Marquess of Anglesey, *A History of the British Cavalry 1816 to 1919, IV: 1899 to 1913* (London: Leo Cooper, 1986), pp. 388–423. For a more positive view, see S. Badsey, 'Cavalry and the Development of Breakthrough Doctrine', in P. Griffith (ed.), *British Fighting Methods in the Great War* (London: F. Cass, 1996),

has called the 'gentlemanly officer tradition'. The officer corps was, almost entirely, made up of those who could claim to be 'gentlemen'. As a group they cherished a heroic and chivalric concept of war, valued 'character' and morale over intellect and professional training, and attached a high importance to sporting activities.[3] The Edwardian debates over the place of sport in the officer lifestyle, hitherto largely unexamined, therefore provide a revealing sidelight on the ethos of the pre-1914 army.[4] This chapter explores the role of equestrian sport in the 'gentlemanly officer tradition' and describes the prolonged and ultimately futile campaigns before 1914 to restrict it in the cause of a more diverse and meritocratic officer corps.

Despite the abolition of purchase in 1871, the officer corps of the British army retained a 'high degree of social homogeneity' through recruitment from the public schools and the need for officers to possess private incomes. Rates of pay were so low that, except in India, it was impossible for officers to live only on their pay, especially as the army also expected them to buy their own uniforms, furniture and – in the case of cavalry officers – two chargers. Officers required an additional annual income of between £100 (minimum – for an infantry officer) and £700 (for a cavalry officer in an 'elite' regiment). The officer corps therefore came largely from the ranks of the landed gentry, which Razzell suggests consistently provided one-third of the officer class across the period 1830–1912. In addition there was a high rate of self-recruitment from military families, and an increasing proportion from the 'gentlemanly' professional classes. The aristocracy maintained a diminishing but significant presence: by 1912 only 9 per cent of all officers were from the aristocracy, but this rose to 24 per cent for officers ranked major-general or above. Moreover, certain regiments became steadily more socially exclusive.[5] The cavalry's traditional

---

and *Doctrine and Reform in the British Cavalry 1800–1918* (Aldershot: Ashgate, 2008); also G. Phillips, 'Douglas Haig and the Development of Twentieth-Century Cavalry', *Archives* 28 (2003), 142–62.

[3] Spiers, *The Army and Society*, pp. 1–2; Spiers, *The Late Victorian Army*, ch. 4.

[4] Post-Boer War concerns over officer sport are discussed briefly in Lowerson, *Sport and the English Middle-Classes*, pp. 285–9. Campbell, 'Training for Sport Is Training for War', 22–7, and 'The Army Isn't All Work', ch. 1, puts the case for officer sport. P. F. McDevitt, *May the Best Man Win: Sport, Masculinity and Nationalism in Great Britain and the Empire 1880–1935* (New York: Palgrave Macmillan, 2004), ch. 3, discusses polo in the Indian context. See also J. A. Mangan and C. McKenzie, '"Pig-Sticking is the Greatest Fun": Martial Conditioning on the Hunting Fields of Empire', in J. A. Mangan (ed.), *Militarism, Sport, Europe* (London: Frank Cass, 2003), pp. 97–119.

[5] Spiers, *The Late Victorian Army*, pp. 94–9, 103–5; G. Harries-Jenkins, *The Army in Victorian Society* (London: Routledge and Kegan Paul, 1977), ch. 2; P. E. Razzell, 'Social Origins of Officers in the Indian and British Home Army: 1758–1962', *British*

social and military prestige as 'the gentleman's arm – an elite bound together by the cavalry spirit' further contributed to the perpetuation of aristocratic values.[6]

This continuing connection between the army and the land meant that the 'military life-style, ethos, norms and standards were primarily based on the principal characteristics of the landed interest'.[7] Sport, and especially equestrian sport, was central to this lifestyle and one of the markers by which the socially desirable were distinguished from the undesirable. In several cases in which 'unsuitable' junior officers were bullied or ostracised by their peers, inability or refusal to participate in equestrian sport made up part of the evidence against them. Of an officer whose treatment by the 4th Hussars was raised in the House of Commons in 1896 it was said that 'on its becoming clear that Mr Hodge could not keep racehorses and hunters it was apparent that his brother officers were determined to get rid of him'; in a similar case in 1903 three subalterns of the Grenadier Guards were 'brought before the senior subaltern, who told them that, unless they rode with the Brigade drag at Windsor, they would be flogged'.[8] If, as Spiers has commented, 'a paramount concern of the officer gentleman tradition was the maintenance of social standards – not simply the possession of a private income but a pattern of expenditure which met with the approval of brother officers and sustained the customs of the mess', equestrian sport constituted an essential component of this pattern.[9]

Officers spent an extraordinarily large proportion of their time hunting. Percival Marling, 18th Hussars, remembered of Cahir in Tipperary in the 1880s that hunting was available six days a week, with a drag on Sundays. Transferred to Aldershot, he found that 'in the winter there was no soldiering at all, except one route march a week ... We were hunting five and six days a week. We hunted with the Queen's Staghounds, De Burgh's Harriers, the Garth, HH, Chiddingfold, and the Vine, to say nothing of the Staff College drag once or twice a week'.[10] In the 1890s officers expected two days' hunting leave a week during the season in addition to their two and a half months' annual leave. Evelyn Wood was accustomed to hunt forty-six

---

Journal of Sociology 14 (1963), 248–60, at 253–5; C.B. Otley, 'The Social Origins of British Army Officers', *Sociological Review* 18 (1970), 213–39.
[6] Bond, 'Doctrine and Training', p. 100; DeGroot, 'Educated Soldier', p. 52.
[7] Harries-Jenkins, *Army*, p. 43.
[8] *Times*, 20 June 1896, 10 February 1903.
[9] Spiers, *The Late Victorian Army*, pp. 338–9.
[10] Marling, *Rifleman and Hussar*, pp. 167–73.

days a year.[11] Many cavalry regiments and some infantry regiments maintained a regimental pack of hounds. There were close links – and considerable overlap of personnel – between the county yeomanry regiments and the hunting field.[12]

Racing was also a popular occupation for soldiers. The Grand Military Race Meeting, including what became the Grand Military Gold Cup steeplechase, was first held in 1841. It was run at a variety of courses, most often at Rugby, before settling in 1881 in the more luxurious surroundings of Sandown Park, where it became a 'fashionable *réunion*'. Officers often attended this and other races in the 'regimental drag', or stagecoach. The major Aldershot races were also sufficiently fashionable to attract royalty and the 'Upper Ten'. The South Western Railway ran special trains from Waterloo for the Aldershot Divisional and Cavalry Brigade steeplechases, which combined open military and regimental races. The *Badminton Library* commented approvingly on the severity of the Aldershot course, which, with its wide water-jump, open brook and drop fences, 'more nearly resemble[d] the typical "fair hunting country"' than most courses. Individual regiments also held point-to-points wherever they happened to be stationed.[13] But the glory days of military steeplechasing were over by the late nineteenth century. Flourishing in the mid-nineteenth century (when races were held even in the Crimea), it perhaps peaked in the 1870s – since when, one writer complained, it had been discouraged by the military authorities.[14]

This was probably because of its connection with gambling. W. E. Cairns, though approving of steeplechasing as an activity for soldiers, deplored the annual toll of cavalry officers lost through 'the fascination of the betting-ring'. Occasionally it led to accusations of foul play. In March 1895 Winston Churchill, as a young officer in the 4th Hussars, rode in that regiment's Subalterns' Challenge Cup at the Cavalry Brigade Meeting at Aldershot under the name of 'Mr Spencer' (probably because he had just assured his mother he wouldn't be racing). He came third out of five runners, the favourite came second, and the

[11] Lieutenant-Colonel R. L. A. Pennington, 'Army Reform from a Battalion Point of View', *Fortnightly Review* 69 (1901), 312–29, at 326; Farwell, *Mr Kipling's Army*, pp. 68–9 and 206–7.
[12] N. Mansfield, 'Foxhunting and the Yeomanry: County Identity and Military Culture', in R. W. Hoyle, (ed.), *Our Hunting Fathers: Field Sports in England after 1850* (Lancaster: Carnegie, 2007).
[13] 'The Grand Military', *Country Life*, 11 March 1899, 318–19; *Bell's Life*, 4 March 1882; *Horse and Hound*, 17 April 1886; *Country Gentleman*, 14 March, 14 November 1896; Earl of Suffolk and Berkshire *et al.*, *The Badminton Library: Racing and Steeplechasing* (London: Longmans & Co., 1886), p. 347.
[14] 'Outpost', 'Recollections of Steeplechasing – VIII', *Country Life*, 3 February 1900, 152–3.

winner was Mr A. O. Francis's Surefoot, which had started the race at 6–1 against. A year later the National Hunt Committee, having been alerted to 'certain irregularities' in the running of the race, declared it null and void and perpetually disqualified all the horses that had run in it. Henry Labouchere's radical journal *Truth* claimed that there had been collusion between the competing officers to profit from the race by running a 'ringer'. Churchill protested that the National Hunt Committee had, in correspondence with the War Office, 'expressly vindicat[ed] us from any charge of ... dishonourable behaviour' and threatened to sue Labouchere, but nothing came of this. The case provides a useful reminder that officer sports were not invariably carried out in accordance with 'gentlemanly' ideals.[15]

Sport was one of the main attractions of overseas service. Big-game hunting is somewhat outside the scope of this study, but it was certainly pursued avidly by officers. In India between January 1902 and December 1912 2/Gordon Highlanders accounted for '674 big game of thirty-six species, including three elephants, six tigers, twelve panthers and eighty-four boars' not to mention 4,256 pigeons, 7,549 ducks and 9,354 snipe. Many a regimental mess accumulated an impressive array of trophies – and many an officer writing his sporting reminiscences mentioned that his victims looked down at him from the walls as he wrote.[16] Officers went to enormous lengths to reproduce English field sports overseas. Foxhounds accompanied regiments to stations across the Empire so that hunting (with some necessary modifications, such as the replacement of foxes by jackals) could proceed as normal. The Royal Calpe Hunt of Gibraltar was established in 1813 by the Duke of Wellington's Peninsula troops. Packs were also formed at the Cape (1820) and by garrisons throughout India. The oldest was the Madras Hunt, first recorded in 1776; another famous pack, founded in 1844, was based at Ootacamund. The Peshawar Vale Hunt, established in the 1860s by the Green Howards, continued its activities almost unaffected by the vicissitudes of life on the North-West Frontier until 1947.[17] In

---

[15] Cairns, *Social Life*, p. 53; R. S. Churchill, *Winston S. Churchill, Vol. I: Youth 1874–1900* (London: Heinemann, 1966), pp. 246–52; see also *Sporting Times*, 29 February 1896 and *Freeman's Journal and Daily Commercial Advertiser*, 22 October 1896. Labouchere emphasised that the five subalterns accused of rigging the race were the same group who had been guilty of the brutal bullying of two 'unsuitable' junior officers in the 4th Hussars.

[16] Farwell, *Mr Kipling's Army*, p. 207; MacKenzie, *The Empire of Nature*, p. 191. See also 'The Big-Game Trophies of the Royal Engineers' Mess', *Country Life*, 3 October 1914, 448–50, and 'The Royal Artillery Mess, Woolwich, and Its Big Game Trophies', *Country Life*, 2 January 1915, 9–11.

[17] MacKenzie, *Empire of Nature*, pp. 177–8; Captain Lionel Dawson, RN, *Sport in War* (London: Collins, 1936), pp. 75–9.

more densely cultivated areas officer hunting could cause problems with civilians. In 1901 the Abbassiyeh Fox Hounds, accompanied by officers mainly of the 11th Hussars, entered Wilfrid Blunt's Egyptian estate in disputed circumstances and became involved in a fracas with Blunt's Egyptian servants, leading to a court case, a highly acrimonious correspondence between Blunt and the British authorities, letters to the press and questions in Parliament – after which the army was directed that 'all possible care should be taken to avoid acts of trespass by British officers on inclosed or cultivated property'.[18]

Both Egypt and India had fairly well-developed racing scenes. Egyptian racing was centred around the Alexandria Sporting Club and the Gezira Sporting Club in Cairo. In the 1870s Indian racing, led by the army and the Indian Civil Service, was an essentially amateur affair involving ponies rather than horses. 'The bookie had not yet invaded the land', and betting took place through a lottery system which tended to circulate the money among a small group. Racing took place between September and February on a recognised circuit, in Bengal starting at Dehra Dun in the Himalayan foothills, where many racing men had their stables, moving south through Umballa, Meerut, Lucknow and other stations to Calcutta for the Christmas meeting, then north again. There were also a number of 'Sky Races', confined to runners from the local district. Elaborate handicapping arrangements compensated for the very mixed quality of runners – Arab and country-bred ponies, 'Walers' from Australia and imports from Britain. By the early 1880s racing was changing as the Turf Clubs of Calcutta, Bombay and Madras tightened the rules and introduced official handicappers, starters and judges. Bookies and professional jockeys began to appear.[19] But officers continued to take an active part in Indian racing both as owners and riders. Hubert Gough, weighing just over nine stone, rode regularly in the 1890s for Smith-Dorrien (then a major) and Major 'Kitty' Apthorp, both of whom had extensive racing stables. In steeplechasing he won both the 'Grand Military' and the 'Pony Grand Military' before a bad fall 'on the then very small Simla race-course' led him to concentrate on flat racing, twice winning the Army Cup, the most important pony race in India after the Civil Service Cup. Big races carried substantial prizes. Bigger money was made through gambling.

---

[18] Published at Blunt's request as Cd. 796 (1901), the correspondence relating to this case has recently been reprinted as *Wilfrid Blunt's Egyptian Garden: Fox Hunting in Cairo* (London: The Stationery Office, 1999).
[19] Captain Hayes, *Indian Racing Reminiscences* (London: W. Thacker, 1883), ch. 2; Colonel T.A. St Quintin, *Chances of Sports of Sorts* (Edinburgh: Blackwood, 1912), pp. 276–85, 313.

Gough's victory on Smith-Dorrien's pony Shannon in the Army Cup was described in the sporting press as 'very popular ... the winner having been backed for many thousands [of rupees], and a bad race for the bookies'. Gough commented that 'Smith-Dorrien and all my friends won a nice packet'.[20] Both Churchill's mother and his commanding officer, Colonel Brabazon, expressed concern that racing in India was 'not square' – though Churchill assured them that 'everyone out here possesses an animal of one sort or another which they race in the numerous local meetings'. St Quintin's memoirs, full of stories of crooked dealing on and off the course, certainly suggest some truth in their assertions.[21]

More of a 'gentleman's game' was pig-sticking – pursuing wild pigs across country on horseback armed with an eight-foot spear. Natural hazards included rough ground, canals, hidden wells, the occasional tiger and the pigs themselves, which grew to over three feet in height, had eight-inch tusks and when attacked became extremely aggressive. Originating in Bengal in the late eighteenth century, pig-sticking became 'more highly regularised and institutionalised' in the post-Mutiny period with the development of hunt clubs (known as Tent Clubs), pig-sticking competitions and cups and pig-preservation policies. Tent clubs were based on the model of foxhunting (some club rules specified expulsion for shooting a pig), each having a recognised territory, a master, and an Indian *shikari*, or huntsman, whose job included organising the Indian beaters who drove the pigs out of cover. The season ran from November or December to the rains in June. Although penalties were imposed for killing immature pigs, bags were often substantial. Wardrop claimed to have ridden and killed 'between 700 and 800 boar' over twenty-one years. MacKenzie suggests a late Edwardian flowering of pig-sticking as pig-preservation policies began to pay off. Though not the experience of all Tent Clubs, this was certainly spectacularly true of some: at Delhi preservation efforts by British and Indian army officers increased annual bags from fewer than sixty in 1907–9 to 385 in 1912.[22]

Competition began from the 1870s, the Kadir Cup being run from 1874 (after an earlier incarnation as a steeplechase), and several other cups from the 1880s. The competitors ran off in heats of three or four,

[20] General Sir Hubert Gough, *Soldiering On* (London: Arthur Barker, 1954), pp. 44–6; *Sporting Times*, 25 January 1896.
[21] Churchill, *Winston S. Churchill, Vol. I*, pp. 308–10; St. Quintin, *Chances of Sports*, chs. 13 and 16.
[22] MacKenzie, *The Empire of Nature*, pp. 186–90; A.E. Wardrop, *Modern Pig-Sticking* (London: Macmillan, 1914), pp. 2, 12, 22–4, 40, 54, 206–7. See also R. Holmes, *Sahib: The British Soldier in India 1750–1914* (London: HarperCollins, 2005), pp. 167–71.

accompanied by an umpire, who gave the word to ride when a pig was found and judged the winner (the one who first speared – rather than killed – the pig). Spectators watched from their horses, or from elephants. The Kadir Cup – named after the riverbed country on the Ganges near Meerut over which it was run – was the premier pig-sticking trophy, a social occasion that took place over three days in March with up to 150 horses competing. Wardrop described the scene on the first morning

> with 50 elephants crowded with competitors, spectators and a fair sprinkling of ladies. In front is the line of 150 coolies, with the flag elephant [from which the results were signalled], signallers, and shikaries on their camels. Ahead are the three heats with their umpires.

It was won by the horse rather than the rider – so that, although Baden-Powell technically won the 1883 Kadir Cup with his horse Patience, he was actually riding his second horse in the final (and ended in the river).[23] Some pig-sticking purists, like Gough's commanding officer Colonel Babington, disapproved of competitions on principle: though allegedly 'the best man after a pig in India', Babington neither competed himself nor allowed his officers to do so.[24]

In the later nineteenth century the popularity of pig-sticking was challenged by the emergence of a new sport: polo. The British claimed to have invented modern polo. The game had first come to their notice in Manipur (on the India/Burma border) in the 1850s and was quickly taken up by tea planters and army officers. The first polo club was formed in 1859 by Joseph Sherer, a lieutenant in the Bengal army, and Captain Robert Stewart, Superintendent of Cachar; several others followed in the next decade. In 1869 a report in the *Field* encouraged officers of the 10th Hussars camped at Aldershot to experiment with 'hockey on horseback'. The first inter-regimental match was played on Hounslow Heath against the 9th Lancers in July 1871. Famously, it was 'more remarkable for the strength of the language used during it than for the brilliancy of the play' – unsurprisingly since it was played 'eight a-side, without any rules'. By 1878 an annual Inter-Regimental Tournament at Hurlingham had been established. The 'slow, dribbling game' of the early days soon gave way to the 'galloping game' played on bigger ponies with only four players a side, and then to the 'scientific game' with a greater emphasis on combination, in which each position – 1, 2, 3 and Back – was assigned specific duties. In the late Edwardian

---

[23] Wardrop, *Modern Pig-Sticking*, ch. XII: 'The Kadir Cup'; Lieutenant-General Sir Robert Baden-Powell, *Indian Memories* (London: Herbert Jenkins, 1915), pp. 62–5.
[24] Gough, *Soldiering On*, p. 47.

Figure 5. Edwardian pig-sticking: the staff of a Kadir Cup showing the flag elephant from which the results were signalled and the shikaries (huntsmen) on their camels.

period the offside rule was abolished, making the game even faster; a handicapping system was also introduced. In Britain the laws of polo came under the Hurlingham Club. Indian rules were slightly different, reflecting safety considerations in a country where the game's very popularity made bad riding and half-trained ponies more common and the hard-baked ground made falls more serious. Drawn games were decided by 'subsidiary goals' (near misses, in effect) to avoid dangerous scrimmages at the end of hard-fought matches, and there were tighter rules on riding off – the potentially risky strategy of forcing an opposing player away from the ball and off his course. The legal height of polo ponies gradually rose both in India and in Britain, but it was always lower in India until in 1907 it adopted the British standard of 14 hands 2 inches. The movement towards a faster game played on larger ponies had the side-effect of making polo steadily more expensive. More ponies were required per game, while the price of good ponies soared. At the end of the nineteenth century, as polo developed into a focus of regimental activity and pride, it became both an almost compulsory activity for young officers – especially cavalry officers or those stationed in India – and potentially a major addition to their expenses.[25]

It was in India that polo really became integral to army life. India was well known as a 'sporting paradise' for officers, and cheap ponies and cheap grooms made polo accessible to infantry and artillery as well as cavalry. Almost all stations had a polo ground of sorts, and station games were played at least two or three times a week all year round. Churchill recalled of his days in Bangalore with the 4th Hussars that 'the hour of Polo' was 'the hour for which we [lived] all day long'. In peacetime, Patrick McDevitt suggests, 'the main occupation of many officers in India was playing, organizing, training for, and financing their polo'. It was first-class tournament polo that really required financing. The Indian first-class tournaments – the Inter-Regimental (founded 1877), the British Infantry, the Native Cavalry and the Indian Polo Association Championships – became high-profile sporting and social events for which ambitious teams built up substantial and expensive stables. Churchill famously returned from Britain to India in 1899 purely to take part in the Inter-Regimental Tournament; a Captain Kirk of the Queen's Bays did the same a few years later. Kipling's polo story, 'The Maltese Cat', captures the potent atmosphere of dust, Society, temporary racial mingling, fierce competition, gentlemanly sportsmanship, danger and regimental pride these occasions produced.[26]

---

[25] J. Moray Brown, 'Polo', in R. Weir, *The Badminton Library: Riding and Polo* (London: Longmans, 1895), pp. 254–9, 283–94; St Quintin, *Chances of Sports*, pp. 225–32, 439; Major Dalbiac, late R. H. A., 'Polo in the Army', *Navy and Army Illustrated*, 13 November 1896, 251–2, and 'Polo in India', *Navy and Army Illustrated*, 30 April 1897, 300–1; T. F. Dale, *Polo Past and Present* (London: Country Life, 1905), pp. 369–99; Captain H. de B. De Lisle, *The Rules of Polo in India, 1907* (Bombay: Thacker, 1907); 'Polo in India', *Country Life*, 31 August 1912, 298–300; Lieutenant-Colonel Humphrey Guinness, 'Foreword', in Brigadier Jack Gannon, *Before the Colours Fade: Polo, Pig, India, Pakistan and Some Memories* (London: J. A. Allen, 1976), p. 10; Captain G. J. Younghusband, *Polo in India* (London: W. H. Allen & Co., 1890), pp. 20–5.

[26] McDevitt, *May the Best Man Win*, p. 37; Jack Gannon, 'Polo: The Indian Inter-Regimental Tournament Part I', *Royal Armoured Corps Journal* 2 (1948), 130–7, at 135; W. Churchill, *My Early Life* (London: Thornton Butterworth Ltd, 1930), pp. 122, 213; R. Kipling, 'The Maltese Cat', in *The Day's Work* (London: Macmillan,

By the late 1880s polo's all-pervasiveness was causing some official unease in India. There had been a spate of serious accidents, and rapid inflation in the price of polo ponies had tempted officers to balance their accounts by buying poor-quality chargers. The Commander-in-Chief, Sir Frederick Roberts, though an enthusiastic horseman who believed that officers should undertake 'frequent practice in feats of horsemanship', in 1890 issued a general order regarding polo, urging clubs to minimise its dangers and instructing commanding officers to see that officers did not buy expensive ponies 'until they are provided with proper chargers' and that the price of polo ponies was kept within officers' means. The Indian Polo Association was formed to regulate the game but initially had little effect: in 1892 Roberts was forced to threaten 'decisive action' unless his comments on safety and economy were heeded.[27] He was not alone in his concerns. From the Punjab 'A Player' urged the abolition of cavalry tournaments, the main cause of high expenses. Since 'success generally comes to the owners of the speediest ponies – *i.e.*, to the longest purse', he said, junior officers were pressured into buying expensive ponies which were then transported long distances to tournaments 'at a cost of £200 to £300 in some cases'.[28] (Some years later the officers of the 4th Hussars chartered a special train to transport thirty ponies 1,400 miles from Bangalore to the Inter-Regimental Tournament at Meerut).[29] At home the difficulty in finding sufficient officers to staff cavalry regiments raised similar alarms about expenses. One correspondent to the *Times* complained of 'reckless and growing extravagance amongst the younger officers', another that 'a stud of hunters and two or three polo ponies ought not to be regarded as compulsory in order to keep up a certain tone in a regiment'.[30] In 1894 polo was banned from Sandhurst (along with keeping horses, racing and hunting) after a series of reports by the Board of Visitors condemned it as encouraging extravagance.[31]

However, it took the disasters of the Boer War to bring the issue of officer sport to the foreground. While almost all sections of the British

1898). See also Younghusband, *Polo*, and H. de B. De Lisle, *Polo in India*, 2nd edn (Bombay: Thacker, 1913).

[27] Dale, *Polo Past and Present*, pp. 369–71; D. James, *Lord Roberts* (London: Hollis & Carter, 1954), p. 211; *Times*, 1 September 1890, 30 May 1892.

[28] *Times*, 7 October 1890. For a dissenting view, see 21 October 1890.

[29] Churchill, *My Early Life*, p. 221.

[30] *Times*, 30 March 1893, 4 April 1893.

[31] Polo had been played at Sandhurst since about 1874, initially on the football ground. The regulations against keeping horses, hunting and point-to-point races had been relaxed by 1900. *Times*, 12 November 1891, 22 February 1893, 22 November 1893; Major A.F. Mockler-Ferryman, *Annals of Sandhurst* (London: Heinemann, 1900), pp. 256–7.

army proved inadequate in South Africa, the cavalry came under particular criticism for its lack of mobility, initiative and reconnaissance skills, and its extraordinarily high levels of horse wastage. Roberts, who dismissed eleven out of the seventeen cavalry commanders, thought that the failure of the cavalry adequately to perform its basic duties had prolonged the war.[32] The *Times*, heading the charge for army reform, was moved, soon after 'Black Week', to deplore:

> the scandal, for it is nothing less, that no man can hold the QUEEN'S commission except under perfectly intolerable social conditions unless he can command a private income of from £150 to £500. The abolition of purchase was supposed to make the nation master of its Army [but] ... expensive habits, mostly connected with amusements of one kind and another, have made the Army a close corporation just as in the old purchase days.[33]

As the subsequent correspondence demonstrated, the expenditure of cavalry officers on equestrian sports, particularly polo, was the main issue at stake. A typical letter, signed 'General', complained that in a well-known cavalry regiment, 'by no means ... one of the fastest', a private income of £700 a year was thought the acceptable minimum.

> An officer is considered 'a very poor fellow' and one not at all likely to do credit to the regiment if he does not race and keep hunters and polo ponies ... Nearly the whole of this expenditure goes to promote pleasure and amusements, and acts most detrimentally upon the efficiency of officers, who have neither time nor inclination for the serious study of their profession, which has become a vital necessity nowadays.[34]

Officer sport thus became the focus of concerns about two related problems: firstly, the standard of military education; secondly, the difficulty in recruiting sufficient capable officers for the cavalry because of the expenses of the expected lifestyle. In the years after 1900 the War Office and a series of government committees tackled the interconnected issues of military education, officer recruitment, cavalry extravagance and equestrian sport. Their suggestions proved remarkably similar: their ability to force through the proposed reforms proved remarkably weak. The movement for reform took place against a wider debate about the role of the cavalry in modern warfare given recent advances in firepower. Roberts, as Commander-in-Chief of the British army, urged a move away from shock tactics and the *arme blanche*

---

[32] Spiers, 'The British Cavalry', pp. 72–3; Anglesey, *British Cavalry*, chs. 14–15. It is striking that the obsession with equestrian sport had apparently produced no improvement in horsemastership.
[33] *Times*, 14 February 1900.
[34] *Times*, 22 February 1900.

towards a mobile force able to fight dismounted using rifles. In 1903 the lance was retired as a weapon for active service, and the rifle displaced the sword as the cavalry's principal weapon. However, Roberts faced great resistance from cavalry traditionalists led by General French and Colonel Douglas Haig, and his reforms were not destined to last long.[35] The parabola between reform and reaction described by the cavalry debate was echoed in miniature by the debate over polo.

Well aware of the strength of vested interests in the cavalry regiments, the War Office proceeded on the polo question with caution tempered by an increasingly widely felt need for reform. An earlier committee on cavalry organisation led by French had advocated banning neither entertainments at race meetings ('expenses under this head, seemed, of late years, to have greatly decreased in the Cavalry') nor inter-regimental polo tournaments. Good polo was valuable training for cavalry work: as a concession to criticism, tournaments might be supervised by a committee of brigadiers. By late 1899 most members of the War Office Council felt that more radical change was needed. The Adjutant General, Sir Evelyn Wood, came out strongly for restricting officer sport and the associated expense. Describing tournament polo as 'almost professional', he recommended banning regiments from playing in tournaments outside their regimental district, forbidding regimental polo clubs and allowing officers to play only on their own horses. Lord Wolseley, Roberts' predecessor as Commander-in-Chief, agreed that 'tournaments as now carried out do more harm than good'. Support within the Council was sufficient by January 1900 to warrant the drafting of a draconian Army Order:

Regimental polo clubs for providing ponies for polo tournaments are forbidden. Regimental teams in matches, or in polo tournaments are not to be permitted, except within the military district in which the regiment may be quartered, and Officers playing in such teams may only do so on ponies that are *bona fide*, and unconditionally, their own property.

In February tournaments outside regimental districts were forbidden. The other proposals included in the draft order, however, continued to be discussed.[36]

The Secretary of State for War, Lord Lansdowne, seemed disinclined to take on the cavalry regiments. He declared himself 'entirely in favour of putting down extravagance' regarding polo, particularly objecting to regimental clubs funded by universal subscription among officers

---

[35] Bond, 'Doctrine and Training'; Spiers, 'The British Cavalry'.
[36] Proceedings of the War Office Council, 30 June 1898 to 11 July 1900, WO163/4B, TNA.

'which compel Officers who do not play to pay for those who do'. (This was a recognised grievance: in 1899 Sir George Luck, Lieutenant-General Commanding Bengal, ordered all station polo clubs to be disbanded for this reason, after officers at Naini Tal 'submitted a petition complaining that polo's supremacy at the station was despotic'.)[37] But Lansdowne preferred to work through persuasion rather than by regulation. He was certainly not prepared to pick a fight over entertainments at race meetings, though Wood wanted to 'absolutely forbid any Regimental lunch being taken to race meetings, except those of point to point races in which the regiments may be taking part' and prepared a draft Army Order to this effect. Was it, said Lansdowne 'intended to forbid the regiment from going to a race meeting? If it may go, is it to take no luncheon with it? If it may take luncheon with it, are the Officers to be forbidden from giving a sandwich to their friends?' Lansdowne's ridicule cloaked considerable unease about the probable reaction to such reforms. It was essential, he urged,

in framing rules of this kind to obtain as large a measure of support as possible from within the Cavalry itself. There was little doubt that any restrictions imposed upon the mode of life in Cavalry regiments would be difficult to enforce, and would probably encounter a good deal of hostile criticism.

Surely the Colonels of regiments could control any tendency towards extravagance? Wolseley, out of his riper military experience, assured them that they could not, or would not: 'warnings to Colonels had frequently been given, but their effect was but slight, and of short duration, and in six months they were forgotten'. But Lansdowne succeeded in carrying his view that 'stringent sumptuary laws' could not be passed without first ascertaining 'the general opinion of Cavalry Officers', and that sporting expenses could not be considered in isolation from the other costs of military life.[38] A committee was subsequently appointed to investigate officer expenses.

Meanwhile, however, yet another committee added its weight to the attack on officer sport. The Committee on the Education and Training of Officers, headed by the Conservative MP Aretas Akers-Douglas, reported in June 1902, having spent a year taking evidence from military men, public-school headmasters and other interested parties. They found that, although public-school games had improved the physical condition of officers, their intellectual state was less satisfactory. Boys coming out of school knew 'nothing at all properly as a rule', and young

[37] McDevitt, *May the Best Man Win*, pp. 44–5; *Times*, 6 November 1899.
[38] Proceedings of the War Office Council, 30 June 1898 to 11 July 1900, WO163/4B, TNA.

Figure 6. Polo: the Irish Subalterns' Cup, 1896. 10th Hussars versus 13th Hussars. Even minor regimental polo tournaments were social occasions.

officers were astonishingly ignorant on military matters. The committee recognised that the root cause of this problem was that promotion was too rarely by merit, too often by seniority, connections or interest. They were concerned, however, by the fanatically sporty, rigorously anti-intellectual culture that prevailed both at the military colleges and in the army more generally: studying was positively discouraged, 'keenness is out of fashion', and young officers aimed only 'to see how much polo they can play and how soon they can get out of their uniform'. They were also under-employed and consequently idle: a cavalry subaltern, it was said, had 'nothing to do after luncheon' and could potentially spend at least two or three hours a day on study 'without interfering with his games'.[39] The well-known army crammer Thomas Miller Maguire (admittedly an uncompromising opponent of 'athleticism' generally) saw these games, and the emphasis placed upon them, as part of the problem. A young officer, he said, had 'every

---

[39] *Report of the Committee Appointed to Consider the Education and Training of Officers of the Army* [Cd. 982] 1902, 2 vols. (hereafter Akers-Douglas), vol. I, pp. 29, 37–9, vol. II, pp. 93, 30, 69.

discouragement to fit himself for his post by study ... success at polo, or cricket, or tennis, or theatricals, or billiards would have paid him in his career better than learning' – not an unreasonable assertion in an age when commanding officers' reports for the Selection Board could refer only to the applicant's success at polo or field sports or 'in society'.[40]

The committee was particularly concerned by the relationship between military education, the expenses of the cavalry lifestyle and the consequent lack of competition for commissioned posts in cavalry regiments. While a large private income remained essential, it was 'hopeless to endeavour to raise the standard of education among Cavalry officers'.[41] The Committee made several suggestions for cutting expenses, including the government provision of chargers. Much of the evidence given on this point, however, revolved around polo and hunting. Lieutenant-Colonel the Hon. R. T. Lawley, commanding the 7th Hussars, thought a private income of £600 a year necessary for an officer in his regiment: asked on what it was spent, he replied, 'always on horses'. Colonel Fisher of the 10th Hussars thought polo 'a very delicate subject' and a 'difficult thing' – 'a poor fellow who is a brilliant player' might easily, he acknowledged, run into debt. The Inspector General of Cavalry, Major-General Grant, hinted at the social pressures involved when he said that 'if you could arrange so that the man who can afford it plays polo and one who cannot afford it is not pressed in any way to play, I am entirely in favour of it'. Major-General H. R. Abadie, Commandant of the Cavalry Depot at Canterbury, was more direct. Polo he thought a 'good game, especially so for all mounted officers' but polo tournaments were 'a curse owing to the great expenses of ponies, their carriage to and fro as well as their wear and tear'. Regimental packs of hounds, he added, he 'would not tolerate at any price', though he was prepared to allow small regimental point-to-points and race meetings.[42] The committee's recommendations followed Abadie closely in commending polo as a game but advocating the prohibition of tournaments, regimental coaches and regimental packs of hounds.[43]

Nothing had changed, however, by the time the Committee to Enquire into the Nature of the Expenses incurred by Officers (headed by Lord Stanley, the Financial Secretary to the War Office) reported a year later, in April 1903. In those areas where their concerns overlapped, the two committees' recommendations were very similar. After taking

---

[40] Akers-Douglas, Appendix XV, vol. I, p. 79; Spiers, *The Army and Society*, p. 249.
[41] Akers-Douglas, vol. I, p. 36.
[42] *Ibid.*, vol. I, pp. 36, 134–5; vol. II, pp. 304, 67, 298.
[43] *Ibid.*, vol. I, p. 36.

'a large amount of evidence ... almost exclusively of a confidential character', Stanley's committee – refusing to recommend an increase in pay and thereby cementing the need for army officers to possess a private income – concentrated on two main points. Firstly, it recommended that the state should provide some specific necessities of army life currently paid for by officers. For cavalry officers, these were to include two chargers plus saddlery and stable gear, and a second soldier servant to act as groom. (This was calculated as an initial saving of £300 plus an annual saving of £180, reducing the private income needed by a cavalry officer to £120.) As it was 'considered practically essential for all Cavalry Officers to hunt as part of their military training', they were to be allowed to hunt their chargers ('a concession,' said the *Times*, 'which will be greatly appreciated'). While encouraging hunting, however, the report – like that of the Akers-Douglas Committee – advocated that certain familiar areas of officer extravagance should be restricted. All regimental race meetings except one point-to-point per year should be banned. No regiment should be allowed to keep a pack of hounds. Polo 'within certain limits' received modified approval as serving 'a very useful educational end, in the development of qualities of horsemanship and character particularly requisite for service in the mounted arm'. But inter-regimental tournaments should be prohibited; regimental teams should not be allowed to compete outside their regimental district; and polo clubs, and subscriptions, should be restricted to playing members – 'in no case should membership be felt to be compulsory'. The *Times*, still flying the flag of army reform, was delighted by the report, editorialising that, given 'the ever increasing demand upon the intellectual powers of officers of all ranks resulting from the conditions of modern warfare, the very serious limitation of the field of selection by the present high standard of expenditure can be considered nothing less than a national danger'. Inter-regimental tournaments had long been 'simply a competition in wealth between regiments': their prohibition had 'it is well known, been urged by SIR EVELYN WOOD and other zealous officers for years', and the *Times* hoped the War Office would 'lose no time in giving it effect'.[44]

Officer sport, however, could call on powerful supporters, and the debate was played out not only within the army but in the general and

[44] *Report of the Committee Appointed by the Secretary of State for War to Enquire into the Nature of the Expenses Incurred by Officers of the Army, and to Suggest Measures for Bringing Commissions Within Reach of Men of Moderate Means* [Cd. 1421] 1903; *Times*, 9 April 1903; Spiers, *The Army and Society*, p. 25. The suggestion that chargers should be provided at government expense was adopted for cavalry stationed in Britain but not extended to India.

sporting press. The critics of 1893 were met with the arguments that, since the army was not a paying profession, officers joined largely 'with a view of obtaining a comfortable home, pleasant society, and a larger amount of sport than he would obtain in civil life', and that on active service a sporting officer would be of more use than the 'theoretical one' competitive examinations threatened to turn out.[45] Even in 1900 it could be argued that sport and society were the main attractions of officer life and that ('Is it seriously contended that a cavalry officer should live on his pay?') the role of sport as a social gatekeeper should be embraced rather than deplored:

Restrict the sporting instincts of our cavalry officers, forbid them to hunt or play polo ... and in a very short time I venture to predict a very different class of person will offer himself for cavalry commissions; whether this will be to the advantage of the service remains to be seen.[46]

Similarly, W. E. Cairns argued that the unreformed system had created a 'corps of officers, the best in the world', distinguished not so much by the 'scientific military training of the Germans' as by the 'higher military qualities' of 'courage ... devotion ... forgetfulness of self' and the 'indefinable qualities' required to lead men under fire. Raising pay and lowering expenses would open the profession to men of lower social status less endowed with these qualities than the traditional officer class: and 'Tommy Atkins,' he said, would 'follow a "gentleman" much more readily than they will an officer whose social position is not so well assured'.[47] The defenders of the gentlemanly officer tradition therefore saw equestrian sport – and its associated expenses – as usefully ensuring that the officer corps would continue to come largely from the ranks of the aristocracy and landed gentry.

This was scarcely a view to commend itself to army reformers, but officer sport could also be defended as promoting soldierly efficiency. Even the sternest critics agreed that hunting, pig-sticking and polo could serve as a form of military training. In the days of cavalry and mounted infantry there was no doubt some truth in this – if not, perhaps, quite enough truth to justify the lavishness with which leave for hunting was granted. In addition to horsemanship, hunting and pig-sticking were said to develop an 'eye for the country' and the ability to cross unknown territory at speed. Lieutenant-Colonel Graham Seton Hutchison described 'prowess in the hunting-field' as 'an essential

---

[45] *Times*, 4 April 1893.
[46] *Times*, 22 February 1900, letter from 'C.O.'.
[47] Cairns, *Social Life*, pp. xi–xvi. Cairns was subsequently secretary to the Military Education Committee.

part of training' for colonial warfare.[48] Lieutenant-Colonel E. A. H. Alderson's *Pink and Scarlet or Hunting as a School for Soldiering* (1900) was a prolonged attempt to prove that hunting – in Mr Jorrocks' well-known words – really was the image of war. Hunting, Alderson argued, took up 'the fighting education of the young Officer just where the barrack-square and the drill-field can go no further' and in a way that nothing but active service itself could do. As supporting evidence, he pointed out that the German cavalry now hunted 'by order'. Similarly, Baden-Powell thought pig-sticking and polo 'an exceptionally practical school for the development of horsemanship and of handiness in the use of arms while mounted' – an education the more valuable for being undertaken voluntarily.[49]

Not only physical but also moral qualities were said to be produced by polo and field sports. These included pluck, nerve, judgement and (in the case of polo) team spirit and regimental *esprit de corps*. Above all – as befitted officer sports – they promoted leadership ability. 'In war we find our sportsmen natural leaders, men of decision who inspire confidence, and who in consequence will always be respected and followed'.[50] In 1916, in the face of considerable scepticism, Major General Knox declared that no man had 'done so much as has the fox and the foxhound to foster the cult of character, quick decision, and nerve so necessary for leadership in war'. Lieutenant-Colonel E. D. Miller (late 17th Lancers) thought 'the same qualities which bring a man to the front at polo are required by anyone who aspires to lead men'. Baden-Powell agreed, specifying 'quiet, quick decision and dash' – the epitome of the 'cavalry spirit' – as the qualities in question. In 1889 he argued that the British cavalry's 'superior qualities of dash and horsemanship' were under threat as the French and Germans gave more encouragement to similar sports in their armies. After his triumphs at Mafeking, Baden-Powell himself was frequently cited as an example of how sport prepared men for war. ('I knew Baden-Powell in India as a first-class man to "pig", and a most successful shikari, and am therefore not in the least surprised that he is now making game of the Boers'.) The skills acquired in breaking and schooling horses were thought to be transferable to the

[48] Hutchinson quoted in Harold E. Raugh, Jr, 'Training Ground for a Future Field Marshal: Wavell in the Boer War and Edwardian India, 1901–1908', *Journal of the Society for Army Historical Research* 72 (Spring 1994), 8–18, at 16.
[49] Lieutenant-Colonel E. A. H. Alderson, *Pink and Scarlet or Hunting as a School for Soldiering* (London: Heinemann, 1900), pp. 1–2, 209–10, 216; Baden-Powell, *Indian Memories*, p. 31. Lionel Edwards' watercolour illustrations for the second (1913) edition of *Pink and Scarlet* still hang in the Officers' Mess at Sandhurst.
[50] General Sir Beauvoir De Lisle, *Reminiscences of Sport and War* (London: Eyre & Spottiswoode, 1939), p. 272.

training of enlisted men ('Men ... like horses ... have tender mouths, therefore "hands", tact, temper, justice, confidence in them, boldness, judgement, and self-reliance are required to lead them successfully, just as they are to ride horses properly'); the habit of ensuring a horse's comfort before one's own could also be usefully transferred to the care of one's men. The business of organising regimental polo provided useful experience in man-management and administration.[51] Moreover, polo (as its supporters were glad to see the German military journal *Militär Wochenblatt* point out) could be played by the middle-aged as well as the young, keeping older officers in condition and providing an opportunity for senior and junior officers to mingle. If it was 'unthinkable' in the early 1880s for a colonel to be in the regimental polo team it was by no means uncommon by 1914 to see 'a colonel of a regiment playing Back, and urging his officers on to victory in a hard-fought match'.[52]

Even the question of expense was disputed. Polo, claimed its champions, was not how young officers wasted money – or if it was their parents should be thankful. In later life Churchill claimed that 'no one ever came to grief – except honourable grief – through riding horses'. Miller thought that debts allegedly incurred by officers through polo had probably been acquired in a less creditable fashion 'on amusements of a much less reputable nature'. Sport was surely preferable to the 'crapulous, unwholesome café haunting' of the continental officer. Some suggested that polo should be seen as an economy and as an agent of moral regeneration, especially in India. Baden-Powell, surely optimistically, thought that polo and pig-sticking had 'completely driven out from the British subaltern the drinking and betting habits of the former generation', and Sergeant-Major John Fraser (who did not indulge in these sports himself) called them 'the salvation of many a young officer' for

---

[51] *Times*, 29 May 1916; Lieutenant-Colonel E. D. Miller, *Modern Polo*, 4th edn (London: Herbert Jenkins, 1922), pp. 348–9, 356; Baden-Powell, *Indian Memories*, pp. 31–3; Captain R. S. S. Baden-Powell, *Pigsticking or Hoghunting: A Complete Account for Sportsmen; and Others* (London: Harrison & Sons, 1889), p. 7; 'Outpost', 'Recollections of Steeplechasing – VIII', 152; Alderson, *Pink and Scarlet*, pp. 86–7, 175–6; McDevitt, *May the Best Man Win*, pp. 40–1; Winston Churchill to St John Brodrick, 7 June 1902 (copy), in Randolph S. Churchill, *Winston S. Churchill*, 8 vols., vol. II Companion Part 1: *1901–1907* (London: Heinemann, 1967), pp. 142–4.

[52] 'Polo and Cub-Hunting', *Country Life*, 13 September 1902, 346; Baden-Powell, *Indian Memories*, p. 104; Miller, *Modern Polo*, p. 350. Successful regimental teams with Commanding Officers playing included the 17th Lancers (Haig and then Portal), 16th Lancers (Gough) and the 10th Hussars (Vaughan). Unusually, in the 10th Hussars equestrian sport also provided a link between officers and men: the rank-and-file were provided with polo ponies, and the NCOs had their own annual polo tournament and were taken pig-sticking by the officers (St Quintin, *Chances of Sports*, pp. 93–5; Jack Gannon, 'Polo: the Indian Inter-Regimental Tournament Part II: 1900–1914', *Royal Armoured Corps Journal* 2 (1948), 207–20, at 212).

the same reason. Even in Britain polo was said to keep officers with their regiments and dissuade them from racing and 'more expensive and less desirable distractions in London'. Polo thus promoted thrift, self-control and 'careful living'.[53]

Invariably the example used to support this argument was the success of the Durham Light Infantry, winners of the Indian Inter-Regimental Tournament 1896–8: a poor foot regiment beating the cavalry at its own game.[54] This triumph was the product of a decade's-long campaign spearheaded by Henry de Beauvoir De Lisle, a mere lieutenant when, with the support of his commanding officer, he carried through his proposal to start a regimental polo club against considerable opposition. A successful amateur jockey, he devoted himself to polo after being offered the adjutancy of the regiment on condition he gave up racing. De Lisle was central to all aspects of the team's success. His tactical innovations – derived from the DLI's football team – brought in a new style of play that emphasised teamwork, accurate passing and pace. His horsemanship and eye for a horse not only meant that the regiment's polo ponies were unbeatably well trained: the team was largely funded by the profits made from buying raw ponies, training them and selling them on. His 'iron discipline' forced team members to devote themselves to a regime of keep-fit routines, clean living, constant individual practice and intensive team practice at speed.[55] Justly famous, the DLI polo team was less a demonstration that regimental polo need not be expensive than it was the exception that proved the rule. When in 1898 De Lisle left the regiment the DLI left the annals of polo history forever.[56]

[53] Churchill, *My Early Life*, p. 59; Miller, *Modern Polo*, pp. 351, 356; C. Stein, 'Soldiering and Sport', *Baily's Magazine* 74 (1900), 235–40, at 237; Baden-Powell, *Indian Memories*, p. 31; Farwell, *Mr Kipling's Army*, p. 205; T.F.D., 'Polo prospects in 1901', *Baily's Magazine* 75 (1901), 270–3, at 272; Dale, *Polo Past and Present*, pp. 94–5; McDevitt, *May the Best Man Win*, pp. 54–5.

[54] This did not make them universally popular: some cavalry regiments 'went out of their way to show resentment over the fact that an infantry regiment should even compete in the Regimental Cup – much less win it' (Gough, *Soldiering On*, p. 47).

[55] 'History of the Polo Club, 2nd DLI', *Bugle* (weekly journal of the 2nd Battalion Durham Light Infantry), vol. I, 21 June 1894, pp. 63–4, 28 June 1894, p. 75, 5 July 1894, pp. 89–90, 19 July 1894, p. 111, 26 July 1894, p. 122, 2 August 1894, pp. 36–7; reprint from *The Pioneer*, *Bugle*, vol. IV, 12 March 1896, p. 993; General Sir Beauvoir De Lisle, *Tournament Polo* (London: Eyre & Spottiswoode, 1938), pp. 1–4, *Reminiscences*, pp. 57–62; Gannon, 'Polo: Part I', p. 136.

[56] Polo undoubtedly benefited De Lisle's military career. Though he lived entirely on his pay, his profits from selling trained polo ponies were sufficient to let him take a year's leave, 'pay his expenses at a crammer's and pass into the Staff College'. His polo fame surely eased his later path as commander of mounted infantry and cavalry. (Lieutenant-Colonel E.D. Miller, *Fifty Years of Sport* (London: Hurst & Blackett, 1925), p. 201.)

Proponents of polo and pig-sticking argued that their sports enhanced British-Indian relations. One ex-army officer even suggested that polo alone could 'break down the barriers of race, and bind together in amity the fellow-subjects of the East and West'. At the top of the social hierarchy polo – along with pig-sticking and big-game hunting – did indeed perform the useful function of providing 'a locus for social interaction between the leaders of the great princely states and the British establishment'. Many officers recorded their gratitude for princely hospitality, though princely wealth could sometimes grate: having framed their rules to 'put a poor man on equal terms with a rich man' the organisers of the pig-sticking Guzerat Cup were taken aback when the Maharana of Dholpu and the Maharaja of Patiala turned up in 1892 with forty-five horses between them.[57]

For ordinary Indians the evidence is less convincing. In Bombay between 1879 and 1884 Indian cricketers engaged in a protracted and ultimately fruitless battle to protect their ground on the Maidan from British army polo players. As Guha notes, their petitions were written in the language that became characteristic of early Indian nationalism, adopting British notions of justice and 'fair play' and turning them against the Raj.[58] On pig-sticking, Baden-Powell insisted that it was 'a boon to natives': a meet brought villagers work for men and boys as beaters, provided customers for their horses and forage, bullocks and carts, and (splendidly ignoring pig preservation policies) removed the pigs which damaged their crops. He also thought that through pig-sticking 'governor and governed are brought into relations of a personal and friendly character of the utmost value to our hold in India'. Perhaps there was some truth in the idea that villagers benefited from pig-sticking: Wardrop described how the Meerut Tent Club, which often included a doctor, held impromptu surgeries and dispensing clinics every evening during a camp. But Baden-Powell undermined his case by adding that it was 'fatal to the interest of sport to ill-treat the villagers or to let your servants or Shikaris do so, as they are very apt to do under cover of your prestige'.[59]

By showing ability in field sports Englishmen in India were, in Baden-Powell's view, proving themselves 'a different and superior order

---

[57] T.F. Dale, 'Polo and Politics', *Blackwood's Magazine* 165 (1899), 1032–6, at 1033; McDevitt, *May the Best Man Win*, p. 37; Wardrop, *Modern Pig-Sticking*, pp. 174–5.

[58] R. Guha, *A Corner of a Foreign Field: The Indian History of a British Sport* (London: Picador, 2002), pp. 20–8.

[59] Baden-Powell, *Pigsticking* (1889 edn), pp. vii, 12–13; Sir Robert Baden-Powell, *Pig-Sticking or Hog-Hunting: A Complete Account for Sportsmen and Others* (London: Herbert Jenkins, 1924), pp. 35–40, 45, 70–1; Wardrop, *Modern Pig-Sticking*, p. 211.

of beings' and demonstrating 'a proper prowess in the dominant race'. Sport, in fact, was one of the ways in which the British maintained the 'prestige' of the Raj and demonstrated to supposedly 'effeminate' Indians their superior manliness.[60] Certainly sport in India was not exclusively a male activity. Procida highlights the extent to which women participated in the sporting life of the Raj, part of a version of 'imperial femininity' that 'incorporated traditionally masculine attributes without completely eradicating fundamental gender distinctions'.[61] Nevertheless the predominant impression of Anglo-Indian sport is of a largely sex-segregated zone in which relationships between men were paramount. Wardrop, though he dedicated *Modern Pig-Sticking* to his mother and included a lengthy description by her of the Kadir Cup, insisted that 'ladies are quite out of place at ordinary meets of a Tent Club'. The male-bonding aspect of officer sport is illustrated in a curious short story by Baden-Powell, 'The Ordeal of the Spear'. Two officers of the 6th Hussars discover that they are in love with the same woman. ('How evenly matched we are at this new game just as we are said to be at polo and pig-sticking!') To preserve their friendship they decide that whichever gets first spear at the Meerut Christmas meet will win the right to propose to her first. This is duly carried out and the 'wrong' man wins. It transpires, however, that the woman, watching the contest in ignorance of its significance, has been killed by her elephant – effectively solving the problem.[62]

Officer sports both certified the 'manliness' of the imperial rulers and provided reassurance to those who feared creeping effeminacy. The crowning argument in favour of polo, as McDevitt argues, was that polo was a 'masculine' sport, 'the most manly of games'. Polo, said J. Moray Brown, called forth:

all those manly qualities that make Britons what they are, and what, please God, they ever will be ... In these days of luxury any sport that tends to take away our youth from enervating influences, that trains their physical powers, and makes them *men*, ought surely to be encouraged and fostered.[63]

---

[60] Baden-Powell, *Pigsticking* (1889 edn), pp. 5–6; E. M. Collingham, *Imperial Bodies: The Physical Experience of the Raj c.1800–1947* (Cambridge: Polity, 2001), 124–6, 141–2. See also M. Sinha, *Colonial Masculinity: The 'Manly Englishman' and the 'Effeminate Bengali' in the Late Nineteenth Century* (Manchester University Press, 1995).
[61] M. A. Procida, 'Good Sports and Right Sorts: Guns, Gender, and Imperialism in British India', *Journal of British Studies* 40 (2001), 454–88, at 455.
[62] Wardrop, *Modern Pig-Sticking*, p. 219; 'The Ordeal of the Spear', in R. S. S. Baden-Powell, *Sport in War* (London: William Heinemann, 1900), pp. 81–118.
[63] McDevitt, *May the Best Man Win*, pp. 37–8, 44; J. Moray Brown, 'The Training of Polo Ponies', *Blackwood's Magazine* 149 (1891), 645–51, at 650.

Sport provided an arena for the demonstration of tough masculinity. Pig-stickers proudly flaunted their injuries. One entry in a Tent Club journal read 'Result of meet – Twenty-four boar, two panther, one sahib badly mauled, one coolie ditto, one broken collar-bone, one dislocated shoulder, one back injured and (only) four horses *hors de combat*'.[64] Baden-Powell's *Pig-Sticking* includes advice on dealing with sunstroke, broken bones, dislocated shoulders, punctured wounds, large cuts, concussion and fracture of the skull (Wardrop added fever, cholera, plague and snake-bite). Curiously, however, pig-sticking fatalities were rare. Aside from a handful of well-remembered incidents in which pig-stickers were impaled on their own or their comrades' spears, the sport killed very few officers.[65] Fatal accidents happened much more frequently to their horses, or to their Indian beaters, who, dismounted and usually armed only with sticks, were far more vulnerable to the tusks of enraged boars. For officers, therefore, pig-sticking, gratifyingly, looked more dangerous than it actually was. Polo, though less dramatic, was really far more perilous despite repeated efforts to make it safer. Between 1880 and 1914 the *Times* reported the deaths of thirty-six officers from polo accidents – over one a year on average – mostly in India and of all ranks up to Lieutenant-Colonel John Sladen, commanding officer of 2/East Yorkshire Regiment, killed in a station game in 1910.[66] The deaths and injuries produced by officer sports must have gone some way to counteracting their perceived contribution to military efficiency.

The battery of arguments produced to present equestrian sports not as frivolous, extravagant, wasteful of men and prohibitive to military talent but as manly, moral, conducive to thrift and self-control, and a useful form of military training, nonetheless had its effect. In conjunction with their overwhelming popularity in the Edwardian officer corps it meant that the War Office's attempts to restrict them were destined to fail. Even as the Committees on Military Education and on

---

[64] L. E. [?Lionel Edwards], 'Pig Sticking in Northern India', *Country Life*, 30 May 1914, 780–3, at 783. Baden-Powell, *Pig-sticking* (1924 edn), p. 293, cites the same entry, which is presumably exceptional: it refers to a seven-day meet of the Meerut Tent Club involving fourteen men and sixty-seven horses.

[65] For the death of Lieutenant Startin, 10th Hussars, in an accident involving another officer's spear, see *Times*, 28 December 1875, Baden-Powell, *Pig-Sticking* (1924 edn), p. 226, and St Quintin, *Chances of Sports*, pp. 190–4.

[66] Miller, *Modern Polo*, p. 355; *Times*, 7 March 1910. This figure includes seven British officers of the Indian army, one of the Egyptian army and one Royal Navy officer: it is clear from other sources that the actual death rate was rather higher. A search of the *Times* for deaths from pig-sticking (or hog-hunting) 1880–1914 finds only two: those of Frederick W. L. Birdwood, RA, and John Blackwood, 8th Hussars (19 August 1884 and 4 May 1912 respectively).

the Expenses of Officers recommended the banning of inter-regimental polo tournaments, a campaign was beginning to revive them after the hiatus of the Boer War. In mid-1902 Winston Churchill, claiming that it was 'wealthy civilians' who had 'so greatly increased the price of polo ponies', told St John Brodrick (Lansdowne's replacement as Secretary of State for War) that the problem could be solved by dissociating army polo from civilian polo. A British Army Polo Association should be set up and inter-regimental tournaments not banned but used as a weapon to reduce the cost of army polo. Churchill suggested regulations 'to discourage the use of very high priced polo ponies' and 'to prevent altogether the sort of practice lately indulged in by some regiments of buying a great many expensive ponies shortly before a match', and urged that 'not less than half of the ponies should have been actually trained to polo in the regiment and not bought as made ponies'. With these rules the tournament would be won by the 'finest masters of horsemanship', not 'merely the most wealthy or the most sporting'. All this seems a trifle ironic from Churchill, whose former regiment had won polo success through precisely the methods he now deplored. Yet Churchill had personal reasons to support such reforms: he had left the army partly because his £500 annual income was inadequate to fund 'polo and the Hussars'.[67] In any case he was clearly not the only person thinking along these lines.

That September De Lisle sent Roberts a memorandum on regimental polo, arguing that the Boer War had proved that the best polo players were the best soldiers. There was, he said, 'a peculiar similarity between the characteristics required to "run" a Regimental Polo Team and to excel as a leader of men in the Field'. Polo trained officers for war as effectively as hunting, big-game shooting or pig-sticking, with the added advantage of promoting *esprit de corps*. Far from discouraging polo the military authorities should give every inducement to young officers to play a game which encouraged horsemanship, horsemastership, organisation and 'personal character'. Polo's one drawback being its expense in England, he submitted a scheme to run the Inter-Regimental Tournament as cheaply as possible. Roberts, who had always felt that polo as a game was a good activity for mounted troops, was not difficult to persuade. Soon afterwards he told Brodrick that, rather than banning inter-regimental tournaments as the Akers-Douglas report

---

[67] Churchill to Brodrick, 7 June 1902 in Churchill, *Winston S. Churchill*, pp. 142–4; Churchill, *My Early Life*, p. 213. The 4th Hussars on arrival in India had taken the unprecedented step of buying the Poona Light Horse's entire polo stud of twenty-five trained ponies as a short-cut towards winning the Indian Inter-Regimental Tournament (*My Early Life*, pp. 120–1).

Officer sports and their critics

recommended, he intended to get new rules drawn up by a committee of experienced officers and give them one year's trial to see if tournaments could be run without 'undue expense'. Closely echoing De Lisle, he justified this decision in terms of military utility:

amongst the officers, who distinguished themselves in the war, several were noted as leaders of Polo in their regiments, whilst I can only remember one good Polo player amongst the many who proved failures. Polo certainly teaches officers to become good horsemen and careful horsemasters; it develops the powers of organisation, and trains men to think quickly and act on the spur of the moment – all valuable qualities in a mounted officer.[68]

The rules produced by the polo committee, which included De Lisle, included a number of cost-cutting measures: a restriction on the number of ponies allowed per team; preliminary ties to be played in regimental districts; the Hurlingham Club to defray the expenses of teams competing in the semi-finals and finals from gate money (reflecting the tournament's standing as a social function). Roberts had suggested a price limit for ponies, but the Committee felt this would result only in 'evasion and consequent unpleasantness'. If Roberts insisted (which he did not) they were prepared to set a limit of £80, the price of a good untrained pony, to foster horsemanship and make polo 'a school for cavalry soldiers'. Formally applied to by Haig, a well-known polo player, Roberts approved the new rules in January 1903, though the Adjutant General, Sir Thomas Kelly-Kenny, was 'afraid of trouble' with Brodrick.[69] Perhaps because of this Roberts 'forgot' to tell Brodrick that he had agreed to let the 1903 Inter-Regimental Tournament go ahead until March – by which time the War Office had received the Stanley report, again recommending a crack-down on polo. Roberts presented his decision as a deal with the cavalry commanders who, 'in return ... promised me to do all in their power to reduce the expense of living in their regiments'. If this was a genuine deal Roberts certainly got the worst of the bargain: the cavalry commanders were prepared to reduce the minimum private income required for young officers only to £300, rather than the £120 recommended by Stanley.[70]

[68] H. de B. De Lisle, 'Memorandum on Regimental Polo', 30 September 1902, Roberts Papers, 7101/23–221/2, NAM; Roberts to Brodrick, 3 October 1902, 7101/23–124–3, Roberts Papers, NAM.
[69] 'Rules [for the Inter-Regimental Tournament]'; Correspondence between members of the Army Polo Committee, December 1902–January 1903; Proceedings of a Meeting held at the Cavalry Club on 18 January 1903 to discuss questions relating to Inter-Regimental and army Polo generally; Minutes by Roberts and Kelly-Kenny, January 1903. 'Polo Papers', Roberts Papers, 7101/23–191–20, NAM.
[70] Roberts to Brodrick, 7 March 1903, Roberts Papers, 7101/23–122–5, NAM; Minute on Condition of Competitions for Cavalry Commissions, 30 March 1903, Roberts Papers, 7101/23–124–3, NAM.

Roberts hoped that this would still be sufficient to allow the abolition of the separate standard of examinations for cavalry candidates.[71] But his retirement in early 1904 as a result of the abolition of the post of Commander-in-Chief led to a 'cavalry counter-reformation' in this area as in others.[72] By 1905, following the Hutchinson report on the Deficiency of Officers in the Cavalry, the Army Council was again discussing the same old problems and meditating upon the same old solutions. Extravagant living still needed to 'be repressed by some means'. The Chief of the General Staff, Sir Neville Lyttelton, thought that, although it was unnecessary to prohibit racing and polo, 'it must be made quite clear to officers commanding that these are luxuries, and are not to be forced upon young officers of slender means'. The Army Council was increasingly concerned about the need to relax educational tests in order to ensure a sufficient supply of cavalry officers, with the result that many possessed 'a low standard of general education and intelligence'. The Adjutant General, Major-General C. W. H. Douglas, felt that strong measures were needed to reverse this situation:

> The monied classes must be eliminated from the cavalry, and a poorer class of officer sent in, letting the officer commanding know that if a young officer with, say 200*l*. a year, cannot live in the regiment, the officer commanding will be removed ... hunting and polo may improve the cavalry officers [but] ... the choice between money and brains must be made, and if we elect for brains the hunting and polo must go.[73]

With Roberts gone, however, traditional cavalry values were rapidly reinstated. Under French and Haig the rifle was de-emphasised, the lance was restored as a weapon of war, and the focus of training placed once more on the charge and the *arme blanche*. It is no coincidence that this period also saw the resurgence of officer sport. Faced with a choice between brains and polo – that is, between meritocracy and professionalism on the one hand and gentlemanly values and the 'cavalry spirit' on the other – the cavalry regiments of the Edwardian army unhesitatingly chose polo.[74]

---

[71] Minute on Condition of Competitions for Cavalry Commissions, 30 March 1903, and Memorandum on Entry of Cavalry Officers, Roberts Papers, 7101/23–124–3, NAM.
[72] DeGroot, 'Educated Soldier', p. 61.
[73] Anglesey, *British Cavalry*, pp. 471–2; Minutes of Proceedings and Précis Prepared for the Army Council for the Year 1905, WO163/10, TNA.
[74] As DeGroot, 'Educated Soldier', argues for Haig, a few exceptional officers of course managed to combine the two.

Officer sports and their critics

Continuing War Office attempts to curb officer expenditure on sport met with a mixture of evasion and defiance. Asked for their own solutions to the recruiting problem cavalry officers recommended more pay, more polo and more leave for hunting. The 10th Hussars responded to a circular on cavalry expenses asking, *inter alia*, whether the regiment kept a pack of hounds by simply transferring the pack – on paper – to the ownership of a Captain Mitford.[75] The *Cavalry Journal*, a bastion of cavalry traditionalism, bullishly promoted equestrian sport, deriding 'the recent mania to cut down expenses, regardless of whether it makes for efficiency or not'.[76] In 1905 an Army Polo Committee was set up in the teeth of War Office opposition; it was immediately dissolved by the Army Council but revived in March 1906 under the new War Secretary, Richard Haldane – perhaps as a sop to officer feeling at a time when he was presenting wide-ranging reforms. By 1910 the polo lobby was sufficiently confident to suggest that some of the restrictions on the Inter-Regimental Tournament agreed to in 1903 for 'diplomatic' reasons could now safely be abandoned.[77] In India the 1899 order from the Lieutenant General of Bengal banning regimental polo clubs proved similarly short-lived.[78]

While the belief that equestrian sports had military utility was held even by moderate reformers like Roberts it was further encouraged by the renewed emphasis on traditional cavalry tactics such as the charge. Haig's 1909 report on cavalry training placed 'great importance' on 'young officers being encouraged to hunt and play polo ... These pursuits have a very real value as training for war'. Polo was actively promoted at the new Cavalry School, and under Major-General John Vaughan hunting was included in the syllabus disguised as 'Memory Training'.[79] By 1911 (Douglas having left to take over the Southern Command) the Army Council had softened sufficiently on officer recreation to pronounce that hunting should be accepted as having 'special military value', and that polo possessed 'distinct military advantages,

---

[75] Summary of Answers given by 23 Cavalry Officers, including 14 Commanding Officers of Regiments Stationed at Home, 1905, WO163/10, TNA; Major-General John Vaughan, *Cavalry and Sporting Memories* (Bala: Bala Press, 1954), p. 115.
[76] 'Sporting Notes', *Cavalry Journal* 1 (1906), 380; see also in the *Cavalry Journal* e.g. 'Cavalier', 'The Height of Polo Ponies', 1 (1906), 109–11; Colonel F. V. Wing, 'Foxhunting and Soldiering', 1 (1906), 495–500; 'Ubique', 'The Value of Foxhunting', 8 (1913), 443–50.
[77] *Times*, 9 July 1910; T. B. Drybrough, *Polo*, 2nd edn (London: Longmans, 1906), pp. 370–2.
[78] *Times*, 11 March 1911.
[79] *Times*, 16 February 1910; 'Sporting Notes', *Cavalry Journal* 8 (1913), 126; Vaughan, *Cavalry and Sporting Memories*, pp. 149–50.

and should therefore be officially encouraged'.[80] At the outbreak of the First World War equestrian sport was as central to army life as it had ever been, and even during the conflict it was pursued as vigorously as circumstances allowed. Packs of hounds joined several regiments at the front, despite the complaints of French farmers; polo was played behind the lines; the boar of the Ardennes were found suitable for pig-sticking; at a pinch partridges could be ridden down and dispatched with polo-mallets. In Salonika the Scottish Horse formed a scratch pack to hunt hares just behind the trenches which met every Saturday, 'war permitting', and 'a good deal' of polo was played, sometimes within range of the Bulgarian guns.[81]

The debate over officer sport took place at a time when sport for other ranks was increasingly accepted as having military value. Equestrian sport, which took officers away from their men (the 10th Hussars seem to have been unique in encouraging polo and pig-sticking in the rank-and-file) and acted to restrict the social composition of the officer corps, was perceived to have the opposite tendency. There was certainly some truth in the accusations that polo had been unfairly singled out as a scapegoat for all the problems of officer recruitment and education. Polo and hunting were not the only things on which officers wasted time and money. In the absence of any political will to raise officer pay it was inevitable that the commissioned ranks would continue to be drawn mainly from the narrow band of those with substantial private incomes.[82] Yet the polo debate provides ample evidence to support Travers' assertion that behind the 'reluctance to insist on basic structural changes … lurked, among many officers, a simple desire to perpetuate the privileges and attractions of the late Victorian and Edwardian army, with its pleasant life, social networks and amateur ideals'.[83] Moreover, if for the Edwardian cavalry 'the lance was a "state of mind" and "the

---

[80] Minutes of Proceedings and Précis Prepared for the Army Council in the Year 1911: Précis No. 502, 'Provision of Facilities for Officers' Recreation, other than Golf', WO163/16, TNA. The Chief of the Imperial General Staff, General Sir William Nicholson, a man of long Indian experience, nevertheless remarked that polo had been 'anything but an unmixed advantage to the Army'.

[81] 'Hounds at the Front', *Baily's Magazine* 103 (February 1915), p. 86; R. Hargreaves, 'Divertissement', *Cavalry Journal* 31 (1941), 204–25; Miller, *Fifty Years of Sport*, pp. 255–6; A. Buxton, *Sport in Peace and War* (London: Arthur L. Humphreys, 1920); Dawson, *Sport in War*, pp. 84–98; C. Gibson, 'The British Army, French Farmers and the War on the Western Front 1914–1918', *Past and Present* 180 (2003), 175–239, at 189–91.

[82] Officer pay was finally raised in 1914, but only marginally: 'one receives the impression', said the *Times*' military correspondent, 'that one is reading some change in the rates of pay authorized by some rather shabby company to an inferior class of tram-conductors' (*Times*, 1 January 1914).

[83] Travers, 'The Hidden Army', p. 538.

charge" connoted not merely a tactical movement but a whole way of life', belief in equestrian sport as training for war was part of the same mind-set as the lance, the charge and the 'cavalry spirit'. The conviction once attributed to British officers by a Frenchman that 'the art of war' was 'precisely the same as that of fox-hunting' clearly survived into the twentieth century. With all its improvements in organisation, training, horsemastership and even musketry, the cavalry entered the Great War 'as wedded to shock tactics as it had been in 1899'.[84] For Bond, the 'cult of the horse and the *arme blanche*' can be seen as a 'last desperate effort to withstand the de-personalization of war'.[85] It also testifies, like the triumphant ascendancy of equestrian sport in the Edwardian army, to the survival of aristocratic and chivalric values in the face of repeated attempts to establish a more meritocratic and professional officer corps.

---

[84] Bond, 'Doctrine and Training', p. 99; L. Wolff, *In Flanders Fields* (London: Longmans Green, 1959), p. 33; Spiers, 'The British Cavalry', p. 79.
[85] Bond, 'Doctrine and Training', p. 120.

3   Sport in the Great War

> The assiduous and organized cultivation of sport, and what is more important the spirit of sport, has become one of the most distinctive marks of the British Army, and it will be a task worthy of the greatest historians to record what this sporting spirit has done, not only for the British Army, not only for the British Empire, but for the whole civilized world during the present war.
>
> *Field*, 16 March 1918

Sport has provided some of the most abiding images of the Great War. The impromptu football played between British and German soldiers during the 1914 Christmas Truce, the British troops kicking footballs across No Man's Land at Loos and at the Somme, still resonate in the public memory. For the British army the war marked the point at which sport, hitherto widely popular but unofficial in the armed services, became formally integrated into the military system, both as 'recreational training' and as an officially sanctioned form of leisure for other ranks. The British example was followed by other Allied forces – by the Dominion armies, by the United States and, despite considerable initial scepticism, by the French. The experience of the First World War had an enduring influence on the organisation and ideology of modern British military sport. When in 1931 General Harington declared that the war had been won by 'leather' in the shape of footballs and boxing gloves he was only expressing in exaggerated form the official recognition of sport's military value.[1] This chapter traces the process by which sport in the British army was transformed from a mainly spontaneous and improvised pastime in the early stages of the war into a compulsory activity for troops out of the line by the last months of the conflict. It examines the ways in which sport was seen to have military utility in improving fitness, relieving boredom, providing distraction from the

---

[1] General Harington, 'Preface', *Games and Sports in the Army*. This handbook was published annually by the Army Sport Control Board from 1931–2: Harington's remarks on sport in the First World War were repeated in the preface of every volume.

80

horrors of war and building morale, officer–men relations and *esprit de corps*. Finally it demonstrates how the amateur model of sport, promoted energetically but largely unsuccessfully by army sports reformers before 1914, came to be imposed on service sport on the Western Front.

Over recent decades, and particularly since the release of documents from the National Archives after 1965, military historians (if not the general public) have begun to move away from the notion of the Western Front as an arena of mud, futility and military incompetence towards a more considered examination of such subjects as command, control and communications in the British army.[2] One result of this new work has been to emphasize that not all soldiers experienced the war in the same way. For one thing some 16 per cent of the army were in non-combatant units from the beginning of the war, and this would grow to 33 per cent by 1918.[3] These men fought the war not in the trenches but behind the lines, providing the supplies and services crucial to the military effort. Even those on the front line were not subject to its horrors all the time. Not only was there a rotation system, whereby units went from the front line to the support line then into the reserve and finally to a rest area, but different parts of the front varied widely in conditions and activity. Some were often quiet, well ordered and comparatively safe. Dan Todman has reminded us of the routine of Charles Carrington, a junior infantry officer who in 1916 spent less than a third of the year under fire either in the front line or in immediate support: the largest proportion of his time, 145 days, was spent away from the front 'resting, or at schools of instruction, in hospital or on leave' or on the move between them. Carrington did twelve tours in the trenches out of sixteen for his battalion and was in action four times. A recent biographer of Siegfried Sassoon has calculated that, although he was in the army throughout the war, he spent barely one month out of a possible fifty-one actually in the front line.[4] Indeed, as J. G. Fuller has commented, some three-fifths of an infantry serviceman's life on the Western Front was typically spent behind the lines.[5]

---

[2] See D. Todman, *The First World War: Myth and Memory* (London: Hambledon and London, 2005) for an overview of changing perceptions of the war. For a distinguished example of this new work see G. Sheffield and D. Todman (eds.), *Command and Control on the Western Front: The British Army's Experience 1914–18* (Staplehurst: Spellmount, 2004); see also, e.g., G. Sheffield and J. Bourne (eds.), *Douglas Haig: War Diaries and Letters 1914–1918* (London: Weidenfeld & Nicolson, 2005).

[3] R. Holmes, *Tommy: The British Soldier on the Western Front* (London: HarperCollins, 2004), p. 191.

[4] Todman, *The First World War*, pp. 4–5; J. M. Wilson, *Siegfried Sassoon: The Making of a War Poet* (London: Duckworth, 1998), p. 209.

[5] J. G. Fuller, *Troop Morale and Popular Culture in the British and Dominion Armies 1914–1918* (Oxford University Press, 1990), p. 6.

In fact, as has often been remarked, boredom was the most frequent experience of the war. The army was well aware that 'morale had particularly to be nourished during time out of the line', when, with the enemy out of sight, boredom, drink and fatigues were apt to induce 'mischievous thoughts' in the private soldier. Yet, as John Bourne has persuasively shown, civilian soldiers' earlier life in the urban working class had provided them with the skills and stoicism to cope, not only with the terrors of war but also with its tedium and discomforts.[6] Moreover it should not be forgotten that even in war there were compensations. The most important were probably the bonds of comradeship, a form of male love, built up through the months of training, fighting and resting together and encouraged by the almost tribal regimental system which was such a powerful source of group identity. As Todman pointed out 'laughter, drunkenness and camaraderie were as much a part of the war, for many men, as terror, violence and obedience'.[7] And so was sport.

If the more mainstream military historians have tended to neglect the social fabric of military life, a new generation, influenced by the wider developments of social and cultural history, has begun to explore this important area of wartime experience. Nevertheless, the 'behind-the-lines' experience – and the part sport played in it – has, despite the *Field*'s optimistic prediction, been less examined. Even historians of sport have largely focused on the impact of the war on civilian sport at home, such as the debate over the continuation of professional football in 1914–15.[8] Gary Sheffield's *Leadership in the Trenches* is one exception to this neglect; so, and most notably, is J. G. Fuller's study of morale and popular culture in the British and Dominion Armies. In a chapter on 'leisure' Fuller places sport alongside the concert party as the most enjoyed and important participant and spectator activities, with the canteen, cinema and excursion some way behind. His conclusion is that all were part of a culture of consolation, diverting, preoccupying and an affirmation of a kind of creativity. There is also a sense of the British believing themselves to be more 'sportsmanlike' than other nations,

---

[6] *Ibid.*, pp. 79–80; J. Bourne, 'The British Working Man in Arms', in H. Cecil and P. Liddle (eds.), *Facing Armageddon: The First World War Experienced* (London: Leo Cooper, 1996), pp. 336–52.
[7] Todman, *The First World War*, p. 6.
[8] For civilian sport in Britain during the First World War, see C. Veitch, 'Play Up! Play Up! And Win the War! Football, the Nation and the First World War 1914–15', *Journal of Contemporary History* 20 (1985), 363–78; D. Birley, 'Sportsmen and the Deadly Game', *British Journal of Sports History* 3 (1986), 288–310; N. Young, 'A Splendid Response? Cricket and the First World War', *Imperial War Museum Review* 12 (1999), 36–47; also A. Diaper, 'Kicking Football to the Front. An Investigation into the Role of English Football during the Great War 1914–1918', unpublished MA thesis, University of Central Lancashire, 1997.

particularly the Germans – a reflection of the moral superiority of a nation that believed it 'conquers less for herself than for humanity'.[9] Yet Fuller's findings have not made their way into the mainstream: even Richard Holmes' recent book *Tommy: The British Soldier on the Western Front* has no reference to sport in the index – though in the final section, entitled 'Heart and Soul', he does quote 2nd Lieutenant Bernard Martin's comment that 'on every possible occasion the men turned to sport'.[10] Yet, as we have seen, by 1914 sport was already an important part of military culture. Indeed, if, as Bourne suggests, the 'system and values' of the British army 'owed little to the values of British society', sport was the great exception that proved the rule and helped significantly to bridge the gap between the military and civilians.[11] During the war troops continued to pursue a variety of sporting activities whenever opportunity arose.

The outbreak of war understandably led to the temporary collapse of much of the pre-war organisation of army sport. The annual Army Athletic Meeting with a record entry of 600 was called off, the Army Cup was abandoned for the duration, and the new playing fields at Aldershot became training grounds. Members of the Army Gymnastic Staff were initially returned to their units, though it was soon realised that this was a mistake, and the AGS was rapidly reformed – with important consequences for army sport.[12]

However, the revival of military sport at home owed much to civilians, in particular to Charles Otway, honorary secretary of the National Cross-Country Union and the Southern Area Cross-Country Association and a contributor to *Sporting Life*, and the Aldershot-based journalist Frank Starr. Both had been repeatedly turned down for the army on account of their age, Starr forty-one times by January 1915. Anxious to find an avenue of usefulness, they resolved to bring recreation to the thousands of recruits undergoing training in the big military centres. In a series of articles in the sporting press they stressed the benefits of sport – especially boxing, cross-country running and football – and recommended

---

[9] Sheffield, *Leadership in the Trenches*, esp. pp. 44–9; Fuller, *Troop Morale*, pp. 93–4, p. 140. See also Campbell, 'The Army Isn't All Work', J. Roberts, '"The Best Football Team, The Best Platoon": The Role of Football in the Proletarianization of the British Expeditionary Force, 1914–18', *Sport in History* 26 (2006), 26–46; and, for Australian troops, D.J. Blair, 'The Greater Game: Australian Football and the Army in Melbourne and on the Front During World War I', *Sporting Traditions* 11 (1995), 91–102, and M.G. Phillips, 'Sport, War and Gender Images: The Australian Sportsmen's Battalions and the First World War', *International Journal of the History of Sport* 14 (1997), 78–96.
[10] Holmes, *Tommy*, p. 604.
[11] Bourne, 'The British Working Man', p. 337.
[12] *Athletic News*, 21 July 1914; Oldfield, *History*.

a weekly half holiday on which it should take place for the troops in training for the New Army. Many commanding officers clearly agreed. An unknown soldier described such an afternoon during training in October 1914: 'Strong sou'wester blowing, with lashings of rain. Two pick-up games, Rugger and Soccer; I played in the former ... We played in our trousers, puttees and shirts, just as we were, in the pouring rain, all very wet and muddy and happy.' At the Aldershot Training Centre, organised and unorganised football was soon in full swing, and a military league had been formed by the end of October 1914. Meanwhile Otway and his colleagues were busy fostering distance running among the troops. Their first military cross-country race was run from Aldershot in December 1914, with Otway 'starter, judge, recorder and donor of prizes, all in one'. His initiative soon developed into the Military Race Committee, which organised sport in training camps all over the country, with the emphasis strongly on mass participation and the encouragement of physical fitness. Otway's reward was a letter of thanks from the Army Council.[13] Frank Starr, who had been campaigning for almost a decade for an 'Army Association which should be the ultimate board of control and appeal for all military sports', saw his idea realised on a small scale in October 1915 with the foundation of the Aldershot Command Athletic Association, Starr being one of the two civilians on the committee. When it organised its first championship in August 1916 all the events were, for the first time in the history of army athletics, open to both officers and men.[14]

By this time there was enough spectacular sport, both civilian and military, to fill the pages of sporting newspapers such as the *Athletic News*, *Sporting Life* and *Sportsman*. Matches and tournaments were often used to mount recruiting drives, but their main purpose was to raise money for the growing number of war charities and provide a cheap source of entertainment, not only for those in the armed forces training at home but also for those working in war industries. The 17th (1st Football) Battalion, Middlesex Regiment played against both Birmingham and Cardiff City in the autumn of 1915, and in May 1916 teams of professionals representing English soldiers and Scottish soldiers met at Goodison Park, Liverpool, home of Everton Football Club, with the

[13] F.J.S. [Frank Starr], 'Charles Otway', *Aldershot Command News*, 17 January 1928; 'Obituary: Captain F.J. Starr', *Times*, 6 February 1931; *Athletic News*, 14 December 1914, 17 February 1919, 8 December 1919; *Times*, 13 October 1914; *Sporting Life*, 8, 14, 20, 26 October, 30 November, 12, 19, 28 December 1914; Anon., *A Soldier's Diary of the Great War* (London: Faber & Gwyer, 1929), pp. 44–5.
[14] *Athletic News*, 1 May 1916; 25 October, 22 November 1915; 14 August, 11 September 1916.

proceeds going to the Lord Mayor's Roll of Honour Fund. The Belgian army team played a series of matches against British army teams in Glasgow, Liverpool, Manchester and Birmingham in November 1917.[15] Meanwhile, scores of civilian clubs and military teams embarked on regular programmes of fixtures. The arrival in Britain of Dominion troops with overlapping sporting traditions not only brought new games – like baseball and Australian rules football – to the attention of the British public but also offered new challenges to established military teams. Rugby Union received a particular boost, especially once the Rugby Football Union had reluctantly conceded that Northern Union and Rugby Union players could mix, in military and naval teams only, for the duration of the war. The Army Service Corps team stationed at Grove Park was a formidable mixture of leading amateur and professional players brought together and managed by Captain R. V. Stanley, Oxford University's representative on the RFU. They were unbeatable during 1916–17, amassing over 1,000 points until, after a close shave against a New Zealand fifteen, they finally succumbed to another strong combination of union and 'league' players disguised by the name United Services. The Grove Park games attracted big crowds but also some criticism, not so much about how these leading players had been recruited as about how they were kept together in 'soft jobs' at home. After adverse press comment the team was broken up in 1917.[16] The organisation required for all this sport was considerable and just occasionally became unravelled. In 1917 the Canadian Pay Office thought they had arranged a rugby match with the Royal Naval Depot at Crystal Palace, but found the RND football team waiting for them. Apparently they took it in a sporting spirit – which did not prevent them losing 12–2.[17]

Even among fighting troops sport had become informally re-established by the end of 1914. As early as October the 'daily routine' for Lieutenant-Colonel Jack's Cameronians included 'games – chiefly football' after dinner and a few months later, in reserve, he commented that 'games, mainly football, in the afternoons keep them fit and cheery … however tired the rascals may be for parades they have always energy enough for football'.[18] By December the *Athletic News* was running regular reports of football behind the lines in France and in other theatres

---

[15] *Ibid.*, 4 October, 1 November 1915; 15 May 1916; 13, 20 November 1917.
[16] Collins, 'English Rugby Union'; *Athletic News*, 9, 16, 30 October, 13 November 1916.
[17] *Athletic News*, 5 January 1917.
[18] J. Terraine (ed.), *General Jack's Diary* (London: Eyre & Spottiswoode, 1964), pp. 57, 91.

such as Egypt. In Ismailia, for example, the 1st Field Ambulance RAMC (T) East Lancashire Division took on a civilian club composed chiefly of French, Italian and Soudanese (*sic*) players. The game was watched by a 'large number of Indian soldiers' who were 'delighted' with a 7–0 victory.[19] The improvised nature of these sports is emphasised by the equally regular appeals for footballs – there was said to be a 'famine in footballs' at the front, and one soldier reported playing with a wet sack. Several football clubs, especially Heart of Midlothian, most of whose pre-war players had enlisted to form the nucleus of McCrae's Battalion (16th Royal Scots), began sending regular supplies of footballs to France.[20] Since soldiers usually played in hobnailed army boots, the balls didn't last long. In the summer of 1915 impromptu cricket matches were arranged: a former Northamptonshire captain organised one with hop poles for bats, bully beef tins for wickets and a tennis ball. Two platoons of the 1/7th (Robin Hood) Battalion Sherwood Foresters managed to play a match actually in the trenches near Sanctuary Wood: 'the ball was an old jam tin, the bat one of the good old army spades; the game was keenly contested'.[21] Some were luckier: an RE unit receiving 'large quantities of cricket gear' through the *Daily Express* Cheery Fund set about forming 'rival elevens entertaining many hundreds of khaki-clad spectators to a proper match'.[22] Football continued through the summer months: in July 1915 Haig famously complained that men were falling asleep on night sentry duty because instead of resting during the day 'they run about and play football'.[23]

While improvised sport continued throughout the war, by early 1915 competitions and tournaments had been established in France as the military situation stabilised and the huge 'back of the front' organisation began to be set up. In January the ambulance men of the RAMC appealed for a football cup. That spring there were reports of matches

---

[19] *Athletic News*, 7 December 1914.
[20] *Ibid.*, 7, 14, 21 and 28 December 1914; 22 February, 12 April, 7 June, 6 December 1915; J. Alexander, *McCrae's Battalion: The Story of the 16th Royal Scots* (Edinburgh: Mainstream, 2003). McCrae's Battalion had been raised in Edinburgh in the autumn of 1914 by Sir George McCrae, a local businessman and politician.
[21] *Athletic News*, 26 July 1915; *'The Robin Hoods': 1/7th, 2/7th & 3/7th Battns. Sherwood Foresters 1914–1918: Written by Officers of the Battalions* (Nottingham: J. & H. Bell, 1921), p. 76.
[22] *The Sapper* 21 (August 1915), p. 24.
[23] Terraine, *General Jack's Diary*, p. 91 fn. 1. Haig subsequently changed his mind about the value of sport for other ranks and encouraged it in the British Expeditionary Force. His 1919 Rectorial Address to the University of St Andrews eulogised team games as promoting 'decision and character on the part of the leaders, discipline and unselfishness among the led, and initiative and self-sacrifice on the part of all' (quoted in Sheffield, *Leadership in the Trenches*, p. 44).

for the 'Bishop of Khartoum's Cup' in France. By November it was said that 'every section has its team'.[24] Competitions were arranged from platoon to divisional level. In January–February 1915 forty-five teams from troops and sections of the 1st Cavalry Brigade competed for a trophy provided by Brigadier General C.J. Briggs. The final was played before a large crowd, and the winning team was chaired off the field and photographed by their Colonel.[25] At Christmas 1915 the 138th Brigade ran a football cup competition which was won by 1/5th Leicestershire Regiment, the trophy being a clock mounted into a French '75' shell.[26] Not surprisingly the 17th (1st Football) Battalion, Middlesex Regiment, with its high concentration of professional footballers, dominated the 2nd Divisional Cup competitions in the spring of 1916, going through five rounds without conceding a goal and beating a team from the Royal Field Artillery 11–0 in the final. However, the team suffered serious casualties in the Somme fighting later that year (the medals for the cup victory won by two of the players, both formerly with Clapton Orient, were later presented to their widows). The battalion team was still able to reach the final for a second time in December, but this time the winning margin against the same opponents was only 2–1.[27]

Boxing was also a popular sport behind the lines and had the advantage over most other athletic activities that it could take place indoors during the frost-bound Northern French winters. Many officers had been members of the National Sporting Club and were keen to promote the sport. Captain Temple Clarke, the sports officer for the Advanced Horse Transport Depot near Abbeville, promoted several boxing tournaments, often with the help of the YMCA. His method was to construct a programme of one top-line fight and a couple of good supporting bouts together with a group of novice fights, these latter usually consisting of one two-minute round. There were always good houses and enough income to meet expenses, including paying the fighters, with the surplus going to the Company Games and Sustenance Fund.[28]

---

[24] *Athletic News*, 25 January, 15 March, 5 April, 1 November 1915.
[25] *XI Hussar Journal* 6 (October 1915), pp. 42–4.
[26] Captain J.D. Hills, *The Fifth Leicestershire: A Record of the 1/5th Battalion the Leicestershire Regiment, TF During the War 1914–1919* (Loughborough: Echo Press, 1919), pp. 102–3.
[27] *Athletic News*, 31 January 1916, 1 May 1916, 15 May 1916, 26 February 1917; War Diary, 17th Middlesex Regiment, WO95/1361, TNA. See also M. Eksteins, *Rites of Spring: The Great War and the Birth of the Modern Age* (London: Papermac, 2000), pp. 125–6. The battalion was disbanded in February 1918 as part of a widespread reduction in the BEF: by then only about thirty ex-professional footballers remained out of an initial figure of over 200.
[28] Capt. A.O. Temple Clarke, *Transport and Sport in the Great War Period* (London: Garden City Press, 1938), pp. 174–7. The purses were sometimes provided by the two

Horse shows and horse racing were staged whenever possible. Typically these included not only jumping competitions and contests for the best-turned-out draft horses and mules, but wrestling on horseback (or muleback).[29] Athletic sports were *de rigueur*. Some might contain a large proportion of 'fun' events like those of B Company, 1/5th Gloucester Regiment, in July 1916 which included not only a three-legged race but a hobble skirt one in which the competitors were handicapped by a pair of puttees around their knees. But there was plenty of serious competition with officers usually putting up the prizes.[30]

The impression is still largely of a grass-roots and unofficial movement. In 358 Company ASC Motor Transport the moving spirit was Sergeant-Major Grimshaw, without whom 'we, one of the largest MT units in France ... would undoubtedly be in the shameful condition of being without a "footer" team'.[31] Nevertheless (and despite Haig's early strictures) commanding officers were generally glad to promote sport, either by providing prizes or by facilitating competitions. W.J. Grant, serving near Port Remy with the 154th Brigade RFA, reported in December 1915 that the 'commander-in-chief let us have a wagon and six horses to take a football team from A & B Batteries to play C & D Batteries'.[32] Non-official support came from army chaplains, who were often important in sports organisation, and from the YMCA, which organised football leagues. Equipment was still being provided largely by the players themselves, or by civilians at home, and was still scarce. In 358 Company Lance Corporal Woodlands and Private Parsons provided the cricket kit: an experimental 'franc subscription' for sports equipment proved 'certainly not ... a success'. A football match between companies of the 5th Gloucesters in January 1916 was played 'on a very greasy ground, which the lack of football boots accentuated. (Kind friends at home please note)'.[33] Sport, however, was about to become an official part of military life. After some initial hesitation the army hierarchy came to approve sport as making a useful contribution to fitness, morale and *esprit de corps*, and even to military training.

As the *Field*'s reference to both 'sport ... and the spirit of sport' suggests, not only practical but also ideological reasons lay behind this

---

Misses Yewdell, voluntary helpers at the YMCA hut No. 5 Veterinary hospital. See also N. Clark, *All in the Game* (London: Methuen, 1935), ch. 5.
[29] See, e.g., 'The Robin Hoods', p. 223.
[30] *5th Glo'ster Gazette* 13 (July 1916).
[31] *Open Exhaust* 1 (January 1916), p. 4.
[32] War Diary of W.G. Grant, 27 December 1915, 97/16/1, Department of Documents, IWM.
[33] *Open Exhaust* 7 (July 1916), p. 8; 8 (August 1916), p. 3; *5th Glo'ster Gazette* 9 (February 1916).

development. The concrete physical advantages of sporting activity and the alleged moral advantages of sport, particularly sport on the amateur model, are often hard to disentangle in contemporary thought. By 1914, after nearly forty years of organised military sport, it was widely accepted within the regular army that sport could have a number of practical benefits: that it could increase fitness, decrease drunkenness, help build regimental identity, enhance relations between officers and other ranks, and between the army and civil society, and improve morale. Experience of the particular conditions of the Western Front demonstrated that sport could similarly be useful to a largely civilian army engaged in total war. At the same time, however, the advocates of army sport were strongly influenced by the public-school belief in games as a means of character formation and moral discipline. The realities of mass warfare did not immediately curb the Edwardian tendency to see sport and war as versions of each other. A Territorial officer heading for the front in late 1914 wrote that, 'personally, I feel less excited and interested than when travelling down to play in some important Rugger match. I think we all treat it as a bit of a game, and I am quite sure we shall give a good account of ourselves.' In 1915 a Yorkshire Rugby Football Union official pronounced that its players would 'fight as hard, and as keenly in this, the greatest game of their lives, as ever they did on the football field ... And they will sacrifice themselves, too, as cheerfully on the field of battle.'[34] The belief that sport possessed military utility – that 'a sportsman is already half a soldier' and 'the best sportsman is the best soldier' – thus arose both from demonstrable practical realities and from the habits of thought induced by public-school 'athleticism'.

Sport obviously promoted fitness and stamina. One soldier thought that it was thanks to his experience in cross-county running that the retreat from Mons 'scarcely affected him at all'. But, unlike physical training, it was not a *necessary* part of a soldier's preparation for war. Some specific sporting skills might be useful on the battlefield: cricket, for example, was not bad practice for bomb-throwing. (An officer thought his lacrosse training 'of the greatest use' at Gallipoli – but did not specify how.) These benefits, however, were very much prone to exaggeration: only a civilian could seriously have suggested that 'the feints and swerves of the football field' would help a soldier 'weaponless in no-man's land'.[35] Boxing, often compared to bayonet training, was the

---

[34] Anon., *A Soldier's Diary*, p. 54; 'Yorkshire Sportsmen and the War – II', *Country Life*, 23 October 1915, pp. 559–62.
[35] *Athletic News*, 1 February 1915, 17 April 1916, 31 January 1916.

sport to which concrete military utility was most often attributed. R. B. Campbell, the leading advocate of bayonet training, admitted after the war that its chief importance was to stimulate controlled aggression in front-line troops: bayonets were rarely used in actual fighting. It is easy to see how boxing could be used in the same way.[36] Nor was it always necessary to take part. Even watching boxing matches was thought to inculcate fighting spirit in the spectators, and marks were awarded to 'plucky losers' in the hope of communicating to the watching troops a 'grim determination to "hang on"'.[37]

For American observers, the experience of the British army showed that athletics did help develop the 'fighting spirit'. 'Troops developed a quality of courage and aggressiveness not only from their physical training but from their experience in personal contests and games.' Sport also encouraged persistence by teaching men 'how to get bumped and not to mind it'. In this belief, as well as in acknowledgement of sport's usefulness as a distraction from less wholesome activities, an extensive athletic programme was introduced into all US army training camps at home and overseas. As Nancy Bristow has suggested, an additional motivation was that sport was thought to make men 'manly', counteracting the perceived 'feminisation' of men in white-collar jobs.[38] The British army had similar concerns, although its main focus was on converting working-class spectators of sports – pale, narrow-chested and prone to mass hysteria (as Baden-Powell and other middle-class commentators described them) – into healthy, independent players of 'He sports' (aggressive contact sports like boxing and rugby). The public-school model of the 'manly Englishman', to which sport and war were central, certainly influenced the middle-class men who designed the army's sports programme, if not necessarily the soldiers who encountered it. This concern with 'military masculinity' is seen most clearly in post-Armistice anxieties, apparently widespread, about competing boxers embracing each other in the ring instead of shaking hands – a habit attributed variously to 'low-class boxing' and to the effeminate example of the French. During the Second Army Boxing Tournament at Cologne in March 1919 offenders were rebuked by the referee with the words 'It's very un-English'. ('You can get plenty of people to kiss outside', he added.)[39]

[36] J. G. Gray, *Prophet in Plimsoles: An Account of the Life of Colonel Ronald B. Campbell* (Edinburgh: Edina Press, 1978), p. 28.
[37] *Athletic News*, 29 December 1919.
[38] Wakefield, *Playing to Win*, pp. 13–14; N. Bristow, *Making Men Moral: Social Engineering During the Great War* (New York: New York University Press, 1996), pp. 38–40.
[39] 'Rugbiana', *Aldershot Command News*, 20 December 1927; Temple Clarke, *Transport and Sport*, p. 195; 'Boxing on the Rhine', *Times*, 28 March 1919. *Games and Sports in*

Despite such class-based cultural differences, sport clearly did provide a common language and frame of reference which all men could be expected to understand. Gary Sheffield suggests that 'treating training as a form of sport' gave officers a way to 'make training comprehensible to their fellow sports-enthusiasts in the ranks'. S.S. 185 *Assault Training*, issued in September 1917, made 'a close analogy' with cricket. The players 'play the game under agreed laws' and 'under the orders of their Captain', the platoon commander. Meanwhile the umpires adhere strictly to their allotted role and spectators 'keep away from the pitch'. A more direct sporting element was introduced to training by the inclusion of military events like bomb-throwing in military sports days. Nor was it just training that could be sweetened by competition and prizes. In June 1915, with the 3rd Cavalry Brigade entrenching a second line between Dickebusch and Kemmel, Major-General John Vaughan offered a barrel of beer and a cup (engraved '1915. Spades are trumps') for the Champion Diggers.[40]

But it is the more concrete benefits of sport, to which we have already alluded, which surely need to be underlined here. It did provide relief from the 'boredom unspeakable' of which most servicemen – not only in the army – endured long periods. After the Battle of Jutland Admiral Jellicoe encouraged the development of sports facilities at the naval base at Scapa Flow. A football ground was built by fleet labour, together with a golf course for officers, and a boxing ring was installed on the canteen ship *Ghourko*. Jellicoe believed this helped prevent the unrest which boredom could promote, although one ordinary seaman still found Scapa Flow 'monotonous' and the football pitch too boggy.[41] Similarly an RAF squadron stationed in 'a most desolate and god forsaken part of Italy' in 1918 pleaded for sports gear to alleviate the tedium of their lives.[42] Such monotony occasionally tempted soldiers to play sport under extremely hazardous circumstances. Boxing tournaments were held not just in forward areas but almost up to the front line itself. At one brigade meeting three semi-finalists were killed by a bursting shell; the survivor won by default.[43]

---

the *Army* similarly insisted in its guidelines for boxing that 'embracing and other forms of a demonstrative nature are strongly deprecated and should be openly reproved'.

[40] Sheffield, *Leadership in the Trenches*, p. 47; Vaughan, *Cavalry and Sporting Memories*, p. 184.

[41] *Country Life*, 2 November 1918, p. 380; Admiral Viscount Jellicoe of Scapa, *The Grand Fleet 1914–1916* (London: Cassell, 1919), pp. 85–7; William Hales quoted in Baynham, *Men from the Dreadnoughts*, p. 217.

[42] Lieutenant Arthur C. Mann, Sports Secretary, 224 Squadron, to Hon. Sec., RAF Central Sports Committee, 1 October 1918, AIR 2/95, TNA.

[43] *Athletic News*, 29 December 1919.

92   Sport and the Military

Figure 7. Scene at a boxing tournament organised by the Grand Fleet, July 1918: middleweight contest – Chief Carpenter's Mate Gartner (US Navy) versus Leading Stoker Roberts (Royal Navy).

Sport played an important part in distracting the troops from the imminent horrors of war, a role recognized both by the soldiers themselves and by the military authorities. Bombardier Cornfoot, serving in France, told his girlfriend in 1915 that 'we are arranging football matches and boxing to keep our minds off this terrible war as much as possible'. In the shadow of the 1918 German spring offensive the 138th Infantry Brigade, encouraged by its commanding officers, took to football:

> The German offensive was expected to start any day, and the 'wind' was terribly 'up'. This, however, did not prevent the Infantry from amusing themselves whenever possible ... General Rowley gave a cup for a Brigade Company Competition, and ... 'A' Company [1/5th Leicestershires] beat Brigade HQ in the 'final', after which 'Tinker' Evans, the captain of the team, received the cup from the Brigadier.
> The following morning we went once more to the line ... [44]

---

[44] IWM, 97/37/1, Cornfoot papers, 17 December 1915; Hills, *The Fifth Leicestershire*, p. 242.

Sport in the Great War 93

Sport also provided an important link with home, a reminder of civilian life and identity. Sporting papers were in great demand at the front as soldiers sought to maintain links with Blighty. Private W. Fiske, 1/Norfolk Regiment, formerly a goalkeeper with Nottingham Forest, wrote to the editor of the *Athletic News* in October 1914, telling him that the paper was being sent by his wife. 'You ought to see the boys how they hound me for the news and rolling up to borrow it. There isn't much left of it after they have read it. I hope to get it every week as it cheers one up.'[45] For the author of a poem entitled 'Cricket, The Catch' published in the *5th Glo'ster Gazette*, sport brought back 'Happy days long dead, Childhood that is fled'. A supporter of 17/Highland Light Infantry's football team travelling 'by "motor" in the early hours of Saturday afternoon to a football match' thought it 'one of the nearest approaches we have had to the old days before the war'. Even in battle sport could provide a comforting reminder of home and civilian identity: one former athlete wore his running kit under his uniform for an assault 'in case it was my last race'.[46] It is in this context – the role of sport as distraction and as a link with home – that the well-known incidents of soldiers kicking footballs into battle, at Loos and on the Somme, should be understood.[47]

Many officers were committed to an ideology of amateurism which placed a high premium on participation and was somewhat scornful of the spectator. Nevertheless most were prepared to embrace sport as spectacle for the duration, recognising that it could legitimately provide entertainment and escape very necessary to young males embedded in an apparently endless struggle with death and destruction. In early 1916, for example, the 48th Division, a Territorial Division originally largely recruited from the rural South Midlands, organised a football knockout competition for which their General Officer Commanding, Major-General Fanshawe, presented a cup. Ten regimental teams took part, and the matches attracted many spectators. The seriousness of it all was indicated when, after 1/7th Worcestershire Regiment lost to 1/6th Gloucestershire Regiment in a second round tie, Quarter Master Sergeant Neale, the team's manager, lodged a complaint against the referee. The complaint was upheld and the match replayed, the Worcesters winning 4–0.[48] That these were matches to be watched as

---

[45] Catton folders, Tityrus scrapbooks, Arsenal Football Club Archive, Highbury, London.
[46] *5th Glo'ster Gazette* 5 (August 1915); Fuller, *Troop Morale*, p. 89; *Athletic News*, 15 November 1915.
[47] See Sheffield, *Leadership in the Trenches*, pp. 47–8.
[48] Roberts, 'The Best Football Team', 40.

well as played is well illustrated by the final tie, when a crowd of about 2,500 soldiers saw the 1/7th Worcesters beat the 1/1st Buckinghamshire Battalion (Oxfordshire and Buckinghamshire Light Infantry), 2–0. 'The Divisional Band was in attendance and whiled away the time of waiting for the kick-off. It was a typical cup final crowd, and tin cans, clappers and the proverbial mouth organ were very much in evidence ... The cup and medals were on view in the officers' enclosure'.[49] The Fanshawe Cup was also played for in 1917 and in 1918, when the final was held in Trissino, Italy.

Horse racing also attracted big crowds, not least because of the opportunities it provided for betting. Before the Third Battle of Ypres, the 2/7th (Robin Hood) Battalion Sherwood Foresters took part in a brigade race meeting 'at which countless five franc notes changed hands and the horsey element had a magnificent and lucrative day'.[50] At the 138th Infantry Brigade sports and race meeting at Bazeque Farm in September 1916 the bookies' wagon was one of the features of the day, 'two officers disguised with top hats, yellow waistcoats and pyjamas' carrying on a successful business as 'turf accountants'.[51] While the 7th Division were in training at Hendecourt-les-Ransort in August 1917 they put on a divisional fair.

> No pains were spared to make this a tremendous success, and such it was. Lieut.-Col. Beauman, of the 1st South Staffords, rode horses to victory in two exciting flat races, to the excited cheers of all his officers, nearly all of whom had taken tickets at the totalisator machine, over which a medical officer very well known throughout the Division presided with marvellous efficiency. There were foot races, obstacle races, tugs-of-war, mule races and a mounted steeplechase, refreshments in plenty, an enormous gathering of spectators, and side shows that would have done credit to Hampstead Heath on the busiest of Bank Holidays; and at the end of a perfect day the troops and their officers seemed thoroughly pleased with themselves and the war, although at this time the prospect of an early move to Flanders was looming gloomily.[52]

There seems little reason to doubt that sport improved morale and that from an early stage it was recognised to do so. 'How many times,' asked General Harington rhetorically, 'did one see a Battalion which had come out of the line in the Ypres Salient and elsewhere, battered to pieces and sad at heart at having lost so many Officers and men, hold up its head again and recover in a few hours by kicking a football

---

[49] *5th Glo'ster Gazette* 11 (April 1916).
[50] *Robin Hoods*, p. 355.
[51] Hills, *Fifth Leicestershire*, p. 159.
[52] G. Goold Walker (ed.), *The Honourable Artillery Company in the Great War* (London: Seeley & Co., 1930), p. 319.

Sport in the Great War 95

Figure 8. Football final of the 48th Divisional (Fanshawe) Cup between the 1/7 Battalion, Worcestershire Regiment and 1/7 Battalion, Warwickshire Regiment played at Trissino, Italy, 1918.

or punching with the glove? It had a magic effect on "moral" [sic]'.[53] Certainly it seemed to work for 7/Bedfordshire Regiment, enjoying a much needed rest after the Somme: 'the general routine has been to work extremely hard from 9 A.M. to 1 P.M. daily, Games in the afternoon, lectures, Concerts, Boxing Entertainments & other forms of enjoyment being indulged in every evening, which has resulted in the battalion appearing very Smart, Merry & Bright & very fit for fighting'. Playing sport served to indicate good morale in a unit. In January 1915 Colonel Treffry of the 1st Battalion Honourable Artillery Company was told by his Corps Commander: 'It is a real tonic to me to see your men. Here they are just out from twelve very hard days and nights and are hard at it playing football, and all look in the highest spirits and so clean. It does me good to see them'.[54] Regimental footballers, like

[53] Harington, 'Preface'.
[54] War Diary, 7th Battalion Bedfordshire Regiment, December 1916, X550/8/1/1612, Bedfordshire & Luton Archives & Records Service, Bedford (hereafter BLARS);

regimental bandsmen, were recognised to contribute to unit morale and were sometimes deliberately kept out of the front line. Quarter-Master-Sergeant Neale looked after the 1/7th Worcesters team like 'pieces of china, never letting them do any duty in the front'.[55]

As we have seen, in the Edwardian army sport had been valued partly for its apparent ability to forge links between officers and men, and to provide a safe arena in which the strict hierarchies of military life could be temporarily forgotten. Junior officers in particular were constantly urged to involve themselves in the games of their men, though how successful these appeals were is not clear. Just before the First World War, for instance, J. H. W. Knight-Bruce, an officer in the Royal Warwickshire Regiment, urged officers to become involved in regimental boxing. An officer who refereed his men's boxing, he claimed,

> has established the same bond of sympathy between himself and his men that exists between the officer and private who shove together in the pack, who run together between the stumps, or who pass together on the wing of an Army 'Soccer' eleven. He establishes a trust and faith that, when the day comes, will take his men, if needs be, to Hades for him.[56]

During the war officers were similarly encouraged to 'take a personal and active interest' in unit sport, with the further incentives that it would provide them with 'an insight into the characters of their men which they could obtain by no other means' and an opportunity to 'develop those powers of leadership which are absolutely essential to military success'. (That sport also served, or was believed to serve, to *demonstrate* leadership qualities is illustrated by Robert Graves' recollection of officer-cadet selection in Oxford in 1917: 'our final selection was made by watching the candidates play games, principally rugger and soccer. Those who played rough but not dirty, and had quick reactions, were the sort we needed.')[57] Fuller comments that 'officer involvement in sport did something to break down the

---

Goold Walker, *The Honourable Artillery Company*, p. 30. The war diaries of the Bedfordshire Regiment for 1914–18 are available online both at http://blars.adlibsoft.com/ and at http://www.bedfordregiment.org.uk/.

[55] Quoted in Roberts, 'The Best Football Team', 40. Similarly during the 1918 German Spring offensive Lieutenant-Colonel Potter, King's Liverpool Regiment, 'used very carefully' his battalion's football team, recent winners of the 55th Division championship (T. Travers, *How the War Was Won* (London: Routledge, 1992), p. 97). Cf. R. Feilding, *War Letters to a Wife: France and Flanders, 1915–1919* (London: Medici Society, 1930), p. 313: 'Our band is thirty-three strong. We do not risk it in battle unless we are absolutely tied up for stretcher bearers'.

[56] 'Navarm' (J. H. W. Knight-Bruce), 'Service Boxing', *Sporting Life*, 18 October 1912.

[57] *Recreational Training*, S.S. 137, October 1917, pp. 6–7; R. Holmes, *Firing Line* (London: Penguin, 1987), p. 55.

dehumanizing barriers of military protocol'. At sports, one soldier remembered, 'officers descended from their giddy altitudes of discipline and became almost chummy. They held the tape for you in the different heats, fielded the cricket ball or loaned you their shorts and sweaters, and you rubbed "flashes" with them in the crowd without having to salute and look as though you realized the enormity of your offence'.[58] Sport was often a mutual interest – instructing his platoon in the evenings, George Sherston (Siegfried Sassoon's fictional alter ego) confined himself to 'asking them easy questions from the infantry training manual ... and reading the League Football news aloud'. Gary Sheffield, in his study of leadership in the trenches, notes a soldier bringing his officer the result of the 1915 FA Cup Final during the 2nd Battle of Ypres. He also quotes G. H. Cole, an officer in the 1/20th London Regiment, realising that he had been accepted by his men 'when he heard a spectator call him by a (fairly respectful) nick-name while Cole was playing football'.[59]

Sports in which officers took part – like officers performing in unit concerts – could produce a brief carnival atmosphere, a strictly limited period in which the world was turned upside down and military superiors became the subject of licensed ridicule and mirth. In October 1916 the 1/7th (Robin Hood) Battalion Sherwood Foresters held 'some most enjoyable sports at Bailleulval' at which the officers' mule race caused 'much merriment'. So did rugby union, primarily a middle-class game and therefore little played by other ranks. Ian Hay's no doubt somewhat exaggerated account of an officers' rugby match gives an idea of its novelty and amusement value.

The lookers-on ... were to a man devoted – nay, frenzied – adherents of the Association code ... To these, Rugby Football – the greatest of all manly games – was a mere name. Their attitude when the officers appeared upon the field was one of indulgent superiority – the sort of superiority that a brawny pitman exhibits when his Platoon Commander steps down into a trench to lend a hand with the digging.

But in five minutes their mouths were agape with scandalised astonishment; in ten, the heavens were rent with their protesting cries. Accustomed ... to demand with one voice the instant execution of any player (on the other side) who laid so much as a finger on the ball or the man who was playing it, the exhibition of savage and promiscuous brutality to which their superiors now treated them shocked the assembled spectators to the roots of their sensitive souls ...

---

[58] Fuller, *Troop Morale*, pp. 90–1.
[59] S. Sassoon, *Memoirs of a Foxhunting Man* (London, 1971), p. 286; Sheffield, *Leadership, in the Trenches*, pp. 45–6, p. 80.

More common were football matches between officers and other ranks. It is noticeable, however, that these games were almost always between officers and sergeants – 'this Homeric contest between the Immortals and the Mortals' as the 5th Gloucesters described it. A rare exception was a match between officers and officers' servants in 2/Bedfordshire Regiment, which the servants won 5–1. Like the strict segregation of boxing competitions for officers and for other ranks this carefully controlled breaking down of ranks recognised that the use of sport in breaching military hierarchies needed to be closely monitored if it was not to undermine military effectiveness.[60]

Sporting success had become part of a regiment's tradition and history for regular soldiers well before 1914, and certain regiments pursued long-standing sporting rivalries. During the war sport was used to inculcate a sense of *esprit de corps* among new men, or in new battalions. Since 1903 Royal Engineers units had won the Army Football Cup three times and been runners-up twice: the *Sapper* reported in 1915 that 'our new comrades are being told tales of the Army Cup, and having obtained a football, hunting the leather is the order during the times of relaxation from military duties'. This was the kind of regimental tradition to which civilian soldiers could relate. A *Times* correspondent, probably Frank Starr, thought that in new battalions too team sports could establish team spirit –

the very spirit which the Service battalions need. They have no century-old traditions behind them ... and though the new men are winning laurels on the field of battle, it is doubtful whether they prize these intangible awards so much as the cup or shield won at a boxing meeting or football match. Besides ... one may not brag of victories in battle; but no law forbids a man saying, 'Anyhow, we whacked you at football'.[61]

But it was not only the crack regimental team which helped shape identities and solidarities. It was participation within and between the smaller primary groups, the platoon and the company boxers, footballers and runners which contributed to that sense of community, that solidarity in adversity which John Bourne has suggested were the working-class qualities particularly well suited to the soldier's lot in 1914–18. After the Somme battle of 1916 a reorganisation of infantry units began in which the platoon (a group of from twenty-eight to forty-four other ranks)

---

[60] *Robin Hoods*, p. 227; 'Ian Hay' (John Hay Beith, Argyll and Sutherland Highlanders), *Carrying on After the First Hundred Thousand* (Edinburgh: Blackwood, 1917), pp. 110–13; *5th Glo'ster Gazette* 16 (December 1916); War Diary, 2nd Battalion Bedfordshire Regiment, 16 April 1916, X550/3/WD/1604, BLARS. For concerts, see Sheffield, *Leadership in the Trenches*, p. 140.
[61] *Sapper*, 20 (January 1915), p. 153; 'Boxing in the BEF', *Times*, 19 April 1917.

became the 'basic tactical building block'. From February 1917 each platoon comprised a Headquarters (or administrative) section plus one section each of Bombers, Lewis Gunners, Riflemen and Rifle Bombers. Thus all infantry weapons were represented within it. The devolution of command that accompanied this new emphasis on smaller fighting groups meant that the role of platoon commander (normally held by a junior officer) became 'a key tactical command appointment'.[62] Subsequent manuals on infantry training reflected these developments in emphasising that 'true soldierly spirit must be built up in sections and platoons. Each section should consider itself the best section in the platoon, and the platoon the best in the battalion'. *Esprit de corps* had become 'esprit de section' and 'esprit de platoon'. Sport, especially football, became, as James Roberts has argued, a 'significant vehicle' for propagating platoon spirit. The 1918 version of the General Staff's instructions on training platoons was very clear:

> too much attention cannot be paid to the part played by games in fostering the fighting spirit ... [The platoon commander] should not only personally and actively arrange for games and competitions for his men, but take part in them himself. If he induces his platoon to be determined to produce the best football team in the battalion, he will have done a great deal to make it the best platoon in every way.[63]

Inter-platoon and particularly inter-company football competitions possessed an additional purpose: to find the best players for inter-battalion matches. For sport also provided a means of cementing relations with other units. When 10/Royal Welch Fusiliers was dispersed in early 1918, Lieutenant Colonel J. L. Likeman, commanding 2/Suffolk Regiment, lamented the 'termination of our close friendship. For two years the battalions have fought side by side, and have striven in friendly rivalry [*sic*] in the cricket and football fields. In these and many other ways we have learnt to appreciate the Royal Welch Fusiliers'.[64] On occasion even long-standing animosities could be temporarily breached. In May 1917, at Locre, the Connaught Rangers played a battalion of the

---

[62] C. McCarthy, 'Queen of the Battlefield: The Development of Command, Organisation and Tactics in the British Infantry Battalion during the Great War', in Sheffield and Todman (eds.), *Command and Control on the Western Front*, pp. 173–93, esp. pp. 181–2.

[63] Bourne, 'The British Working Man in Arms', p. 220; Roberts, 'The Best Football Team', p. 37; S.S. 143 *Instructions for the Training of Platoons for Offensive Action*, 1917 issued by the General Staff February 1917; S.S. 143 *The Training and Employment of Platoons* 1918.

[64] Lieutenant-Colonel F. N. Burton assisted by Lieutenant A. P. Comyns, MC, *The War Diary (1914–1918) of the 10th (Service) Battalion Royal Welch Fusiliers* (Plymouth: William Brendon, 1926), p. 95.

36th (Ulster) Division before more than 2,000 spectators, rather too close to the front line for comfort. Colonel Feilding, the senior officer present, was apprehensive that the crowd might be spotted by an enemy aeroplane and shelled, but

> to stop a match in process of being cleanly fought before a sporting audience between the two great opposing factions of Ireland, in a spirit of friendliness which, so far as I am aware, seems unattainable on Ireland's native soil – even though in sight (or almost in sight) of the enemy – was a serious matter; and I decided to let the game go on ... During the game a wag on the Ulster side was heard to say: 'I wonder if we shall get into trouble for fraternizing with the enemy!'[65]

W. J. Grant notes in his diary that an inter-battery boxing match was staged in a cinema in Bayeux in an attempt to settle some dangerous rivalry. Yet sport sometimes crystallised rather than dissipated tensions, between combat and support troops for example. 'Can't understand it,' wrote one soldier of a divisional cup semi-final on the Western Front, 'everybody is up against the ASC boys and don't want them to win the competition.'[66]

Games were also played against the French army, though perhaps with mixed results for Allied relations. Resting during the final advance, in October 1918, 1/5th Leicestershire Regiment played two football matches against the French. The first, against the 55th Infantry, ended 5–1 to the Leicestershires, 'a fact which merely increased the fervour of the welcome we received from our opponents'. Later they beat a team of French sappers 5–0 'in an excellent game watched by many people. The language on both these occasions would sound as foreign in London as in Paris, but this did not in the least diminish the cordiality of the Entente'. However, a rugby match between the Tank Corps and the French army in Paris during the spring of 1918 was embittered, for the Tanks at least, by a defeat they attributed to a biased French referee. The French army, which had initially been 'sceptical' about sport, 'feeling that such a matter was not a vitally serious one in time of war', was nevertheless persuaded by the British example to encourage it. By early 1918 the British authorities had supplied the French with 15,000 footballs, and in the post-war period sport became part of the training of French soldiers and unit participation in military sporting championships was made compulsory.[67]

[65] Feilding, *War Letters*, pp. 169–70.
[66] War Diary of W. J. Grant, 18 February 1916, 97/16/1, IWM; War Diary of A.G. Parker, n.d., 82/25/1, IWM.
[67] Hills, *Fifth Leicestershire*, p. 360; Lieutenant-Colonel G.J. Dean, 'Notes on Royal Tank Regiment Rugby', Liddell 9/28/92, Liddell Hart Centre for Military Archives,

As the army had long been aware, competitive sport of the kind that could bring kudos to units could be actively detrimental to military training – witness the admission of the 2/7th (Robin Hood) Battalion Sherwood Foresters, whose football team in January 1918 'achieved considerable fame' by winning both their Brigade Cup and their Divisional Cup.

Their training, which was carried out in unconventional uniform and in which a leather spheroid played a much greater part than a Mills' bomb or box-respirator, took place in the most secluded and least likely spot to be visited by any Red Hats. Their success and physical fitness perhaps justified their temporary neglect of military training.[68]

As the Grove Park rugby team suggests, even in wartime sporting stars sometimes had the rules bent in their favour. Corporal Willie Applegarth, ASC, a former Olympic sprinter turned professional, spent much of his early wartime service running exhibition races around Britain. After being posted to Salonika he ran a three-race series for the 'world championship' against another sprinter, Private Eastman, in 1917.[69] Albert Hill, one of Britain's best middle-distance runners, became a wireless operator with the Royal Flying Corps. On posting to France his athletic ability soon got him noticed by his superior officers. He found plenty of time to train and entered races in a variety of sports meetings, often as a result of challenges from other officers who felt they had their own unbeatable champions. The only thing that could not be arranged was a transfer back to England to enable him to run for the RAF. His running certainly brought pleasure to many of those who saw him. How far it was detrimental to the overall military effort is hard to say.[70] And favouritism did not happen everywhere. When 1/14th London Regiment (London Scottish) played the Royal Engineers in the semi-final of the 56th Divisional Cup they left the trenches on the day of the match, travelled to the game by lorry and returned to the line the same night.[71]

Wartime sport was therefore not wholly unproblematic. Nevertheless, by 1916 it was clear to the military authorities that sport could play

London; Minutes of the Royal Navy and Army Boxing Association, 29 January 1918, Royal Navy and Royal Marines Sports Control Board, Portsmouth (hereafter RNSCB); *Times*, 21 November 1927.
[68] *Robin Hoods*, p. 403.
[69] *Athletic News*, 19 June, 31 July, 7 August, 14 August, 21 August, 4 September, 18 September 1916, 3 July 1917; *Times*, 15 May 1916.
[70] Albert Hill, unpublished MS autobiography, copy in the possession of Tony Mason. The Royal Air Force was formed in April 1918 by a merger of the Royal Flying Corps and the Royal Naval Air Service.
[71] *London Scottish Regimental Gazette* 23 (July 1918), p. 100.

an important part in sustaining the morale and *esprit de corps* of an army increasingly made up of civilian soldiers. More than that, sport became increasingly accepted as constituting a form of military training in itself. A discussion in the House of Commons on pensions for disabled soldiers in March 1916 raised the hypothetical issue of whether a man who broke his leg playing football in France was eligible for a pension. By September the War Office had decided it was 'so important that every man should be kept up to the highest pitch of physical fitness, that it is virtually a military duty to take part in and encourage such sports', and soldiers injured in 'properly organised military games' should be compensated accordingly.[72] These discussions reflected the beginnings of a formal recognition of the value of sport for front-line troops. In August 1916 General Gough, commanding the 5th Army, ordered that there should be a football ground in each Brigade Area. It was probably around this time that the duties of Claims Officers came to include finding sports grounds, often a thankless task as many French farmers objected to troops playing on their land. ('We are ... apt to have tremendous rows with them on the question of football fields,' wrote one officer, '... One old fellow frankly told me ... that he would really rather have the Germans here than us.') A soldier of the 1/20th London Regiment, returning to his unit in autumn 1916 after a six-month absence, found a change: 'we have longer spells in the trenches, but our "rest" days are far better. In the morning we have parades, but our afternoons are devoted to sport, such as football matches and company running.'[73] By the end of 1916 sport had become an official part of the army system.

These developments were part of a more general process of improving the training given to soldiers in a range of evolving techniques and tactics in signalling, wiring, trench building, the use of machine guns and artillery. They also underlined the growth of a more widespread belief among military authorities in the importance of physical training. An early indicator of this shift was the reorganisation of the delivery of physical training on the Western Front. In March 1916 Major R. B. Campbell of the Army Gymnastic Staff, a former army middleweight

---

[72] *Hansard's Parliamentary Debates*, HC Deb., 14 March 1916, vol. 80, cc. 2027–30, 2039–42; *Appropriation Account of the Sums Granted by Parliament for Army Services for the Year 1918–19* (1920), p. 83. This decision was reiterated by ACI 445 of 1926. The issue had been raised before the war but without success: see *Hansard's Parliamentary Debates*, HC Deb., 16 November 1911, vol. 31, cc. 524–5.

[73] '"Monsieur Le Clams" Looks Back', in Major-General Sir Ernest Swinton (ed.), *Twenty Years After: The Battlefields of 1914–18 Then and Now*, Supplementary Volume (London: Newnes, n.d.), p. 88; Gibson, 'The British Army', 218; Fuller, *Troop Morale*, pp. 88–9.

boxing champion, was sent to France with fifty-one instructors for two months to set up demonstrations at the base camps of Etaples, Rouen and Le Havre. The group was later transferred to the Third Army School at Flixecourt and in May 1916 relocated with them to Auxi-le-Chateâu. Early in 1917 the Physical Training and Bayonet School moved to St Pol and became a permanent part of the BEF's establishment. The School put on short courses for junior officers and NCOs, who would then return to their units as P&BT instructors.[74]

Campbell became notorious for his bloodthirsty lectures on the 'spirit of the bayonet'. His influence in cementing the place of sport in the BEF has been less remarked. Campbell was a vocal believer in the link between sport and war ('What qualities prevail in games?' he asked in a lecture in 1915, '... Physical fitness, executive action, and confidence – the three essential qualities for war').[75] Several famous professional boxers became sergeant-major and sergeant instructors at St Pol including Johnny Basham, Jim Driscoll, Jimmy Wilde and the British heavyweight champion Billy Wells. In September 1916, the P&BT staff were given overall responsibility for organising sport and providing the appropriate equipment in the BEF. (Funding for sports gear, amounting to £20,000 by January 1918, was raised by the Expeditionary Force Canteen, 'largely from the Dripping Fund'.) In December Frank Starr – who had been running a campaign in the *Athletic News* for sports organisation at the front – joined the staff as assistant to the Superintendent of Physical and Bayonet Training in France, with the temporary rank of captain and responsibility for organising 'Recreational Training'. Courses were given on sporting organisation and ideology, and Starr encouraged the establishment of competitive structures where they did not already exist. He was particularly keen on promoting boxing and football, and a system of team boxing was introduced to encourage mass participation and 'playing for the side'.[76]

---

[74] See P. Griffith, *Battle Tactics on the Western Front: The British Army's Art of Attack, 1916–18* (London: F. Cass, 1994), pp. 71–2; Campbell, 'The Army Isn't All Work', pp. 197–220; Oldfield, *History*, pp. 26–7.

[75] Quoted in J.M. Osborne, 'Sports, Soldiers and the Great War', *Proceedings of the Eighth Annual Meeting of the British Society of Sports History* (1991), 17–34, at 18.

[76] Oldfield, *History*, ch. 2; Minutes of the Royal Navy and Army Boxing Association, 29 January 1918, RNSCB; *Athletic News*, 23 October, 30 October, 25 December 1916; 'Starr, Lieut. F.J. (1916–21)', WO374/64933, TNA. With the German spring offensive in 1918 the school retreated hurriedly to Hardelot Plage but the courses continued: see the school journal, *Sport and Spuds*, June–October 1918. Starr later estimated that 2,000 officers and 22,000 NCOs had been trained as instructors and superintendents at the various training centres at home and in France (Campbell, 'The Army Isn't All Work', p. 193).

Early in 1917 'areas behind the lines began to cry out for more recreational training', and more instructors were sent from Britain and overseas. What had doubtless appeared to many of the higher command to be a case of a small unit getting too big for its army boots suddenly took on a new importance. In March 1917 the General Staff took over responsibility for the school which now had a personnel of 10 officers and 152 other ranks. Their responsibilities were expanded to include the rehabilitation of injured troops, not only by restoring the mental and physical condition of war weary men by physical training and games but also through a programme of remedial work in the hospitals.[77] This seems to be a more definite attempt to incorporate sport into the military training programme, something that can also be identified in the General Staff's 1917 instructions for training platoons for offensive action. Along with drill, bayonet fighting, grenade throwing and musketry, physical fitness programmes were to include 'recreational training such as football and paper chases'. These were to take place on Wednesday and Saturday afternoons and be presented as 'half holidays'.[78] These instructions codified what was already standard practice: as we have seen, units out of the line by now typically spent mornings training and the afternoons playing sport – and not only on Wednesdays and Saturdays. The army's example now began to attract the attention of other Allied forces and other services: after visiting St Pol in 1917 Commander Coote, head of the Naval School of Physical Training at Portsmouth, introduced a similar scheme of 'recreational training' for the navy.[79]

The Physical and Bayonet Training Staff not only increased the amount of sport being offered, they also changed the context in which it was played. At the first monthly conference of Superintendents of Physical and Bayonet Training, in December 1916, it had been decided that no money prizes should be given for any kind of 'recreational training'. This was in direct opposition to long-standing army traditions of awarding money prizes to other ranks at regimental sports and service boxing matches: it is significant that R.B. Campbell, now in

---

[77] Oldfield, *History*, pp. 28–9 and (for work with convalescents in Salonika) pp. 39–40. For the use of sport and games in rehabilitation, see also Gray, *Prophet*, pp. 28–30; K. Digby Bell, 'An Address on the Position of the Medical Profession in Relation to National Physical Education', *Lancet*, 31 January 1920, 231–5; also W. Muir, 'Summer Days in a War Hospital', *Country Life*, 16 June 1917, 598–600.

[78] *Instructions for the Training of Platoons for Offensive Action*, February 1917, General Sir Ivor Maxse papers, 69/53/13 File 53, IWM.

[79] Commander P.F. Newcombe, 'Physical Training in the Services', *The Fighting Forces* 12 (1935–6), 588–92; see also 'Physical and Recreational Training of the Royal Navy', 1919, ADM 1/8549/16, TNA.

Figure 9. Physical and Bayonet Training Headquarters Staff, St Pol, 1917. Lieutenant-Colonel R. B. Campbell, middle row, left; Commander Coote, RN, middle row, centre. Captain Frank Starr, author of the *Athletic News*' 'Service Gossip' column, front row, right.

overall charge of sport in the BEF, had been prominent in the pre-war movement to introduce amateur values into army sport. Campbell secured Haig's approval for the superintendents' decision, which was confirmed – but for boxing only – by G.R.O. No. 2059 of January 1917. Subsequently Training Pamphlet S.S. 137 on Recreational Training of October 1917 laid down a general rule that 'money prizes must not be given. They kill good sport, encourage selfishness, and destroy the spirit of individual sacrifice which games are intended to foster'. (The echo of the values fostered by public-school 'athleticism' is unmistakable.) The Physical and Bayonet Training Staff supplied a variety of cups, medals and other prizes (watches, razors, tobacco boxes and so on) to be awarded instead of money. By early 1918 there were 'no less than six engravers in France solely engaged in designing' sports medals for the British army.[80] Some observers, notably Sir George Newman,

---

[80] Oldfield, *History*, p. 28; *Recreational Training* S.S. 137, October 1917, p. 6; Minutes of Royal Navy and Army Boxing Association, 29 January 1918, RNSCB.

chief medical officer to the Board of Education, saw the work of the P&BT Staff in France as pointing the way to a future in which Britain would become 'a nation of players', scorning professionalised spectator sport in favour of mass participation and amateur enthusiasm.[81]

This assessment was over-optimistic. It is not clear even how far the P&BT corps was able to enforce the 'no money prizes' rule. Starr – a devoted advocate of amateurism – later insisted that, despite the scepticism of their officers, even professional boxers preferred to win medals as a memento of sport behind the lines.[82] However, Campbell admitted that 'the abolition of money prizes was at first very unpopular and a great deal of opposition was experienced from men in the ranks interested either directly or indirectly with professional boxing ... The professional was the chief difficulty'.[83] It certainly took time to establish the new rule, and it seems unlikely that money prizes were fully eliminated from the BEF before the Armistice. In October 1917 – months after they had been banned in boxing – the 173rd Brigade RFA (36th Division) held an inter-battery boxing match on the Western Front for a prize of 100 francs. News of the general ban on money prizes had evidently not reached 1/Leicestershire Regiment by November, since it held a cross-country run at Manin with a prize of thirty francs. Looking back twenty years after the end of the war one officer at least regretted that professional boxing in the army was a thing of the past. 'If a man, by reason of brains, hard work and perseverance, becomes eminent in a particular art, surely he should be allowed to capitalise his skill.' Moreover boxing champions brought prestige to the army.[84]

By the later years of the war sport – both as a leisure pursuit and as 'recreational training' – had become part of military routine. With victory in sight the authorities began to turn their minds to the likely problems attending the gradual demobilization of a huge civilian army. Meeting with army commanders on 11 November 1918, Haig 'pointed out the importance of looking after the troops during the period following the cessation of hostilities ... I suggested a number of ways in which men can be kept occupied. It is as much the *duty* of all officers to keep their men amused as it is to train them for war'. Along with a great expansion in army education, sport was the major tool used by the

[81] J. Bourke, *Dismembering the Male: Men's Bodies, Britain and the Great War* (London: Reaktion Books, 1996), pp. 183–4.
[82] *Athletic News*, 2 February 1919; Starr, 'Army Boxing History', *Aldershot Command News*, 10 January 1928; Oldfield, *History*, p. 28.
[83] Minutes of Royal Navy and Army Boxing Association, 29 January 1918, RNSCB.
[84] War Diary of W. G. Grant, 14 October 1917, 97/16/1, IWM; War Diary, 'A' Company, 1st Battalion Leicestershire Regiment, 8 November 1917, DE 5670, Leicestershire Record Office, Leicester; Temple Clarke, *Transport and Sport*, p. 178.

army to keep the men occupied and reasonably content: officers were instructed to 'keep troops busy, especially with games'.[85]

One week after the Armistice that movement for a central authority to control army sport which had begun just before the war reached its goal when the first meeting of the Army Sport Control Board was held in the War Office.[86] The new Board circulated a letter to General Officers Commanding in all theatres of war, stressing that

> during the process of demobilization and the period which must necessarily elapse between that process and the reorganization of our future Army, the earliest possible efforts should be made to organize sport in all its branches; the intensity of military training carried on throughout the War will, on the conclusion of peace, be considerably relaxed, the leisure of the soldier consequently increased and it is considered that a great part of such leisure cannot be more profitably employed than by the universal participation of all ranks in the National sports of the Country.[87]

In January 1919 a British Expeditionary Force Sport Board was established in France to coordinate existing Divisional Sports Associations and exercise overall control. The Board included some of the major figures of pre-war army sport such as Brigadier General Kentish, former honorary secretary of the Army Football Association, and representatives of the Dominions forces and of the RAF and each branch of the army. Frank Starr became honorary secretary of the Board and editor of the *BEF Sports Journal*, which, along with sports results and histories of army sport, blended propaganda for the 'sporting spirit' with exhortations to troops to bear the long period of demobilization patiently. The 'Games Spirit' that won the war should, it urged, 'keep us from "grousing" at little troubles during demobilization'. Later Starr claimed that Kentish's article on sportsmanlike conduct in army football, which fronted the *Journal*'s first number, had proved a 'remedy for discontent'. Read out at hundreds of matches, it ensured – said Starr – that the 'spirit of the football teams permeated the army', helping to prevent the mutinies over slow demobilisation seen in the United Kingdom.[88]

---

[85] Sheffield and Bourne, *Douglas Haig*, p. 487; Temple Clarke, *Transport and Sport*, p. 114.
[86] The founding of the Army Sport Control Board is discussed in more detail in chapter 4.
[87] Major-General H. C. Lowther, GHQ Great Britain, to All Commands and London District, 25 November 1918, File 114/General/6042, Army Sport Control Board Records, Aldershot.
[88] 'Sport in the BEF', *Times*, 5 March 1919; *BEF Sports Journal* 1 (8 February 1919), 5; 2 (20 February 1919), 1; Brigadier-General R. J. Kentish, 'Army Association Football. Its Present and Its Future', *BEF Sports Journal* 1 (8 February 1919), 1; *Athletic News*, 12 January 1920. For the 'crisis in morale' among British forces on the Rhine in 1919,

The Board codified the principles of amateurism and mass participation fostered by the recreational training programme, aiming to 'improve the physical fitness of the troops', organise competitions 'in which men compete for the honour of their unit', and 'instil the root principle of true sport, viz., "Play for your side and not for yourself".' Football, rugby and boxing matches were held at every level, culminating in Brigade, Division, and 2nd Army championships. On Boxing Day 1918 a 'Tactical Rugby' match was played near Amiens with teams of 200, no boundaries and two villages as goals. An Inter-Theatre of War sporting championship was held in Britain in April–May 1919: the process of selecting teams to represent the BEF helped to provide sporting incentives. The amateur spirit suffered in the process, however, since, once selected, the teams were removed from their units and duties for intensive training.[89] Similar developments occurred in other theatres. The diary of the 5th (Territorial) Battalion Bedfordshire Regiment, stationed in Egypt, for the early months of 1919 records an unbroken round of drill, education and sport, football, hockey, cross-country running and boxing being carried out on a daily basis at all levels from platoon to division and finally at the Egyptian Expeditionary Force sports at Gezira and in trials to find the team to represent the EEF in Britain. 'The principal interest has been sports and the men have taken it up well & trained hard,' the diary comments, also remarking that 'the Sports have undoubtedly done a great deal in keeping the men fit & free from sickness'.[90]

In Britain it was the services who kick-started post-war sport. In December 1918 a British Empire and American Services Boxing Tournament took place at the Albert Hall, with the British army the eventual winners. So attractive was the programme – the teams including numerous big-name professionals in the services for the duration – that hundreds of spectators left outside forced the east doors to get in.[91] In March–April 1919 the Army Rugby Union organised an imperial inter-services rugby tournament between teams representing New Zealand, South Africa, Canada, Australia, the RAF and the British army playing as 'The Mother Country'. It was eventually won by New Zealand, who went on to play – and defeat – the French army at

see D. G. Williamson, *The British in Germany 1918–1930: The Reluctant Occupiers* (Oxford: Berg, 1991), pp. 32–7.
[89] *BEF Sports Journal* 2 (20 February 1919), 7; 'Sport in the BEF', *Times*, 8 April and 24 April 1919.
[90] War Diaries, 5th (Territorial) Battalion Bedfordshire Regiment, January, February and March 1919, X550/6/8/1901, X550/6/8/1902, X550/6/8/1903, BLARS.
[91] *Times*, 13 December 1918.

Twickenham. The matches were deliberately distributed across Britain, and the tournament was, as W.W. Wakefield recalled, 'almost the only organised Rugby football played in the spring of 1919'.[92]

The finals of the Inter-Theatre of War games in boxing, cross-country, football and rugby took place in England late in April 1919. The British army in France won most of them, but the Egyptian Expeditionary Force carried off the cross-country race with four runners in the first six: all of them Indians running with bare feet.[93] In the bouts to choose the Home Army's boxing representatives one of the competitors was a former army heavyweight champion, Major M.P. Leahy, who fought (at welterweight) despite having lost a leg in the war.[94] An even more ambitious Inter-Allied Games was organised in Paris by the American Expeditionary Force. Styled a 'military Olympics', it too was designed to 'absorb the interest of the troops during the somewhat restless period of waiting their return home'. The Americans promoted, directed and financed the operation including building a 25,000-seat stadium in the Bois de Vincennes – the Pershing stadium – in a few weeks during April and May 1919. About a thousand athletes from eighteen nations eventually competed. The British, however, declined to take part, merely sending a token force of golfers and rowers from the British Army on the Rhine – a decision that may be explained by Wanda Wakefield's suggestion that the Games were intended to demonstrate to Europe the dominance of the United States and the superiority of American manhood.[95] The process of demobilisation meant that this sporting renaissance, though intense, was brief. By late April sport was 'almost dead in the BEF'. Nevertheless sport continued to be actively fostered in the Army of the Rhine: it is an indication of the importance attached to it that Starr, to his disgruntlement, was not released from the army until December 1919.[96]

If sport, despite the assertions of its enthusiasts, did not quite win the war, it nonetheless played an important part in the experiences of many soldiers between 1914 and 1918. As a distraction from the horrors of the conflict, as much-needed amusement and diversion, and as a link with home and civilian life, sport helped to make war bearable.

---

[92] W.W. Wakefield and H.P. Marshall, *Rugger* (London: Longmans, Green & Co., 1927), pp. 13–15. The tournament was reported in depth by the *Times* and the *Athletic News*.

[93] *Times*, 29 April 1919.

[94] *Ibid.*, 25 April 1919; Gray, *Prophet*, p. 48. He lost on points.

[95] Major G. Wythe *et al.*, *The Inter-Allied Games, Paris 22nd June to 6th July 1919* (Paris: The Games Committee, 1920); Wakefield, *Playing to Win*, pp. 37–51.

[96] 'Sport in the BEF', *Times*, 24 April 1919; 'Starr, Lieut. F.J. (1916–21)', WO374/64933, TNA.

(This is not to argue that *all* soldiers found solace in sport – the men of 358 Company Army Service Corps Motor Transport were presumably not alone in offering only 'scant support and encouragement' to their unit football team.[97] There is no doubt, however, that for the majority it did provide some enjoyment and consolation.) This wartime sport drew on two strong and converging traditions: the well-documented civilian obsession with sport and (which has been less recognized) the sporting tradition that the British services themselves had established by 1914. If, as Fuller argues, British troops 'carried over from civilian life many institutions and attitudes which helped them to adjust to, and to humanize, the new world in which they found themselves',[98] it is important to emphasize that sport was already an institution within the army as much as it was outside it. Indeed, part of sport's value in the Great War may precisely have been that it provided a rare arena in which military and civilian preoccupations overlapped, a familiar point of contact for the civilian soldiers who made up the majority of the wartime army. The conjunction is illustrated by the way in which the old army habit of shouting 'HLI!' at football teams considered to be wasting time – a tradition that dated back to an 1890s Indian cup final involving the Highland Light Infantry – became generally adopted on the Western Front.[99]

Sport was valuable not only to individual soldiers but to the army as a whole. The First World War marks the point at which sport, formerly all-pervasive but largely unofficial in the British army, became an integral part of the military system. In upholding morale, cementing *esprit de corps* and officer–men relations and encouraging fitness and the 'fighting spirit', sport appeared – not only to the British but to the French and American troops who followed the British example – to have substantial military utility. It is a small indication of the developing ability of the British army to adapt to the demands of mass warfare that in the last two years of the war sport became officially adopted as part of military life and training, reflecting a recognition of its ability to contribute to military effectiveness. The experience of the First World War had a major impact on service sport, not least in enabling the formal laying down of the principles of amateurism, grounded in the public-school code, which shaped it – if sometimes more in the breach than the observance – for decades thereafter. As a result of its experiences on the Western Front the Army Gymnastic

---

[97] *Open Exhaust* 1 (January 1916), p. 4; see also 9 (September 1916), p. 9.
[98] Fuller, *Troop Morale*, p. 175.
[99] Ibid., p. 136; Richards, *Old-Soldier Sahib*, p. 41.

Staff also began incorporating team games into physical training, part of its ambitious post-war resolve to treat 'mind, body and spirit' as one unified whole.[100] In the inter-war period sport became an increasingly important part of service life.

[100] 'L.C.', 'Modern Developments in Physical Training', *Journal of the Royal United Service Institution* 67 (1922), 678–81, at 681.

4 The amateur era, 1919–39

> The Army Sport Control Board has ... been constituted to encourage and assist sport in the Army by eliminating the taint of professionalism and gambling which resulted so often in unhealthy antagonism rather than healthy rivalry ... by providing the facilities for universal participation by officers and other ranks; [and] by ensuring that the game is played in the proper spirit for the game's sake and for the side, remembering that this great war has been won by all from nations to platoons 'playing for the side'.
> *Games and Sport in the Army (Issued by the A.S.C.B.)*, 1919

The inter-war years were difficult ones for the services, especially the army, yet curiously propitious for service sport. For most of the period the armed services remained small, subject to increasing financial stringency, and unclear about the roles they were intended to serve. The Ten Year Rule, laid down in August 1919 and renewed in 1928 on a rolling basis, stated that no major war was to be expected within the next decade. Until it was abandoned in 1932 the services were subject to repeated economic cuts of which the army bore the brunt. The Geddes Axe of 1922 led to the disbanding of twenty-two infantry battalions, while the cavalry were reduced, in part by amalgamations, from twenty-eight to twenty regiments; the national crisis of 1931 brought all servicemen and officers a 10 per cent pay cut. Rearmament began only in 1934 and was hamstrung by continuing uncertainty about the army's priorities. How far, if at all, should it prepare for a commitment on continental Europe? Or should it confine itself to the 'limited liability' of imperial defence?[1] These were not circumstances to encourage a forward-thinking, professional army. For the Royal Artillery, Bidwell and Graham chart a decline from pre-war professionalism and a successful adaptation to the challenges of the Western Front to an organisation that by the 1930s was marked by conservatism, suspicion of innovation

---

[1] B. Bond, *British Military Policy Between the Two World Wars* (Oxford: Clarendon Press, 1980); R. Higham, *Armed Forces in Peacetime: Britain 1918–1939: A Case Study* (London: G. T. Foulis & Co. Ltd, 1962).

and, for officers, adherence to a narrow social code that included 'an affectation of professional ignorance'. The causes of this deterioration included uncertainty about the Artillery's future role, understaffing, poor prospects of promotion, and the deficiencies of officer education. One of its main symptoms was the 'swingletree factor' – an obsessive interest in horses (the Artillery was overwhelmingly horse-drawn for most of the inter-war period) coupled with a striking lack of interest in gunnery.[2] Most of this analysis is applicable to the army as a whole. Brian Bond has emphasised how the situation tended to produce a 'narrow and unintellectual' officer corps who compensated for the boredom of peacetime soldiering by a fanatical pursuit of sport.[3] To a remarkable extent the social and sporting atmosphere of the Edwardian army was recreated between the wars, especially in India but also at home. Nor was it only officers who were affected. Alec Dixon, an unsporty private in the Tanks Corps, found Tanks Central Schools at Bovington in the early 1920s 'little better than a manufactory of athletes'; under pressure from above he too became one.[4] It was only in the late 1930s, with the international situation increasingly threatening and rearmament at last under way, that the place of sport in the army was challenged.

The inter-war years saw the consolidation in service sport of the amateur ideology that had been preached in the Edwardian period and made official policy during the war, with a permanent ban on money prizes and greater emphasis on sport's moral value. Central to this success was the establishment of official structures to regulate and control service sport. Here the army led the way: the campaign begun in 1913 for a body to oversee 'all forms of Army games and recreation' finally prevailed in late 1918.[5] The experience of sport's military utility in wartime clearly played a part in this; also important was the promotion of some of the key figures of pre-war army sports into positions of influence. As Major V. A. Jackson, one of the group of Edwardian army sports reformers led by Reginald Kentish, recalled,

In 1913–14 I was very keenly interested in army games etc. and did a certain amount of work with Kentish in this direction. On one occasion when he was a Territorial Adjutant in London he said to me, 'if any of us ever get into any position at the W[ar] O[ffice] whence we can further our ideals we must do so'. I always remembered this and made a written note of it which

---

[2] S. Bidwell and D. Graham, *Fire-Power. British Army Weapons and Theories of War 1904–1945* (London: George Allen & Unwin, 1982), ch. 9. The swingletree was 'the point of attachment of the traces connecting the team of horses to the gun limber'.
[3] Bond, *British Military Policy*, esp. ch. 2.
[4] A. Dixon, *Tinned Soldier* (London: Jonathan Cape, 1941), pp. 167–9, 191–5, 280–1.
[5] 'Army Athletic Association – proposed formation', 1912–14, WO32/5492, TNA.

I reread when I was sent to W.O. from France in 1918. I knew my boss [General Charles Harington, Deputy Chief of the Imperial General Staff] ... was keen on games – hence a screed I drew up and presented to him & with which he agreed.[6]

The idea of 'a central authority to control Sport and Athletics in the Army' was pitched to the War Office in September 1918, in what was presumably Jackson's 'screed', in terms that blended efficiency with the promotion of the amateur ideology. Such an organisation would encourage army sport, improve financing and liaise with the other services and with civilian sporting organisations. The sporting soldier was currently 'not well catered for with results that tend to discountenance amateur sport in the Army. The soldier is inclined to join the civilian organisation, generally professional.' Moreover, better control of army sport would 'do away with controversies such as have occurred in cases where soldiers have taken part in professional competitions and receive[d] money prizes. (To the detriment of sport and to the loss of prestige in Army Athletics)'.[7]

The War Office clearly shared Jackson's concerns about the degrading influences of professionalism and civilian sport generally. Major General Sir A. L. Lynden Bell remarked that 'recent events, more particularly competitions organised by civilians in connection with boxing have shewn the necessity of having a central controlling body for the Army, which shall be powerful enough to have a strong influence over sports both within and outside the Army'. Major General Sir W. T. Furse commented loftily that he was 'all for doing anything that will raise the tone of the Civilian Athletic Associations to that which obtains in the Army'.[8] The foundation of the Army Sport Control Board was officially notified on 20 November in Army Council Instruction No. 1299 of 1918, which set out the objects of the Board as:

(a) To assist the organizations now existing in the Army for the various branches of sport.

---

[6] V. A. Jackson to B. C. Hartley, 12 June 1935, attached to ASCB file 69/3209, 'Army Sport Control Board – Grant for', Army Sport Control Board records, Aldershot (ASCB). For Harington's own claim to be 'founder' of the ASCB, see Harington, *Tim Harington Looks Back*, pp. 98–9. For an attempt earlier in 1918, also prompted by Kentish, to raise funds 'so that the Athletics of the future Army ... may vigorously be pursued on sound and properly controlled lines', see 'Appeal for Funds for the Army Boxing, Army Football, and Army Athletic Associations', Central Registry File No. 21020, ASCB.

[7] 'Formation of a Central Authority to Control Sport and Athletics in the Army', 114/General/6042, ASCB. For the formation of the Army Sport Control Board, see also Campbell, 'The Army Isn't All Work', Conclusion.

[8] Minutes on the Proposal, September–October 1918, 114/General/6042, ASCB.

The amateur era   115

(b) To control the conduct of sport in the Army.
(c) To assist the organizations for sport in the various Commands at Home and Overseas.
(d) To deal with questions arising from organizations outside the Army, in which sport in the Army may be connected.
(e) To maintain the necessary co-operation in sport between the Army and the other Forces of the Crown, both at Home and Overseas.

Among the first members of the Board's executive committee were Harington (as president), Major Jackson, and Colonel R.B. Campbell, now Inspector of Physical Training. The first secretary was the rugby international Captain B.C. Hartley, Hertfordshire Regiment, who remained in post until 1939, when he became director of the Board with the honorary rank of colonel.[9]

Where the army had led the way the two other services followed. For the post-war navy – facing an increasingly militant lower-deck movement and an outbreak of serious disciplinary cases in 1919 – sport seemed most valuable as an aid to discipline. Wartime recreational training, it was felt, had helped improve officer–men relations – particularly important in an uneasy post-war world in which it was anticipated that 'general unrest will be prevalent ... the value of the right type of discipline in the Navy will have a steadying effect which will be felt far beyond the confines of the Navy itself'. These concerns help to explain the Navy's adoption in 1919 of an elaborate, not to say eccentric, scheme of 'physical, recreational and morale training' put forward by Commander Coote[10] of the Naval School of Physical Training. The scheme drew in about equal proportions on public-school athleticism, muscular Christianity, wartime ideas of recreational training (adopted by Coote from the army's School of Physical and Bayonet Training at St Pol) and the new 'mind, body and spirit' approach being adopted by the Army Physical Training Staff.[11] 'Perfect morale' would be produced through mass participation in sports and games (the '90 per cent

---

[9] 'Meeting of "Sports Control Board" held at War Office on 18th November 1918', 114/General/6042, ASCB; one page history headed 'The Army Sport Control Board', n.d. and 'The Army Sport Control Board', Enc. 15 to 261/Pubs/9913, both in file labelled 'ASCB History', ASCB. The duties and membership of the executive committee were set out in ACI 1387 of 1918; for the sporting credentials of its first members see *Athletic News*, 30 December 1918.
[10] Staff officer at the Naval School of Physical Training at Portsmouth 1903–6 before leaving the service to study at the Royal Gymnastic Central Institute of Stockholm, Coote became superintendent of gymnasia at Eton and then Harrow. Re-enlisting in 1914, he spent the war on physical training duties at Portsmouth. *Times*, 5 September, 8 September 1955.
[11] As the Army Gymnastic Staff was renamed in 1918.

system'), encouraged by providing a wide variety of sporting activities and rewarded by a scoring system which awarded points for taking part. For Coote, sport provided simple lessons for the 'Game of Life': 'don't play foul'; 'don't chuck up the sponge'; 'go allout [sic] to win'; 'play for your side and not for yourself'. It was thus both in emulation of the ASCB and in the context of a wider rethinking of the roles of physical training and sport in the post-war navy that the Royal Navy Sports Control Board was founded in July 1919.[12]

Though some of the details of Coote's scheme may have been eccentric there is persuasive evidence that by the 1930s the idea that sport should play a part in the physical, organisational and recreational training of men on board ship was widespread. Leonard Harris, who served on seven different vessels during the decade, found that sport was always encouraged with most ports and stations offering good facilities. Individual ships held their own sports days and teams would take part in squadron and flotilla events. The pursuit of high standards for the few was accompanied by the provision of opportunity for the many: each part of every ship had its own football team which usually competed in an inter-part league with the results posted up on the ship's sports board.[13] When the cruiser HMS *Penelope* embarked on her first commission between 1936 and 1939 in the Mediterranean with the Third Cruiser Squadron the range of sports organised for the twenty-eight officers and 468 men was impressive. It included athletics, billiards, boxing, cricket, fencing, football, hockey, rowing, rifle and pistol shooting, rugby, sailing, swimming and water polo. Fifty-eight cricket matches 'of all sorts and sizes' were played in 1937, though only twenty-eight in 1938, the decline due to 'cruises, crises and catastrophes'. The Squadron had its own football league and there was also a Mediterranean Fleet league. Fixtures with local teams at Malta, and at ports such as Fiume, Lanaka and Trieste, were regular events.[14] In these warmer climes many of the ship's company took every opportunity to enjoy bathing, sailing and 'banyan parties' (excursions to the beach) in the 'delectable bays on the Majorcan coast'. Rowing and water polo also took place 'against our great friends the German Cruiser "Koln"', the

[12] 'Physical and Recreational Training of the Royal Navy' (1919), ADM 1/8549/16, TNA; 'Games and Sport in the Royal Navy. Proposal to form Central Committee' (1919), ADM 1/8566/237, TNA; *Handbook of Physical and Recreational Training for the Use of the Royal Navy 1920 Volume II Recreational Training* (London: HMSO, 1922), pp. 5–48. See also Fox, 'The Royal Naval Physical Training Branch', pp. 133–42.
[13] Chief Petty Officer Leonard Harris, Memoirs 1923–47, 'Without Regret', pp. 84–9, 1999/102, Royal Naval Museum, Portsmouth (RNM).
[14] *Souvenir Book of HMS Penelope's First Commission*, pp. 69–73, RNM; for matches against Malta teams see also Harris, Memoirs, p. 87, RNM.

water polo in the swimming bath at Tangier. *Penelope* lost 5–4 but the team were entertained on board the *Koln* after the match.[15]

But the sun did not have to shine for shipboard sports to flourish. The battle cruiser *Hood* based at Rosyth during its three-year commission from 1933 spent much of its time in the cooler waters and ports around Ross and Cromarty. None the less sport played an important part in both the recreation and training of the 1,300 officers and men on board, who competed vigorously with and against each other especially in cross-country running and football. Almost 20 per cent of the ship's company, over 200 men, ran in the inter-part cross country race on 30 September 1933 from which a team of thirty was selected to run for the Arbuthnot Trophy, competed for annually by the crews of capital ships. The *Hood* team won, which would have delighted their commander, Captain Rory O'Conor. The author of what became the post-Invergordon handbook on ship management, *Running a Big Ship on 'Ten Commandments'*, O'Conor saw sporting success – along with discipline, cleanliness and contentment – as one of the key markers of a 'Good Ship'. Himself a rugby player, O'Conor thought the pulling regatta the Fleet's principal sporting event because of the mass participation it involved. In the big ship regatta almost 300 officers and men represented each ship and it was 'no wonder, therefore, that the Cock is the most highly prized of trophies; it is the reward of arduous training and of massed effort on a grand scale … There is nothing in the world to surpass the heartfelt satisfaction and delight when the Cock comes on board – it is a moment worth living and working for.'[16]

For the new Royal Air Force, finally setting up a Sport Control Board in late 1921, the main motivation was anxiety that it was 'falling behind the other Services in matters of sports and games'.[17] Sport was deliberately fostered in the RAF as a way of creating corporate identity in the youngest service. Even before the war ended efforts were being made to endow the RAF with its own sporting traditions. In October

---

[15] *HMS Penelope's First Commission*, pp. 81–2, RNM. Water polo could also be played alongside one's own ship, the goal nets being suspended from spurs – see Harris, Memoirs, p. 87, RNM.

[16] *The Chough, Hood News* 2 (15 October 1933), Scrapbook compiled by Captain Rory O'Conor, 1993/54/1, RNM; Captain Rory O'Conor, RN, *Running a Big Ship on 'Ten Commandments'* (Portsmouth: Gieves Ltd, 1937), pp. 141–2, 149–50. HMS *Hood* was sunk by the *Bismarck* with heavy loss of life in 1941. O'Conor was killed on HMS *Neptune* in the same year.

[17] Minutes of 1st meeting of the RAF Sports Board, 21 December 1921, RAF Sports Board Records, RAF Halton (RAFSB). RAF sport had previously been organised by a Recreational Council bringing together officials from the various game associations; it was hoped that a stronger body would carry more weight with the Air Council.

1918 Sir Charles Wakefield, a businessman and philanthropist with a special interest in aviation, offered challenge cups and medals for an RAF boxing competition, 'recognising the beneficial effects of Boxing to men in training and the interest taken by the Officers and men of the Royal Air Force in the Sport'. Air Marshal Trenchard commented that 'a gift of this nature is of especial value to us in building up the traditions of the Force on sound and healthy lines'.[18] Inter-service matches were especially important to the RAF as it strove to put itself on equal terms with the two older and bigger services. Trenchard used his royal connections to pressure the navy into agreeing a rugby fixture with the RAF on the same terms as their match against the army. When in 1921 W. W. Wakefield's team beat the army it was a landmark victory, 'the first occasion on which an RAF team had beaten either the Navy or the Army in a representative game' at any sport – though this triumph was dwarfed by their victory in the Inter-Service Rugby Championship two years later.[19] Something of the same anxious keeping up with the sporting Joneses is evident in the RAFSB's decision in 1922 to build an RAF stadium at Uxbridge at a cost of almost £10,000. Before the Second World War the stadium never came close to paying its way – the rent payable by Uxbridge Town FC for its use had twice to be reduced, and the RAF Football Association was reluctant to play there at all because of the difficulty in attracting crowds and therefore gate money.[20]

But, as so often in service sport, it was the army which set the tone for the inter-war years. The new Army Sport Control Board set out its manifesto in a leaflet of 1919. Citing Wellington's apocryphal saying that the battle of Waterloo had been won on the playing fields of Eton as its 'governing idea', the Board stated that 'sport in all its branches furnishes in miniature many of the conditions which confront a soldier in battle'. Pre-war army sport, however, had come dangerously close to being 'enfolded by the corrupting tentacles of professionalism'. Regimental football teams, excused parades and given special diets and separate quarters, had 'ceased to be soldiers and became regimental gladiators'. Reshaped on the model of mass participation, amateurism and the public school spirit, army sport was to be made explicitly a tool for producing good soldiers. The 'principles' with which the Board set to work echoed both the preoccupations of pre-war army sports reformers and the rules by which wartime 'recreational training' had

---

[18] 'Boxing: Gifts of Cups etc. by Sir Charles Wakefield', AIR 2/71 F6510, TNA.
[19] J. Mace, *The History of Royal Air Force Rugby 1919–1999* (Oxon: RAF Rugby Union, 2000), p. 3; Wakefield and Marshall, *Rugger*, pp. 18–19, 28, 45–6.
[20] RAFSB minutes, 1 May 1922, 6 September 1922, 17 April 1923, 14 May 1924, 26 January 1925, 9 June 1925, 9 July 1925, RAFSB.

The amateur era   119

been run. Indeed, the wording of S.S. 137 on Recreational Training of October 1917 was echoed very closely in the sections banning money prizes ('they kill good sport and encourage selfishness') and encouraging officers to 'take a personal and active interest' in army sport ('officers can thus gain an insight into the true characters of their men, which they can obtain by no other means during times of peace; they will, at the same time, develop in themselves powers of leadership which are absolutely essential to military success'). Repeated annually in the ASCB's publication *Games and Sports in the Army*, the 'principles' enshrined the spirit of the Great War and the Edwardian public schools well into the Cold War period.[21]

If military sport was to produce the effects aimed at by the ASCB it was important that it should be played in the 'right spirit'. During the 1919 Inter-Theatre-of-War Championships a meeting of all ranks was held to define 'a good sportsman'. It was decided that a 'sportsman' was one who:

(1) Plays the game for the game's sake
(2) Plays for his side and not for himself
(3) Is a good winner and a good loser, i.e., is modest in victory and generous in defeat
(4) Accepts all decisions in a proper spirit
(5) Is chivalrous towards a defeated opponent
(6) Is unselfish and always ready to help others to become proficient
(7) As a spectator, applauds good play on both sides
(8) Never interferes with referees or judges, no matter what the decision.

This definition featured prominently in *Games and Sports in the Army* and was widely published elsewhere. The evidence from the *Aldershot Command News*, however, suggests that enforcing these standards was a running battle. In 1927 the editor deplored the behaviour of 'young soldiers who come straight from civil life and whose experience of the ethics of games has been gathered very largely from professional sport. It is they who bring into the Command the practice on the field of chanting the number of goals gained by their own football club and

---

[21] *Games and Sport in the Army (Issued by the Army Sport Control Board)* (1919), ADM1/8566/237, TNA; 'Meeting of "Sports Control Board" held at War Office on 18th November 1918', ASCB. Published annually from 1931, *Games and Sports in the Army* included rules for all the games played by servicemen plus practical hints for organising and judging them and advice about the spirit in which they should be played; the *Royal Navy and Royal Marines Sports Handbook*, and *Royal Air Force Athletic and Games Handbook* were both modelled closely on it.

of "booing" a decision given by a boxing referee which is not of their liking.' A *Young Soldier's Catechism*, displayed in recreation rooms and soldiers' institutes, aimed to accelerate their transformation into 'full-fledged Army Sportsmen'. The *Catechism* asked why each of the eight points in the 'Definition of a Sportsman' should be observed and supplied answers – including 'because no other way is possible to a pukka sportsman', because unsporting behaviour 'isn't done in the Army', and 'because they're British'.[22] 'Sportsmanship' thus united chauvinism, public-school protocol and adherence to institutional norms. Ensuring 'gentlemanly conduct' in players and spectators none the less proved an uphill struggle.[23]

A more concrete result of the new emphasis on amateurism in service sport was that in the 1920s service boxing became almost entirely amateur. Frank Starr suggested that this development had long-term benefits for servicemen, since few who left the forces to box as professionals were successful, whereas 'the Police Force, the Fire Service, and scores of business houses run amateur boxing clubs … and are ready to allow a period of semi-apprenticeships to the time-expired soldier who brings with him a first-class boxing reputation'. It was nevertheless a gradual process. In late 1923 the Army Boxing Association rejected a proposal to make all army boxing amateur, only to accept it less than a year later. In the mid-1920s it was still possible for a serving soldier to box professionally, though only with the permission of the Army Boxing Association. The Association's handbook stated in 1925 that 'a boxer who has won the Army Amateur Championships and then the Amateur Championships of Great Britain and has shown exceptional skill and ability may have a career before him as a professional and no obstacle then would be put in his way'. (This paragraph had disappeared by 1928.) In 1924 and 1925 the army held parallel championships, one open and one for amateurs only. The move towards amateurism necessitated the creation of the category of 'Service Amateur': an ex-professional who formally severed his links with professional boxing was then able to compete as an amateur in service tournaments, though not in civilian contests. The idea was that they would be gradually squeezed out, and in 1937 the RAF banned them from its championships.[24]

---

[22] *Aldershot Command News*, 13 December 1927, 20 December 1927.
[23] For other pleas for 'sportsmanship' see e.g. *Aldershot Command News*, 21 February 1928, 2 January 1934, 25 September 1934, 1 January 1935.
[24] F. Starr, 'Army Boxing History', *Aldershot Command News*, 6 March 1928; Martel, *An Outspoken Soldier*, p. 43; Minutes of the Imperial Services Boxing Association, 23 July 1925, RNSCB; *Times*, 10 March 1924, 20 April 1925, 24 February 1937.

The amateur era   121

The drive for amateurism was led by the army, supported by the RAF, and strongly resisted by the navy. The issue came to a head in 1925 when the Imperial Services Boxing Association discussed making its championships all-amateur. The army case for amateurism was forcefully presented by Major Giffard 'Q' Martel. Amateurism encouraged a 'more sporting spirit' and provided better 'moral training', since without money prizes as an incentive greater 'self-denial and determination' were required. It also dispensed with the civilian manager, a species long regarded with disgust by army boxing reformers. It was unfair, Martel argued, that in the ISBA championships army amateurs should have to face professionals from other services and have 'the prestige of the Army boxer ... lowered' by a likely defeat. Nor was the present system likely to encourage amateurism: 'the professionals at these meetings often speak openly of the "foolishness" of the Army boxers in fighting for "nothing"'. The RAF, following closely in the army's footsteps, had banned professionals from RAF contests, but thought it 'unfair' to stop the professional boxing altogether 'in view of the encouragement we have given him in the past'. The navy alone remained wedded to professionalism: most of its other ranks boxers were *de facto* professionals having fought for money prizes in foreign ports. Its protests were over-ruled, however, and from 1926 the ISBA championships were entirely amateur.[25]

Amateur boxing was a sport that had done well out of the war. Another was that bastion of amateur values, rugby union. In civil society, rugby's war record of willing enlistment and patriotic sacrifice bolstered its claim to be 'a school of true manhood and leadership' and hastened the 'rush to rugby' in public and grammar schools in the 1920s.[26] Despite the rarity of rugby games on the Western Front, the war also encouraged the promotion of rugby in the services. Boxing and rugby were often bracketed together as sports which promoted tough masculinity and had particular military value. In 1919 a group of ASPT officers awaiting demobilisation constructed a table (giving points for physical, mental and moral benefits) to decide which were the best games for soldiers: the winner was team boxing, with rugby only one point behind.[27] Martel persuaded his Experimental Bridging Company to take up rugby rather than football by emphasising the 'bellyaching'

---

[25] ISBA Minutes, 23 July 1925, including reports from the three services boxing associations on 'Amateurism v. Professionalism', RNSCB.
[26] Collins, 'English Rugby Union', 815–16.
[27] Frank Starr, 'Which is the Best Game?', *Aldershot Command News*, 20 December 1927. The next three games were Team Wrestling, Lacrosse (unexpectedly) and Football, in that order.

practices of professional football compared with the fortitude expected at rugby where 'if a man was hurt he did his best to carry on without interrupting the game at all. If, however, he was so bad that he could not do so, then he crept away and died quietly on the touch line' – thus providing a good example for soldiers. Having persuaded the War Office to allow him to select four young officers with a 'mechanical bent' from Woolwich, Martel boosted the team by choosing 'two three quarters, a fly half and a forward' – all of whom, 'though the reader will hardly believe it', also turned out to have the necessary engineering skills. With this help the small unit got to the semi-final of the 1919–20 Army Rugby Cup before being beaten by the eventual winners, the Welch Regiment. Martel claimed that without the 'rugger spirit' they 'could never have carried out the work that has left its mark on the Army to this day'.[28] In the RAF, rugby got preferential treatment, players 'almost invariably' being given leave to play in important matches, whereas 'in the case of other games it is somewhat frequently stated that owing to official duties personnel cannot be spared'.[29] The RAF went to enormous lengths to play rugby wherever it was stationed, in the Middle East binding sandy pitches with waste sump oil from aeroplane engines, and at Habbaniya in Iraq even diverting the Euphrates to flood the ground.[30]

Between the wars overseas sports tours and matches against foreign armies became regular events. Partly the result of the widespread belief that sport could help foster the international cooperation and friendship that seemed so necessary in the immediate post-war years, it also reflected a desire to develop in peacetime the alliances and friendships forged during the war – and to patch up some long-running hostilities. In 1926 a team of British army boxers made an apparently well-received goodwill visit to the Irish Free State to compete against the Irish army.[31] Boxing teams representing the army, the Imperial Services and the RAF made regular visits to Scandinavia between the wars, and in 1938 the RAF Boxing Association made a more ambitious tour of South Africa competing against teams from the South African police, armed services and Amateur Boxing Association.[32] In cricket, army teams played

[28] Martel, *An Outspoken Soldier*, pp. 24–6. His unit developed what came to be the standard army bridge.
[29] RAFSB minutes, 12 March 1937, RAFSB.
[30] Mace, *History of Royal Air Force Rugby*, p. 137.
[31] David Fitzpatrick, 'Unofficial emissaries: British Army Boxers in the Irish Free State, 1926', *Irish Historical Studies* 30:118 (1996), 206–32.
[32] *RAF Sports Yearbook* (1939), pp. 146–55. Otherwise successful, the South African tour was marred when three boxers and the team trainer were killed in an air crash between Bulawayo and Pretoria.

The amateur era 123

India, the West Indies and Australia at Aldershot in the early 1930s.[33] Most significant was the series of football matches between the British, French and Belgian army teams beginning in 1919 which became a competition for the Kentish Cup from the 1920–1 football season.[34] It was in this context that the disadvantages of service amateurism became most apparent.

The Kentish Cup games quickly became important social as well as sporting occasions, attended by royalty, diplomats and generals. In 1931 the French Ambassador, the Secretary of State for War and the Adjutant General all greeted the players as they came out onto the Crystal Palace ground at Selhurst Park to the strains of the 'Marseillaise' and the 'British Grenadiers'.[35] After the matches players and accompanying dignitaries dined well at one of London's best hotels and went on afterwards to a West End show. A journalist who attended several of these events recalled them fondly some thirty years later.

> At the top table, in a blaze of decorations, were the general officers of both armies, military attachés and other members of the diplomatic service. At the two middle tables were the teams in full-dress uniform – each Frenchman or Belgian, as the case might be, seated next to an Englishman. At the start of the saturnalia they were rather shy, but as the champagne began to flow they would begin to converse vigorously, mainly by signs, and by the end of the evening they would appear to understand each other perfectly.[36]

Toasts to 'Our Allies' were drunk and extravagant speeches made which, from the visitors to Britain at least, were designed to tell us what we surely wanted to hear. In 1928, for example, the Belgian Ambassador told his audience that 'the British nation had been in the matter of football as in so many others their leaders and instructors'.[37]

By the 1930s, though, it was the Belgian and French army teams which were dishing out the lessons. Between 1919 and 1929 the French army had only beaten the British army once. During the 1930s one match was drawn, the British team won twice, the French won seven times. Against the Belgians the British army won only six matches out of twenty played between the wars. Between 1936 and 1939 the British

---

[33] Harington, *Tim Harington Looks Back*, p. 181.
[34] The cup was presented by Brigadier-General R. J. Kentish, who had been secretary of the Army Football Association 1912–14 and 1919–21.
[35] *Times*, 23 February 1931.
[36] N. Ackland, 'The Forces', in A. H. Fabian and G. Green (eds.), *Association Football*, 4 vols. (London: Caxton, 1960), vol. I, p. 378. Contributions from the offices of the Adjutant General, the Army Sport Control Board, the War Office and the theatre owner Oswald Stoll helped fund these jamborees. Minutes of the Army FA, GC 3 June 1924, EMC 28 January 1930, EMC 14 February 1933, AFA.
[37] *Times*, 17 February 1928.

team scored only three goals against twenty-one by the Belgian army team. Even in the early matches of the series the signs were already there. Though the British army won 1–0 in 1922 it was the Belgian team who had the 'cut of a professional League side rather than a Service eleven' and 'their speed in control of the ball and their headwork were of themselves sufficient evidence of a professional instructor lurking somewhere in the background'.[38] By the 1930s, both Belgium and France were developing their own professional football leagues and both had conscription, which meant their best and improving players had to serve a period in the army. Unlike the players in the British volunteer army, therefore, both the Belgian and French soldier footballers were regularly taking part in a higher standard of play even if they were 'true amateurs' – and many were not. When the French army beat the British army 5–0 in the Parc des Princes before 15,000 spectators in March 1938 most of the team were professionals playing for teams such as Lens, Lille, Marseilles, Sète, Antibes, Metz and Belfort.[39] Committed to amateurism, there was little the Army FA could do – and it refused to introduce one change which might have helped because it was opposed to the employment of coaches or trainers in regimental football.[40] At least the tournament remained on the fixture list. The British army rugby team had also played the French army regularly in the 1920s. But two rival unions were in conflict there and in the wider game they had been acquiring a reputation for violent conduct on the field. Evidence of professionalism led to the International Board breaking off relations with the French, a decision with which the army could only concur.[41]

As the foundation of the Sport Control Boards suggests, between the wars sport attracted a greater level of official approval and support than ever before. Another indication of this development is the new use of sport for recruitment purposes. Even as post-war demobilisation continued, a series of posters emphasising the sporting opportunities of military life was produced to attract young recruits and persuade those already in the army to re-enlist for a further period of service.[42] Most famously, 'The Army Isn't *ALL* Work' (July 1919) depicts an

[38] *Times*, 31 March 1922.
[39] *Times*, 4 March 1938.
[40] Minutes of the Army FA, Gen. Com., June 1930, 11 June 1937, 25 February 1938, 13 June 1939, Emergency Com., 6 December 1932, AFA.
[41] See David Smith and Gareth Williams, *Fields of Praise: The Official History of the Welsh Rugby Union* (Cardiff: University of Wales Press, 1980), p. 303.
[42] All the posters mentioned below are held at the Imperial War Museum and viewable on its website at www.iwmcollections.org.uk/. For post-war demobilisation and recruitment policies see Higham, *Armed Forces*, ch. 1; Bond, *British Military Policy*, ch. 1.

The amateur era   125

infantryman with rifle flanked by two other soldiers, one in football kit, the other in cricket whites, with football and cricket matches taking place in the background. 'Re-Enlist Now' (May 1919), includes six images of army life, one illustrating the chance to 'see the world', the other five showing soldiers taking part in football, water polo, cricket, athletics and boxing. Lionel Edwards' 'Are You Fond of Horses? Then Join the Cavalry' (July 1919) features a full-length illustration of a polo-player. The theme was taken up at regimental level. In 1919 the Royal Munster Fusiliers offered 'To Sportsmen and Smart Men A Good Clean Sporting Life … with an Assured Future', a promise illustrated with pictures of soldiers engaged in football, cricket, boxing, cross-country running and hockey (the last against the backdrop of the Pyramids since the 2nd Battalion was then stationed in Egypt). How far this emphasis on sport actually attracted recruits is unclear. A *Times* correspondent in 1937, signing himself 'Serving Soldier' and evidently one of the rank and file, listed as grievances (along with more serious issues such as poor pay, bullying discipline and bad food) deductions from pay for regimental sports funds and 'unofficial compulsion to attend regimental sports events' such as battalion football matches.[43] But, with life in the services marked for most of the inter-war period predominantly by declining pay, poor promotion prospects, trivial discipline increasingly out of line with civilian society and public unpopularity, the well-founded promise of almost unlimited sport was one of the army's better draws.

Similarly, recruiting for the reconstituted Territorial Army opened in 1920 with a flourish of sports-related posters. 'Are You Fond of Games? … Then Join the Territorial Army' shows a smiling Territorial, his arms crammed with equipment for cricket, football, hockey and tennis. In another poster a Territorial swimming in the sea shouts 'Coming In? It's Great!'; the text promises 'Free Holidays, Sports, Social Amusements'. The most striking example, 'Learn to Defend Yourself and Your Country', depicts an evening Territorial boxing match in a barn watched by a crowd of officers and other ranks. As Peter Dennis has commented, 'sports programmes and a busy social life, topped off by the annual camp – at the seaside if possible – were the Territorial Army's answer to the competitive attractions of civilian leisure' between the wars. A Territorial Army Sports Board founded in 1920 organised competitions and attempted to ensure units had access to sports grounds. The *Times* hailed the Board as an excellent way of promoting a 'desirable spirit of comradeship' between Territorials and

[43] *Times*, 2 January 1937.

Figure 10. 'The Army Isn't ALL Work', recruiting poster, July 1919.

Regulars, and increasingly Territorial sport was incorporated into the regulars' world, either by holding parallel competitions simultaneously at the same venue, or by allowing Territorials to participate in competitions against the regular services. The Imperial Services Boxing Association tournament was expanded in 1931 to include the auxiliary services; in 1939 the Territorial Army were joint winners with the RAF. The King presented a challenge cup for competition between TA units. In the late 1930s the TASB launched an ambitious fund-raising drive to equalise access to sports facilities across the country and allow Territorial soldiers to 'receive training in sport in the same way as they receive training in war'. By May 1939 it had raised £79,000, of which £50,000 was donated by Lord Nuffield and another £20,000 by a single anonymous donor.[44]

The more supportive official attitude towards service sport in the interwar years can also be seen in a new approach to sports funding. From being paid for purely by games subscriptions and gate money, army sport in the inter-war period came increasingly to be supported by centrally controlled non-public service funds. The original source of funding for the ASCB was the accumulated profits of the Navy and Army Canteen Board (the predecessor of NAAFI), then being liquidated, together with a one-off grant in 1920 of £80,000 from the United Services Trust Fund, also derived from wartime canteen profits. It also received an annual grant, and occasional substantial loans, from the Central Regimental Institute Funds (maintained from canteen profits and after 1921 from NAAFI) disbursed by the Central Funds Representative Committee. This body became a major source of army sports funding: its annual grant to the ASCB had risen to £11,000 by 1938.[45] Harington later attributed the Army Council's willingness to spend money on sport to his claim that sport had won the war. But there remained strict limits to the Council's support. In 1920, refusing to grant Aldershot additional funding to cover the wages of staff involved in sports administration, Sir Charles Harris, Assistant Financial Secretary to the War Office, insisted that 'the first condition of efficiency is that the Army shall learn to run [sports] itself, in the way that any other large organisation of Britishers the world over always has done and always will, without being "nursed" by a special staff paid by the taxpayer'.[46]

The navy fought a prolonged but ultimately successful battle with the Treasury on precisely this ground. Its planned post-war reorganisation of physical training involved a new Physical Training & Sports Branch run by a director (replacing the post of Superintendent of Physical Training), whose duties would include sports organisation, and an assistant-director, who would also act as secretary of the RNSCB.

---

[44] *Times*, 19 May 1920, 17 December 1920, 10 November 1931, 6 April 1939, 4 May 1939; 'Territorial Army, Sports Fund 1938–9', WO 32/12936, TNA; Kirke Papers, 5/5 and 5/6, Liddell Hart Centre for Military Archives, King's College, London (LHC); P. Dennis, *The Territorial Army 1906–40* (London: Royal Historical Society, 1987), p. 216 – see also ch. 8 for the problems of inter-war recruitment, though Dennis does not discuss the TASB.

[45] 'Army Sport Control Board – Grant for' (1918–19), ASCB; *Games and Sports in the Army* (1939–40), p. 39.

[46] Harington, *Tim Harington Looks Back*, pp. 98, 237; ASCB minutes of April 1920, 114/General/6230, ASCB.

128   Sport and the Military

Ever-greater reasons were produced to justify spending public money on navy sport, with emphasis on the 'cramped conditions of Naval life' and the importance of recreation 'in the promotion of discipline in the Royal Navy'.

> Important as undoubtedly is the development of Sports and Athletic Exercise for the general well-being of the Soldier, to the Navy, with the unnatural life on board ship and the lack of possibilities of exercise and recreation, the matter stands on a different plane, and the encouragement and development of all forms of Physical Exercise, Games and Sports is a vital essential in our Naval Training.
> The development of the modern ship with its almost entire replacement of manual labour by machinery, the use of oil fuel instead of coal, the construction of the Submarine, have all acted to restrict the physical development of the seaman from his normal duties. If therefore the fighting capacity and inclination and the physical and moral character of the Seaman is to be maintained in the future as in the past, some effort must be made and some assistance afforded by the State.

Confronted with the argument that sport in the navy would develop not only physical fitness but also discipline, fighting capacity and moral character, the Treasury could only submit. The Physical Training and Sports Branch was established in March 1920, with the rugby international Engineer Commander E. W. Roberts as assistant-director and RNSCB secretary.[47]

It was still unclear, however, how the Navy Sports Board was to be funded. There was some concern lest it be 'undesirably dependent on voluntary aid from Funds controlled by the vote of the Lower Deck'.[48] In theory the top players were to fund facilities for 'the masses' through gate money – to which end a number of grants were made to fence in football grounds. But what really kept the Board solvent was being granted the rights over Admiralty war films: cinema rights and the exhibition of films like *The Exploits of a German Submarine* raised thousands for navy sport in the early 1920s. With a grant of £5,000 from the Lower Deck Ratings this enabled the NSCB to establish a capital fund which, together with regular donations from ships and shore establishments, became the main source of funding for navy sport.[49]

Unlike the other services, RAF sports funding emerged from the war in a state of controversial prosperity. The RFC Central Mess

[47] 'Games and Sport in the Royal Navy. Proposal to form Central Committee' (1919), ADM 1/8566/237, TNA.
[48] Memorandum by Rear Admiral Hugh Watson, 29 December 1919, ADM 1/8566/237, TNA.
[49] 'The Financing of the Physical Training and Sports Branch' (1922), ADM 1/8619/24; *Royal Navy and Royal Marines Sports Handbook* (1930), pp. 2–7.

Fund (renamed the RAF Officers' Sports Fund in April 1918) had been financed since its foundation in 1912 by officers' subscriptions of four days' pay per annum. The expansion of the RFC after 1914 thus resulted in an equally great expansion of the Fund, which by July 1918 amounted to over £25,000, despite recent disbursements to the RAF at home and overseas totalling £14,000. Although the voluntary principle had recently been reluctantly accepted ('the subscription is to be *entirely voluntary*; in view of the object of the Fund the loyal support of *all* Officers is expected'), subscriptions continued to be collected unless officers gave instructions to the contrary. After the Armistice many officers demanded their money back when the press exposed this 'scandal' of compulsory subscriptions. In 1919 the Fund, still amounting to some £12,000, ceased to collect subscriptions, and distributed its assets as grants towards permanent sports facilities or as loans (repayable at 2 per cent) to encourage officer sport; the residue was divided between RAF stations overseas and a fund to encourage inter-service sport.[50] From 1921 sport in the RAF was supported by a capital fund of £9,000 derived equally from a new Officers' Sports Fund, the Central Institute Fund (Officers) and the Central Institute Fund (Other Ranks). The profits of the annual RAF Display were also earmarked for sport. Immediately before the Second World War the Board received a £10,000 windfall from Lord Rothermere, who had chosen this way of commemorating his role as Air Minister at the time of the RAF's formation in 1918.[51]

As a result of the Great War the state came to recognise some monetary obligations towards the infrastructure of service sport. In 1919 the War Office agreed that it was liable to provide 'standard [recreation] grounds to the scale laid down in the Barrack Synopsis'. The 1924 War Office Committee on Public Liabilities in Respect of Army Sport decided that, since 'the General Staff and the training manuals advocate voluntary games as a valuable training both for the recruit and the trained man', the War Office should subsidize grounds maintenance and sports administration.[52] In practice, however, constant funding shortfalls meant that sports facilities were largely underwritten by the Sports Boards. Between the Armistice and the end of 1927 the ASCB distributed £207,000 'to aid games, grounds, and sport generally', of which around half went to 'the main stations at Aldershot and in the Eastern

---

[50] 'RAF Sports Board and RAF Officers' Sports Fund', AIR 2/71 F8465, TNA.
[51] RAFSB minutes, 21 December 1921, 7 February 1934, 15 August 1939, RAFSB; *Times*, 8 July 1939.
[52] *Second Report of the Committee on Public Liabilities in Respect of Army Sport* [C. 24] in file labelled 'ASCB History', ASCB.

and Southern Commands' and about £34,000 to garrisons overseas.[53] The Navy SCB also spent much of its income on sport facilities. In 1920–2 alone it spent over £12,000 on grounds in Britain (including the Rectory Field rugby ground at Devonport, bought and refurbished at a cost of £9,000) and overseas at Malta, Bermuda and Simonstown.[54] The RAF Sports Board was particularly anxious to make its bleak, isolated stations more attractive by providing recreational facilities – especially squash courts, which also provided an effective way of keeping officers fit all year round.[55] The rapid increase in the number of RAF stations after 1936, and their reorientation towards the eastern side of Britain, stretched the resources of the Board to its limits. In July 1939 the Treasury agreed to advance funding for new squash courts, the Board paying off the debt over time.[56]

For army officers, as Brian Bond has noted, inter-war soldiering was still very much 'a horse-dominated way of life', and not just for the cavalry. Mark Henniker recalled of Woolwich in the mid-1920s that 'riding was, at once, one of the most important and enjoyable subjects taught at The Shop … Gunners and sappers were mounted officers and good horsemanship was still almost synonymous with military proficiency'. Even in 1937, 125 hours of instruction in the eighteen-month Woolwich course were still devoted to 'the horse'.[57] It was only in the late 1930s that artillery officers ceased to be granted a government horse plus forage allowance, and as late as 1938, *after* mechanization, cavalry officers were still provided with chargers – the War Office having successfully argued to the Treasury that 'both polo and hunting have a definite military value'.[58] Even infantry officers were sometimes enthusiastic equestrians. The Royal Irish Fusiliers went through a polo craze at Malta in the late 1930s, as Brigadier W. Carden Roe recalled. One officer from the Buffs transferred to the Fusiliers purely for the polo, somehow managing to wangle accelerated promotion from subaltern

---

[53] *Times*, 23 February 1928
[54] 'The Financing of the Physical Training and Sports Branch' (1922), ADM 1/8619/24, TNA.
[55] *RAF Quarterly* 1 (1930), 411; 2 (1931), 689.
[56] RAFSB minutes, 24 July 1939, RAFSB. For the development of the RAF from the mid-1930s see D. Richards, *The Royal Air Force 1939–1945*, vol. I: *The Fight at Odds* (London: HMSO, 1953), 'Prologue: The Awakening'.
[57] Bond, *British Military Policy*, p. 64; M.C.A. Henniker, *Memoirs of a Junior Officer* (Edinburgh: Blackwood, 1951), p. 48; Brigadier Sir J. Smyth, *Sandhurst. A History of the Royal Military Academy, Woolwich, the Royal Military College, Sandhurst and the Royal Military Academy Sandhurst 1741–1961* (London: Weidenfeld and Nicolson, 1961), p. 200.
[58] Bond, *British Military Policy*, pp. 64–5; *Reports from the Committee of Public Accounts* (55, 148) 1936–37, pp. 453–4; see also *Times*, 1 December 1937, 9 December 1937.

to captain en route. In 1938 Carden Roe and two other officers visited Hungary to play polo against the army, returning in a hurry after Munich 'as the Hungarian Army with its polo players and ponies was mobilising, very regrettably, to possibly fight against us'.[59]

The cavalry in particular retained decidedly Edwardian attitudes towards equestrian sport. At the cavalry school at Weedon it was still considered 'a vital part' of students' training to hunt three or four days a week. Cecil Blacker recalled of the 5th Royal Inniskilling Dragoon Guards in the 1930s that 'each winter we all departed for two months to hunt; in the spring we rode in point-to-points to the accompaniment of not very exacting military duties, and during the summer we were mainly concerned with polo'. Mike Ansell was unrepentant about the amount of time he spent hunting while nominally that regiment's Equitation Officer: 'for a cavalry officer it made a superb training ... and while I was away, a younger or non-commissioned officer would be only too happy doing my job and learning thereby ... I don't think it an accident that, during the [second world] war, the "hunting" Inniskillings had more commands than any other British regiment'. In 1931 Ansell toured America and Canada show-jumping with the 'British Team' (made up of four cavalry officers); in 1935 he visited America to play polo for the Hurlingham team, leaving Britain again for India immediately on his return to play polo for Kashmir – for all of which he was granted leave.[60]

For Liddell Hart, the cavalry's 'sentimental devotion to the horse' was the prime reason for the British army's delays in mechanisation. In evidence he quoted Haig's 1925 comment that aeroplanes and tanks were 'only accessories to the man and the horse ... as time goes on you will find just as much use for the horse – the well-bred horse – as you have ever done in the past', and the officer who wrote in the 1935 Staff College exam that 'the horse must inevitably disappear from the Army in time, but this sad event must be delayed as long as possible'.[61] Recent writers, lacking Liddell Hart's sentimental devotion to the Tank Corps, have preferred to emphasise broader structural issues, while pointing out that for much of the inter-war period Britain actually led the way in mechanisation. For Brian Bond it was the 'perpetual doubt about the army's role in war' and particularly about continental war,

---

[59] War Diary of Brigadier W. Carden Roe, pp. 1–12, 77/165/1, Imperial War Museum.
[60] General Sir Cecil ('Monkey') Blacker, *Soldier in the Saddle* (London: Burke, 1963), p. 8; Colonel Sir Mike Ansell, *Soldier On* (London: Peter Davies Ltd, 1973), pp. 23–4, 33–6, 41–5.
[61] B. Liddell Hart, *The Tanks*, 2 vols. (London: Cassell, 1959), vol. I, pp. 200, 234, 309, 343–4.

coupled with the inflexibility of the Cardwell system and its orientation towards imperial defence, that caused Britain to lose its lead. David French argues that mechanisation of the cavalry was delayed until the mid-1930s less because of cavalry intransigence than because of the technical shortcomings of early tanks combined with insufficient funding for tank production.[62]

The evidence for the role of equestrian *sport* here is mixed. It is scarcely encouraging to find the commander of the first artillery brigade to be mechanised assuring the Staff College that officers should not only keep their chargers but should spend half their time hunting ('did I say half? ... I meant three-quarters'); nor to find conservatives still arguing in the mid-1930s, as they had before 1914, that the success of the British army depended on its ability to attract 'gentlemanly' officers to whom equestrian sport was a way of life – and that therefore both the cavalry and the artillery should retain their full complement of chargers even after mechanisation.[63] Certainly Percy Hobart, trying to turn three cavalry regiments into the 7th Armoured Division in Egypt in 1939, found their sporting preoccupations trying:

> Unless someone upsets all their polo, etc, for which they have paid heavily – it's so hard to get anything more into them or any more work out of them. Three days a week they come in six miles to Gezirah Club for polo. At 5pm it's getting dark: they are sweaty and tired. Not fit for much and most of them full up of socials in Cairo.[64]

But Mike Ansell demonstrates that an obsession with polo and show-jumping need not prevent a wider view. When in 1935 he was appointed an instructor at the cavalry school at Weedon he was 'pleased and proud', but he knew that the cavalry 'was finished, would never again be used in modern warfare – and yet we felt war coming'. It was this thought that made him reject Weedon in favour of a polo tour – 'polo might take me away for a year, but Weedon would take me away for three during the vital stages of the cavalry's change-over to mechanization'. Liddell Hart's own view on equestrian sport is unexpectedly positive. He pointed out that the cavalry had been fighting dismounted for more than a generation by the 1930s, so that with mechanisation

---

[62] Bond, *British Military Policy*, pp. 187–9; D. French, 'The Mechanization of the British Cavalry between the World Wars', *War in History* 10 (2003), 296–320.
[63] E. Harrison, *Gunners, Game and Gardens* (London: Leo Cooper, 1978), p. 65; 'The Army, the Officer, and the Horse' by 'You Have Been Warned', *Journal of the Royal Artillery* 64 (1937–8), 323–39 (reprinted from the *Cavalry Journal* (April 1937)).
[64] Quoted in W. Murray, 'Armored Warfare: The British, French and German Experiences', in W. Murray and A. R. Millett, (eds.), *Military Innovation in the Interwar Period* (Cambridge University Press, 1996), p. 23.

they had to start as 'two-fold novices – learning to fight mounted as well as to manage a mechanized mount'. Those who made a success of it did so, he suggested, 'because of their personal qualities helped by the quickening effect of games such as polo, of hunting, and of other activities outside their military work'.[65]

That technology and 'the horse' could happily coexist is illustrated by the emphasis on traditional officer sports in the RAF between the wars. Wing-Commander A. W. H. James even tried to get riding included in the curriculum at Cranwell, on the grounds that flying, like riding, required 'good "hands"'; that 'following hounds, quick decisions and chances have to be taken, and manoeuvres executed, closely comparable to making a forced landing, and quite the best possible training for such an event'; and that in the event of a crash a horse was useful to get back to base.[66] Though this suggestion was not followed, many in the RAF shared James' enthusiasm for horse and hound. In 1919 it was urged that the RAF should immediately begin 'the equestrian education of officers' since 'Polo and Hunting are recommended by the Medical Authorities as most beneficial recreations for Flying Officers, and ... foster the qualities most useful for War Pilots'.[67] In the immediate post-war years the Officer Sport Fund was largely devoted to beagle packs and hunt clubs. In May 1920 an RAF Beagles Association was formed with the aim of having a pack at each station within five years. OSF loans enabled Hunt Clubs to be formed at Cranwell and Spittlegate (there was already one at Halton) and funded the construction of stables. From the early 1920s an annual RAF point-to-point was held (though this gradually dwindled into a single race held at the race meeting of an accommodating hunt and run for all three challenge cups available). Repeated and expensive attempts were made to establish polo in the RAF. Halton was granted £1,400 in the early 1920s to form a polo club offering ponies to hire. In 1929 the RAFSB, having written off £700 of the club's debts, nevertheless agreed that 'every encouragement should be given to stimulate polo in the RAF'; but five years later the club still had so few members it had to hire its horses to civilians. Undaunted, the RAFSB approved a proposal for an RAF Polo Association in 1935. It also made private loans to officers to allow them

---

[65] Ansell, *Soldier On*, pp. 41–2; Liddell Hart, *The Tanks*, vol. I, pp. 358–9.
[66] Wing-Commander A. W. H. James, 'Equitation as an Aid to Efficiency in the Royal Air Force', *RAF Quarterly* 1 (1930), 534–8. He was disgusted to be foiled by the 'educational experts' who insisted on training 'for a purely mechanical war, to be fought in a civilized country'.
[67] 'RAF Polo c. 1919–20', AIR 2/129, TNA.

to buy polo ponies and hunters.[68] Even in the navy polo had its enthusiasts. Admiral Keyes was notorious for his 'addiction' to the game. It has been suggested that his failure to become First Sea Lord can be attributed in part to a widespread feeling that, during his time as Commander-in-Chief of the Mediterranean Station in the 1920s, he had favoured and promoted those who played polo above those who did not.[69]

'The joys that horses brought to soldiering were very great,' Henniker remembered.

The link they forged between officers and men was one that is hard to forge today. In Aldershot we soldiered with the jingle of harness in our ears ... There would never be a war because of The League of Nations. So the *arme blanche*, chivalry, polo and hunting, would go on for ever; or so it all seemed when, in December 1928, I set sail for India.[70]

India did not disappoint. Though old-timers grumbled that neither polo nor pig-sticking were what they had been before the war,[71] Henniker had no complaints. The Commandant of the Bengal Sappers and Miners at Roorkee, it transpired, chose his officers partly by 'their willingness to play polo. In a small station this was necessary, for unless everyone played the same game, there were insufficient numbers to play any game'. Henniker and his fellow officers duly 'applied all our resources, both mental and physical, to the game ... It was seldom far from our minds'. As well as playing three evenings a week they were allowed a week's tournament play at New Year at one of the local cantonments, this counting not as leave but as duty. Frederick Morgan's commanding officer – after a survey of the local gravestones – preferred to encourage pig-sticking, as being less frequently fatal than polo or big-game hunting. Indian sport was still comparatively cheap, especially since polo ponies could be passed off as chargers, with keep and grooms provided by the government; officers could also hire government horses, on a

---

[68] Officers' Sport Fund minutes, 17 December 1919, 3 February 1920, 16 March 1920, 7 May 1920, 29 September 1920, 22 February 1921; AOC Cranwell to Secretary OSF, 26 August 1921, AIR2/71 F8465, TNA. RAF Sports Board minutes, 2 March 1925, 17 March 1927, 26 March 1929, 2 July 1929, 15 October 1929, 8 October 1935 (other loans included £500 for the formation of a polo club in the Middle East Command (2 February 1927) and £50 for a polo club at Dhibban, Iraq (21 October 1938)), RAFSB. See also 'RAF Polo Club, Halton', *RAF Quarterly* 5 (1934), xxvii.

[69] P.G. Halpern (ed.), *The Keyes Papers*, 3 vols. (London: Navy Records Society, 1979–81), vol. II, p. 122; Commander R. Travers Young, 'Mischiefs in My Heart', unpublished memoir, pp. 158–60, 11487 P103, IWM. We are grateful to Neil Young and Roderick Suddaby for these references.

[70] Henniker, *Memoirs*, pp. 86–7.

[71] R.W. Henderson, 'Twenty-Five Years of Indian Polo', *Fighting Forces* 1 (1924), 622–9; 'The Future of Pig-Sticking', *Journal of the Royal Artillery* 61 (1934–5), 544.

short-term or long-term basis, for a nominal fee. Henniker calculated that over six years he had 'hunted and played polo to my heart's content for £260 ... well within the pay of a subaltern drawing the higher rates of pay allowed for Indian Army service'.[72] Big-game hunting was still possible. The officers of 1/Leicestershire Regiment, stationed at Kamptee, did their bit to reduce the tiger and panther population of Central Provinces, the commanding officer bagging an extra tiger as the battalion marched the 235 miles to Saugor. Philip Neame devoted much of his autobiography to the small game, bears and tigers he slaughtered in Northern India, Waziristan and Tibet. (Eventually a wounded tiger took its revenge by mauling him so badly he spent two months in hospital, subsequently marrying his nurse.)[73]

Indian sport for other ranks became more organised between the wars with the advent of the Army Sport Control Board India, formed in March 1919 with the Director of Military Training as president. (In the 1920s there were still nearly 60,000 British troops in India, typically serving a six-year tour of service.) As at home, the ASCBI aimed to develop and control army sport, enforce amateurism and coordinate with civilian bodies (here primarily the Indian Olympic Association, the Indian Hockey Association, the Board of Control for Cricket in India and the All-India Lawn Tennis Association). It also administered the British Troops Fund for establishing permanent sports facilities (a capital fund of Rs. 60,000 yielding a rather meagre annual income of Rs. 3,000, about £225, per annum). The Inspector of Physical Training for India was the ASCBI's honorary secretary, and it is no coincidence that the Board's early years coincided with a resurgence of the PT staff in India. Indeed, the post of Inspector was only instituted in 1922, part of a reorganisation that involved the merger (in 1923) of two separate Indian Schools of Physical Training to form one central school for all India, based at Ambala in winter and the hill station of Kasauli in summer.[74]

---

[72] Henniker, *Memoirs*, pp. 93–8, 126–7, 235–6; Lieutenant-General Sir F. Morgan, *Peace and War* (London: Hodder & Stoughton, 1961), pp. 67–8. For evidence that Morgan's C. O. was probably right to choose pig-sticking, see chapter 2.

[73] *Green Tiger*, August 1929, 78; November 1929, 118–19; February. 1930, 165–6; Lieutenant-Genenral Sir Philip Neame, *Playing With Strife* (London: Harrap, 1947), esp. chs. 9, 10, 16, 17. Uniquely, Neame had won both the VC (during the First World War) and an Olympic gold medal (for shooting, Paris 1924).

[74] *ASCB Handbook India* 1936–7, pp. 1–9, 328; Oldfield, *History*, ch. 8. 'Army' in this case incorporated the small units of the RAF and the Royal Indian Navy, both of which were included in Army Championships in India. Sports grounds for Indian troops were provided from a separate Expeditionary Force Canteen Profits Fund of Rs. 3,660,000 (*ASCB Handbook India* 1936–7, p. 6). The value of the rupee had been reset at 1s 6d in 1927.

Sporting enthusiasm was at least as great as it had been in pre-war days, and the constant round of inter-platoon, inter-company and inter-regimental competitions established before 1914 continued. Spike Mays, a trooper in the Royal Dragoons, arrived in India around 1930 to be told that 'everybody is sports mad. Football, hockey, swimming, boxing, the lot! There's no parades for the sports wallahs ... no fatigues, guards or picquets. A bit of training twice a day and every bloody weekend off ... Special diets, too. Bleedin' great steaks and as many eggs as they can bolt, and that's only for breakfast!' (All of this was of course strictly against the rules.) Cricket is notably absent from this list but there were other ranks who played it well, as in the 70th Field Battery, stationed at Lucknow, where the NCOs ran a cricket team so serious that they were not prepared to include their battery commander, even at his request, because he was not good enough. (The major responded with 'a humble request that he might be included in the 2nd XI'.)[75] The British army in India produced some notable athletes. Sergeant Jack Hart, 1/Cheshire Regiment, developed such a reputation as a sprinter in military and civilian sports that in 1936 he was posted home 'with a view to a trial for the British Team entering for the Olympic Games'. This never materialised, but in 1936 and again in 1937 he won both the 100 and 220 yards championships at the Aldershot Army Athletic Meeting as well as running successfully in civilian races for Salford AC. It has even been suggested that the times Hart recorded in India (9.7 seconds for 100 yards in 1934, 10.6 seconds for 100 metres in 1935 and again in 1936 – all record-equalling performances) make him 'Britain's unrecognised sprinting star'.[76] Boxing in India was initially hit hard by the imposition of amateurism, but in 1931 an Army and RAF Boxing Association, India, was formed which soon came under the chairmanship of Brigadier Gort, then director of military training at army headquarters. Individual and inter-unit team championships were reorganised, and within a few years 'nearly every regiment in India' had entered and there had been 'a vast increase in the number of military boxing tournaments all over India'.[77]

Sports for British and Indian soldiers were still highly segregated. The 1909 order forbidding British and Indian troops to compete against

[75] S. Mays, *Fall Out the Officers* (London: Eyre & Spottiswoode, 1969), p. 198; Morgan, *Peace and War*, pp. 93–5.
[76] B. Phillips, 'Is Sergeant Jack Hart Britain's Unrecognised Sprinting Star?', *Track Stats* 39 (2001), 25–31; 'Sergeant J. Hart', *Oak Tree* (1936), 301; 'Sergeant J. Hart. An Appreciation of an Outstanding Athlete', *Oak Tree* 31 (1946), 242–5. Acceptance of Hart's status as a 'sprinting star' of course requires faith in army timekeeping.
[77] *Times*, 22 December 1934, 17 February 1936. See also Brigadier J. C. K. Barnard, 'My Impressions of Boxing in India', *Aldershot Command News*, 9 January 1934.

The amateur era 137

Figure 11. Sergeant Jack Hart, star sprinter of the inter-war army, competes in the Inter-Allied Athletic Championships in Berlin in 1946.

each other was still in force, and the ASCBI reiterated that 'a British team shall not compete against an Indian team, nor shall it include any of its Indian personnel in its team, in any competition held under the auspices of the ASCB India'. The ASCBI ran boxing championships for British troops only, wrestling championships for Indian troops only, and football, hockey and athletics championships for British and Indian troops separately. Yet the times *were* changing, at however glacial a rate. At lawn tennis – the sole official exception to the rule – officers and other ranks of the British and Indian armies all competed together, and the list of winners features Captain D. Datt (Medical Services, Rawalpindi District) and Lieutenant R. N. Mulla (1st Punjab Regiment).[78] These were perhaps beneficiaries of the 'Indianisation' policy begun in 1923. As it was usual for Indian army officers newly graduated from Sandhurst (or, after 1932, the Indian Military College at Dehra Dun) to spend a year with a British regiment stationed in India, Indianisation also

[78] *ASCB Handbook India* 1936–7, pp. 12, 16–17, 180–1.

meant the introduction of Indian officers to British army regiments. Thus in 1934 1/Leicestershire Regiment's cricket team benefited from the batting prowess of 2nd Lieutenant Rajkumar Baghel Singh. A further small sign of changing *mores* was the bursting into print in 1937 of the 'Followers' of 1/Leicesters – the Indian servants, drivers and cooks – to announce their own sporting victory at Jubbulpore: 'Yes, sir, for the second year in succession we have lifted the coveted Govind Raj Cup (Soccer).' As a result they were invited to take part in the battalion's inter-platoon league; they ended second from the bottom but redeemed their reputation by winning another Jubbulpore competition, the Karim Beg Tournament, beating a team of Europeans in the final and being congratulated by the colonel.[79]

The rules banning competing against Indians did not of course apply to civilian competitions. In a context of rising nationalist tensions, British troops and Indian civilians seem to have met at sport much as they had always done, largely unaffected either by Gandhi's non-cooperation campaigns or by nationalist terrorism – though the murder of Mr Burge, district magistrate, in 1933 as he entered Midnapore football ground 'to play for the town against a Moslem team' demonstrates that sporting events were not always immune from politics.[80] Certainly 1/Leicesters found playing Mohun Bagan in the 1931 IFA Shield in Calcutta an uneasy as well as an exasperating experience (they lost by a disputed goal in extra time). With some 28,000 Indian spectators inside the ground and another 30,000 watching from the banks of the Fort just outside, 'really we were very fortunate, as only one brick-head was thrown into the field of play'. Gandhi's 1930 Salt March did cause some irritation to troops who were kept on the hot plains to control the 'disturbances' when they had expected to be in the hills; battalion sports had to be postponed and few competitors turned out for the Kasauli Boxing Tournament. 'Needless to say, our opinion of Gandhi is not what it was.'[81] But such annoyances were few. The cancellation in 1936 of the Wucha Jawar Football League matches in Rawalpindi on the North-West Frontier due to the 'unsporting attitude of the tribesmen who were indulging in sniping at players and spectators' is a rare example of military sport being directly affected by political disturbances. Playing hockey in Amritsar (of all places) in 1933 'A' Company, 1/Leicesters were surprised to find 'how popular our team was with the crowd, though playing against the Sikh national college, in

[79] *Green Tiger*, February 1934, 180; August 1937, 99–100; November 1937, 141.
[80] *Times*, 4 September 1933.
[81] *Green Tiger*, November 1931, 119; August 1930, 241–2; November 1930, 282.

The amateur era 139

the Sikh capital' (and the site of General Dyer's 1919 massacre). As late as 1938–9 2/Border Regiment stationed in Calcutta was still playing friendly matches against Mohun Bagan and Mohammad Sporting.[82] Spike Mays, based around Meerut in the early 1930s, recollected that 'Hindu and Muslim soldiers would invite us to their sporting events and their merry-making'; he also went game-shooting with them. Mays had his hockey stick autographed by two members of India's Olympic gold-medal-winning hockey team. Less plausibly, he claimed to have met Gandhi – and to have been given a sip of orange juice by the great man – at a village cricket match near Delhi.[83] This impression of generally peaceful sporting coexistence is in contrast to other troubled regions of the Empire – Ireland in 1921, for example, where the officers of 1/Royal Scots Fusiliers played polo under armed guard, or Palestine, where in 1938 2/Black Watch's polo team had to be escorted the thirty miles from their base in Jerusalem to their polo ground at Sarafand by RAF armoured cars (the polo season ending early after most of their ponies were stolen from the club stables).[84] It perhaps helps to explain the apparent lack of perception among officers and other ranks that the British Raj was coming to an end.

In 1926 2nd Lieutenant Mark Henniker was told by the Regimental Sergeant-Major at Chatham that in peacetime the 'professional side' of army life could be left to the sergeants. 'The officers' best contribution to the unit was to win races, shoot goals, score runs, or take wickets' – privileges they were to pay for in wartime by 'leading the way'. But army sport was never wholly uncontroversial between the wars. J. F. C. Fuller complained repeatedly in the 1930s that the army:

lives almost exclusively in the past – a past of fox-hunting squires, week-end shooting parties, village cricket fields … The prevailing idea is not, as might be expected, the inculcation of leadership (though this is much talked about), but the establishment of team work; football and cricket, polo and hunting being exalted to a military art … is it to be wondered at that our army is never prepared for war, which is not a game; that is to say, never prepared spiritually and intellectually.[85]

---

[82] *The Gunner* 17 (January 1936), 257; *Green Tiger*, May 1933, 54; *Border Regiment Regimental Association News Sheet* 2:7 (June 1939), 14.
[83] Mays, *Fall Out*, pp. 215–17.
[84] Colonel J. C. Kemp, *The History of the Royal Scots Fusiliers 1919–1959* (Glasgow: Robert Maclehose & Co., 1963), online at http://rhf.org.uk/Books/KEMP'S%20History%20of%20the%20RSF%201919%201959.doc, accessed 20 September 2007; *Red Hackle* 71 (October 1938), Palestine supplement.
[85] Henniker, *Memoirs*, p. 63; Major-General J. F. C. Fuller, 'You Forget the Army', *Evening Standard*, 5 January 1934, Liddell 15/3/58, LHC. See also Fuller's *The Army in My Time* (London: Rich & Cowan, 1935), pp. 17, 62, 75–6, 96–9.

However predictable Fuller's attacks, he was by no means the only dissenting voice, and even those who advocated army sport were aware that it was by no means unproblematic.

The topicality of the issue is indicated by the subject for the *Journal of the Royal Artillery*'s prize essay in 1921–2: 'Sport. Its uses and abuses as an adjunct to the training of the Soldier'. Two winning essays, by Captain P. I. Newton and Captain D. J. R. Richards, both of the RGA, were published in the *Journal*.[86] Predictably they agreed that sport could promote fitness, morale, officer–men relations and *esprit de corps*, as well as preventing men from 'becoming bored with soldiering'. More originally, Newton thought that sport could help to produce more 'up-to-date' soldiers, self-improving and more educated and independent while still accepting of military discipline. Other ranks sport should be expanded to include game shooting, tennis and even golf – 'rather fanciful suggestions' perhaps but 'I would rather see the men playing [tennis] themselves, than cutting up their officers' courts because they cannot see why their officers should play, while they do not'. Both Newton and Richards, however, were well aware of the possible 'abuses' of military sport – particularly 'the Competition Bogey'. Both deplored what was apparently still a widespread habit of letting men off military duties for sports training (Newton cited cases where men had refused to form a team when this privilege was refused) and Richards suggested that higher authorities should intervene since the temptation was sometimes too much for commanding officers to resist. Clearly many of the problems of sport for other ranks identified in the Edwardian period had survived the Great War and the reorganisation of service sport. As in the Edwardian period, however, it was officers who became the main target of criticism. But while Edwardian critics had primarily objected to officers' preoccupation with equestrian sport, the main focus now was on the time and energy demanded to supervise and run the games of their men.

For the Indian Army, 'F.M.' complained in 1926 of 'Surfeit in Games and Starvation in Study'. In an average week, he suggested, a British officer would take part in three hockey matches, an afternoon's running or football, two or three polo sessions, 'tennis and golf to fulfil one's social obligations', plus Sunday cricket and weekday net practice. All this left little time either for military study or for keeping 'in touch with matters of Imperial and world-wide interest', though the 'great social

---

[86] Captain P. I. Newton, 'Sport: Its Uses and Abuses as an Adjunct to the Training of the Soldier', *Journal of the Royal Artillery* 48 (1921–2), 250–7; Captain D. J. R. Richards, 'Sport: An Essay', *Journal of the Royal Artillery* 48 (1921–2), 409–15.

The amateur era

upheaval' of recent years made it imperative for officers to understand them. Certainly in 1934 Field-Marshal Sir Philip Chetwode, departing the post of Commander-in-Chief India, deplored the 'brain slackness' of his officers.

> Their narrow interests are bounded by the morning parade, the game they happen to play, and purely local and unimportant matters. I have found men all over India who evidently scarcely read the papers, and are quite unaware of the larger aspects of what is going on in India around them, and still less of the stupendous events outside this country that are now in process of forming an entirely new world.

It is not clear, however, that it was lack of time that was the problem. Many officers, no doubt, like Henniker, were proud to possess 'three interests alone ... soldiering, polo, and shooting'. [87]

Criticism intensified in the late 1930s as the German threat became more apparent and rearmament a matter of urgency. In 1936 G.W. Lathbury, a lieutenant in the Oxfordshire Light Infantry, suggested that officers had too little time to train for war because one-third of their working life was spent maintaining the army as 'a glorified sports organization ... organizing the men's games, playing games with the men, teaching the men how to play games, and, worst of all, watching the men play games. Innumerable inter-company and inter-regimental competitions follow one another in never-ending array.' Lathbury argued that the benefits of games – in terms of physical fitness and officer–men relations – had been much exaggerated, and claimed that it was impossible to treat sport light-heartedly 'because many senior officers judge a regiment on its athletic record'. His solution was simple, if severe: all sporting competitions should be scrapped and games used purely as recreation.[88] Clearly this was never going to happen, but when in April 1938 the number of sports competitions in Aldershot Command was substantially cut back, the War Office found it necessary to issue a denial of 'certain reports which have appeared in the Press' that army sport was being 'drastically curtailed' because it was interfering with military training; on the contrary, they claimed, the aim was to *increase* sporting opportunities for the non-experts.[89]

Another critic, signing himself 'Lieut.-Colonel' and claiming thirty years' army experience, complained in 1937 that sport undermined

---

[87] 'F.M.', 'Surfeit in Games and Starvation in Study. An Indian Army Officer's Point of View', *Fighting Forces* 3 (1926), 486–8; Bond, *British Military Policy*, p. 68; Henniker, *Memoirs*, p. 92.
[88] Lieutenant G.W. Lathbury, 'Wasted Time in Regimental Soldiering', *Journal of the Royal United Service Institution* 81 (1936), 826–30.
[89] *Times*, 21 April 1938.

military efficiency in two ways. First, because regiments chose young officers for their sporting, rather than mental, abilities: he quoted an infantry officer as saying that, after family connections with the regiment, they looked 'for a man suitable to take charge of the regimental cricket, boxing, football, and so on'. Secondly, like Lathbury, he felt that the average infantry subaltern was now little more than 'a glorified games coach'. Pressure for better-educated and more professional officers, he argued, must come from within the army itself. 'So long as young officers are encouraged to think that by acting as games coach for a particular game they are justifying their existence we shall not make any progress towards getting a better educated type.'[90] Both of these criticisms seem to have had some basis in fact. Sporting ability was evidently still a route to success for young officers. Newton described it as a 'custom common in Army games' for a talented sportsman 'to step from one soft job into another, or worse still into some more or less important post with no other qualification for it'. And the 'games coach' role was officially recognised by Sandhurst which, 'realis[ing] the value to a unit, not only of a keen playing boy, but also of a young officer who understands the theory and organisation of games and sports', ran a compulsory course on it conducted by the physical training officer.[91]

The pressure for better-educated officers meant that the sporting preoccupations of the cadet colleges also came under renewed criticism in the mid-1930s. A precocious cadet whose critique of Sandhurst is among Liddell Hart's papers complained that 'the instructors should be more carefully chosen, more for their intelligence and less for their prowess at sports' (he also objected to being lectured to on the value of hunting).[92] The Massy Committee came to similar conclusions about Woolwich in 1938, finding 'too high a tendency to select officer instructors for their prowess at games and their smartness, rather than for their knowledge of the subjects in which they had to instruct or their qualifications as teachers'.[93] As much as the War Office's disinclination to fund the cadet colleges properly, this tendency to put sport before intellect fundamentally undermined official intentions of raising their courses to university level. An officer who graduated from Sandhurst in 1935 considered the course 'intellectually, an almost complete waste

---

[90] *Times*, 20 April 1937.
[91] Newton, 'Sport: Its Uses and Abuses', 256; 'Lecture given by the Assistant Commandant [Sandhurst] to the Junior Division of the Staff College, 12 Feb. 1930', Liddell 15/3/58, LHC.
[92] 'The RMC' (n.d., *c.* 1934–8), Liddell 15/3/58, LHC.
[93] Smyth, *Sandhurst*, p. 199. See Shepperd, *Sandhurst*, pp. 145–6 for sport at Woolwich in the 1930s.

of an important 18 months of his life. There were plenty of physical, but no mental challenges'.[94] Presumably in response to these criticisms, in the mid-1930s Sandhurst–Woolwich matches were cut down, and a 'tilting of the balance towards education and away from athletics' began.[95]

If service sport came under attack in the last years before 1939, for most of the inter-war period sport was central to service life, and particularly army life. Better organised and better funded than ever before, sport provided a necessary compensation for the inevitable tedium of peacetime soldiering. Yet the reduced size of the services meant that between the wars the forces became marginal to the national sporting life – as they were to national life as a whole. Sports where amateurism still held sway – track and field, equestrianism and amateur boxing, for example – could still find a place for military performers, sometimes even at Olympic level. Rugby union still had its service international players, though no service team could compete with the top club sides. But football and cricket were increasingly no-go areas: even in the FA Amateur Cup service teams were by no means as competitive as they had been before 1914. It would take another world war and the introduction of conscription to bring the services back into the mainstream of British sport. For that a pragmatic accommodation with professionalism would be required.

---

[94] French, *Military Identities*, pp. 71–2. For officer education between the wars see also D. French, 'Officer Education and Training in the British Regular Army, 1919–39', in G.C. Kennedy and K. Neilson (eds.), *Military Education: Past, Present and Future* (Westport, Conn.: Praeger, 2002).

[95] Smyth, *Sandhurst*, p. 192.

5 Soldiers, sailors and civilians

> I don't think that before I came to Hampshire, I had ever talked to a soldier. They were a race apart to me.
>
> William Pickford, Secretary of Hampshire Football Association in his 'Veterans' Column in the *Portsmouth Football Mail*[1]

David French has recently reminded us that one of the ideas behind the reforms of the army in the second half of the nineteenth century was to raise the status of the regular soldier in the eyes of the rest of the population.[2] French has pointed to the paradoxical attitudes held by many late Victorians who embraced a 'pervasive popular militarism' largely based on the role of the army and navy in constructing and maintaining the British Empire while at the same time having a very low opinion of those soldiers and sailors who made up the bulk of the other ranks in both services. While toy soldiers and *Boy's Own* stories of imperial adventures were popular among the young, the older generation were excited by the exploits of military heroes such as Gordon, Roberts and Baden-Powell. Moreover military parades and regimental bands were often part of public displays which appealed across class, generation and locality. But the ordinary soldier was often criticised for drunkenness, hooliganism and sexual immorality. Largely recruited from the lowest of the low, they were not respectable and often refused entry to parts of theatres, coffee shops, hotels and even some public houses. When R.J. Kentish joined the Royal Irish Fusiliers he thought the men 'giants' but noted that 'they had the ... habit of drinking an average of at least 15 pints of beer per man on pay-days', which 'occasioned much crime and a ... very long orderly room daily'.[3] The Cardwell-Childers reforms of the 1870s aimed to embed regular infantry regiments within their county and city communities

---

[1] Pickford Files (n.d., *c.*1903–5), Hampshire Football Association, Southampton (HFA). See also *Navy and Army Illustrated*, 12 October 1901.
[2] French, *Military Identities*, esp. pp. 234–8.
[3] Papers of R.J. Kentish, 98/12/1 RJK 2, Accounts of Early Life, IWM.

with the establishment of a permanent depot and a clear, geographical recruiting area. The hope was to develop a shared sense of identity between civilians and their local regiments. This chapter will explore the relationship between the development of modern organised sport in Britain between the 1880s and the 1930s and the growth and role of sport in the armed services. Sport was one of the ways in which regiments might mix more or less freely with their civilian neighbours. The aim of this chapter will be to look in more detail at these sporting relations, first at the local level, then at the level of the key national sporting organisations such as the Football Association, the Amateur Athletic Association and the Rugby Football Union. We will try to explore military influences on civilian sport and attempt to estimate the impact of civilian sport on the military.

As we have seen in the discussions around the setting up of the Army Sport Control Board, the attitude towards civilian sport at the War Office was often wary or even hostile. This attitude certainly pre-dated the war. In 1913, with the proposal for a central committee to organise army sport under consideration, Sir Edward Ward, Permanent Undersecretary at the War Office, describing himself as having been 'intimately connected for many years with sports and competitions in the Army', warned that it was

> not ... fully understood how complicated are the questions which arise in connection with the various games played by soldiers ... not so much as regards the soldiers themselves but from the watchful action of the various Associations which now rule over Athletics in this country. Hardly a match of any importance takes place without some question arising which has to be settled by authority, and on the manner in which these frequently difficult questions are decided rests a great deal of the reputation of the Army among the civil population for fairness in sports.

The Chief of the Imperial General Staff, Sir John French, agreed that 'the difficult questions which arise are within all our experiences'. The Assistant Adjutant General, R.J. Strachey, disliked the idea of an official director of army sport because he feared that it 'might result in embroiling the Army Council with all sorts of outside athletic and sporting leagues and associations, some of which are not perhaps very desirable company'. This warning – heavily marked in the margin and repeatedly referred to in later minutes – encapsulates War Office anxieties about involvement with civilian sports organisations.[4]

---

[4] 'Army Athletic Association', WO32/5492, TNA.

At regimental level, however, soldiers were often actively encouraged to participate in sport alongside civilians. Commanding officers were very influential figures who could promote or retard just about anything in their units. In the mid-1880s the CO of the Guards Depot at Caterham (Surrey) had the idea of arranging an athletic meeting at the barracks for both the 'amusement of the men under his command' and the 'edification of the residents in the neighbourhood'. It was held on Easter Monday and by the end of the decade was attracting 5,000 spectators. Some of the events were open to civilians as well as soldiers. When Private Musson won the 440 yards in 1889 he had stiff competition from the winner of the year before, a well-known local pedestrian named Potter.[5] In similar fashion Colonel G. E. Gordon gave a challenge cup 'with a view to encouraging football between the residents of Windsor and Eton and the Scots Guards' who were stationed there.[6] Sometimes civilian clubs were allowed to use military grounds. In 1883–4 on the Royal Engineers' ground at Chatham, three matches in the first round of the FA Cup were played simultaneously. The home teams were RE, Chatham and Rochester, and all lost![7] It was not long before military footballers were taking part in local civilian competitions, providing interest for people both inside and outside the barracks. An early example was provided by 1/Grenadier Guards, who won the Berkshire and Buckinghamshire Junior Cup, beating Abingdon in 1893. The team and 200 supporters, including the commanding officer Lord Arthur Wellesley, who had apparently seen nearly every match, travelled to Reading by special train. The team had been trained by Sergeant Instructor Pritchard, who was also the goalkeeper, and, playing 'a splendid passing game', won the match 3–0. Presenting the cup, the president of the Berks and Bucks FA, the Reverend Newhouse, noted that this was the first time a military team had won the trophy. What followed was a military version of the celebrations which had come to mark the homecoming of cup winners everywhere. The team and friends adjourned to the Tudor Arms (kept by an ex-Guards sergeant-major), where the cup was filled with 'something stronger than water'. When they arrived home at Victoria Barracks the welcome was strongest in the Sergeants' Mess, and the party did not break up until the 'football edition' of the local paper had been read and discussed. On the Sunday morning, the officers of the battalion together with 'a large number of civilians' inspected cup and medals which were on

---

[5] *Brigade of Guards Magazine* 2 (1889), 315.
[6] *Brigade of Guards Magazine* 4 (1891), 296.
[7] Brigadier-General W. Baker Brown, *History of the Corps of Royal Engineers vol. IV* (Chatham: The Institution of Royal Engineers, 1993 (1st printed 1952)), p. 374.

display in the Sergeants' Mess 'surrounded by vases of flowers'.[8] Some commentators began to think that sporting activities not only were one of the things that got a regiment noticed but also improved its reputation with the local civilian population. It was sometimes a matter of assertion rather than evidence. In the 1910–11 season 1/East Yorkshire Regiment, stationed in York, won the East Riding Cup, the York Senior and Junior Cups, the York Charity Cup and the championship of the York District League. The following season they won the Senior Cup again and were beaten finalists in the Army Cup.[9] All these triumphs brought favourable comment from local and national newspapers.

Even more impressive were the footballing achievements of the Royal Marine Light Infantry stationed at Gosport in Hampshire before the outbreak of the Great War. This was a football team which had had little success until it was taken over and managed by Sergeant Gowney, who had previously helped with the running of the Portsmouth Naval Depot eleven. How he turned a losing team into a winning one is not entirely clear but according to local newspapers he gained the support of the officers and introduced organisational improvements such that in his first season, 1906–7, the RMLI won the Portsmouth United Services League and reached the final of its Charity Cup.[10] The following year produced victories in both these competitions together with success in the First Division of the Portsmouth League and victory in the Portsmouth Cup, both primarily civilian competitions. RMLI were also beaten finalists in the Hampshire Senior Cup and competed in the national competition for the FA Amateur Cup. The team was obviously playing a lot of football. This successful run was continued in 1908–9, when the First Division of the Portsmouth League, with a membership of eleven teams, was won again, and second place was obtained in the United Services League First Division, while the reserve team – an interesting concept itself this – won the Second Division of the same competition, a feat repeated in 1909–10.

The 1909–10 football season was certainly the *annus mirabilis* for RMLI football with both the Army and FA Amateur Cups won, and it brought considerable notice to the unit both in and around Portsmouth and further afield.[11] The FA Amateur Cup was won without playing a match in Gosport. Rail journeys were made to Worthing, Bournemouth,

---

[8] *Brigade of Guards Magazine* 6 (1893), 218–21.
[9] *Lloyd's Weekly News*, 14 December 1913.
[10] *Portsmouth Football Mail and News*, 26 March 1910.
[11] What follows is largely based on the *Portsmouth Football Mail and News*, 19 March, 26 March, 2 April, 9 April, 23 April 1910, and B. Barton, *Servowarm History of the FA Amateur Cup* (Newcastle: Barton, 1984), esp. pp. 59–61.

Bromley and East London and although the semi-final was played in Portsmouth the final was in Bishop Auckland (Co. Durham). It all must have involved not only plenty of travelling but a good deal of rearranging of military duties. After the match at Bishop Auckland against the tough South Bank team from Teesside, which the RMLI won 2–1, Sergeant Gowney received a letter from the local MP congratulating both him and the team and emphasising the credit which such sporting triumphs brought not only to the team but also to the town of Gosport.[12] The RMLI team clearly had quite a few supporters among the local population. Many marines had attachments with local women and through them with the community more generally. Few supporters could have afforded the trip to Bishop Auckland, but a large crowd of Gosport people did go to nearby Aldershot on Easter Monday to see the Marines beat 1/Royal Irish Fusiliers to win the Army Cup. In the Portsmouth League there was quite a rivalry between the RMLI team and Gosport United: it was the RMLI–Gosport United fixture that attracted the record crowd that season.

In many respects this footballing triumph of the RMLI was the pinnacle of a process which had been in train for the previous three decades. It was also probably the most visible part of a much larger set of civilian–military sporting contacts. These athletic relationships can be most clearly seen in association football because it was the most popular winter sport both in civil society and among the other ranks in both the army and the navy. The number of civilian clubs had grown rapidly during the 1880s and beyond, many joining with others in a structure of county football associations all under the overall supervision of the London-based Football Association. After the formation of the Football League by twelve professional clubs in 1888 a plethora of other competitive combinations rapidly developed, the whole a stunning manifestation of the voluntary principle. In theory the services could have remained outside of this process and just played amongst themselves but in practice it was no surprise that many military teams chose to test themselves in a civilian sporting landscape that just could not be ignored. These developments were slower in the more rural south, west

---

[12] The RMLI were the last military team to win the FA Amateur Cup. As the two leading areas of amateur football, in London and north-east England, gradually developed both the infrastructure and playing side of the game their leading clubs would become too strong for most outsiders. 2/Coldstream Guards reached the semi-final in 1910–11, and HMS *Victory* (Portsmouth) had an encouraging run to the third round in 1934–5. The RAF officers training college at Cranwell (Lincolnshire) also entered the competition regularly in the 1920s and 1930s but had few victories. But by then most military teams had given up entering the leading football competition for amateurs in England because they were no longer competitive enough.

and east, and there the military could sometimes play an important part. In Colchester, for example, in the late 1880s, 1/Somerset Light Infantry 'revolutionised' the local style of football presumably by developing passing movements rather than merely kicking the ball forward and running after it, setting an example to the local teams against which they played. When the Sherwood Foresters joined the garrison they were good enough to persuade leading civilian teams such as Woolwich Arsenal, Luton, Stockton and the Casuals to play them. Their games often attracted mixed crowds of soldiers and civilians of more than 5,000.[13] In Ireland it was the military who often led the civilians to the football field. In Athlone, for example, between 1887 and 1905 of 241 football matches mentioned in local newspapers, 119, almost half, involved military teams.[14] As we shall see it was the example of the military which illustrated the potential for the establishment of professional football in Portsmouth in the 1890s.

We can see this relationship between civilians, soldiers and sailors in a little more detail reflected in the activities of the Hampshire Football Association. Hampshire was probably the most important military county in England, including as it did the garrison towns of Aldershot and Portsmouth and the port of Southampton. Hampshire was something of a late developer itself so far as football was concerned. The local FA only broke away to independence from Dorset in 1887 and in some respects local football, both civilian and military, grew together. The role of William Pickford was especially important. A Bournemouth journalist, he was secretary of the Hampshire FA for over twenty years. He used that influential position together with his regular football columns in local newspapers, especially the Portsmouth ones, to encourage service clubs to become part of local civilian football and to take part in both local league and cup competitions. Pickford also did much through his sporting columns in the local press and doubtless behind

---

[13] French, *Military Identities*, pp. 238–9, citing 'Bantam', 'Reminiscences of Colchester Garrison', *The Abbey Field Review. A Monthly Record of Garrison Life in Colchester* 1 (1926), 96–7. The Sherwood Foresters actually reached the semi-final of the first FA Amateur Cup competition in 1894, having beaten the Old Etonians 5–2 on the way.

[14] T. Hunt, 'The Development of Sport in County Westmeath, 1850–1905', unpublished PhD thesis, De Montfort University (2005), p. 262. See also N. Garnham, *Association Football and Society in Pre-Partition Ireland* (Belfast: Ulster Historical Foundation, 2004), pp. 18–21; N. Garnham, '"The Only Thing British That Everybody Likes": Military–Civilian Relations in Late Victorian Ulster', *Eire-Ireland* 41 (2006), 59–79, at 66–8. Garnham also notes dissatisfaction from civilians at the 'unfair advantages' (in terms of facilities and practice time) enjoyed by military teams. It was not long before Irish nationalists were campaigning against 'barrack-room British sports': see Garnham, *Association Football*, pp. 27–9; Hunt, 'The Development of Sport in County Westmeath', p. 279.

the scenes to help bring about the formation of the Royal Navy Football Association in 1904, which not only provided a stimulus to the development of the game in the senior service but also meant that another sector of organised football was brought under the overall control of the Football Association. Army players were chosen for the county team,[15] and soldiers were soon sitting on the Executive Committee and Council.[16] The minutes of the meetings were regularly permeated by encomiums to the excellent relations that existed between the Army FA and the Hampshire FA 'to the mutual benefit of both'.[17] By 1936 the Army FA would have representatives on the English, Irish and Scottish FAs and the County FAs of Devon, Dorset, Kent and Wiltshire as well as Hampshire.[18]

Of course there were occasionally problems but generally not serious ones. For example after military teams had won the Hampshire Junior Cup for three years in succession between 1895 and 1897 some of the civilian clubs argued that they should be removed from the competition because their players were older and stronger than the youths in the average junior club. Moreover opinion, both civilian and military, seemed to accept that in the 1890s servicemen, especially in the army, had more and better opportunities to practise than the average working-class young man, and were probably physically fitter.[19] William Pickford pointed out to the critics of military teams in the junior cup that the association always reserved the right to refuse the entry of any military

[15] One of the first was probably D. B. Hames, Royal Engineers (Aldershot), who played right back against Berks and Bucks in 1888. Minutes Exec. Committee, Hants FA, 3 March 1888, HFA.
[16] See Minutes of Council 18 October 1898, 10 February 1899, HFA.
[17] Royal Navy Football Association, Gen. Com. Minutes, 1 February 1907, RNSPT; *Portsmouth Football Mail*, 29 December 1906. See the Hampshire FA 18th Annual Report 1905. One example of RNFA willingness to help the Hampshire FA was provided by the 1905 semi-final of the Hampshire Senior Cup. When the RN Depot Portsmouth was drawn against Portsmouth FC reserves the match was to be played on neutral ground in Southampton, but when it was pointed out to the RNFA that a bigger crowd, and therefore an increase in revenue for the HFA, would be obtained if it was played in Portsmouth the sailors agreed to the change. Earlier the 11th Annual Report of Hampshire FA had noted that the Association's favourable financial situation was largely due to a match between Portsmouth RGA and Southampton and thanked by name Sergeant-Major Windrum, Sergeant Bonney (both RGA) and Quartermaster Sergeant Line of the Rifle Depot. It also mentioned that the Army Cup had been won again by 'a Hampshire club, the 2nd Battalion Gordon Highlanders of Aldershot', and that RA Portsmouth had won the Southern League Second Division and gained promotion to the First.
[18] Army Football Association Gen. Com. Minutes, 9 June 1936, AFA.
[19] See 'Football in the Army by a Footballer at Head-Quarters', *Navy and Army Illustrated*, 11 December 1896, and Callum Beg, 'The Soldier at Play', *Navy and Army Illustrated*, 5 November 1898. Pickford seems to have agreed in the early twentieth century. See his cuttings, mostly undated, HFA.

club deemed to be too strong but also emphasised that the average military football team was not stronger than the average junior one and that it would be a pity to shut the soldiers out. Perhaps these debates did lead to more careful monitoring. The AGM of the Hampshire FA in 1900 decided that three military teams, the RMLI, HMS *Excellent* and the Royal Engineers (Aldershot), *were* too strong for the junior cup competition and would therefore have to compete with the seniors.[20] As for the Senior Cup itself, by the early years of the twentieth century, military teams made up one-third of the total of sixty-three entries.[21] Many of the early winners of the Aldershot Senior Cup, presented by a firm of local printers, were military teams.

The military were also able to exploit the links between sport and philanthropy in ways which could only improve the reputation of sailors and soldiers with local civil society. Sport and charity had a long, if not always close, relationship and many examples of military involvement could be given. The United Services League in Portsmouth in 1899 organised a football match between teams drawn from members of the army and navy, with the proceeds going to charity. Both at Aldershot and at Colchester permission was regularly given by commanding officers and sporting bodies to play matches against local teams in order to contribute to local good causes. At Aldershot in 1908, for example, it was in aid of a fund for the poor children of the district and in Colchester in 1911 for the benefit of both military and civilian charities.[22] Nor did the initiative for such activities always come from the servicemen. In 1904 the Hampshire Football Association voted £5 from their benevolent fund set up to aid necessitous and injured players to a sailor who had broken his leg in a match and had, as a consequence, been discharged from the navy without pension or gratuity.[23] In 1912 Plymouth Argyle played two matches against navy teams to raise funds for the dependents of seamen killed in the A 3 and B 2 submarine disasters.[24]

Sport was, of course, a national phenomenon run by a growing number of specialist organisations, responsible for rules and standards of conduct and naturally concerned to bring all organised practitioners

---

[20] Hampshire FA Minutes, AGM 1900, HFA.
[21] Pickford Cuttings, undated, HFA.
[22] *Navy and Army Illustrated*, 13 May 1899; Army FA Com. Minutes, 14 January 1908, 17 April 1911, AFA.
[23] Pickford Cuttings, 3 September 1904, HFA. Later, in 1937, the Football Association made a grant of £20 from its National War Fund to Staff Sergeant-Major J. W. Whelan of the RASC, who had suffered the loss of a leg through injuries primarily caused by his football activities. Army FA Minutes, 26 January 1937, AFA.
[24] *Times*, 14 March, 21 November 1912. A 3 sank in February 1912 after being rammed by a gunboat; B 2 in October after colliding with a German liner.

under their control. There were obvious advantages to the sporting sailor and soldier of being part of this structure. Well before 1914 a significant sporting infrastructure of cricket and football grounds, swimming pools, athletic tracks and boxing halls had grown up. In contrast the facilities for sport in the army and navy, especially for the other ranks, were relatively underdeveloped before 1914. With military facilities in short supply regimental footballers often depended on permission to use civilian stadiums, particularly for important games. On their way to winning the Army Cup in 1898–9, 1/South Lancashire Regiment played on civilian grounds in Glasgow, Sheffield, Preston and Birmingham with the semi-final held at Villa Park. Semi-finals of the Army Cup were often held at civilian venues, as in 1908, when they were played on the grounds of Sheffield United and Woolwich Arsenal.[25] In 1912 the Committee of the AFA thanked Preston North End for allowing army cup-ties to be played on their ground at Deepdale with no charges nor expenses.[26] Similarly the inter-port match between Devonport and Chatham in 1905 was played on the ground of Plymouth Argyle, a young and struggling club to whom the Royal Navy FA paid a hiring fee of £5.[27] The good relations between the Association and the clubs were further illustrated in 1913, when it was agreed that the Honorary Secretary of the Devonport Port Management Committee be allowed to make a small presentation to the Argyle club 'in view of services rendered' to the RNFA.[28] The first Army v. Navy game played in 1905 at the Queen's Club in London was also the first occasion on which a reigning sovereign attended a football match. The annual Army–Navy match was often played on the grounds of professional clubs such as Chelsea and Portsmouth.[29] It must have been exciting for young servicemen to play and watch on what were becoming important features of the urban landscape. Free admission to civilian football matches was frequently allowed for soldiers and sailors in uniform. Many English county associations agreed to this privilege, although the Football Association of Wales stipulated that payment would be required for all ranks above sergeant. Interestingly the Scottish FA refused to allow it.[30]

[25] *Navy and Army Illustrated*, 20 May 1899; Army FA Minutes, 10 February 1908, AFA.
[26] Army FA Minutes, 29 January 1912, AFA.
[27] RNFA Minutes, 10 October 1904, RNSPT.
[28] RNFA Minutes, 10 April 1918, RNSPT.
[29] RNFA Minutes, 22 January 1906, 11 March 1908, RNSPT.
[30] The Hampshire FA charged men in uniform half price. Army FA Minutes, 3 November 1891, AFA.

Playing with civilians probably helped to improve service standards of sporting performance. Many army and navy officers were members of the National Sporting Club in London, and service boxers often fought on its largely professional programmes. Similarly footballers and rugby players were able to test themselves against leading, as well as local civilian, elevens and fifteens. The Army football team first played the Corinthians on Christmas Eve 1892 and soon had regular fixtures with county football associations such as London and Surrey. In the years between the wars matches were often played against professional clubs, and the Army FA seems to have had particularly cordial relations with both Aston Villa and Everton. These games were doubtless good preparation for the annual fixtures against the Belgian and French armies, which were begun after the First World War.[31] In the early days of the RNFA, so many games with good clubs ended in defeat that the Devonport Management Committee proposed that matches with 'first class clubs' should be abandoned until the play of sailors improved, but most other members of the RNFA Committee felt that the only way navy footballers would improve was to test themselves against better teams.[32]

Similar arguments were heard in service rugby circles. 1/Leicestershire Regiment's prowess at the sport was partly due to Leicester itself being a rugby-playing centre supporting a top club side but was also partly due to the arrival of Lieutenant W. C. Wilson, who had played for England against Scotland in 1907. The battalion team soon claimed to have 200 playing members. Many began to turn out regularly for top southern sides, which helped to produce a competitive regimental team.[33] On the other hand when William Wendell Wakefield tried to build up the RAF fifteen in the early 1920s by encouraging players to hone their game with good club sides he found himself opposed by other members of the RAF Rugby Union Executive. In some respects it was a persistent problem for a sport which mistrusted the pursuit of winning as the top priority.[34] As we have seen the RFU was keen to encourage rugby in the services, presenting the trophy for the Army Cup even though they frowned upon structures of competition themselves.[35]

---

[31] With the coming of the RAF, tournaments involving all three services began in several sports from 1921.
[32] Minutes RNFA, 30 April 1906, RNSPT.
[33] *Lloyd's Weekly News*, 24 August 1913; W. J. A. Davies, 'Service Rugby', *Fighting Forces* 13 (1936), 95–102.
[34] Wakefield and Marshall, *Rugger*, pp. 17–20.
[35] McLaren, *Army Rugby*, pp. 5–7.

It made sense for service sporting organisations to become affiliated to the civilian national governing bodies of sport. This can be clearly illustrated by looking at the case of association football, the most popular game among other ranks in all three services. Civilian clubs with ambition were always on the look-out for better players, especially after the legalisation of professionalism in 1885. As service football became both more organised and more public it was not surprising that their scouts began to look at service players with an eye to a bargain. Two related, but separate, issues rapidly emerged. One was the relatively straightforward one of who had first call on a service player – his unit or any civilian club to which he might be attached? The other was more complicated and, from the military point of view, more disturbing. Servicemen could buy themselves out of their engagements in the regular forces: what if football clubs provided the money for this transfer, collecting some of the better physical specimens and contributing, in however small a way, to the perennial problem of service recruitment?

The first of these issues was more or less easily and simply dealt with. Representative fixtures involving the Army or Navy and the Command or Fleet took precedence over the unit, and all of these came before the commitment to any civilian club. But there were often examples of these priorities being rejected by the players. The Army Football Association was pleased when Corporal Lease, 2/Coldstream Guards, was chosen to keep goal for England in an amateur international with France in 1910 but they were less enamoured of his preference to play for his regiment rather than to turn out in the army 'international', the title given to the annual match between the army in England and the army in Ireland.[36]

The approaches of civilian clubs to service footballers drew attention to a potentially more difficult issue. Other ranks soldiers were permitted to purchase their discharge on payment of a sum which varied between £18 and £35. A new recruit could claim his discharge at any time within three months of his attestation for £10.[37] The buying out of football-playing soldiers seems to have begun at least as soon as the Army Cup. In May 1890, for example, a football newspaper reported that two soldiers

---

[36] Army FA Minutes, 16 April 1910, AFA.
[37] See Lieutenant-Colonel S. T. Banning, *Administration, Organisation and Support Made Easy* (Aldershot: Gale & Polden, 1908), pp. 100–1; *King's Regulations for the Army* (1928), p. 126; and Colonel W. G. Lindsell, *Military Organisation and Administration* (Aldershot: Gale & Polden, 1932), p. 202. By this time the figure was £20 for the purchase of discharge within the first three months and a sum varying between £35 and £100 for all others. By 1955, the cost of purchasing discharge had been made dependent on age, rank, amount of service and qualifications. Major R. C. W. Thomas, *The Soldier's Pocket Book* (1955).

from 2/Black Watch, the first winners of the Army Cup, had signed for Preston North End. They had been spotted by the Preston manager as he refereed the Army Cup semi-final against 2/Gordon Highlanders.[38] Joseph Powell was bought out and signed by the Royal Arsenal after he had been seen playing for the Army against the Corinthians in 1892.[39] Linfield of Belfast paid £18 in order that Robert Hill could leave his regiment to play for them, but these speculations were not always successful. In 1893, the supporters of the Distillery football club of Belfast raised £21 to buy out a soldier from the Lancashire Fusiliers who had played for them and was about to go to India with the regiment but 'he degenerated into one of the lowest, if not the lowest loafer in the city' and was expelled from both team and club.[40] Cases such as these must have been part of the reason why the Army FA affiliated to the Football Association in 1894. But even military teams were sometimes prepared to poach good players from each other. After an Army Cup tie the officer in charge of the Lincolnshire Regiment team complained that a member of the opposition Highland Light Infantry had served in the Royal Artillery from which he was discharged by purchase on 30 October. The next day, 31 October, he played for the HLI in the match having never appeared in regimental orders or done any duties.[41] This led to the Army FA constructing a new rule forbidding a soldier who was transferred to, re-entered in or re-engaged in another corps from playing in the Army Cup team of the said corps for three complete years from the date of such transfer and the ruling that any team playing such a man would be disqualified from the competition.[42]

The FA were sympathetic to these problems of military football and were prepared to make changes in their rules which would both reassure the service football authorities and enable the FA to punish those civilian clubs who infringed them. An early attempt was to make civilian clubs obtain the consent of the officer in charge of a military club before making an approach to one of its players. If permission to play for them was granted it was valid for the current season only. This was further tightened by insisting that any approach had to be made to the service club giving at least seven days' notice. But of course it was the question of the purchase of a soldier's discharge by a professional club that the

---

[38] *Football Field*, 17 May, 14 June 1890.
[39] He would later captain the side from right back. See B. Joy, *Forward, Arsenal!* (London: Phoenix House, 1952), p. 10; *Woolwich Herald*, 4 December 1896. The Arsenal were especially keen on signing ready-made army players as they tried to build one of the first professional teams in London.
[40] Garnham, *Association Football*, pp. 70–1.
[41] Army FA Minutes, 30 April 1891, AFA.
[42] Army FA Minutes, 1 May 1893, AFA.

service football authorities found most irksome. The answer was FA rule 34, which laid down that a soldier while serving with the colours or a sailor with the fleet should not be registered as a professional player and that any player whose discharge was obtained by purchase could not be registered as a professional until twelve months had elapsed from his date of release.[43]

It is impossible to know how many times these regulations were breached, but it was an issue which surfaced regularly before 1914. The FA fined Leicester Fosse £5 in 1907 for having played Lance-Corporal Benfield of 1/Leicestershire Regiment without having given his club the requisite notice. Southampton were punished for a similar offence when selecting Private Gowers of the 16th Lancers to play for them, and Exeter City were fined 2 guineas after they had bravely asked Lieutenant E. C. Purchas of the 137th Battery Royal Field Artillery if he would turn out for them. An offence by Swindon Town was considered more serious and they were fined £10 for having approached Private Puddefoot of 2/South Lancashire Regiment to sign for them. He had just appeared in the army team which had played against an amateur XI captained by V. J. Woodward to mark the opening of the new Aldershot ground in 1914.[44] Larger fines were handed out to Manchester United and Bristol City. The former were fined for having approached and played Sergeant Rowe of 1/East Surrey Regiment in violation of FA Rule 37 and the latter were fined £50 for buying out Private Howarth, late of 2/Lancashire Fusiliers. The player was suspended for twelve months in 1914, and the FA Council were moved to notice 'the increasing number of offences relating to soldiers and sailors' and to warn member clubs that punishments would be tougher in future.[45] The Army FA were certainly severe on Sergeant C. E. McGibbon of the Army Ordnance Corps. Stationed at Woolwich, he was found to have received two guineas a week beyond what could be considered legitimate expenses while playing for Leyton FC. He was declared a professional and suspended from taking part in any football or football management.[46] It would be interesting to know how such details came to light.

[43] Army FA Minutes, 20 December 1909, AFA; FA Rules (1907 edition).
[44] Army FA Minutes 3 December, 16 December 1907, 23 June 1913, 23 June 1914, AFA. Benfield played for the Army against the Navy in March 1909, scoring two of their three goals. On leaving the army in 1910 he signed as a professional for Leicester Fosse, making his debut in a Second Division match against Hull City on 12 November 1910. In 1914 he was transferred to Derby County but rejoined the Leicestershire Regiment soon after the outbreak of war. Promoted to sergeant, he died from wounds in France on 20 September 1918. *Green Tiger*, April 1909, 57; *Leicester Mercury*, 8 November 2008.
[45] Football Association Council Minutes, 30 March 1914, Football Association, London.
[46] Army FA Minutes, 29 January 1912, AFA.

To those officers who gave up their time to running what was essentially the voluntary activity of service football, membership of the civilian national governing body provided some protection against the poaching of the better service players by civilian clubs. It is easy to see how men might be tempted not only by the money but also by the chance to play in a better standard of football.[47] Of course it was inevitable that membership of, and often strong personal links with, civilian sporting organisations did involve some of them with the complexities and controversies of civilian sport and in particular important definitions of who was an amateur and who was not.

This became of some importance in track and field athletics after 1880, when the Amateur Athletics Association, dominated largely by ex-public- or grammar-school boys and university graduates, tried to outlaw money prizes, competing against known professionals and even receiving money for teaching the sport. In 1882 the general committee excused a man who had run in the army a year earlier for some 'money prize of trifling value' but when discussing sports meetings of the Volunteers at which money prizes were often awarded they decided that anyone who had run for a money prize at any sports must be a professional and in April 1883 they disqualified a soldier.[48] This led to a special meeting to consider the proposition 'that N.C.O.s, private soldiers and sailors in Her Majesty's Army and Navy, who may have competed for money prizes only at regimental sports but who are in all other respects strictly amateurs, may be allowed to compete at all athletic sports held under the laws of the A.A.A.' Some of those present urged that the military were a separate case and there was even a petition presented at the meeting and signed by members of the Stock Exchange but to no avail. The motion was lost by sixteen votes to eighteen.[49] A similar motion was also lost in 1889.[50]

---

[47] Able Seaman O'Hara gave that as his reason for playing with Gosport United rather than his navy team. RNFA Minutes, 4 October 1912, RNSPT.

[48] Amateur Athletics Association Miscellaneous General Committee, 30 September 1882, 14 April 1883, Amateur Athletics Association records, Birmingham University Library Special Collections (BULSC).

[49] AAA Minutes of Special Meeting, 29 June 1883, BULSC. Engineering students at HMS Marlborough who had competed at the Portsmouth Garrison Sports were excused on the grounds of their ignorance, but it was made clear that the Portsmouth meeting would not be recognised in future. A letter was also sent out to 600 Volunteer Corps warning them of the consequences of continuing to award money prizes, and to the organisers of naval and military athletics meetings against awarding cheques on tradesmen to winners of their officers' races. AAA Minutes, 11 February 1888, 31 October 1890, BULSC.

[50] See AAA Minutes, AGM 24 March 1889, and General Meeting, 30 March 1889, BULSC.

By the AGM of 1903 it was recognised by some delegates that penalising the recipients of money prizes at purely naval and military sports meetings 'under the absolute control of the military' made little sense, but an attempt to exempt those in uniform from the rules of the AAA again failed to get a majority.[51] This had one especially noteworthy victim when Private Dunne, 1/Royal Irish Fusiliers, selected to represent Britain at the 1908 Olympics in the long jump and the triple jump, was subsequently turned down, the AAA 'having decided that as he had competed last year in the Army Championship for a money prize' he was not eligible to compete as an amateur.[52] Critics of the severity of the rule complained that in military centres such as Portsmouth or Plymouth amateur athletic meetings were almost impossible as most of the would-be competitors would be soldiers or sailors who had taken or at least competed for small money prizes at their own sports. Nothing, it seemed, could be done, although the AAA offered a paternalistic solution to the Army Athletic Association that the value of a prize awarded at a regimental sports day should be sent to the winner's commanding officer 'to enable him to expend it on some article for the winner, not a necessity and on the distinct understanding that no orders on tradesmen be given'. The fate of this proposal is unknown.[53] There was some relaxation at the end of the First World War: although there was no general amnesty for those who had competed for money prizes in wartime, the sin was forgiven if it had been committed while serving and competing in military events before 1 May 1919, and if no other AAA rule had been broken.[54] By this time several regimental athletic clubs had become affiliated directly to the AAA, the Army Athletic Association was represented at the AGM by Captain Wand-Tetley (who would represent Britain in both fencing and modern pentathlon in the 1920 Olympic Games and who in 1939 became Inspector of Physical Training), and even the athletic association of the Territorial Army had been allowed two representatives on the General Committee.[55] Interestingly though in 1942 the AAA sent a letter to all the service Sport Control Boards noting its decision that promoters of athletics meetings could send any

---

[51] AAA Minutes, AGM 18 April 1903, BULSC; *Times*, 20 April 1903. It was delegates from the north and midlands who opposed it because, they said, it would create an anomaly in that soldiers or sailors might win money prizes at a military meeting one day and run as amateurs the next, whereas a civilian who had run for and not even won a small money prize would be disqualified from competing with a military money prize winner.

[52] *Faugh-a-Ballagh* 7 (July 1908), 17–18.

[53] AAA Mins Gen. Com., 17 October 1914, BULSC.

[54] AAA Mins, 12 April 1919, BULSC.

[55] AAA Mins, 12 April 1919, 17 April 1920, 21 February 1932, BULSC.

money allocated for prizes to the Association who would use it to buy National Savings Certificates to be converted into prizes of equivalent value after the war, to be handed to the winners. It was agreed by the RAFSB to send the letter to all RAF sports associations though not before a comment had been made about the disappointment involved in receiving 'empty envelopes'.[56]

Army footballers were able to play a more significant role in what could be described as one of the last hurrahs of the more extremist wing of civilian amateurism. As service teams themselves were discovering by 1900 not only were professional football teams superior to most amateur sides but even in amateur football standards were rising especially among the largely working-class clubs of northern England. By 1906, all county football associations except those of London, Middlesex and Surrey had accepted professional clubs into membership. But many in the south were unhappy at the growing influence of the professional clubs not only in county FAs but within the Football Association itself. When in 1906-7 the FA Council insisted that each member association must admit professional as well as amateur clubs, attitudes hardened when the London FA agreed. Some clubs and individuals from the southern suburban and old boys sections began to talk of breaking away from the FA to secure, as they put it, the future of football as a sport. In effect they were rejecting what they considered to be some of the more unappealing aspects of popular culture. In April 1907, after a meeting called to oppose the FA's policy of compelling Middlesex and Surrey to accept professional clubs, the breakaway Amateur Football Association was formed.[57] The FA at once prohibited clubs and players in membership with it from playing against the rebels and this quickly had a serious impact on the quality of the fixture lists of many of those who joined the breakaway group, which was never as strong as its activists hoped or claimed. In these circumstances the question 'What would the Army do' was an important, probably a crucial one. Surely the Football Association would not insist that civilian associations and clubs must not play against army teams? It seems clear that the representatives of army football thought that too and tried to persuade the Football Association to exempt military footballers from the new regulations. The FA, however, declared a policy of no exemptions on which

---

[56] RAF Sport Control Board minutes, 4 June 1942, RAF Sport Control Board records, RAF Halton.
[57] The best account of the AFA's brief history is D. Porter, 'Revenge of the Crouch End Vampires: The AFA, the FA and English Football's "Great Split" 1907-14', *Sport in History* 26 (2006), 406-28. For a belated defence, see W. Greenland, *The History of the Amateur Football Alliance* (Harwich: Amateur Football Alliance, 1965).

the committee of the Army FA decided to 'take a poll of the Military Clubs in Great Britain, Ireland and the Channel Islands' to seek their views. They were obviously aware that some officers sympathised with the rebels and had social as well as sporting relations with many school, university and old boys' clubs. The necessity of 'adhering to one policy' was stressed. In the event a postal ballot and a general meeting saw 160 clubs vote in favour of continued affiliation to the Football Association and twenty-two against, sixteen of whom were willing to accept the views of the majority.[58]

There was some evidence of dissent. The 35th Brigade of the Royal Field Artillery were found to have played against rebel teams during the 1907–8 season and warned not to repeat it and 1/Queen's (Royal West Surrey) Regiment were actually expelled from the Army Cup for membership of the Amateur Football Association.[59] It was also clear that the split was causing a good deal of unease both amongst those who ran military football and in the civilian game especially among southern amateurs. For one thing the boycott worked. Even prestigious clubs such as the Corinthians, who had reluctantly joined the breakaway, found the quality of their fixture list much diminished, both at home and abroad. It brought a stop to those enjoyable and profitable summer trips to Europe where the leading national associations were members of the international body FIFA, who supported the FA in their struggle. The Corinthians went twice to Brazil, who had yet to join what was to become the football's world governing body.[60] It was inevitable that as time went on there would be more unease inside the military football world and attempts to solve a problem which they did not want. By 1911 there were moves to get negotiations started between the Football Association and the breakaway faction in which the Army FA played a significant part.

On 3 March 1911, Major R. McCalmont (Irish Guards), the Honorary Secretary of the Army FA, wrote to the treasurer of Oxford University FC suggesting that the military might be able to broker a settlement. It is hard to believe that Frederick Wall, Secretary of the FA, did not

---

[58] Army FA Minutes, Special Meeting 9 August 1907, 27 August 1907, AGM 20 April 1908, AFA. The Royal Navy FA agreed as it was 'always considered expedient' to stick with the army on football matters. Minutes RNFA Emergency Committee, 21 July 1908, RNSPT. See the resolution of the Household Brigade FA that it was 'strongly of opinion that ... it is necessary for the Army FA to remain affiliated to the Football Association ... their only protection against professionalism' (Army FA Minutes AGM, 20 April 1908, AFA).

[59] Minutes Army FA Committee, 10 May 1911, AFA.

[60] See P. Lanfranchi et al., *100 Years of Football: The FIFA Centennial Book* (London: Weidenfeld and Nicolson, 2004).

know that these discussions were going on. At a committee meeting of the Army FA on 10 May 1911 it was proposed by Colonel Couper, the Inspector of Army Gymnasia, and seconded by Captain Kentish, 1/Royal Irish Fusiliers, that as it was not the Army FA's quarrel, the time had now arrived when the Army FA should be conducted as 'a separate and independent association'. McCalmont and Paget Tomlinson produced an amendment which deserves quotation:

> The time has now arrived when the differences of opinion, with which the Army FA has no concern, but which prevent their clubs from playing with clubs of the Amateur Football Association, should be adjusted; but that in the meantime the Army FA shall for the present remain affiliated to the Football Association Limited, for the benefit of the units in the numerous small stations where there are no Amateur FA clubs, and for the protection of Army players against professional clubs.[61]

At the Annual General Meeting on 1 June 1911 it was this amendment that was carried by sixteen votes to three and as a substantive motion, passed with only one dissenting hand. The Committee then decided that the support for the original resolution was insufficient to merit it being put to a vote of the membership.[62]

McCalmont later obtained the approval of the Committee for resolutions to be moved by him at the next Council meeting of the Football Association suggesting the appointment of a small commission with representatives from both sides and a neutral chairman to work out a basis for a settlement. The Football Association insisted that the rebels make the first move.[63] Of course it wasn't only the opinion of the military which counted. By 1912 the weakened condition of southern amateurism's elite had prompted particular individuals and clubs such as Cambridge and Oxford Universities to push the militants of the Amateur Football Association towards a resolution of the dispute. But what was demonstrated to activists and members alike was that the national organisation could only be influenced if you were in it.[64]

In the letter to the Honorary Treasurer of Oxford University FA, McCalmont had emphasised that the service associations had stuck to

---

[61] Minutes Army FA, 10 May 1911, AFA.
[62] It is interesting that of the representatives of twenty-four units who were present at the AGM, six were NCOs.
[63] Minutes Army FA, 13 November, 4 December 1911, 29 January 1912, AFA.
[64] The final outcome involved the Amateur Football Association retaining its identity and gaining four seats on the FA Council, forming a wing of purist amateurs which would have more influence on the FA inside it than they would have done as exiles. See Porter, 'Revenge of the Crouch End Vampires'.

the FA 'for the sake of the rank and file'.[65] The *Athletic News* was more outspoken. 'The Army had remained loyal to the FA due to the overwhelming vote of the private soldier and he voted as he did because FA clubs were mainly recruited from his own class ... whereas AFA clubs were composed largely of men who would not sit at the same table with him which was a hard saying in a democratic age'.[66] This was a clear recognition of the importance which football had attained among the other ranks and it was echoed after the First World War by a not dissimilar intervention. The occasion was the well-publicised action of certain public schools giving up association football in favour of rugby union. It provoked some excited letters to the *Times*, mostly, though not all, in favour of the change. The Army FA Committee discussed this at some length at their meeting on 4 February 1919, and the result was a letter sent to the headmasters of the public schools. Although the matter was in many respects a domestic one it was not entirely so,

> owing to the fact that the Public Schools supply a big percentage of the future Officers of His Majesty's Army; and if the policy referred to became general ... the young Officers of to-day and to-morrow will join their regiments knowing nothing whatever of the game that figures so largely in the life of the private soldier which would be injurious to the interests of the game in the army.[67]

The heads were asked to take these points into consideration, though it is not clear that the Army FA succeeded in making much impact.

Of course there was always the possibility that military sport and military sportsmen would be seduced by the challenge and the glamour that became attached to its civilian counterpart. From the 1880s sport was growing rapidly in size and significance in both the civilian and military worlds and it was inevitable that the one would want to test itself against the other. It was probably also inevitable that standards in civilian sports would outstrip those in the army and navy as investment expanded and competitive structures became more demanding. If service sportsmen wanted to improve they needed to test themselves against the best, and this, together with the publicity that sport was attracting, especially football, also provided its own temptations. But there would be a price to be paid for too much sporting ambition and

---

[65] Major McCalmont to C.N. Jackson, 3 March 1911, Oxford University Association Football Club MSS, Dep.d.822–824, Bodleian Library, Oxford. We are grateful to Dilywn Porter for this reference.
[66] *Athletic News*, 14 February 1910.
[67] Minutes Army FA Committee, 4 February 1919, AFA; *Times*, 26 February, 1 March 1919. By the 1930s the officer training college at RAF Cranwell found it impossible to field more than one football team because there were only twenty cadets in residence who were regular players. *Times*, 19 October 1934.

the complexities which it produced when a military team tried to conquer a civilian sporting world. The example of the Royal Garrison Artillery Football team from Portsmouth is especially instructive not only because it shows what could be done but also because it demonstrated the limits of what service players could achieve.

If the south of England was relatively slow to be infected by the late Victorian virus of football as spectacle, when it did arrive it was the military who were partly responsible for bringing it and most notably in Portsmouth. There was a team calling itself Portsmouth Town by 1891 and in that year it met 1/Oxford Light Infantry in the final of the local cup competition. Three times they played and three times the matches were drawn, each game reported in detail in local newspapers and each attracting several thousand spectators. The eleven from Portsmouth won at the fourth time of asking, but attempts to elevate it to professional status failed. This left a gap for an elite football team which would catch the imagination of Portsmouth's developing football public, and for almost five years a team of soldiers filled it.

The origins of the Royal Garrison Artillery side are slightly obscure. There were several company artillery teams in the Portsmouth area in the 1890s and several of the players who would later turn out for the Portsmouth Garrison played for them. The 15th Company at Fareham, for example, had a good team, and the Royal Artillery team based at the Gosport Depot which reached the Army Cup Final in 1894 contained eight players who would later play for Portsmouth RGA,[68] and most of them were in the team which won the Army Cup in the following season. It is not clear what happened next. There appears to have been some footballing rivalry between the Fareham Company and the Depot team in Portsmouth which may have been partly the result of the latter unit persuading some of the players of the former to transfer to them. Certainly as the Portsmouth RA team appeared to go from strength to strength there were rumours about their status and talk in some journals of their being a 'manufactured team'.[69] Were they becoming footballers first and soldiers second?

They certainly had five remarkable seasons playing a level of football and making a mark not only in the Artillery and Army Cups but in both local and national civilian competitions that was unequalled among military teams. The Army Cup was won in 1894–5, but only twenty-one other games were played that season. The following season thirty-seven

[68] It did not prevent them losing the cup final to 2/Black Watch 7–2.
[69] *Athletic News*, 9 December 1895; *Truth*, 14 November, 5 December, 19 December 1895. See also K. Smith, *Glory Gunners: The History of Royal Artillery (Portsmouth) FC* (Bognor Regis: K.S. Publications, 1999), pp. 29–31.

matches were played as the semi-finals of the Army Cup was reached together with the final of the FA Amateur Cup on the way to which the Gunners knocked out the holders Middlesbrough, the furthest distance which the club had travelled to that point. Moreover their players began to be chosen, not only to represent the army – five of them were in the team which lost 4–1 to the Corinthians at the end of 1896 – but also by the Portsmouth Football Association. Six of the artillery team played for the Portsmouth FA XI which beat the Brighton Association 5–0 at the end of 1895. Due to their long runs in two or three cup competitions the team was playing two cup-ties a week for two months and all this excitement was reported in the local newspapers and reflected in the crowds of several thousands of soldiers, sailors and mostly civilians who turned up to watch a team that was clearly being thought of as representative of the town of Portsmouth. In 1896 they were the first Portsmouth team to win the Hampshire Senior Cup and on their return to Portsmouth Town station they were met by the men and band from their Cambridge Barracks and congratulated by Colonel Wynne and the officers to the strains of 'See the Conquering Hero Comes'. There was one significant piece of intelligence attached to reports of their FA Amateur Cup semi-final against Shrewsbury at Reading. The Artillery players had prepared for it by a short stay at Margate.[70]

The triumphant progress for the team continued in 1896–7. Thirty-four matches were played in a season which began in September and ended in April. The team had now become members of the Hampshire Senior League, which provided them with their first regular set of fourteen fixtures and in which they finished runners-up to Cowes. The Army Cup was won for a second time, as was the Portsmouth Senior Cup, and they were now running a reserve team. After the victory at Aldershot the team and supporters returned to Portsmouth in two long trains and were greeted, as was now to be expected, by the RA band and by many well-wishers who carried the captain of the team on their shoulders through the rain-doused streets. It was in this season that they became direct members of both the Hampshire Football Association and the national FA itself. There were some critics, including a writer in the *Daily Chronicle* who after the Artillery had beaten the Old Etonians in the first round of the FA Amateur Cup thought that 'few teams would have given as unworthy a display as the winners'.[71] There were similar criticisms of their later match in the competition in which they were defeated by the Casuals.

---

[70] *Ibid.*, p. 38.
[71] *Daily Chronicle*, 12 February 1897; *The Field*, 13 February 1897, 20 February 1897.

Figure 12. 'Two gunner football champions': Private Reilly (goalkeeper) and Sergeant Coleman (right wing) of the Royal Artillery Portsmouth football team.

The Portsmouth soldiers fulfilled forty-seven fixtures in the 1897–8 season when there was so much football to be played that the club did not enter for the FA Amateur Cup. It did reach the final of the Army Cup again although it lost to 2/Gordon Highlanders. But the real reason for the expanding fixture list was the growing ambition of those who ran the club: they had applied for a place in the Southern League. They were not admitted to the First Division but were accepted into the Second, where they joined one other military club, the Royal Engineers Training Battalion based at Chatham. The other ten clubs were civilians with a mixture of moderate amateurs and the odd semi-professional probably thrown in. Most of them were no match for the Portsmouth Gunners, who won the championship with the loss of only two games. Moreover following a play-off between the top two in the Second Division and the bottom two in the First, RA Portsmouth won promotion to the top division of the Southern League, a group of clubs which included the ambitious elite of southern professionals apart from Woolwich Arsenal. Teams like Southampton, Bristol City, Millwall Athletic and Tottenham Hotspur would bring a much more serious challenge to the apparently all-conquering soldiers from Portsmouth. How had a group of soldier footballers risen to such athletic heights?

First, and probably most important, they were well managed. In 1895 professional football had only had a short history and there was no pool of experienced ex-players with specialist knowledge about this emerging spectacle. A photograph of the RA team who won the Army Cup in 1895 included Sergeant Bonney as secretary, Sergeant-Major Windrum as trainer and Lieutenant Haynes as treasurer. Four officers were apparently on the committee, but it is clear that it was the two NCOs, Bonney and Windrum, who effectively managed the club. Bonney was thought by the leading football authority, William Pickford, to be the key figure, a master tailor by trade who knew a good player when he saw one, an intelligent man and 'straight'.[72] Windrum was also impressive. He would later be commissioned and posted to Plymouth, where he would become one of the first directors of the newly professional Plymouth Argyle. Both had been very active in the administration of football. Bonney was a vice-president of the Portsmouth FA and on the committee of the Hampshire FA. Windrum was a vice-president of the latter body and also president of the Portsmouth United Services League.[73] It is not surprising that senior NCOs were attracted to football as they were not far removed both economically and socially from those clerks and skilled workers who made up the bulk of its support in civil society in its early days.[74]

They were obviously fortunate in having a collection of good players from the start, but they also made shrewd attempts to strengthen the side with the transfers of Sergeant Coleman from Shoeburyness and Woodard from Yarmouth. Even more interesting was the move of Clarke, a promising forward who played for local team Southsea Rovers, who was allegedly given a commission in the Royal Artillery and was expected to play regularly in 1898–9. Two of the other players would be chosen to play for Ireland. The team also trained regularly and their

---

[72] See Pickford Cuttings, 3 December 1904, HFA.
[73] See Gibson and Pickford, *Association Football*, vol. IV, p. 72.
[74] There are other examples of NCO interest in the running of clubs. When Lancaster City issued a share prospectus in 1905 two of the named directors were a sergeant and a quarter master sergeant from the King's Own Royal Lancashire Regiment. Clubs issued such a prospectus when they became limited companies and wanted to sell shares to the public. 'Lancaster Association Football Club Ltd', BT31/11270/86164, TNA.

fitness and the opportunity to practise clearly gave it the edge over less-organised opponents. As the club had grown in stature, Secretary Sergeant Bonney received help from Quarter Master Sergeant Manley to cope with the extra work now involved. Moreover the performance and reputation of the team attracted increasing numbers of spectators to the Men's Ground in Portsmouth which had to be improved in order to provide more appropriate accommodation.[75]

The team struggled in the tougher competitive atmosphere of the First Division of the Southern League. It is possible that relegation might have been avoided had not more serious misfortune befallen the Artillery footballers. A good run in the Army Cup was accompanied by success in the FA Amateur Cup with the semi-final apparently reached after a 3–1 win at Harwich and Parkeston. Portsmouth RA had made no secret of the fact that, although amateurs, they used what opportunities service life offered to take their training seriously. In 1895, as we saw, they had prepared for their semi-final by spending a week at Margate. Before playing at Harwich, they enjoyed a week's training up the coast at Aldeburgh, staying at the White Lion Hotel. But after their defeat, the Harwich club protested to the Football Association that, as this had not been paid for by the players themselves, it made them in effect, professional and in breach of law 26. The FA Amateur Cup Committee agreed, expelling the gunners from the competition and awarding the match to Harwich. Not surprisingly, the RA team appealed against the decision which was heard before a special delegate meeting of the Football Association, attended by over 120 people. But a majority confirmed the original decision, and the Portsmouth team were suspended for professionalism.[76]

Some military critics felt that the Portsmouth RA managers had been sailing too close to the wind. A writer in the *Household Brigade Magazine* thought that it would be 'a salutary lesson to many clubs who have long skirted along the treacherous edge of professionalism ... When we hear of teams including cigars and brandy and sodas among their "necessary expenses", we are driven to the conclusion that cupboard love is undermining affection for true sport.'[77] This severe opinion was not shared by two of the most vigorous supporters of amateurism in the country namely the *Field* and *Pastime*. Both made similar points, that no one had charged the players with receiving 'remuneration or consideration' for playing. There was a wide

---

[75] Smith, *Glory Gunners*, pp. 60–1, 66, 74.
[76] *Hampshire Telegraph*, 15 April 1899; *Portsmouth Evening News*, 13 March, 10 April, 29 April 1899.
[77] *Household Brigade Magazine* 2 (1899), 287.

distinction between the payment of players and the payment of training expenses or indeed the provision of entertainment. Moreover the FA rule was vague on the subject, talking of 'necessary' payments, and the insecurity generated by the decision is clearly shown by the President of the Football Association informing the Artillery players that they would be justified in applying for reinstatement as amateurs at the earliest opportunity.[78]

The club was relegated from the Southern League and never recovered its former glory. The players were reinstated as amateurs, but several turned professional on leaving the service. Rather surprisingly the affair does not appear in the formal agenda of the Army Football Association. During the winter of 1899–1900 a series of discussions with local business and sporting interests led to the formation of the professional Portsmouth Football Club with Sergeant-Major Windrum joining the board of directors. Sergeant Bonney left the army at the end of 1903, first becoming a director, and then being appointed manager of the club, a post he held until 1910. The *Portsmouth Evening News* provided a stirring epitaph for a soldiers' team which had captured the attention of civilian as well as military supporters:

The team has done so much for the Association game in Portsmouth and has been providing several thousands of people almost weekly with interesting and exciting contests against the crack professional teams of the South. Next year it will probably have to take a back seat before the new Portsmouth professional team but they will not be forgotten ... as a unique Army team, a collection of brilliant players ... and as the club which made the Association game in Portsmouth.[79]

All of this illustrates the dangers for military sportsmen in becoming too closely involved with the relentless spectacle of civilian professional sport. The Olympic Games would prove to be another matter, although there were some War Office anxieties early on. The fact that the British

---

[78] *Field*, 11 March, 15 April 1899; *Pastime*, 15 April 1899. Writing ten years later, Gibson and Pickford thought it a trivial breach of the rules and a punishment that didn't fit. Gibson and Pickford, *Association Football*, pp. 68–9. The expenses totalled £60 and included payments for wines, cigars, carriage drives and billiards and a paid trainer who had been engaged at 32s. for the week.

[79] *Portsmouth Evening News*, 7 January, 10 April 1899. William Pickford talked of a 'brilliant chapter in military football', Pickford Cuttings, 3 December 1904, HFA; *Athletic News*, 14 March 1910. There was a slightly mysterious footnote to the Portsmouth (RA) affair. In 1904 several players were suspended by the Army FA, which expressed dissatisfaction with the way the affairs of the club had been conducted. It was severely cautioned and warned as to its future management which must be placed under the direction of a senior officer. Two of the players remained barred from 'playing or managing' until they told the Committee the 'name and address of the author of the bogus message sent from Muswell Hill'. Minutes Army FA, 29 August 1904, AFA.

Olympic Association was founded in May 1905 at a meeting held at the House of Lords which selected Lord Desborough as its first chairman gives a clear indication that it was an upper-class organisation from the start. You were never elected to the BOA but nominated or co-opted. It would not be long before the BOA Council was decorated with retired high-ranking military officers which by 1924 would include as vice-presidents Admiral of the Fleet Earl Beatty, Field-Marshal Earl Haig and General Sir Charles Harington, while its Honorary Treasurer was a lieutenant-colonel and its Honorary Secretary a retired brigadier-general. The Council included representatives from all three service sport control boards as well as the inspectors of physical training from army, navy and air force. British equestrian teams were packed with military men, and when the Amateur Athletic Association decided to compete in the Antwerp Olympics in 1920 the special committee which was formed to choose the team included one representative from each of the three services.[80]

For some time before 1914 the War Office had not been able to agree who should meet the expenses of officers competing in international horse shows, but in 1910 the War Office Council decided, following representations by the Swedish Minister in London and endorsed by the British Foreign Office, that the 1912 Olympic Games in Stockholm should be officially recognised and that officers should be permitted to participate in riding competitions, 'their attendance being regarded as military duty' and therefore 'regulated travelling expenses' would be allowed. This was the first occasion on which the British Army had been officially represented at the Olympic Games.[81]

Meanwhile Baron de Coubertin had been seeking the support of the military leaders of all the leading nations to introduce a modern pentathlon. This bore little resemblance to the event run in ancient Greece to find the best all-round athlete but rather was overtly military in its concept as it was designed to portray the task of a military hero who had to deliver a message through enemy territory. The competition took four days to complete and involved a 5,000 metre cross-country horse ride, fencing with an épée, pistol shooting, a 300 metre swim and a 4,000 metre cross-country run. Nearly all the British competitors were

---

[80] Minutes AAA, 31 May 1919, BULSC.
[81] *Times*, 6 April 1912. For more detail see 'Minutes of Proceedings and Précis Prepared for the Army Council for 1913', WO 163/18, TNA. A team of four officers was sent and travelling expenses allowed for each officer, two horses and one groom to and from the point of disembarkation in Sweden. See also M. Polley, '"No Business of Ours"? The Foreign Office and the Olympic Games, 1896–1914', *International Journal of the History of Sport* 13 (1996), 96–113.

cavalry types until well after the Second World War.[82] Interestingly, Lieutenant-General Sir Brian Horrocks noted in his memoirs that after receiving selection for the modern pentathlon team for the Paris Olympics in 1924, the four young officers were 'struck off all duties in order to train' for four months.[83]

The strength of the military influence with some of the highest echelons of British sport is most clearly illustrated by the career of Reginald John Kentish. Born in 1876, he was an active games player at Malvern school. In 1894 he failed the exam for Sandhurst; he had to make use of a crammer the following year and even then only just scraped through. In 1897 he joined the Royal Irish Fusiliers for whom he played football, being the first staff officer to appear in an Army Cup final.[84] We have already noticed his work as secretary of the Army FA and his pioneering efforts to extend and develop the facilities for sport at Aldershot begun before 1914, a task which was extended to other commands in 1919–20. From 1921 to 1925 he was secretary of the British Olympic Association and he was commandant of the British team at the Games in Antwerp in 1920 and Paris in 1924. He served on the International Olympic Committee for thirteen years from 1920 and was committed to the idea that the Olympic movement was a force for better international understanding in the world. Having retired from the army with the rank of brigadier-general in 1923, he embarked on what he would later claim to be his most important work: the setting up of the National Playing Fields Association, the purpose of which was to raise funds to provide grounds for sport and recreation for all and not only the well-off. It was an organisation of the great, the good and the rich and has flourished to this day. The band of the Grenadier Guards played at its inaugural meeting in 1925, at which Kentish became the Honorary Organising Secretary.[85]

---

[82] The first time Britain won the team event in 1976 the only military member was Jim Fox, a sergeant in the Royal Electrical and Mechanical Engineers (REME). He had also taken fourth place in the individual event in 1972, the best placing by a Briton up to that time.

[83] Lieutenant-General Sir Brian Horrocks, *A Full Life* (London: Collins, 1960), p. 66. Only officers were allowed to compete in Olympic equestrian events, a rule not overturned until 1956. As the French president of the Fédération Equestre International said, 'if non-commissioned officers were allowed to compete, how could the social standard be maintained? What would happen at the receptions?' Ansell, *Soldier On*, pp. 137–8.

[84] *Athletic News*, 28 March 1910.

[85] He left the post two years later because the work had increased so much. He was offered £600 a year to continue but said he did not wish to become a paid servant. Kentish Papers, Box 1 File 1 98/12/1, IWM.

Apart from war itself, sport was one of the activities of the services that the media most liked to write about, and the civilian press usually presented the military sporting world in the most positive of lights. We have already noticed that local papers in garrison towns often featured soldiers' sport, but the specialist sporting press such as the *Field*, *Sportsman*, *Sporting Life* and *Athletic News* also had their sections on military sportsmen and their doings. The *Field* had regular reports of matches and races both from home and abroad, some of the latter clearly sent in by the serving participants. Some regiments actively encouraged the media: *Sporting Life* commented approvingly on the 'accommodation for the Press' provided at the 1908 Royal Irish Fusiliers Athletic Meeting, 'the first battalion to make such provisions in the Aldershot Command'.[86] In the Edwardian years the Army Football Association made a point of notifying papers like the *Sportsman* and *Sporting Life* of the outcome of the draws for the various rounds of the Army Cup. By 1910 the *Athletic News* had a regular column entitled 'For Soldiers and Sailors' which not only registered the state of play but picked out the particular sporting hero such as the Navy's Lieutenant G. H. D'Olyon, who had not only been the pick of the navy's 'rugger' team in a recent match with United Hospitals but had trained and played full-back for the football team of HMS *Dido* in their Navy Cup victory over HMS *Superb*.[87] Even the *Times* often reported army football and rugby cup final games in considerable detail.

The new journalism also saw in service life a chance to increase its range of more or less specialist periodicals. In 1895 George Newnes brought out the *Navy and Army Illustrated*, a sixpenny magazine 'Descriptive and Illustrative of Everyday Life in the Defensive Services of the British Empire' edited by Commander Charles N. Robinson, RN, which specialised in high-quality photographs.[88] Promoting itself as an advertising medium, it claimed that it was 'found in every Service Mess and Club, [and] appeals directly to a wealthy and leisured class of readers'.[89] Though read by the services, it also aimed at a civilian audience. In 1898 it described itself as 'devoted to popularising the services', and when it was modernised and reissued in May 1906 it claimed its purpose was to familiarise 'the public with the everyday sights and scenes,

---

[86] *Faugh-a-Ballagh*, October 1908, 6–8 (also quoting from the *Aldershot News* and the *Broad Arrow*).
[87] Minutes Army FA, 14 March 1911, AFA; *Athletic News*, 31 January 1910.
[88] *Navy and Army Illustrated*, 1 December 1895. Originally published fortnightly, it soon became a weekly. It merged with the *King* in March 1903 and folded in December 1905, reappearing in 1906 as the *Navy and Army*.
[89] Advertisement in *Hart's Annual Army List* (1900).

the work, the play, the inner life and the personnel of our great Fighting Services', to show 'the sports, amusements and pastimes, as well as those pursuits which form the more striking part of their profession, their everyday life, the functions and ceremonies which they attend, their habitations afloat and ashore, the social side of their existence'.[90] It was certainly effective in publicising the sporting life of the services: in the decade after 1895 it must have published well over 100 pieces on service sports from cycling and cricket to racquets and rowing. The photographs were novel and particularly impressive in providing both an ordinary and extraordinary snapshot of life in uniform at home and abroad. An example from 1896 was a group of pictures of 2/King's Own (Royal Lancashire Regiment), stationed at Plymouth and emphasising, as well as the officers and the battle honours of the regiment, a group of the oldest and youngest members of the battalion, and the winners of the inter-company football championship.[91] The *Navy and Army Illustrated*, presumably with an eye to recruiting, portrayed service life as respectable, modern, professional – and fun. Focusing on service sport was one of the key ways in which it did so.

Most of the papers which we have been discussing had fairly small circulations. A popular Sunday newspaper such as *Lloyd's Weekly News* was a very different matter. *Lloyd's* was the first newspaper to sell one million copies a week and on 30 March 1913 it began a series entitled 'Famous Sporting Regiments' which started with the Grenadier Guards and ended with the Welch Regiment on 3 May 1914. These long articles appeared on one of the pages devoted to sport. They were regularly illustrated by a picture of some notable champion and often featured exceptional items of a regiment's sporting history while clearly trying to include a mention of most sports and their leading contemporary protagonists. The style was admiring and uncritical. As the writer said of the Grenadier Guards,

If the officers have done well, the other ranks have done even better. The regiment stands among the best in football as played in the Army, the 2nd Battalion team having for several years past been pre-eminent, winning the Army Cup in 1904–5 beating the famous team of the 'Sappers' when they were on the top of their form in the final. Their other football successes have been very numerous, for they have won the Household Brigade Cup four times in eight years, and … the Hampshire Senior Cup, the Aldershot Senior Cup, the Championship of the Aldershot League, the Aldershot Charity Cup, besides several other trophies in London and Windsor.[92]

[90] Advertisement in *Pall Mall Gazette*, 7 July 1898; *Navy and Army*, 26 May 1906, iii.
[91] *Navy and Army Illustrated*, 21 August 1896.
[92] *Lloyd's Weekly News*, 30 March 1913.

The series did not end until May 1914, by which time fifty-seven regiments had been featured, providing enough free publicity to satisfy even the War Office let alone any local commanding officer. Regimental sports achievements were catalogued both at home and abroad, many articles ending with a variation on a regular theme. As the writer said of the Essex Regiment,

> behind the sport which is so keenly followed ... is the one great aim and object of all – to fit all ranks by a healthy outdoor life and a clean mode of living, for their great responsibility, that of being ever ready to take the field in defence of King and Country, and in this the men of Essex are in no way behind their comrades of the British Army.[93]

In more concrete ways too, service sportsmen and physical trainers made an impact on the civilian world. In British elementary and secondary schools physical training was largely the preserve of ex-servicemen, given the absence of any physical training colleges for men before the 1930s. Many military physical training instructors whose time in the services had expired at a comparatively early age found jobs in the nation's schools and often encouraged sport as part of their PT programmes. In the immediate aftermath of the Boer War and the anxieties it raised about 'physical degeneration' a new 'model course' of physical training was introduced into the elementary schools; it was based largely on military drill, schools were urged to employ instructors 'trained in the Army Gymnastic Course', and Colonel Malcolm Fox, former Inspector of Army Gymnasia, was appointed Inspector of Physical Training at the Board of Education. After intensive criticism, the 'model course' was quickly declared unsuitable (by an inter-departmental committee which included Fox) and replaced by a syllabus which drew more on the gymnastics taught in the women's physical training colleges. Nevertheless, the service influence remained. The second Inspector, in 1909, was Lieutenant Commander F. H. Grenfell, RN, who had introduced the Swedish system into naval physical training and remodelled the school syllabus along the same lines. In 1919 he produced a new syllabus for physical training in schools which placed more emphasis on games and appointed two new inspectors, both former soldiers.[94] The

---

[93] *Lloyd's Weekly News*, 13 May 1913.
[94] J. Owen and B. Furlong, 'AE Syson: The Military as a Major Influence on PE 1919–1939', unpublished paper n.d.; Commander P. F. Newcombe RN (retd), 'Physical Training for the Nation: How the Services Can Help', *Fighting Forces* 13 (1936), 141–6; P. C. McIntosh, *Physical Training in England Since 1800* (London: G. Bell & Sons, 1968), chs. 9–10. See also the Report of the Physical Education Committee of the British Medical Association, April 1936, p. 31. By the inter-war years interested parties both inside and outside education were underlining the need for specialist

influence of the services was felt well beyond the school system. The main promoters of 'recreational training' in the wartime army and navy respectively, Colonel R. B. Campbell and Commander B. T. Coote, both went on to civilian positions, Campbell as the first Director of Physical Education at the University of Edinburgh and Coote as a member of the Industrial Welfare Society and as technical advisor to the Miners' Welfare Commission, where he promoted the introduction of canteens, pithead baths and playing fields.[95]

There were also signs that influential members of the military were beginning to add their voices to those in the civilian sporting world who wanted to see more serious attitudes towards coaching and training, particularly given a context which saw international events such as the Olympic Games expanding in importance. In 1927 Lieutenant General Gerald Ellison wrote to the *Times* claiming that the success of American track and field athletes could be explained largely by their use of coaches. He even quoted the example of a British regiment whose recent improvements on the athletics track could be linked directly to their appointment of a professional coach. He advocated not only the establishment of a college which would train PT teachers but also a training centre for the coaches of Olympic sports.[96]

In the inter-war years the armed services began to take more seriously their responsibility to help discharged airmen, sailors and soldiers find decent jobs. A small but significant number began to do so in civilian sport. Bill Gopsill, for example, had been a sergeant in the RAMC during the war and the skills he learned there persuaded West Bromwich Albion to appoint him as their trainer in 1922. Similarly Wolverhampton Wanderers appointed a former RAMC corporal to look after their reserve team in 1931.[97] A few time-expired men made careers as professional sportsmen like the private in 1/Leicestershire Regiment who wrote to his regimental welfare officer in 1934:

I am trying in this small letter to convey my thanks to you for what you did for me when I was serving under you, not only bringing me out a bigger man, but the soccer that was taught me and encouraged and the chances given me to prove my ability to play.

    institutions to train subsequent generations of male PT teachers. Carnegie College opened in Leeds in September 1933 followed by Loughborough in 1936.
[95] *Times*, 5 September, 8 September 1955; Gray, *Prophet*, pp. 44–6.
[96] *Times*, 2 August 1927.
[97] West Bromwich Albion, Minutes of Directors' Meetings, 22 July 1931. A Captain Muller was also a physical training instructor at Charlton Athletic: Charlton Athletic, Minutes of Directors' Meetings, 1 December 1932. We are grateful to Neil Carter for these references.

After failing to make the grade with his local club, Lincoln City, he was signed by Tranmere Rovers, where 'the success I had is due to you and the different men you told to coach us and get us fit, so I shall never forget the Tigers and I wish them the best of luck ... I thank you for what I owe to you and others.'[98]

The services also produced a significant number of sporting champions who had notable success in the civilian sporting world both on and off the field. The Marquis of Exeter was a serving officer in 2/ Grenadier Guards when he won the 400 metre hurdles at the 1928 Olympic Games.[99] He also won five AAA titles as well as three gold medals in the first British Empire Games. He captained the British team at the 1932 Olympics and in the same year came top of a poll held by a national newspaper to find the ten most popular young men in Britain, beating Noël Coward into third place. He became the youngest ever president of the AAA in 1936 and chairman of the British Olympic Association in the same year, continuing in both positions until 1976. Herbert Prince joined the RAMC as a boy entrant before the First World War and rose through the ranks to lieutenant-colonel. He won the army 880 yards championship in 1913 and also played tennis and cricket to a high standard. As a footballer he was good enough to be selected for the England amateur international eleven and was a member of the team which competed at the Antwerp Olympic Games in 1920. He was secretary of the Army Football Association from 1947 to 1952. Sam Ferris was a career airman and one of Britain's great distance runners who won the marathon championship of Great Britain in 1925, 1926 and 1927. Sergeant Ferris ran in three Olympic marathons, winning a silver medal at Los Angeles in 1932. He was an influence on many later British long-distance runners and contributed to a book on the subject as late as 1965.[100] The RAF also produced Donald Finlay, another international athlete who rose through the ranks, from aircraftman to group captain. Finlay won the AAA 120 yards hurdles championship seven times in a row between 1932 and 1938 and again, at the age of forty, in 1949. He also won a silver medal in the 110 yards hurdles championship at the 1936 Olympic Games. Finlay was also a footballer good enough to play for the RAF several times in the 1930s.[101]

---

[98] *Green Tiger*, November 1934, 297.
[99] On his return to London he was lifted on the shoulders of the crowd who had gone to Liverpool Street station to meet him. P. Lovesey, *The Official Centenary History of the Amateur Athletic Association* (Enfield: Guinness Superlatives, 1980), pp. 167–8.
[100] *Training for Road Running* (Walton on Thames: Road Runners Club, 1965).
[101] Ackland, 'The Forces', pp. 383–4.

One of the objects of the setting up of the Sports Control Boards for the armed services at the end of the First World War was to form connections with sports organisations outside the services in all matters which might affect service sports and games. It seems clear that a substantial network of contacts at both national and local levels existed already and that what the new service-wide bodies intended was to provide what had grown up organically with the formal mark of authority. There had been moments of tension in the relationships between the civil and military, usually involving those sportsmen in uniform who were good enough to be wanted by civilian clubs and associations, but most appear to have been settled by the application of regulations drawn up as a result of pre-existing contacts. This process was undoubtedly helped by the fact that the leaders of most national and many local sporting associations were run by what might be termed the officer class. Differences of opinion on the values of amateurism as against those of professional sport existed within both of these groups but generally they shared a belief in fair play and sportsmanship together with the idea that sport should be elevating. Team games were especially thought to be the vehicle most likely to bring this about. There were still many in both the civil and military worlds who recognised the fragility of the Corinthian spirit and were anxious to preserve it but not at any price. As we have seen, the Army Football Association supported the established authority of the FA in its battle with the Amateur Football Association when some were urging it to throw in its lot with the rebels.[102]

And of course there were all the more practical reasons for service sportsmen to play with their civilian counterparts: the competition, the raising of standards, the pleasure and prestige to be had when service sportsmen reached the highest levels of a particular sport. England had four rugby union captains who were naval officers in the 1920s: Scotland had two. When England played Wales in January 1923 the navy provided five and the RAF two out of the fifteen. And there was usually a respectable number of service men representing Great Britain at the Olympic Games.

Despite the reservations about civilian sport expressed by the War Office in setting up the Army Sport Control Board, the inter-war years saw many examples of exchange and overlap in personnel and ideas between its military and civilian versions. An early post-war example came from the Commander-in-Chief of the Mediterranean Fleet, who requested the Royal Navy Sports Control Board to arrange with the Reuters news agency to cable the results of English League football

---

[102] *Times*, 20 August 1907.

matches to Malta on the day they took place, a service appreciated by the personnel serving on the station. Military bands remained a feature at many British sporting events such as the FA Cup finals and the annual meetings of the Amateur Athletic Association.[103] Service championships were often played at prestigious civilian venues. By the mid-1920s, for example, the Inter-Services Lawn Tennis championships were being played at Wimbledon, while by the 1930s the RAF squash championship was being held at Queen's Club.[104] Whether or not all of this did much for recruiting is hard to say. The military sports lobby thought it did and often said so. Perhaps in a culture where there was no citizen army, the fact that the military played with and against civilian sportsmen and played a role in the organisations which ran civilian sport made life in the services seem less remote from civilian life. Sport was one of the sub-cultures in which representatives of the military and civilians regularly came together. It was a relationship soon to be tested by war.

[103] 'The Financing of the Physical Training and Sports Branch, 1922', ADM1/8619/24, TNA; Lovesey, *Official Centenary History*, p. 81.
[104] *Times*, 25 July 1925, 10 July 1928; *RAF Quarterly* 4 (1933), 340.

6 A different kind of war

> Some of you chaps who had a rough time during the war may consider that because we were footballers we had a much better time. So we did, and I should be the last man to deny it.
>
> Ron Burgess, *Football – My Life* (London: Souvenir Press, 1952), p. 62

Recently a number of historians have emphasised that from the point of view of the fighting man there were at times striking similarities between the Second and First World Wars. Trench warfare and 'shellshock' were not confined to the Great War; the experience of combat was often equally traumatic; and at times (especially in Normandy) casualty rates equalled or even exceeded those of the Western Front.[1] Yet these similarities should not perhaps be overstated. One significant difference in the Second World War was the concentration of hundreds of thousands of servicemen in Britain between Dunkirk and D-Day; another was the much higher proportion of non-combatant soldiers. These men, most of whose war service was characterised largely by boredom and frustration, represented a rather different morale problem from that seen in 1914–18.[2] The Second World War also saw a much greater recognition by government of the importance of civilian morale.

---

[1] P. Addison and A. Calder (eds.), *Time to Kill: The Soldier's Experience of War in the West 1939–1945* (London: Pimlico, 1997), especially chapters by J. Ellis, D. M. Henderson, G. D. Sheffield, R. Holmes and H. Strachan.

[2] For a discussion of army morale in the Second World War see the work of Jeremy Crang, who concludes that it improved as the war progressed and as the army became more efficient in manning and more responsive to the needs of its civilian soldiers: *The British Army and the People's War 1939–1945* (Manchester University Press, 2000); 'The British Army as a Social Institution, 1939–1945', in H. Strachan (ed.), *The British Army, Manpower and Society into the Twenty-First Century* (London: Cass, 2000); 'The British Soldier on the Home Front: Army Morale Reports, 1940–45', in Addison and Calder, (eds.), *Time to Kill*, pp. 60–70. See also D. French, *Raising Churchill's Army: The British Army and the War against Germany, 1919–1945* (Oxford University Press, 2000), ch. 4, which emphasises that, despite a nadir in 1941–2, discussed below, morale was by no means 'uniformly poor or fragile'. Neither author includes any mention of sport.

These factors produced somewhat different approaches towards sport than had been seen in the first war, when professional football in particular had come under attack as frivolous and unpatriotic. In 1939–45 it was largely accepted that professional sport could help lift the morale of servicemen, war workers and civilians alike. It was only after the fall of Singapore that wartime sport came under attack both in the *Daily Express* and in Parliament as demonstrating the 'smugness' and 'complacency' that were undermining the war effort, and the restrictions subsequently introduced (effectively confining sport to weekends) were gradually eased as the war situation improved.[3]

In the armed forces' attitudes towards sport both similarities and differences can be seen between the two wars. To a considerable degree the uses of sport by the services in the Second World War did replicate those seen in the Great War. Despite the introduction of increasingly sophisticated psychological testing for officer selection the army's faith in sport as a measure of officer qualities seems, at least in the early days of the war, to have burnt almost as brightly as ever. According to Tony Pawson, when he was interviewed for officer training soon after Dunkirk, "'I see you captained the Winchester College cricket team. What was your batting average?" was the only query from the General presiding. "108, Sir". "Splendid, just the sort of man we want".'[4]

Once again sport was used to create *esprit de corps* in new men and new units. Craig French notes how Major General Wimberley, given the difficult job of creating morale and a distinctive group identity in the reformed 51st Highland Division, after the surrender of the original 51st at St Valéry in June 1940, used sport both to create fruitful competition between battalions and 'to promote the 51st to the public' while training in north-east Scotland.[5] Traditional regimental anniversaries continued to be marked with sport and alcohol. In 1943 2/Middlesex Regiment, stationed near Dumfries, celebrated Albuhera Day (16 May) 'in great style' with a sports meeting in which the colonel took part,

---

[3] *Hansard's Parliamentary Debates*, HC Deb., 24 February 1942, vol. 378, cc. 49–50, 160, 314; N. Baker, 'A More Even Playing Field? Sport During and After the War', in N. Hayes and J. Hill (eds.), *Millions Like Us? British Culture in the Second World War* (Liverpool University Press, 1999), pp. 129–32. See also P. Lanfranchi and M. Taylor, 'Professional Football in World War Two Britain', in P. Kirkham and D. Thoms (eds.), *War Culture: Social Change and Changing Experience in World War Two Britain* (London: Lawrence and Wishart, 1995).

[4] T. Pawson, *Indelible Memories: Playingfields and Battlefields* (privately printed, n.d.), p. 26 (see ch. 13 for army sport in Austria at the end of the war); *Observer*, 19 December 1999.

[5] C.F. French, 'The Fashioning of *Esprit de Corps* in the 51st Highland Division from St Valery to El Alamein', *Journal of the Society for Army Historical Research* 77 (1999), 275–92, at 289.

with a machine-gun assault course competition, a football match in which the battalion team beat the local RAF side and an 'inter-rank pass-ball competition' won by the officers. In May 1944, however, plans for similar celebrations with 'sports and barrels of beer' were overtaken by preparations for D-Day.[6] But even on active service overseas such festivities were sometimes possible. In Italy on 1 August 1944 the Hampshires, as Captain Oakley recorded in his diary, organised a 'Hell of a sports programme ... for Minden day' – along with other celebrations ('What a day. I am half gone as I write this').[7]

Again sport helped to cement inter-service and inter-allied bonds. 4/Black Watch, stationed on Gibraltar, forged strong links with the HMS *Ark Royal* through 'many a football match and many a party'. After *Ark Royal* was torpedoed, in November 1941, one last match was played to mark her passing, kicked off by Captain Maund, her last commanding officer, 'witnessed by five thousand men, of whom perhaps a thousand were survivors of "Old Ark"', and won 5–2 by the Black Watch.[8] *Union Jack* hailed reports of games against the French Garde Mobile in North Africa under the headline 'Football is Aid to Allied Relations'.[9] Sport was also used to demonstrate British dominance over her minor allies. In Iraq in 1943 the Commander-in-Chief of the Persia and Iraq force led the search for a British football team to meet and beat a team of Poles who were proclaiming themselves local champions.[10] In 1944 Stan Cullis was ordered to raise a team from Central Mediterranean Forces to play a Yugoslav Partisan team which had been sweeping the board against British army teams in Italy: they were duly beaten 7–2 at Bari before a huge crowd of British troops assembled from all over southern Italy.[11]

As a result of the Great War, the value of wartime military sport was now generally accepted. The 1922 report of the War Office Committee into Shell Shock had acknowledged the usefulness of sport in preventing 'neurosis'. In its list of the chief factors that diminished 'the incidence of nervous and mental disorders in the Field', 'organised recreation

---

[6] Major R. B. Moberly, *Campaign in N.W. Europe, June 6th 1944–May 7th, 1945: Second Battalion the Middlesex Regiment (DCO)* (Cairo: R. Schindler, 1946), pp. 13–14, 18.
[7] Quoted in R. Holmes, 'The Italian Job: Five Armies in Italy, 1943–45', in Addison and Calder (eds.), *Time to Kill*, p. 211.
[8] B. Ferguson, *The Black Watch and the King's Enemies* (London: Collins, 1950), pp. 49–50. *Ark Royal* had won the Navy Cup in 1939, the first ship (as opposed to shore establishment) to do so.
[9] *Union Jack*, 9 June 1943.
[10] T. Purcell and M. Gething, *Wartime Wanderers: Bolton Wanderers – A Football Team at War* (Edinburgh: Mainstream, 2001), pp. 101–2.
[11] S. Cullis, *All for the Wolves* (London: Rupert Hart-Davis, 1960), p. 19.

A different kind of war 181

Figure 13. Stanley Cullis leads out a British Forces team which played and lost to a Yugoslav army team just after the liberation of Split in 1945. The photograph was in an album inscribed 'death to fascism and liberty to the People!'

behind the line' ranked ninth out of fourteen – well below morale, discipline, *esprit de corps* and good officers, but above home leave, early diagnosis and 'the controlled use of rum'. Sport was particularly commended as 'promoting fitness, stimulating the spirit of competition and providing variety for both mind and body'.[12] Although many of the Committee's recommendations were forgotten in the early stages of the Second World War – officers in the inter-war army tending to dismiss 'shell-shock' as a distinct product of the static warfare of the Western Front – the value of sport for fighting men seems to have been much more widely accepted.[13] Those who had been young officers in 1914–18 had direct experience of sport's value behind the lines, and the lessons of the Great War were reiterated in every edition of *Games and Sports in the Army*.

[12] *Report of the War Office Committee of Enquiry into "Shell-Shock"* 1922 [Cmd. 1734], pp. 151, 153 (see also pp. 64, 157).
[13] D. French, 'Tommy Is No Soldier: The Morale of the Second British Army in Normandy, June–August 1944', *Journal of Strategic Studies* 19 (1996), 154–78, at 161–8; French, *Raising Churchill's Army*, p. 136.

Like the government, however, the armed services in the Second World War demonstrated a far greater acceptance of professional and spectacular sport than they had done in 1914–18. Having spent the inter-war years enforcing amateurism, the forces had swiftly to adapt to the influx of hundreds of professional sportsmen. By 1943 the Army Sport Control Board had had to accept that 'to meet war-time conditions, the rules applicable to the strict amateur principles may have to be modified from time to time'.[14] Most striking is the services' acceptance in the Second World War that participatory and spectacular sport were two sides of the same coin. John Ellis emphasises the frequent 'periods of intense boredom' which studded military life even for fighting troops and the 'soul-destroying emptiness' which overtook soldiers out of the line.[15] The army actively used both spectacular and participatory sport to boost morale among servicemen in training, on leave or waiting for action. Indeed, the services' faith in sport as a morale lifter was such that it was sometimes encouraged to the detriment of military efficiency. Keith Douglas claimed that when during the advance on Tripoli his regiment was supplied with filthy, dilapidated tanks 'the men of the other Division who brought them up said they had not had time for maintenance because in their units sport took precedence over it. It is a horrible thought', he added, 'that this may have been true'.[16] Star sportsmen were often kept away from active service (as many professional footballers found to their benefit) to provide entertainment through spectacular sport, or removed temporarily from front-line duties to take part in big games. In 1942, soon after Alamein, ten members of Bolton Wanderers pre-war team, now with the Royal Artillery, were withdrawn from the pursuit of Rommel's forces to take part in a high-profile match in Cairo between the Allies and Egypt. In March 1945 Bleddyn Williams, having landed a glider containing radio equipment on the east bank of the Rhine as part of 'Operation Varsity', was recalled from his slit trench to play rugby for Britain against the Dominions at Leicester.[17]

The roots of this change in attitude towards spectacular and professional sport can be traced to the late 1930s, when General Sir Walter Kirke, Director-General of the Territorial Army, attempted with some

---

[14] 'The Army Sport Control Board', Enc. 15 to 261/Pubs/9913 in file labelled 'ASCB History', ASCB.
[15] J. Ellis, *The Sharp End of War: The Fighting Man in World War II* (Newton Abbot: David & Charles, 1980), pp. 324–5.
[16] Keith Douglas, *Alamein to Zem Zem* (London: Faber and Faber, 1992 (1st edn 1946)), pp. 106–7.
[17] Purcell and Gething, *Wartime Wanderers*, pp. 92–4; Mace, *History of Royal Air Force Rugby*, p. 74.

success to use sport and the Territorial Army Sport Board as recruiting tools. Rugby union, with its traditionally close links to the Territorials, was an obvious target. A conference of thirty rugby clubs held at the War Office in 1937 enthusiastically endorsed the idea of a TA rugby footballer's anti-aircraft unit, a company of the 33rd (St Pancras) Battalion.[18] In terms of numbers association football clearly had more to offer. That year the London Football League clubs agreed 'to encourage the young men of England – and there are hundreds and thousands of them who see your teams play every week – to take an active interest' in the TA by forming special football detachments in units situated close to their respective grounds.[19] In the spring of 1939 the Football Association, approached by the War Office to assist recruiting, circularised all clubs asking them to 'provide a patriotic example to the youth of the country'. It was proposed that players and their supporters should join TA units local to their clubs, 'thus enabling each club to form the nucleus of a footballers' detachment'. A special footballers' company was created attached to the 8th (1st City of London) Battalion, Royal Fusiliers, TA; within a week thirty professional players from London clubs had joined. Elsewhere all the players of Liverpool FC joined to form a club section in the King's Regiment and all the members of Norwich City expressed their willingness to join the Territorials.[20] On Easter Saturday 1939 Bolton Wanderers' captain Harry Goslin made a speech from the pitch to a match crowd of 23,000 urging them to join up; on the Monday he led the entire Wanderers first team to join the 53rd Field Regiment (TA), Bolton Artillery.[21]

As war approached, the Football Association and the army drew up a scheme for enlisting professional footballers into the Army Physical Training Corps.[22] Soon after war was declared Stanley Rous of the FA urged players with coaching experience to join the APTC, promising that they would be given the rank of sergeant-instructor immediately. Here a misunderstanding had occurred. The conditions of service published by the War Office on 30 October 1939 stated that players

---

[18] Collins, 'English Rugby Union', 800; *Times*, 20 November 1937; 'Recruitment Speech at the Saracens Football Club dinner, 23 Feb. 1938', Kirke 5/6, Liddell Hart Centre for Military Archives, LHC.
[19] 'Suggested Speech to Football Club Representatives drafted by Mr Smith, Sporting Editor, *Sunday Express*', n.d. [1937], Kirke 5/6, LHC; *Times*, 28 January 1937.
[20] *Times*, 25 April, 3 May, 4 May, 10 May 1939; T. McCarthy, *War Games: The Story of Sport in World War Two* (London: Macdonald, Queen Anne Press, 1989), p. 33.
[21] Purcell and Gething, *Wartime Wanderers*, pp. 23–5. Goslin, by then an officer, was killed fighting in Italy in December 1943.
[22] The Army Physical Training Staff was reorganised and renamed the Army Physical Training Corps in September 1940: for simplicity we have used the new name throughout this chapter.

would initially be enlisted into the Royal Artillery at gunner rank: only after three weeks' probation at the Army School of Physical Training at Aldershot would they, if approved, join the APTC with the rank of sergeant-instructor. As Joe Mercer remembered, when the first group of nineteen trainees, who had signed up in mid-September, discovered this, 'we mutinied'. A swift compromise was arranged whereby the first group were ranked and paid as temporary sergeants, the FA footing the bill in the first instance.[23] The scheme was sufficiently successful to attract the attention of the RAF, to whom Rous submitted a scheme for 'Recreative Welfare'. As a result, three well-known player/coaches – Walter Winterbottom (of Manchester United and Carnegie College), the amateur J. C. Kilkenny, and T. Whittaker (of Arsenal and the FA's international team trainer) – were commissioned as pilot-officers in charge of Physical Welfare. By the end of the war, Winterbottom was overseeing the department of RAF physical training in the Air Ministry with the rank of acting wing commander. The RAF also began taking footballers as PTIs. By March 1940, 154 men from the FA's list of nominees had become PTIs, 109 in the army and 45 (of which four were now commissioned officers) in the RAF.[24] The system of sending professional footballers straight into the APTC stopped at the end of February 1940, but the FA continued to be asked for the names of suitable footballers serving in the ranks.[25]

The Football Association advised applicants that 'your actual work in the Army will be limited only by your ability and ingenuity to provide and supervise the Recreational activities of the troops during formal P.T. periods and in their free time'.[26] In fact many spent much of the war playing football. The special terms granted to footballers caused some resentment within the APTC. In June 1944, the Directorate of Military Training for Central Mediterranean Forces asked for reinforcements of twenty PTIs including 'at least three well known professional footballers'.

---

[23] Football Association War Emergency Committee minutes, 30 October 1939, 22 January 1940, 12 April 1940; Stanley Rous to the Selected Men (Recreative Physical Training (Army Side)), 14 February 1940 including conditions of enlistment issued by the War Office, 30 Oct. 1939, Football Association Archives (FAA); G. James, *The Authorised Biography of Joe Mercer OBE* (Leicester: ACL & Polar, 1993), pp. 43–4.

[24] Football Association War Emergency Committee minutes, 22 January 1940, 4 March 1940, FAA; T. Mason, 'Winterbottom, Sir Walter (1913–2002)', *Oxford Dictionary of National Biography*, online edn, Oxford University Press, January 2006 at http://www.oxforddnb.com/view/article/76939, accessed 14 January 2008.

[25] Football Association War Emergency Committee minutes, 12 April 1940, FAA.

[26] Stanley Rous to the Selected Men (Recreative Physical Training (Army Side)), 14 February 1940, in Football Association War Emergency Committee minutes, FAA.

My reason for requesting professional footballers with the Mercer-Lawton reputation is that almost all APTCIs out here feel that the professional footballer is having a very comfortable war in UK. I know from personal experience the fine work that many of them have done, but the average APTCI looks upon the whole question in a very different light. To him these Pros without any PT background, came on the Corps direct, in most cases, getting 3 stripes in as many weeks, and then staying in UK and earning 30/- a week for playing for their club on Saturday afternoon. It would be a tremendous uplift to morale if some of the more prominent footballers could be sent out.

Joe Mercer, Tommy Lawton, Stan Cullis and Willie Fagan were specifically requested.[27] Cullis at least was duly posted to Bari in July 1944, remaining in Italy for eighteen months.[28]

There were also occasional suggestions from the home front that being a PTI was a 'cushy number'. The commandant of the APTC took these seriously enough to produce a studied rebuttal emphasising that the reason why only 1,000 out of a total of 3,000 PTIs had gone overseas was that most troop training was done in the United Kingdom. It seems likely that it was he who persuaded the well-known sports writer W. Capel Kirby to write an article in a Sunday newspaper which was effectively the army's response to the grumblers.[29]

By no means all sportsmen went into the Army Physical Training Corps. By April 1940, according to *Picture Post*, 629 professional footballers had joined up, 514 in the army, 84 in the RAF, and 31 in the navy.[30] They too could typically expect to spend a good deal of the war playing sport, both civilian and military. Not everyone approved of service players being released to play games. Some commanding officers had a shrewd appreciation of its publicity value. The Bolton Wanderers' CO allowed the team to play one last game (against Manchester United) in September 1939 'on the condition that they wore the Regimental strip'.[31] Others were more sceptical. Ron Burgess, in the RAF and anxious to obtain leave to play for Wales, was hurt and astonished to find that 'my C.O.s seemed more concerned with discipline than

---

[27] Major G. Cox, SOPT, Directorate of Military Training ADV AFHQ, CMF, to Commandant APTC Aldershot, 19 June 1944, HQPT/607 'Secret. Africa, N, S, E & W incl. Italy. 1940–6', Army Physical Training Corps Museum (APTCM).
[28] J. Holton, *Stan Cullis: The Iron Manager* (Derby: Breedon, 2000), ch. 4. Cullis' work in organising recreational training in Italy was commended by the Staff Officer for Physical Training, though he noted that Cullis' 'one bad fault' was that 'he moans too much about trivial matters that someone in his position should ignore'. The work of Cliff Britton, Matt Busby and Joe Mercer was also singled out for praise. Personnel Files, APTCM.
[29] *Sunday Empire News*, 10 December 1944; Personnel Files, APTCM.
[30] J. Hadden, 'Where the Sportsmen Have Gone', *Picture Post*, 27 April 1940, 38–41.
[31] Purcell and Gething, *Wartime Wanderers*, p. 41.

international football'. Forbidden to travel far from RAF Syerston in Nottinghamshire, 'I missed at least half a dozen Welsh matches in which I might have been selected. I am not grumbling, just stating the facts as they were'.[32] Tom Finney's CO in the Middle East insisted that 'the footballing soldiers were playing a major role in maintaining morale'. But later, in Italy, when he suggested a touring team, his captain there told him that 'all footballers were dodgers'. When Finney protested that he was ready to do his bit 'he took me at my word. The following day I was in action with Queen's Royal Lancers, with a squadron of Honey tanks'. Finney himself had a 'terrible guilty complex' about being pulled out of the fighting to tour the Middle East playing football.[33]

Despite the blackout, the restriction on travel, the long hours of work and the shortages of both materials and facilities, there was no lack of spectacular sport in Britain. Servicemen and even a few servicewomen were heavily involved organising it, playing it and watching it. Over half of the army – some 1.5 million troops – spent most of the war in Britain. 'Even in the spring of 1945 about a million, which at that time was around one-third of the service, were still serving at home' – not to mention the navy and the RAF.[34] Sport was one of a number of diversions designed to entertain and support morale, both of civilians and servicemen. It also boosted the war effort in more material ways by contributing to military benevolent funds and war charities.[35] As early as April 1941 the RAF rugby team met a South Wales XV in Swansea, the match raising £795 for the mayor's Air Raid Disaster Fund. They met again in October, when the gate money was split between the air raid fund and the RAF's own benevolent fund and by the time the last match of the series was played in October 1944 £3,000 had been raised.[36] Similar services internationals and other representative matches were sponsored by the Army Sport Control Board, producing

[32] R. Burgess, *Football: My Life* (London: Souvenir Press, 1952), pp. 46, 72, 58–63.
[33] P. Agnew, *Finney: A Football Legend* (Preston: Carnegie Press, 1989), pp. 37–8; A. Rippon, *Gas Masks for Goal Posts: Football in Britain during the Second World War* (Stroud: Sutton, 2005), p. 204.
[34] Crang, *The British Army and the People's War*, p. 2.
[35] Stanley Rous was transferred back to London from an army posting on an Anti-Aircraft Battery in Fishguard to use his experience as Secretary of the Football Association in organising the Sports Committee of the Duke of Gloucester's Red Cross and St John Ambulance Fund. The Sports Committee contributed a little over £3 million to a total of £53 million raised for the Fund. Rous was also co-opted onto the Army Football Association's War Emergency Committee. S. Rous, *Football Worlds: A Lifetime in Sport* (London: Faber, 1978) pp. 107–11; *Times*, 12 December 1945.
[36] Mace, *History of RAF Rugby*, pp. 23, 34. By the end of 1944 the Swansea and West Wales Rugby Charity Committee had donated £16,600 to war charities with teams representing the army playing in the area four times and the RAF five (p. 44).

£15,000 for distribution among a range of beneficiaries including the three service benevolent funds and the Red Cross.[37] The Inter-Services Rugby Union Committee organised sixteen 'services internationals' between England, Scotland and Wales. All attracted crowds smaller than they would have been pre-war but ranging respectably from twelve to thirty thousand at a variety of venues. For the first time since the First World War, rugby union and rugby league players played with and against each other and first Army Northern Command and then the Inter-Services Rugby Union Committee organised matches between teams representing the two codes. On 23 January 1943 at Leeds a Northern Command Rugby League XV beat a Northern Command Rugby Union XV and in April 1944 a Combined Services match at the Bradford Rugby League ground saw a second victory for league over union before a 14,000 crowd.[38]

Though it might be an exaggeration to say that boxing flourished during the war there were many opportunities for servicemen to take part, or watch others, in organised events. The Imperial Services Boxing Association's wartime rules stated that in service competitions professional boxers turned servicemen could box only against other service professionals, only in six-round contests, and not for money prizes. There was no ban, however, on professionals pursuing their career outside the services. Nor did the rules against officers competing with other ranks apply to civilian competitions.[39] Professional boxing continued throughout the war years with regular promotions at a range of locations including Bournemouth, Glasgow, Leeds, Leicester, Liverpool, Manchester, Newcastle, Oxford, Watford and London. Some indication of what was possible can be seen through the wartime career of Freddie Mills. Mills was a promising middleweight conscripted into the RAF at the end of 1939. He eventually became a physical training instructor serving on a number of home stations. It was during the war that Mills broke into the top rank of professional boxing. Between 1940 and 1944 he had at least seventeen contests, two of which were for British titles. He benefited from sympathetic COs who were generous with leave.[40] Many of these promotions devoted some of the profits to war charities but Mills made money too: £2,000

---

[37] *Times*, 2 August 1944.
[38] Mace, *History of RAF Rugby*, pp. 46–66, 77–8.
[39] *Games and Sports in the Army* (1941), pp. 150–1, 361.
[40] One of them even overlooked a period of absence without leave after Mills' victory over Harvey. The best account can be found in J. Birtley, *Freddie Mills, His Life and Death* (London: New English Library, 1978), esp. pp. 55–99. See also Harding, *Lonsdale's Belt*, pp. 170–88.

was his share, for example, when he lost a British heavyweight title fight with another RAF sergeant, Jack London, in September 1943. By then he had become the British light heavyweight champion after a spectacular knockout of Len Harvey (also in the RAF but as a pilot officer). Mills had taken fourteen days leave to prepare for the contest: his training sessions were open to the public, the money collected going to the RAF benevolent fund. The fight itself, held on a Saturday afternoon in June 1942 at White Hart Lane, Tottenham, attracted a crowd of 30,000. Exhibition fights by top boxers were also commonplace on the home front. Perhaps the most famous series took place shortly before D-Day, when Joe Louis, the world heavyweight champion, came over to entertain the American and British troops awaiting action. One fight was held in the large natural amphitheatre of the Punchbowl near Winchester, where many thousands of Allied troops were distracted and astonished by the scene and the moment as much as by the physical prowess on view.

The official historian of the Amateur Athletic Association thought that the armed forces played a large part in maintaining public interest in track and field athletics between 1940 and 1945. Not only were competitive events organised within and between units but regular matches took place between teams representing the Association, the Universities, leading clubs and the military. Although usually on a limited scale they often featured leading runners such as the sprinter Cyril Holmes, a company sergeant-major instructor in the Army Physical Training Corps, and the famous middle-distance runner Sydney Wooderson, whose poor eyesight kept him out of the armed forces but who served in the Auxiliary Fire Service and later in the Pioneer Corps.[41] Major events were occasionally organised such as the meeting promoted by the Manchester Athletic Club for Mrs Churchill's Aid to Russia Fund in mid-summer 1944. This meeting featured representatives from the RAF and the Army's Northern Command as well as Civil Defence together with teams from the AAA, the Universities' Athletic Union, Glasgow University and the local Victoria Park Athletic Club. The main event was a mile handicap – the Stalin Mile – which Wooderson was hot favourite to win though he finished second behind a student who had started 80 yards ahead. The excellent crowd included not only the Lord Mayor and Lady Mayoress of Manchester but also a deputation

---

[41] Lovesey, *Official Centenary History*, p. 58; J. Crump, *Running Round the World* (London: Hale, 1966), ch. 7. The first post-war meeting to be held at the White City in 1945 between the AAA, Army, RAF and the American Forces drew the biggest crowd seen for athletics since the Olympic Marathon in 1908.

from the Soviet Embassy, who presented the prizes to the winning athletes.[42]

Even cricket, hardly a game to be staged in the austere conditions and time shortages of the war, did its bit and on summer Saturdays and bank holidays could still draw the crowds to Lord's and a variety of outlying centres. Much of it was reduced to one day, one innings affairs which was the type of cricket that most ordinary players were used to anyway. Teams representing the British and Australian services featured heavily in the wartime programmes at Lord's. Several games between the RAF and the Army, and between the Army and the Navy, took place. The RAF and the Army each took on 'The Rest of England', and the Royal Australian Air Force provided the British service teams with competition. Teams representing various RAF stations, a number of Guards regiments, Sandhurst and the ASC also played at Lord's during the war.[43] Teams such as London Counties and the Empire XI, both made up largely of members of the armed services, played regularly at the major London venues and often farther afield, in Coventry and Cardiff, Eastbourne and Southampton. Again war charities benefited from the receipts from many matches.[44]

But when it came to sporting spectacle it was association football which was as prominent and visible in wartime as it had been in peace. With so many young players in the armed forces the bulk of spectacular football was also service football. Of course regular club football suffered as regionally based wartime leagues with complicated structures replaced the familiar Saturday games. Military duties and unpredictable postings meant that it was difficult if not impossible to field settled teams. In the 1943–4 season Notts County used 132 different players, though Arsenal required only forty-five.[45] Because so many of the elite professional group had become, or were training to be, members of the Army Physical Training Corps, Aldershot could often field a team the quality of which far outstripped their humble Third Division South peacetime status. But in spite of their regular sprinkling of stars the club never came close to victory in any of the wartime competitions. Even ordinary footballers could find themselves playing either with or against internationals. A services team visiting Leamington Town

---

[42] *Manchester Guardian*, 24 June, 26 June, 2 July 1944; *Times*, 26 June 1944.
[43] Lists of 'Matches for the Season at Lord's', 1940–5. We are grateful to Neil Young and Roderick Suddaby for this material.
[44] McCarthy, *War Games*, pp. 109–18; R. Genders, *League Cricket in England* (London: Werner Laurie, 1952), pp. 59, 80, 123–6.
[45] Early in the war Arsenal fielded an entire team of men serving in the RAF. Eddie Hapgood, *Football Ambassadors* (London: Sporting Handbooks, 1945), p. 92.

in early 1944 included Tommy Lawton, England's centre forward; a few weeks later he played for England against Scotland at Hampden Park, Glasgow before a crowd of 133,000.[46] The stars profited from playing regularly together not only for their national sides, but also for their respective services, or for combined services teams, in a way which would have been impossible in peacetime. Ronnie Burgess of Tottenham Hotspur and Wales thought later that joining the RAF had been a good football career move because it brought him into contact with so many of the leading players of the day. Playing for teams such as the RAF, Combined Services and Wales made him a better footballer. He believed the keen inter-service rivalries and playing regularly with the same group of players produced a higher standard than had existed in pre-war league football.[47] It seems clear that most celebrated professional footballers had good wars. For those lower down the pecking order experiences were more mixed. Alf Ramsey was in the 6th Battalion Duke of Cornwall's Light Infantry engaged on home defence. Army service brought improved physical fitness and the opportunity to play not only more football than he had done previously but of a better standard. Tim Ward, on the other hand, in 1939 a young professional with Derby County, spent the war with the RAMC in the north of Scotland. Between 1941 and 1943 he played only six games of football and saw his wife four times.[48]

The Army FA was overseen by an Emergency Committee during the war which at first suspended both the Army Cup and the organisation's regional structure. But the Command and District Committees were rapidly reformed to construct a framework of representative matches at command, formation, unit and even company levels.[49] Both the Army and RAF regularly played against teams chosen by the FA and their games against each other became one of the main footballing attractions of wartime. Over 30,000 saw the games at Stamford Bridge in April 1943 and St James' Park, Newcastle was filled by 51,000 in March 1945.[50] The Army in England against the

[46] D. McVay and A. Smith, *The Complete Centre Forward. The Authorised Biography of Tommy Lawton* (Worcester: Sports Books, 2000), p. 107.
[47] Burgess, *Football – My Life*, esp. pp. 56–65.
[48] L. McKinstry, *Sir Alf: A Major Reappraisal of the Life and Times of England's Greatest Football Manager* (London: Harper Sport, 2006), pp. 28–34. A. Ward, *Armed with a Football: A Memoir of Tim Ward, Footballer and Father* (Oxford: Crowberry, 1994), pp. 134–5.
[49] Army FA, *Annual Report*, 1941–2.
[50] Both matches were drawn. Despite being able to field a strong side of professionals in uniform, the RAF never won against the Army during the war. See Army FA War Emergency Committee minutes, 10 November. 1943; Army FA, *Annual Reports*, 1943–4, 1944–5; J. Rollin, *Soccer at War 1939–45* (London: Willow Books, 1985), p. 50.

Army in Scotland was another popular fixture, and many of these representative games not only attracted 'large and appreciative soldier crowds' but reached a wider public from the running commentaries broadcast by the BBC.[51] The Army also took representative football to Northern Ireland playing a series of matches, mainly in Belfast, once every season from 1941. Scottish Command regularly sent teams to play against service elevens based at the more remote camps in the north of Scotland and Orkney. In 1942, for example, the team played five matches in six days, at Wick, Inverness, Stromness, Kirkwall and Lyness on Hoy.[52] Such was the popularity of these fixtures that the Army FA's bank balance reached record levels – over £10,000 by the summer of 1944 – enabling the Association to make regular contributions to the Directorate of Army Welfare. The RAF Football Association also played many representative fixtures which raised over £30,000 for the RAF Benevolent Fund.[53]

From an early stage professional footballers were used to provide entertainment for troops overseas. In February 1940 three matches were played against sides representing the French army in Paris, Rheims and Lille before large crowds of mainly British soldiers.[54] There is some evidence that the authorities had intended to make such games a regular feature of life behind the lines in France. In the event the policy had to be implemented elsewhere. In the Middle East a touring team known as the Wanderers and made up of professional footballers in the forces travelled across Egypt, Palestine and Syria, playing Egyptian teams and service elevens (many of which also contained professionals or promising young men who would later make a career in football). In late 1941 they also played six matches in Turkey, perhaps as part of British attempts to persuade Turkey to abandon its policy of 'benevolent neutrality' towards Germany.[55] From 1944 troops in Italy were entertained by an army touring team run by Matt

[51] Army FA, *Annual Report*, 1940–1.
[52] Army FA, *Annual Reports*, 1941–2, 1942–3. The RAF football team also went on what their yearbook described as a 'missionary' tour to north-east Scotland in May 1945, during which six matches were played, all won, scoring thirty-nine goals with only six against.
[53] Army FA, *Annual Report*, 1943–4.
[54] 35,000 in Paris, 15,000 in Rheims and 13,000 at Lille. The Army FA made a profit of over £900 from the three games. See Army FA War Emergency Committee minutes, 15 March 1941 and *Annual Report*, 1940–1; also J. Arlott, W. Wooller and M. Edelston, *Wickets, Tries and Goals* (London: Sampson Low, Marston & Co., 1949), pp. 197–8.
[55] T. Finney, *Football Round the World* (London: Sportsmans Book Club, 1955), ch. 6; *Times*, 1, 8, 9, 16, 17 December 1941. The only defeat was to Galata Saray [sic] at Ankara before a capacity crowd of 30,000. See also D. Tossell, *Bertie Mee: Arsenal's Officer and Gentleman* (Edinburgh: Mainstream, 2005), pp. 24–5.

Busby, who recalled playing matches 'only a few miles behind the front lines, with the noise of gunfire drowning out the sound of the referee's whistle'; as victory came closer they were joined by an 8th Army team captained by Andy Beattie and including Tom Finney.[56] In the spring of 1945 the British Army arranged to take an eighteen-strong party of well-known footballers to play a series of games in Italy and Greece. They actually arrived in Naples after a six-hour flight from RAF Lyneham one day before the German surrender on 6 May 1945. Five matches against a variety of army and combined services teams resulted in four very easy victories and one rather more difficult win in Rimini over a Naples Area Services eleven billed as the champions of Central Mediterranean Forces. In general the games seem to have been watched by large and enthusiastic crowds, but some of the players remembered hearing cries from the terraces of 'Come on the real soldiers' and 'Where are the D-Day Dodgers?'[57] The team later travelled to Greece, where one of their opponents was the Greek national side.[58]

As the war in north-west Europe entered a more static phase during the late months of 1944 both the need and the opportunity arose to provide spectacular sport for the invading armies in this theatre. That autumn, following a tour of France and Belgium, Brigadier Wand-Tetley, Inspector of Physical Training at the War Office, recommended that 'exchange visits from teams from UK' should be organised 'for each sport such as football, boxing, athletics and swimming'. As early as September an FA Services XI visited Paris, where they beat a French team at the Parc des Princes, and then Brussels, where they beat a Belgian eleven 3–0. Brussels had only just been liberated and fighting continued only 30 miles away: the terraces had to be cleared for mines and the RAF provided air cover. In the spring of 1945 a series of teams representing FA Services and Scottish Services visited Belgium. An Imperial Services Boxing Association team was also flown in to entertain the troops, arriving by happy coincidence on VE Day so that 22,000 soldiers were able to attend the boxing show in Antwerp on VE Day plus 2.[59]

---

[56] Lanfranchi and Taylor, 'Professional Football', p. 191; Holden, *Stan Cullis*, ch. 4; Finney, *Football Round the World*, pp. 34–8.
[57] McVay and Smith, *The Complete Centre Forward*, pp. 111–13.
[58] Arlott *et al.*, *Wickets, Tries and Goals*, p. 199.
[59] Oldfield, *History*, p. 82; 'Report on tour to France and Belgium by Inspector of Physical Training, War Office' (25 September 1944), HQPT/604 Secret BAOR January 44–January 45 (BLA), APTCM; Rippon, *Gas Masks*, pp. 206–7; *Times*, 2 October 1944, 8 January, 21 March, 18 April 1945.

Three weeks before the German surrender, Lieutenant-Colonel Tringham, in charge of physical training for 21 Army Group, had written buoyantly to Aldershot HQ,

> We are ... rapidly approaching a new phase of our work and before long – we hope (*and* believe) – sport and recreation will play an even more important part. At present we are suffering from an inferiority complex. The RAF has recently increased its pool of Fitness officers and instructors and our present prospects in inter-services games are very gloomy. RAF people like Joy, Hapgood, Beattie want a lot of holding in first class Soccer games and our 'known' talent in the Boxing sphere cannot compete with the RAF. I fully appreciate that the stars are limited and you will have regular demands for them, but perhaps the claims of BLA (or Army of Occupation) justify special consideration. Fraternisation *is* permitted in Italy and other CMF areas. We poor blighters in Germany will have no friends – so we'll *have* to play games and watch them!!! Frankly, everyone out here is expecting great things from the sports side. Really good names in Soccer, Cricket, Swimming, Boxing, Athletics will be a godsend to the troops.[60]

There were soon significant numbers of professional and semi-professional footballers in the occupying force, able to form a team which could both provide entertainment for the troops and in a real sense represent the BAOR. By the late summer of 1945, a group of about sixteen players had been brought together in Düsseldorf for fitness training and practice. The team's first match, against visiting Third Division Notts County, was disappointingly lost 5–2 before 30,000 servicemen but the squad was then moved to improved facilities at Wuppertal under the management of Major Tomlinson. By the autumn of 1945 the team was playing at least twice a week, members caricaturing themselves as the 'Vera Lynns' of the football world.[61] Leading British club sides provided most of the opposition. In July 1945 Liverpool FC had been permitted to bring a team of their own service players to Germany to play two matches against 21 Army Group. In September Montgomery approved an FA scheme, largely initiated by Rous, to send over professional teams on a weekly basis to give servicemen 'the opportunity of seeing players from their home towns'.[62] The BAOR team defeated

---

[60] Lieutenant-Colonel J.A. Tringham, Staff Officer for Physical Training, Rear HQ 21 Army Group, BLA, to Colonel. R.W. Littlehales, Asst Cmd, APTC Aldershot, 13 April 1945, HQPT/604 Secret. BAOR January 1944 to January 1945 (BLA), APTCM.

[61] The best account of the BAOR team is in Ward, *Armed with a Football*, pp. 137–46. See also FA Services Association Committee Minutes, 4 December 1945, FA. At that meeting Wing Commander Adams reported that a total of sixty-one international and inter-services matches had been played between 30 September 1944 and 18 November 1945, which had attracted approximately 1,129,000 spectators.

[62] *The Times*, 17 July, 3 September 1945; *FA Bulletin* 1 (1946).

Figure 14. The BAOR team played two matches against a Polish eleven in a frozen Warsaw in November 1945.

Glasgow Rangers – beaten 6–1 at Hanover before 30,000 troops and the pipers of 6/Seaforth Highlanders – Nottingham Forest and Queen's Park (Glasgow). They did lose to an FA XI but then flew to Warsaw for two games against a representative Polish side before returning to Germany to play two games against Scotland, losing 4–2 at Celle and the following day drawing 1–1 in Hamburg, where the crowd of over 40,000 included Field Marshal Montgomery. Later the BAOR team played five games in Italy and Austria, four against CMF Combined Services and one against a team representing British troops in Austria. They continued to play well into 1946.

This was clearly the stuff to give to the troops in Europe but there were many more British and Allied forces in the Far East, fighting in tough climatic conditions against what must often have appeared the most implacable of enemies, and a very long way from home. When the war ended in Europe there was no sign that it was soon to be followed by victory over the Japanese. Serving in India were thousands of men in all three branches of the armed forces, largely involved in training and support roles for the vanguard of fighting men who were directly confronting the Japanese army in Burma. They had already built up a sophisticated competitive sporting infrastructure particularly in and around Bombay and Calcutta.[63] Tours by British forces footballers became a major part of efforts to boost fragile morale. It is not entirely clear how the first tour – described as 'unofficial' and taking place over six weeks between mid-September and late October 1944 – came about.[64] Denis Compton, company sergeant-major, physical instructor in the Royal Artillery had been posted to India late in 1943 and he was chosen to captain the team under the management of a Captain A. A. Record. A party of twenty-three players were selected though injury and illness meant nine replacements had to be drafted in. With the party divided fairly evenly between English and Scottish professionals many of the games were exhibition matches between two teams designated England and Scotland, a footballing rivalry that never seemed to fade. Several matches were also played against local service teams. A Tottenham man present at one of their matches in Katupalong wrote home that 'the boys enjoyed that game more than watching all the BESA and ENSA concerts'.[65] It had certainly been a staggering journey which, beginning in New Delhi and Calcutta, went through Assam to Imphal, Chittagong, and Ranchi before arriving back in Calcutta – where they still had enthusiasm enough to defeat both a team drawn from the combined strengths of the two top sides in Bengal, Mohun Bagan and East Bengal, and an Indian FA XI. Its success was confirmed late in 1944 when an Inter-Services Sports Exhibition Control Committee was set up in New Delhi to 'organise and control touring football, cricket, hockey teams etc' as 'it has been found that touring teams of this kind are an excellent form of entertainment for the troops'. Four more football tours would take place, the last in 1946, and after VJ Day troops benefited from a wide variety of touring sporting entertainment including an Australian services cricket team, a combined British and Indian hockey team and Freddie Mills boxing exhibition fights.[66]

---

[63] I. Nannestad, 'British Services Football in India 1944 to 1946', *Soccer History* 15 (2007), 3–9, at 4. See also http://website.lineone/net~katie-jones/wood8.htm, accessed 28 November 2006. Even in Burma itself the RAF had an inter-unit football league in 1944 called, sardonically, the Monsoon League.

[64] This paragraph is drawn from the minutes of the first meeting of the Inter-Services Sports Exhibition Control Committee, 3 February 1945, WO 203/1248, TNA. The tour was apparently paid for by gate money from 'matches in Calcutta'. The committee stressed that individuals would be allowed to take part in such tours when they could be spared from military duties. The officer i/c HQ Air Command, South East Asia, however, insisted that 'the diversion of 2 or 3 Dakotas for a three months tour is ... not repeat not justified'.

[65] *Tottenham Weekly Herald*, 20 October 1944, quoted in Nannestad, 'British Services Football', 5.

[66] Nannestad, 'British Services Football'; Birtley, *Freddie Mills*, pp. 100–6.

But despite its willingness to adopt spectacular sport as a form of troop entertainment, the army remained convinced that participation was a greater good. The 1941 War Office notes for officers on soldiers' welfare insisted that 'it is far more important that all men should play games, even if the majority play badly, than that a few should play well while the others look on'. It defined the purpose of sport as three-fold: 'to give healthy exercise, interest and amusement to as many as possible', 'to encourage Unit esprit de corps and loyalty' and 'to teach men the team spirit and the art of losing and winning well'.[67] This latter seems a triumph of amateur ideology over military imperatives – by 1941 the British army was surely already expert in the art of losing well. Perhaps more realistic was the attitude captured by Anthony Powell:

'What about organising some football?'
'No other company there is to play, sir' ...
'But there are plenty of our own fellows. Can't they make up a game among themselves?'
'The boys wouldn't like that ... Another company's what they like to beat'.
That was a good straightforward point of view, no pretence that games were anything but an outlet for power and aggression; no stuff about their being enjoyable as such. You played a game to demonstrate that you did it better than someone else.[68]

But of course many men did find sport enjoyable for its own sake. *The Soldier's Welfare* advised, 'always have a football or two with you, wherever you are. Men love to kick a football about, and will enjoy doing so, given food and a short rest, even after the most gruelling march or exertion'.[69] This comment clearly reflected the army's experience on the Western Front, but it was certainly true of enthusiasts like Arthur Ward, a football-mad bricklayer from Yorkshire serving with the Royal Artillery. In addition to more formal matches, Ward's diary records a number of 'scratch' games and kickabouts. Near Tripoli in March 1943 (just before an attack on the Mareth Line) he notes 'maintenance and able to play a bit of football'. Two years later, in Italy, he played two scratch matches with friends from his old battery and a fortnight afterwards 'went on the road practicing quick actions.

---

[67] *The Soldier's Welfare: Notes for Officers, issued by the War Office* (1941), p. 13. The Army Sport Control Board produced a new publication, *Small Side Team Games and Tabloid Sports*, to encourage even 'small sections of troops, such as those manning isolated AA searchlight and gun sites' to play games.
[68] Anthony Powell, *The Valley of Bones* (London: Flamingo, 1983 (1st edn 1964)), pp. 183–4.
[69] *The Soldier's Welfare*, p. 14.

In between we kicked a football about but we were very upset when a truck ran over it and it burst'.⁷⁰

The army's commitment to participatory sport necessitated considerable organisation. The Army Physical Training Corps' extensive wartime responsibilities included arranging soldier sport. In 1943 the Army School of Physical Training, Northern Command, ran a course for officers and NCOs on 'Recreation in Battle'. APTC instructors even organised sport on troopships to keep soldiers fit and alleviate boredom on the long voyages around Africa to India or the Middle East. During HMT *Mooltan*'s two-month voyage in 1942, for example, 'tabloid and other sports were held every afternoon'; a sports competition was held over several days, with events including obstacle relay, tug-of-war and a one-mile race; there was a boxing tournament; and a boxing judging course for officers was run.⁷¹ The supply of sports equipment was organised by the Sports Department of NAAFI headed by Flight Lieutenant A.J. (Bill) Adams, who had previously handled boxing for the RAF and played at centre-half for the RAF football team. Almost as soon as the BEF arrived in France in 1939 it was supplied by air with £40,000 worth of sports kit. This was presumably abandoned, like so much of the army's equipment, in the retreat to Dunkirk. Nevertheless by August 1941 NAAFI had distributed 75,000 pairs of football boots, 40,000 footballs, 20,000 dart boards and a million darts, 3,000 table tennis tables, a million sets of gym clothes, half a million football shorts and 250,000 football jerseys. It had also supplied the services with 300 all-metal boxing rings, 'designed with the aid of Meccano'.⁷² These efforts were bolstered by civilian charities, like the *Daily Sketch* War Relief Fund, which in April 1942 announced that it had kitted out 1,008 service football teams. Shortages – particularly of rubber after British losses in the Far East – meant that the supply of sports gear was increasingly tightly controlled by the government, with priority given to the armed forces: in December 1945 about 55 per cent of equipment for team games was allocated to the services.⁷³ The navy allocated sports kit on a sliding scale from capital ships (fifteen pairs of

---

⁷⁰ 'Life in the Army – Arthur Ward's Diary' at www.bbc.co.uk/ww2peopleswar/categories/c55128/, accessed 14 September 2007 (henceforth 'Arthur Ward Diary'), 6 March 1943, 12 March, 26 March 1945. For similar examples, see e.g. W. Miles, *The Life of a Regiment*, vol. V: *The Gordon Highlanders 1919–1945* (Aberdeen University Press, 1961), pp. 166, 182, 218.
⁷¹ Oldfield, *History*, pp. 72–3, 88; 'Ships' Staffs' Reports (May 1942–): Report on the Progress of Physical Training, Sports etc. on Board HMT "J 12"', HQPT/609, APTCM.
⁷² 'Sport and the Services', *Green Howards Gazette* 49 (August 1941), 105.
⁷³ *Times*, 23 April 1942; *Hansard's Parliamentary Debates*, HC Deb., 4 August 1942, vol. 382, cc. 837–8; HC Deb., 3 December 1945, vol. 416, c. 1898.

boxing gloves, six footballs, one pump and six dozen sets of football kit including boots) to submarines (one dozen sets of football kit, one ball, one pump – no boxing gloves).[74]

Facilities too had to be provided. In June 1940, training and defence works having 'taken a heavy toll' of the army's playing fields, their maintenance was finally accepted as a state liability; in 1941 the Director of the Army Sport Control Board took on a new role, Inspector of Recreation Grounds.[75] New RAF bases developed extensive facilities as the war progressed. RAF Snaith, a bomber station in Yorkshire built in 1940, still had few sports grounds when Arthur Ellis arrived in 1942; but by 1945 there were six pitches, three for football, two for hockey and one for rugby, as well as a concrete cricket wicket and courts for both tennis and squash.[76] Overseas strenuous efforts were made to organise sports facilities. Courses in physical training for officers and NCOs run at the APTC's Middle East base included instruction on how 'to improvise and set up sports grounds – to build under all topographical conditions a 400m running track which surrounded a football field'.[77] The 'Forces Guide to Tripoli' produced in May 1943, four months after the 8th Army had captured the town, advised troops that the town stadium was 'greatly in demand and units and teams wishing to play football or cricket must make application well in advance. A number of very successful international football matches have been played here, and it is hoped to organise a number of sports meetings during the summer season.'[78] In Italy the army requisitioned sports grounds and employed civilian groundsmen. Early in 1945 a winter sports centre at Terminillo, north-east of Rome, was established. In August it was decided to set up a much grander one at Cortina in the Dolomites for British and American forces in 13 Corps. Facilities – including ski slopes for novices and experts, toboggan slopes, skating rinks, cinemas, theatres, clubs and canteens – were to be provided for 100 officers of both sexes, 1,000 male other ranks, and fifty female other ranks, potentially expanding to double these figures.[79]

[74] 'Encouragement of Team Games in HM Ships' 1945, ADM1/18968, TNA.
[75] 'Report on the Administration of the Army Sport Control Board' (1957), 'The Army Sport Control Board', Enc. 15 to 261/Pubs/9913, both in file labelled 'ASCB History', ASCB.
[76] Arthur E. Ellis, *Refereeing Round the World* (London: Sportsman's Book Club, 1956), p. 43.
[77] A. Talbar, 'Sports in the Jewish Brigade', in G. Eisen, H. Kaufman and M. Lammer (eds.), *Sport and Physical Education in Jewish History* (Netanya: Wingate Institute, 2003), p. 179.
[78] *The Forces Guide to Tripoli* (1943).
[79] 'Allied Forces: Welfare and Recreation, Minutes of Central Mediterranean Forces Army Sports Control Board', WO204/2044, TNA.

A different kind of war 199

The troops serving at home, fed up with petty discipline, fatigues, and apparently pointless daily activities against a background of perpetual defeats, experienced a 'crisis of morale' in 1941–2.[80] In January 1942 the Adjutant General, Lieutenant General Sir Ronald Adam, initiated regular reporting on army morale believing that on it the war would be 'won or lost'. At the same time, as president of the Army Sport Control Board, he called a meeting of Command representatives 'to ensure that a sound organization existed throughout the Army for the encouragement of games for as many as possible at the present time and in readiness' – rather optimistically – 'for the demobilization period when games and competitions would play such an important part'. Hereafter sport began to be used systematically to raise morale by providing troops with 'something to do' in their spare time.[81] Command Sports Boards were re-established and the APTC put increasing effort into organising sport for troops, running competitions, and training officers and NCOs in sports organisation.[82] An ENSA sports brainstrust was formed which travelled around Britain and later to France and Belgium 'visiting hospitals, RAF stations and military and naval establishments, talking and arguing about sport'.[83]

In March 1942 Mass Observation asked its observers how the war had affected the amount of time they spent on sport. The response from servicemen suggests an extremely mixed picture, depending on opportunity, location, rank, motivation and preferred sport. One observer, who had clearly absorbed wholesale the ideology of military sport, said that he had

> taken a great interest in sport in the army, a much greater interest than I did in peace time. Boxing, football and athletics have all proved of interest to me and I feel that sport in the services should be maintained at a high level. It is good for morale, keeps up the team spirit, and helps to dispel gloom and boredom attendant on inaction ... I have played football, taken part in a little boxing, and played a good deal of squash. And all this at the age of 36 and after having given up sport for a number of years. I have felt that one should do as much as possible to keep as fit as possible. Physical fitness helps to overcome fatigue and ennui.

Conversely, another observer, an enthusiastic sportsman in peacetime, complained that in the ten months since his call-up he had played only

---

[80] French, *Raising Churchill's Army*, p. 130.
[81] Crang, 'British Soldier on the Home Front', pp. 60–4; Minutes of Conference summoned by the President, ASCB, 1 December 1941, File 114/General/7797, ASCB.
[82] Oldfield, *History*, pp. 87–8, 91–5.
[83] Crump, *Running Round the World*, p. 77.

two games of football and two cricket matches: 'sport has really been cut out of my life and I don't like it'. A third, whose pre-war games were golf, tennis and squash, said that while in the ranks he had played no sport at all but, having been commissioned, he now played 'a very little golf' and some tennis. An ex-journalist now in the army thought that 'comparatively few people in the Army retain their pre-war enthusiasm for sports, either as players or watchers': in his section 'the only sport that has a regular small weekly following' was greyhound racing.[84]

Yet Arthur Ward's diary suggests that a good deal of sport could be played in the army when ability, enthusiasm and opportunity coincided. Called up in December 1939, Ward spent the next two and a half years training in Britain. A good enough goalkeeper to play for his regiment as well as his troop and battery teams, his first instinct on arriving in any new camp was to look around for ground suitable for a football pitch.[85] While training at Hingham near Norwich, and then at Mersham near Ashford, in 1941–2, he represented the 70th Field Regiment RA with mixed success against 58th Anti-Tank Regiment, a battalion of the Durham Light Infantry, 46 Divisional Reconnaissance Corps, some Royal Engineers, 2/5 Sherwood Foresters, 183 Ambulance RAMC and a battalion of the Leicestershire Regiment.[86] In May 1941 his battery team played an RAF team, including Bobby Robson of Sunderland, in a Charity Cup Tournament game in Norfolk: they were beaten 3–0 but 'a good crowd paid 6d each for admission and proceeds were given to hospitals'.[87] A few weeks later the battery won the Regimental Tournament Shield. Ward also took part in cross-country running and attended a boxing tournament at Thorncliffe Barracks in Folkestone in which 70th Field Regiment were easily defeated by 2/5 Sherwood Foresters.[88]

In the Middle East the army recognised that it faced a potentially serious morale problem in those soldiers 'who had served many years abroad, often with the knowledge of personal trouble at home, doing their jobs in the widely scattered and isolated depots and garrisons where life was monotonous and dull'. To tackle this problem competitive sporting structures were organised especially for football, athletics

---

[84] Mass Observation Archive, Directive Replies, March 1942, DR3057, DR2694, DR3053, DR1256. We are grateful to the Trustees of the Mass Observation Archive, University of Sussex, for this material, and to Matthew Taylor for bringing it to our attention.
[85] Arthur Ward Diary, 12 October 1940, 19 November 1941.
[86] *Ibid.*, 16 April, 18 October, 14 December, 24 December, 28 December 1941, 3 January, 14 February, 18 February, 21 February, 29 March 1942.
[87] *Ibid.*, 3 May 1941.
[88] *Ibid.*, 14 June, 10 December 1941, 11 February 1942.

A different kind of war 201

and boxing. In the words of the Army Physical Training Corps, 'recreation to these men often meant resurrection'.[89] It felt that the problem was most serious in 1944–5 once the fighting had moved on to Italy. But even during the Desert War tedium and homesickness were the main features in the lives of the thousands of non-combatant servicemen in the Middle East. The diary of Steve Lonsdale – who spent 1941–5 in Egypt as a dental mechanic in the Army Dental Corps, under-employed in a useful but unheroic job, and desperately missing his wife and small daughter – illustrates how for many sport became the main solace and filler of time. 'Football seems to be the only thing to look forward to now,' he wrote in October 1941 and, a little later, 'Football seems now to be the only thing here to interest me'.[90] Lonsdale's diary is revealing of the sheer volume of sporting activity in the Canal Zone. That autumn he played several matches for his unit and in November a football league began. In addition to the pleasures of playing and spectating, football clearly also provided something to gamble on: of a game against the bakery at Geneifa Lonsdale adds, 'there was a lot of money on this game', and he later records 'winning 15/- on the football sweep'.[91] Though he came under fire while serving with Field Ambulances during the fighting for the Mareth Line, Lonsdale's only war wound was a football injury to his knee. This required a military court of inquiry 'owing to the hospital saying that the injury was serious and may interfere with my future service. Lt Frost and two of the team came as witnesses. All went well and the finding was that it was an accident and done while on military duty'.[92] Thereafter Lonsdale moved increasingly into the roles of spectator, referee and occasional lineman in cup tie matches. During the winters of 1943–4 and 1944–5 he was often able to watch or referee afternoon football matches on an almost daily basis, sometimes two matches a day. In summer cricket took over (Lonsdale was a useful bowler); he also played a little tennis, did some swimming, sailing, and fishing, and attended the Alexandria races. In times of despondency Lonsdale felt that his life was 'beginning to be just an existence … Everything is so deadly and so much the same.'[93] Sport did much to provide some variety and raise his morale.

[89] Oldfield, *History*, p. 128. For recollections of British military sport in the Middle East from an unusual perspective, see Talbar, 'Sports in the Jewish Brigade'.
[90] War Diaries of Private Steve Lonsdale, 13–22 October 1941, 3 November 1941, at www.wartimememories.co.uk/africa.html#lonsdale, accessed 21 September 2007 (henceforth 'Lonsdale Diary').
[91] Lonsdale Diary, 13–22 October, 7–13 November, 16–17 November, 22–4 November, 7 Dec. 1941.
[92] *Ibid.*, 26–9 December 1941, 22 February 1942.
[93] *Ibid.*, 2 September, 23 September 1944.

Figure 15. The victorious RAF team from an airfield in Aden celebrate their victory over an infantry side in the final of a hockey tournament in 1944.

Though non-combatants obviously had more time and opportunity, 'sharp end' troops also played sport whenever they could. During the Desert War units sometimes spent several months out of the line for rest, training and refitting, and much official and unofficial sport took place in these periods. Between Alamein and the assault on the Mareth Line, for example, 1st Armoured Division (including Arthur Ward's artillery regiment) spent about three months at Tmimi, some 50 miles west of Tobruk. Ward's regiment immediately 'levelled out a hard area of sand and marked out a football pitch'. Matches were played against other regiments, and an inter-battery competition was held for the 'Tmimi Cup' which was won by Ward's battery on Christmas Day 1942. The cup, created by the Royal Engineers, was presented by the commanding officer, and the team spent the evening with the Sergeants' Mess swigging dangerously mixed drinks from it.[94]

---

[94] Arthur Ward Diary, 19 November, 14 December, 25 December 1942, 12 January, 13 January 1943. For similar recollections of football at Tmimi (with 'disused camouflage nets' for goalnets), see V. A. Crocker, *There's a Soldier at the Gate: Second World War Memoirs of a Tenth Royal Hussar* (Victoria, BC: Trafford, 2005), p. 44.

During another period of inactivity in late 1943, after returning from Sicily to Bizerta in North Africa, a divisional knock-out football competition took place, and the 'Tmimi Cup' cup was again played for and again won by Ward's battery.[95] Similarly, when the 7th Armoured Division (the 'Desert Rats') spent three months at Homs on the Libyan coast in the summer of 1943, 'great efforts' were made 'to provide entertainment for the troops'. The aerodrome at Leptis Magna was 'turned into a Sports Ground comprising football and hockey and a running track'. Divisional athletics, football, hockey and basketball competitions were organised, individual regiments ran inter-troop and inter-squadron contests, and 22 Armoured Brigade held a swimming sports day.[96]

Even much shorter intervals out of action sometimes provided opportunities for sport. During a month's rest and training at Mrassas in late 1942 4th County of London Yeomanry, a territorial regiment of the Royal Armoured Corps, held an athletic meeting and played four football matches against other regiments.[97] In February 1943, following a 'more or less continuous period of Field Service in the front line since the early days of July', the men of 'A' Squadron, 11th Hussars, were granted a few weeks' training and recreation. In this instance sport acted as physical training as well as amusement:

Football and Pass ball pitches were manufactured and as far as possible the fitness of the men returned. Long periods of work in AFVs [Armoured Fighting Vehicles] not being the best way of keeping men fit ... There can be no doubt that this period of rest and training had done considerable good to the Regt, on the whole the men having been very tired when they arrived.

'A' Squadron's commander was certainly a sporting type and alert to sporting opportunities. That April, finding 22nd Armoured Brigade, to which his unit was now attached, 'parked on a ready made aerodrome', he immediately moved the squadron there 'as I thought what a perfect football ground it would make'. Their first football match (played shortly after the burial of two men from another regiment found in a burnt-out tank near Djebibina) 'met a quick end as the bladder broke',

---

[95] Arthur Ward Diary, 2 November, 1 December, 25 December 1943.
[96] War Diary of 4th County of London Yeomanry, 27 May, 10 June, 9 July, 20 July, 27 July, 29 July, 24 August 1943 at http://warlinks.com/armour/4_cly/4cly_43.html, accessed 18 September 2007; War Diary of the 11th Hussars for the Period 24 May 1943 to 19 August 1943 at http://warlinks.com/armour/11_hussars/11huss_43.html, accessed 19 September 2007.
[97] War Diary of 4th County of London Yeomanry, 26 November, 29 November, 1 December, 7 December 1942, at http://warlinks.com/armour/4_cly/4cly_42.html, accessed 18 September 2007.

but the Squadron still managed to play one more game before moving back into the fighting.[98]

A similar pattern of sport fitted in between military engagements can be seen in Italy. In November 1944 Arthur Ward's 11th (HAC) Regiment RHA were fighting on the Gothic Line. Near Cesena, the enemy having retreated, the regiment stayed where it was for a rest and began playing inter-troop football matches. During another rest period in January 1945 at Pesaro near Rimini the regiment began playing for the Tmimi Cup; they also competed in a Brigade Cup competition, making it to the final before being beaten 7–1 by 325th RASC Company.[99] As the Italian campaign progressed a greater level of army organisation became possible. A few weeks after Rome was occupied by the Allies (on 4 June 1944) an Allied Athletics Meeting was held there; a year later a second 'Allied Track and Field Championship' was held in Florence. In November 1944 a Central Mediterranean Army Sports Control Board was established both to provide sporting events 'as a spectacle on the biggest scale possible' and 'to plan sport for all serving men'. By summer 1945, after the German surrender, official policy had shifted, emphasising 'wider participation for the troops themselves' over 'the spectacular and entertainment type' of sport. A Physical Training and Sports Centre was established at Udine in north-east Italy which ran three-week courses for NCOs on sports organisation. A series of theatre-wide inter-unit sports championships was begun in football, rugby, cricket, hockey, cross-country and water-polo. An Army Swimming Championship and an Army Golf Championship were held in Rome, and an Army Tennis Championship in Venice.[100]

By the time the war moved back to north-west Europe, careful official preparations for soldier sport had become standard. In September 1944, shortly after the liberation of Brussels, Montgomery's 21 Army Group laid down 'the policy regarding the importance of providing the facilities for all types of sport and recreation and of organising a comprehensive programme to include competitions and tournaments'. Brigadier Wand-Tetley recommended an increase of physical training staff 'to provide expert organisation of sport and recreation', the establishment of an Army Group Sports Board and a decentralised system

---

[98] War Diary of the 11th Hussars, February 1943; 15 April, 17 April, 19 April 1943 at http://warlinks.com/armour/11_hussars/11huss_43.html, accessed 19 September 2007.
[99] Arthur Ward Diary, 12 November 1944, 16 January, 17 January 1945.
[100] 'Physical Training and Sports Centre, Central Mediterranean Forces', WO170/7469, TNA; 'Allied Forces: Welfare and Recreation', minutes of Central Mediterranean Army Sports Control Board, WO204/2044, TNA; *Union Jack*, 1 November 1944; Oldfield, *History*, pp. 129–32.

of sports committees. He also suggested week-long courses to train unit sports officers and NCOs, and once an Army Group School of Physical Training had been established at Louvain this was put into practice with sixty or seventy NCOs attending each week's course. A progress report of December 1944 added that:

> in some cases a three tonner is the 'Mobile Gym' of the Div[ision], and contains ... a good supply of sports apparatus. The W[arrant]O[fficer] i/c makes this his Headquarters and when a [Brigade] etc is coming out of the line the 'gym' moves to the area concerned and sets up games pitches etc so that recreation is possible from the word 'go' without wasting time looking for facilities and equipment.[101]

This official endorsement of the value of sport to fighting soldiers both recognised and encouraged sporting activity on the ground. In September 1944, between the end of the battle of Normandy and their move forward into Belgium, 2/Middlesex Regiment spent some enjoyable weeks at Le Thil-en-Vexin in the Seine region, where 'there was football each day on the local village ground ... an inter-platoon knockout competition was organised, and there were several good games'.[102] In October 1944, while assisting with the perimeter defence of Oss, north of Eindhoven, the 11th Hussars managed some inter-squadron football matches on the town's three football grounds. A few weeks later the Hussars went into reserve at Dongen, combining training, maintenance and recreation including an inter-troop seven-a-side football competition. By November the squadrons were taking turns to do four days in the line on the Dutch–Belgian border. At leisure, 'two football grounds were now in use by the Regt and there was remarkable keenness throughout as we had had little opportunity for football since we were at ST ANDRE in the beachhead days [of June 1944]'. In reserve that December, 'Rugby Football was started again (the first time since HOMS, in the summer of 1943)'.[103] The 3rd British Infantry Division even organised a divisional football competition played off mainly in the Maas River area between September 1944 and February 1945 whenever opportunity offered. It was taken sufficiently seriously for one of the semi-finals to be replayed after the game ended drawn 3–3

---

[101] 'Report on tour to France and Belgium by Inspector of Physical Training, War Office' (25 Sept. 1944), 'Physical Training. Progress Report for Period ending 31 Dec. 44', HQPT/604 Secret BAOR Jan. 44–Jan. 45 (BLA), APTCM; Oldfield, *History*, pp. 80–2.

[102] Moberly, *Campaign in N.W. Europe*, p. 69.

[103] War Diary of 11th Hussars (Prince Albert's Own), 16 October, 31 October, 20 November, 1 December 1944, at http://warlinks.com/armour/11_hussars/11huss_44.html, accessed 19 September 2007.

despite extra time in fading light. The final was held six weeks later on 5 February 1945 at the De Valk ground at Venraij while the Division waited to be relieved. 2/Middlesex Regiment beat 1/South Lancashire Regiment 3–1 and the acting GOC, Major-General Galloway, presented the winning team with a cup and individual silver medals made from Dutch coins.[104]

A characteristic of this period was matches against local teams from newly liberated France, Belgium and Holland. In September 1944, at Le Thil-en-Vexin, 2/Middlesex Regiment played a 'most amusing game ... against the local French team', the mayor kicking off in the unavoidable absence of the general.

Unluckily the battalion team was far too strong for the local side, but the difference in style and temperament between the two teams was even more striking than the one-sidedness of the play. French and English then had tea together in the Café de la Gare while 'C' Company played the French second team, also scoring an easy victory.

Later that month, the battalion pressed forward into Holland. At Budel, where 13 Platoon's mortars were stationed on the football field, 'they promptly had a game of football with the local side, and were soundly beaten 3–5, to the great disappointment of the Dutch spectators, who cheered loudly whenever we got the ball'. At Someren Battalion HQ and 'D' Company HQ also played a local team, in this case losing 6–2.[105]

After VE Day, as in 1918, sport was promoted by military authorities anxious to 'occupy the waking hours of the troops with every sort of gainful activity in and out of parade hours' to maintain discipline and morale in a civilian army impatiently waiting demobilisation.[106] The war diary of the 11th Hussars illustrates this process. Arriving in Berlin in July 1945, the Hussars put in 'considerable work ... preparing sports grounds and by the end of the month Regtl sports activities included football, hockey, cricket, athletics, swimming and boating', not to mention riding. By October, 'Sport occupied a predominant position in the activities of the Regt'. Balaclava Day was marked by a gymkhana and a football match in which 'the Sgts narrowly defeated the officers ... the score would have probably been considerably larger had it not been for the formers' exemplary tact'. Snow wound up the cricket season, but

[104] Moberly, *Campaign in N.W. Europe*, pp. 100, 101–2 (Appendix – The Divisional Football Competition); N. Scarfe, *Assault Division: A History of the 3rd Division from the Invasion of Normandy to the Surrender of Germany* (Staplehurst: Spellmount, 2004 (1st edn 1947)), pp. 200–1.
[105] Moberly, *Campaign in N.W. Europe*, pp. 69–70, 75–6.
[106] Kemp, *History of the Royal Scots Fusiliers*, at http://rhf.org.uk/Books/KEMP'S%20 History%20of%20the%20RSF%201919%201959.doc, accessed 20 September 2007.

rugby began, the Hussars fielding 'a very strong side, defeating any team put against it'; it eventually won the Berlin Area Championship 'in a thrilling final against British Troops Berlin'.[107] Athletics was also encouraged, and in September 1946 an Inter-Allied Athletics Championship took place in which teams from seven countries competed. The event was held in Berlin's Olympic Stadium, the symbolism both powerful and unmistakable.[108]

Very soon after the end of the war British troops began to play sport, particularly football, against German sides. Some liberated countries, notably Holland and Norway, felt that this was taking fraternisation too far, and at a meeting of FIFA called for such matches to cease. Stanley Rous duly lodged an objection, instancing matches between the 53rd Division and German teams played before 40,000 spectators, and reiterating that Foreign Office policy was that, while children in occupied countries should be encouraged to play games in accordance with British traditions, no sporting opportunities should be given to adults. However, the Control Office for Germany and Austria maintained that 'the playing of matches between British and German teams can contribute to the democratic re-education of the Germans'. Montgomery stated that, while 'my troops are forbidden to play matches with German ex-military teams ... it is part of my policy to play games with civilian teams, such as miners, boys' clubs and so on'. In January 1946 the Foreign Office confirmed that policy was now to allow British troops to play against 'town, village and club teams'.[109]

There is one further role served by sport in the services during the Second World War that deserves detailed attention: its function within prisoner of war camps. During the war 172,592 British servicemen were taken prisoner. Most British and Commonwealth prisoners of war served their time in Germany and Italy, many captured after Dunkirk in 1940, others in the early North African campaigns, while the remainder suffered severely in Japanese prison camps established after the fall of Singapore.[110] S. P. MacKenzie, in his authoritative study

---

[107] War Diary of the 11th Hussars, July–December 1945 at http://warlinks.com/armour/11_hussars/11huss_45.html, accessed 19 September 2007.

[108] Greece, Norway and the Soviet Union were absent (*Times*, 9 September 1946). The Czechs only had one entrant, who after cycling through the Russian lines in order to take part won the 5,000 metres. His name was Emil Zatopek. M. Sandrock, *Running with the Legends* (Leeds: Human Kinetics, 1996), p. 8.

[109] 'Foreign Office correspondence over Army football in occupied zones, 1946', FO371/55626, TNA.

[110] On the logistical problems the large number of prisoners of war presented to the Germans see S. P. MacKenzie, 'The Treatment of Prisoners of War in World War II', *Journal of Modern History* 66 (1994), 487–520. Of the 172,592, 7,401 were from the navy and 13,115 from the RAF while 152,076 were from the army. A total of 135,009 British POWs served their time in Germany.

of the experience of British and Commonwealth servicemen in German camps, has emphasised the single most significant difference between the officers and most of the other ranks. Under the terms of the Geneva Convention ordinary sailors, soldiers and airmen could be put to work while the officers could not. Whereas the majority of other ranks found themselves working for the Germans all commissioned ranks and a good proportion of NCOs spent most of their time behind barbed wire.[111]

Article 17 of the Geneva Convention of 1929 stated that 'Belligerents shall encourage as much as possible the organization of intellectual and sporting pursuits by the prisoners of war'.[112] Although the experience of individual prisoners varied a good deal, for those in the long-term camps for non-working NCOs and officers, the Stalags and the Oflags, there was usually the time, space and resources to provide a wide range of sporting and recreational facilities.[113] Most of the activities were initiated and organized by the prisoners themselves with the captors offering a certain amount of support – supplying materials to construct theatres, for example and spaces to convert into sports fields. Equipment for the games and sports was provided by a range of international organisations, notably the YMCA and the Red Cross. MacKenzie is probably right to conclude that outdoor sports and games served two main functions for prison camp inmates. Once they were receiving enough food, sports and games helped to keep them physically fit. Second and perhaps equally important they helped to pass the time and stave off boredom, a condition from which few prisoners could ever hope to escape totally. Playing or watching sport or discussing its prospects and aftermath meant that POWs had something on which to concentrate for hours at a time to help them forget where they were.[114]

[111] S.P. MacKenzie, *The Colditz Myth. British and Commonwealth Prisoners of War in Nazi Germany* (Oxford University Press, 2004), pp. 193–200. For the growing historiography reflecting on a much wider range of prisoner experiences see B. Moore and K. Fedorovich, 'Prisoners of War in the Second World War: An Overview' in their edited volume, *Prisoners of War and their Captors in World War Two* (Oxford: Berg, 1996) pp. 1–17.

[112] MacKenzie, *The Colditz Myth*, p. 193. The Geneva Convention also allowed a representative of both the International Committee of the Red Cross and the Protecting Power to visit POW camps in Axis and Allied territories in order to monitor conditions and hear prisoner complaints. Switzerland served as the Protecting Power for both sides after the United States entered the war in December 1941. See V. Vourkoutiotis, 'What the Angels Saw: Red Cross and Protecting Power Visits to Anglo-American POWs, 1939–1945', *Journal of Contemporary History* 40 (2005), 689–706.

[113] Stalag Lufts run by the Luftwaffe for captured airmen and Marinelagers by the Kriegsmarine for captured sailors. Army POWs were contained in the Oflags and Stalags run by the Heer.

[114] MacKenzie, *The Colditz Myth*, p. 201. On the range of recreational activities organised see P. Liddle and I. Whitehouse, 'Not the Image but Reality: British POW

A different kind of war 209

We have chosen to explore the place which sport played in the life of the prisoners in one camp in Germany, Stalag 383 which was located near the village of Hohenfels in Bavaria. Opened in the late summer of 1942, it remained operational until the end of the war. Its facilities seem to have been better than those at many camps. Accommodation was in chalet-type rooms with twelve to fourteen prisoners in two lines of double-decker beds. It may have been originally a summer camp for the Hitler Youth as most of the rooms were fitted with electric light, a stove and water. In March 1943 there were 4,003 prisoners at Stalag 383, all non-working NCOs: 2,838 Englishmen, 520 Australians, 459 Scots, 295 New Zealanders, 76 Welsh and 52 Irish. These figures are taken from the diary kept throughout the period in which the camp functioned by Battery Sergeant Andrew Hawarden, 20th Battery, Royal Artillery. Although he did not write entries every day few weeks passed without some account of POW life. Particularly detailed and insightful is what might be called his running commentary on camp sport, in the organisation of which Sergeant Hawarden played an important role and in which he had what might be termed a professional interest. Hawarden had served in the Royal Artillery during the First World War. He was an enthusiastic football player and a member of the team which won the Western Command Championship in 1920. After leaving the army he played professionally with a number of clubs including Tranmere Rovers. As a reservist he was among the first to be recalled when war broke out in 1939 and was captured in the retreat to Dunkirk on 29 May 1940. After a long and exhausting journey he arrived at Thorn in Poland and remained there until the move to Stalag 383 in mid-September 1942.[115]

His enthusiasm for sport is reflected in an early diary entry only five days after his arrival at Hohenfels. 'I have been looking around the camp and its surroundings and there is a piece of land that will make an

Experience in Italian and German Camps', *Everybody's War: The Journal of the Second World War Experience Centre* 8 (2003), 14–25.

[115] Hawarden's diary was written in pencil in notebooks and on scraps of paper and successfully hidden from his captors. So far unpublished, a typescript version has been lodged in the Imperial War Museum; we are grateful to Sandra Hawarden-Lord for permission to quote from it. For Hawarden, see also Purcell and Gething, *Wartime Wanderers*, pp. 47, 62–3. Use has also been made of M. N. McKibbin, *Barbed Wire: Memories of Stalag 383* (London: Staples Press, 1947). See also the websites www.pegasusarchive.org/pSt_383.htm and www.awm.gov.au/stolenyears/ww2/germany/story3.asp. Hawarden's diary is unique in its detail, but numerous other POW diaries include material on sport. In the IWM Department of Documents see for example the diaries of W. A. Quinney (92/31/1) and A. J. East (87/34/1), both at Stalag IVB; John Jenkins (98/21/1) at Chienti, Italy; and Commander John Frank Dover (99/82/1), at several camps in Italy and Germany.

admirable ground for sports '.[116] Different – often overlapping – communities were quickly established to organise not only sports but education classes, a library and many other recreational activities and social clubs.[117] What this at least partly reflects is that the NCO POWs at Hohenfels were experienced prisoners many having already spent two years behind the wire. Two years in a particular camp was also more than enough to build up loyalties to those who had shared the experience with you. One of the first football competitions at Stalag 383 was a knock-out tournament between teams representing the inmates of former camps. On Christmas Eve 1942 Lamsdorf beat Spittal in one semi-final while Wolfsburg beat Thorn in the other.[118] It was not long before a football league of two divisions, featuring two teams from each of the nine companies into which the prisoners were divided, was playing regular competitive and organised games.[119]

In a situation in which spaces to play were scarce and equipment also in short supply organisation was needed to ensure a fair and efficient distribution. Organising committees for each of the main sports quickly developed. Hawarden was honorary president of the Stalag Football Association. Some of the prisoners received sports goods from home, but most were reliant on items sent by the Red Cross. These were very welcome but never sufficient. It was very difficult, for example, to keep footballs in a usable state. Laces in particular were scarce items as was the dubbin which when applied to the outer leather casing offered some protection from the wet.[120] In the spring of 1943 the football kit for the whole camp consisted of two sets of shirts and shorts which would be in regular use on the many football days. The first match would kick off at 10 a.m., and the shirts and shorts would be handed in and used for a second game at noon. By 2 p.m. two fresh teams would be kicking off with a fourth match scheduled for 5 p.m. and, as the nights grew lighter, yet another at 6.30 p.m. The committee attempted to reserve the kit for international matches and other special games, but after a camp vote the camp's Man of Confidence, a kind of POW ombudsman whose role was to settle such disputes between the prisoners, decided

---

[116] Hawarden Diary, 20 September 1942.
[117] For other camp activities see the report of the Arts and Crafts Exhibition at Stalag 383 in *Prisoner of War*, October 1943, p. 3.
[118] Hawarden Diary, 24 December 1942. On rivalries between those from different Oflags see R. Kee, *A Crowd Is Not Company* (London: Eyre & Spottiswoode, 1947), p. 86.
[119] Hawarden Diary, 28 February 1943.
[120] Some footballers found a German margarine an acceptable substitute. Hawarden Diary, 7 May 1943. For an example of the kind of consignments sent by the Red Cross see McCarthy, *War Games*, p. 152.

Figure 16. Andrew Hawarden (second from right with hands on knees) and fellow POWs at Stalag 383, 13 November 1943.

that as the football kit was provided by the Red Cross for all the prisoners to use, all had the right to use it.[121] Shortages of sports gear were not only a football problem. There were only enough dart boards for each room to have one on one day every three weeks, and there were never enough leather-cased cricket balls. Geneva had sent plenty of table tennis bats and balls, but there was no table.[122]

Maintaining the playing field in good condition was another important job for which most of the sports committees could share responsibility. Basketball and hockey had their own playing areas, but the main football pitch was in more or less constant use from March to Christmas for two of the most popular sports, association football and rugby union. They had to make room for rugby league and Australian Rules football too when the enthusiasts for those games began to organise. Moreover, as the number of prisoners increased in the winter of 1942–3, a German hut-building programme began to encroach on the sports field. By early 1943 the prisoner sports organisations had identified an area which could become a new sports ground with some levelling and removal of stones. Digging and rolling equipment was in short supply, though the Germans offered a mixture of eight picks and spades. By May 1943

[121] Hawarden Diary, 31 March 1943.
[122] *Ibid.*, 14 December 1942, 11 February 1943.

the different sporting organisations were sending out up to fifty men on different days to work on the new ground. Its opening was delayed by the time it took for the Germans to put a barbed wire fence around it; it was afterwards closed for a time having allegedly been used during an attempted escape.[123] But by October 1943 the new Sports Platz was the centre of a lot of serious fun including football, both forms of rugby and Australian Rules. Hawarden noted that 'anyone who wants a game can have one', and during the peak of the summer season inter-company football matches played in the evenings drew crowds which the ex-professional player estimated as being between two and three thousand.[124]

There was even a swimming pool, finally opened in May 1943 after prolonged lobbying. It was twenty-two yards long, eleven yards wide and six feet deep. As Hawarden wrote in the diary, 'we called it a swimming pool because that is what we would like it to be'.[125] It was certainly very popular among the 'kriegies' who lounged around and bathed and swam in the pool throughout most of the summers of 1943 and 1944. Photographs give an impression of a 1930s lido with the difference that it was all-male and with naked bathing.[126] Though small, it soon became the venue for competitive swimming and water polo. England and New Zealand staged an eight-a-side swimming event in August 1943 followed by a triple relay swim including an Australian team.[127] It was also a site of self-improvement, staging swimming lessons for beginners together with a life-saving class for which 200 prisoners had enrolled in May 1944.[128]

Many ex-prisoners and other writers have commented on the level of ingenuity shown by individuals and groups in the long-term camps. This partly reflects the skills which conscripted officers and other ranks brought to their military service. Examples can be found in all areas of camp life from cooking and gardening to education, dance, drama and escape plans. Sport at Stalag 383 made its contribution by the making of a pair of goal nets for the football pitch. Most recreational football in 1930s Britain was played without nets largely for economic reasons. Goal nets were a sign that the game was to be taken seriously. There was something magical about the significance of the

[123] *Ibid.*, 14 March 1943; 29 April 1943; 1, 19, 20 May 1943; 4 June 1943; 3, 4, 10 July 1943; *Prisoner of War*, November 1943, p. 5.
[124] Hawarden Diary, 24 October 1943, 14 June 1944.
[125] *Ibid.*, 17 November 1942; 14, 15, 19 May 1943.
[126] *Ibid.*, 21 July 1943. Prisoners called themselves 'Kriegies' from the German word for prisoner-of-war, *Kriegsgefangene*.
[127] The Australians won. Hawarden Diary, 27 July 1943; 4, 6, 13 August 1943.
[128] *Ibid.*, 4 August 1943, 19 May 1944.

ball climbing up the rigging as a goal was scored. Goal nets perhaps even reminded men of exciting Saturday afternoons watching favoured teams or players. Scrounging for goalposts was a relatively easy task, and German toothpaste, although it was not thought much of as an aid to dental hygiene, was an acceptable substitute for white paint for the goal posts and when squeezed carefully on to the grass made very clear pitch markings. The nets were made with 3,000 pieces of string largely collected from Red Cross parcels. The aim was to use them for the first time for the England–Scotland international football match scheduled for April 1943. To collect the required amount a poster advertising the game and autographed by the players was raffled, the entry fee being one piece of Red Cross string.[129] When the match was played on Sunday 18 April practically everyone in the camp turned out to watch. As the diarist noted, the atmosphere was 'like at home' and the ground looked well with its marked-out pitch, white goalposts and the prized goal nets. Several German soldiers, officers and other ranks, were present 'and expressed their thanks and were more than pleased with the match'.[130]

Sports were one of the ways in which important anniversaries were marked and identities confirmed. When the Red Cross representative arrived he was invited to watch some sport. A year in Stalag 383 was marked by sports. The British August bank holiday was celebrated by a carnival and sports day with a fancy-dress dance in the evening and prizes for the most persuasive outfits. There was a British Empire sports tournament and Anzac Day saw a veritable sporting Olympiad with every event save the javelin (there was no javelin), including heats, veterans' sports, relays and tug-of-war. There were thirty-four runners in the mile and over 300 entries in total.[131] Hawarden thought that such a sports day 'could not have been had at home'. It is not surprising that when the Germans allowed a day for the taking of photographs in August 1943 many sports teams took advantage of the opportunity.[132] The Scottish committee organised a Highland Games in August 1943 which included not only the traditional sports but Highland dancing and the playing of the bagpipes.[133] The other way of finding some sporting excitement was to gamble on it. Camp bookmakers in Stalag

[129] *Ibid.*, 18 March 1943; 6, 7, 14 April 1943.
[130] *Ibid.*, 18 April 1943.
[131] *Ibid.*, 25 April, 30 July, 2 August, 28 September 1943; 1 June, 5 June 1944.
[132] *Ibid.*, 16 August 1943. See also McKibbin, *Barbed Wire*, p. 50. *The Prisoner of War* published several pictures of sporting events and sports teams taken in camps in Germany and Italy. See for example November 1942, p. 7; October 1943, p. 9; February 1944, p. 11; February 1945, p. 3. There are many more pictures of POW sports teams in the archive of the British Red Cross.
[133] Hawarden Diary, 9 August 1943.

383 were preparing stands and betting boards in advance of the Anzac Sports Day in April 1943.[134] Prize draws, with cigarettes as prizes, were organised for the Derby in 1943 and 1944.[135]

Of course there were drawbacks to sport. Stalag sports were often conducted on the cruder side of robust. Injuries did happen, and in the winter of 1943 competitive rugby was temporarily suspended after several players were injured following heavy falls on very hard grounds, leading to the prison medical officer expressing his concern.[136] Individual enthusiasm for physical activity of any kind could be and was inhibited by poor diet and the sheer unpredictability of the food supply. When Hawarden first arrived at Hohenfels he thought the food much better than it had been at his previous camp in Poland. But as conditions deteriorated inside Germany by the end of February 1943 Hawarden's daily ration was one-fifth of a loaf, three raw potatoes the size of eggs and margarine. Sometimes the only drinks issued were hot water. In such circumstances Red Cross food parcels were essential to the maintenance of energy and fitness, and when their arrival was delayed playing sport seemed much less attractive. An Empire Day Boxing tournament had to be postponed in May 1943 because boxers could not train and fight on German rations alone.[137] But shortly after the success of the Anzac Sports Day, just before the Empire Games, and with so many sporting and other recreational activities competing for the attentions of over 4,000 men, Sergeant Hawarden may be forgiven for sounding as though he was having a good time. 'If there is a better entertained Stalag in Germany I would like to see it. Everyday there is a football, rugby, hockey and basketball match; then we frequently have boxing and wrestling shows and every night we have some sort of concert running.'[138]

If sport was a valuable source of solace to prisoners of war much the same can be said both of the services as a whole and of the civilian population during the Second World War. In attempting to understand the role of sport in the British war effort there has been a tendency among historians to divide sport up rather too simplistically into the spectacular and the participatory. The latter's contribution to general

---

[134] *Ibid.*, 22, 25 April 1943.
[135] *Ibid.*, 21 June 1943; 16 June, 17 June 1944. By 1944 some prisoners were able to listen to a running commentary on the race on illicit radios.
[136] *Ibid.* 16, 19, 23 March 1943. Rugby was also abandoned in Stalag Luft III when injuries began to take their toll as players 'let off steam'. Squadron Leader P. A. Ward-Thomas, 'Sport in RAF Prisoner of War Camps', *RAF Quarterly*, N.S. 1:1 (July 1949), 38–43, at 40.
[137] Hawarden Diary, 24 February, 28 April, 10 May, 21 July 1943.
[138] *Ibid.*, 5 May 1943.

fitness and well-being is generally if sometimes reluctantly allowed. The spectacular creates more mixed feelings. But Peter Borsay in his recent history of leisure has reminded us not to forget the theatrical ingredient in the sporting spectacle in which both players and spectators are part of the performance. In modern societies, perhaps especially in time of war, 'occasional releases from contemporary structures are a psychological imperative', and both participative and spectacular sport can provide such release.[139] During the Second World War this fact was recognised by the British services, which actively encouraged the use of sporting stars to provide entertainment to troops behind the lines in North Africa, India, Italy and north-west Europe, as well as to the many thousands of servicemen stationed at home. In so doing they also made a contribution to civilian morale. Recent writers such as Robert Mackay have tended to conclude that watching star players 'was the sort of mental refreshment' that 'effectively disappeared' in wartime Britain and that 'spectator sport, at the highest level at least, was badly impoverished'.[140] We believe that the wartime sporting spectacle was less poverty stricken than previous writers have claimed, in large part because of the willingness of the armed forces to release top players for sporting events.

Nevertheless the services, building on the experiences of the Great War, still placed a premium on participative sport and devoted considerable organisation and resources to ensuring that it was made feasible for as many troops as possible, wherever they were. Their well-founded belief in the benefits of sport for troop morale was echoed not only by their allies but even perhaps by their enemies. In the lead-up to D-Day, thousands of pounds of sports equipment was poured into the sealed camps in south-east England. On the other side of the Channel, if the pro-German Swedish newspaper *Aftonbladet* is to be believed, German troops awaiting the Allied invasion of north-west Europe were similarly diverted by a sports programme organised by the German High Command, including a football tournament for a cup presented by Rommel.[141] For many, of course, especially those whose time was spent largely in preparation for or actually involved in combat, the gruesome reality of war provided few opportunities for either the pleasures or

---

[139] Peter Borsay, *A History of Leisure: The British Experience since 1500* (London: Palgrave, 2006), p. 223.
[140] R. Mackay, *Half the Battle: Civilian Morale in Britain during the Second World War* (Manchester University Press, 2002), p. 117; see also J. Walvin, *The People's Game* (Edinburgh: Mainstream, 1994), pp. 144–51.
[141] Oldfield, *History*, p. 91; *Times*, 13 March 1944. For wartime sports programmes in the US Army see Wakefield, *Playing to Win*, ch. 6.

consolations of sport. Yet it is one of these less fortunate soldiers who best sums up sport's value to fighting men. Bill McLaren eventually became 'the voice of rugby union' on BBC Television but he spent the war as an officer in the Royal Artillery. By 1944 he was in Italy attached to 20/21 Battery, 5 Medium Regiment before the battle for Monte Cassino. His job was finding a forward position from which he could send back radio messages directing the gunners to their enemy targets. He was a keen sportsman and had played good-class rugby for Hawick but as he wrote much later,

I didn't give a thought to rugby football in those days. The war put everything else in perspective. But at the end of hostilities when I got a game for the Combined Services in Italy, I was chuffed to bits. It was such a relief from the tension and anxiety of military action. To get out on a rugby pitch and hoof the ball about in complete freedom was just magical. It's strange how it is the simplest of pleasures that often mean the most to us.[142]

---

[142] Bill McLaren, *The Voice of Rugby: An Autobiography* (London: Bantam Books, 2005), p. 103.

7 The national service years: the summit of military sport?

> There was one certain way to escape the routine of the Army and that was to excel at sports. Anyone who reached a high standard at football or rugby, anyone who could run or jump and especially anyone who could box, was assured of a few short cuts ... In the British Army, squad competes against squad and regiment competes against regiment. The Army competes against the Navy and Air Force and the Combined Services compete against the World – or they did in those days. The horizons of an Army sportsman knew no bounds.
>
> Tony Thorne, *Brasso, Blanco and Bull* (London: Robinson, 2000), pp. 50–1.

It will be clear by now that sport in its many forms had become a well-established part of service life well before the end of the Second World War. Its importance was to be underlined when conscription was reintroduced by the National Service Act of 1947.[1] The loss of India had not only diminished the size of the Empire but deprived the British armed services of a large pool of manpower. As the British government had no intention of giving up the rest of the Empire, sailors, soldiers and airmen were needed to man bases in many areas of the world. The 1947 Act stipulated that all males between the ages of eighteen and twenty-six would serve for one year.[2] The rapid onset of the Cold War changed the context of national service with first the crisis over Berlin in 1948 and then the outbreak of war in Korea in 1950 emphasising the need for further increases in the manpower of the armed forces. The

---

[1] There is a large literature on National Service. The following works have been used for what follows. M.S. Navias, 'Terminating Conscription? The British National Service Controversy 1955–56', *Journal of Contemporary History* 24 (1989), 195–208; S.J. Ball, 'A Rejected Strategy: The Army and National Service 1946–63', in H. Strachan (ed.), *The British Army, Manpower and Society into the Twenty-First Century* (London: Frank Cass, 2000), pp. 36–48; T. Hickman, *The Call-Up: A History of National Service* (London: Headline, 2004); Trevor Royle, *The Best Years of Their Lives: The National Service Experience 1945–63* (London: Coronet, 1988).

[2] Interestingly, although the army was happy with this, the RAF were not because it would mean that many technicians would be released when they had barely finished their training.

government agreed to extend the period of service to eighteen months in November 1948; in September 1950 it was increased to two years. By the time of the Festival of Britain in 1951, half of the manpower of the British army was made up of national servicemen.[3] Conscription could have become a permanent part of the British way of life as it was in many other countries such as Belgium, France and Italy. That it did not was probably mainly due to the development of nuclear weapons with Britain relying first on the American deterrent and then on their own atomic bomb and the V-Bomber force to deliver it after 1955. Of course the main point of nuclear weapons was to prevent a war rather than fight one and so the need for large conventional forces was much reduced (not that the army, in particular, was convinced). From 1955 the continuance of conscription was subject to an annual review, which probably meant that it was not long for this world. In the end it was the new Conservative Minister of Defence, Duncan Sandys, who was able to announce in 1957 that no one would be called up later than 1960 and the last national servicemen would leave in 1962.[4] Politics probably played some part in the timing as the Conservative government was trying to recover from the Suez affair and was doubtless also aware that, whereas 57 per cent of those members of the public asked about national service in 1949 had thought that it was a good thing, by 1957 75 per cent wanted it to end.[5]

So throughout the whole of the 1950s all males, on reaching the age of eighteen, registered with the Ministry of Labour and National Service. They were given a medical in a local office, although many had to travel some distance to reach it. Failure to attend meant a £100 fine or two years' imprisonment. There are many tall tales about these medicals. That some young men tried to persuade the doctors that they were unfit to serve is without question. How many succeeded is unknown. Inevitably, perhaps, there were a number of young sportsmen who seemed very fit but were deemed not fit enough to join the armed services. Colin Cowdrey, the Kent and England batsman, had flat feet, and Howard Winstone was the British and British Empire featherweight boxing champion but had the tips of three fingers missing from one hand, which was enough for the medical board to turn him down. Stewart Imlach, the footballer, missed national service due to a

---

[3] By 1955 the army numbered 223,872 soldiers on regular engagements and 213,075 national servicemen. The figures for the RAF were 183,914 and 66,419 and for the Royal Navy 118,006 and 8,297.
[4] In fact the last man seems to have been demobbed on 7 May 1963 (Royle, *Best Years*, p. 27).
[5] Hickman, *The Call-Up*, p. 217.

perforated eardrum and another winger, Terry Paine, a member of the 1966 England World Cup-winning squad, escaped the uniform when diagnosed with a similar condition which he later claimed he never had.[6] Several groups of workers in key industries were exempt, including coalminers, sea-going fishermen, merchant seamen, agricultural workers in essential food production, graduate science teachers, young men on apprenticeships and students engaged on courses, although in the latter case the privilege of serving in the armed forces was only deferred.[7]

Most national servicemen found themselves in either the army or the Royal Air Force. The Royal Navy took relatively few. Whichever service the new recruit joined his introduction was usually an eight-week course of basic drill and physical training. As many commentators have pointed out, the lack of privacy, the verbal abuse and occasional humiliations made for hard times for young men, most of whom had never been away from home before. All sorts and conditions of men were thrown together and given intelligence and educational tests designed to help them to be put in a job suited to their ability. A few even signed on for an extra year in order to get the trade of their choice. Others were identified as potential officers and sent to separate training camps.[8] After basic training came trade training, particularly important in the RAF which needed large numbers of engineering technicians. The length of these courses varied but it was only after they had been completed that posting to a permanent unit took place. Most national servicemen spent their two years in the United Kingdom. Germany was the second most likely destination but a significant minority went further afield, to Aden, Kenya, Hong Kong, Borneo, Kuwait, Tanganyika and Uganda. Some fought in the Korean War and in all 395 were killed on active service.

But inevitably their uniforms were most visible at home. With evenings and weekends often free, soldiers and airmen especially were frequently seen at railway stations, on trains or trying to hitch lifts in a country where few had cars and there were no motorways. A whole range of activities were also provided on airfields and army camps including educational classes, amateur dramatics, local radio stations and sporting opportunities. One of the first things asked of the recruits at basic training was whether they were active in any sport or whether they played a musical instrument. As we have seen already, the armed

---

[6] *Ibid.*, p. 236.
[7] See B. S. Johnson (ed.), *All Bull: The National Servicemen* (London: Quartet Books, 1973), p. 3.
[8] In the RAF they were nicknamed 'POMS': potential officer material.

services were proud of their sports and their bands. National service meant that, for a couple of years at least, they could have the pick of the talented, and some commanding officers were vigorous in the pursuit of them.

Lieutenant-Colonel Anthony Lascelles of the 6th Royal Tank Regiment appears to have been one of them. An Oxford Blue in athletics, hockey and tennis, he took over an underperforming regiment and in part by placing a big emphasis on sport turned them into a fit and fighting force which outlasted all the competition in NATO's Battle Royal exercise in Germany in the early 1950s. By 1954 the regiment were the holders of the BAOR Hockey and Rugby Cups and extremely competitive in athletics and squash, which, along with boxing, were the five sports into which most effort was put. Physically fit soldiers trained as part of teams made good soldiers and even those soldiers relatively uninterested in playing sport found themselves taking an interest in the sporting activities of the regiment. While they were in Münster the regiment appointed a full-time athletics coach, Ernest Albrecht, who had been part of the training staff of the German national team during the 1936 Olympic Games, and he ran fitness programmes for all the other sports.[9]

Not all COs were able to persuade the army hierarchy that a concentration on sport was entirely a good thing. 1/East Surrey Regiment, stationed in Germany at Braunschweig, also had a commander with a 'ferocious commitment to sport of every kind'.[10] Lieutenant-Colonel Clive Wallis had played rugby for Ireland against the New Zealand All Blacks in 1936 and he was keen to recruit young officers who could run, jump, throw, box, score tries and kick goals. When Tony Thorne arrived at Braunschweig the regimental athletics team had just won the championship of BAOR. 'The championships had lasted for nearly a week and the celebration lasted about as long ... Most of the team were officers, apart from a few physical training instructors, so ... Army duties went into abeyance for several days until the officers all sobered up.'[11] This was not simply a special occasion, but a more regular state of affairs. Naturally enough officers and NCOs who had to do the duties of the absent sportsmen were not always pleased. After a headquarters inspection it was decided that the battalion was deficient in all aspects

---

[9] Private information from two former national servicemen who served with the 6th RTR. Letters 15 February, 2 March 2006. For Lascelles see his obituaries, *Telegraph*, 23 August 2001; *Times*, 21 July 2000.
[10] What follows is based on the memories of national service officer Tony Thorne, *Brasso, Blanco and Bull* (London: Constable and Robinson, 2000), p. 22.
[11] Thorne, *Brasso*, p. 156.

of training and would be banned from sporting competition until it reached a higher standard of military efficiency.[12]

By the 1950s most units in all three services had officers part of whose duties were to be responsible for particular sports. They too used the opportunities provided by conscription to strengthen their teams. Tony Davis, a Major in charge of C Squadron of the 6th Royal Tank Regiment in the mid-1950s, was keen on boxing and would visit amateur boxing clubs and tournaments to persuade useful men to come to the regiment for their national service. The 4th Battalion of the Royal Army Ordnance Corps apparently became known in some quarters as the boxers' battalion, with a Captain Eastlake visiting tournaments in London and signing up future professionals including Henry Cooper and his brother George and Joe Erskine.[13] The Battalion won the Army Inter-Unit Boxing championship several times in succession during the 1950s.[14]

As we have seen in an earlier chapter, there were generally good relations between the organisations running civilian sport and their military counterparts. Many of the former had found places on their councils and executives for representatives of the latter, and during the national service decade this led to civilian–military co-operation in placing conscripted promising sportsmen. A good example comes from the Amateur Athletic Association, who drew up a scheme which enabled athletic clubs to inform the military representatives when their members were coming up for national service. The scheme began in April 1955. By October the navy had had no notifications and the army ten, but the RAF had received thirty.[15]

---

[12] *Ibid.*, p. 173.
[13] Henry Cooper and Erskine would both become British Heavyweight Champions. Cooper had already won the Amateur Boxing Association championships and represented Great Britain at the Helsinki Olympics 1952.
[14] *RAOC Gazette* 33 (1952), 34 (1953), 36 (1955); H. Cooper, *An Autobiography* (London: Coronet, 1972), pp. 48–51.
[15] Amateur Athletic Association Development Committee Mins, 22 October 1955, Birmingham University Library Special Collections (BULSC). It was agreed to give the scheme further publicity. It is interesting that the navy had no takers but then it took relatively few national servicemen. Nonetheless there were more informal arrangements. Gwyn Walters, an international rugby referee from Wales, had an arrangement to divert promising players to 'an unnamed naval officer in Devonport'. This was how Carwyn James found himself in the Royal Navy in 1952. A. Richards, *Carwyn: A Personal Memoir* (London: Michael Joseph, 1984), p. 76. By far the largest number went to the most modern of the services, the RAF, who remained very keen to challenge the two senior services in all fields and especially in sport. This may have partly reflected the view, often expressed in the RAF at that time, that it was the 'Cinderella' service; and it was well known that Cinderella had two very ugly sisters.

There is no doubt that sportsmen with a reputation, especially if they were spoken for by some representative of sporting authority, could find more comfortable billets than the average conscript. Tom Cartwright was a promising young cricketer who had played about ten matches for Warwickshire when his call-up came. It was 1953 and he was anxious that he might end up in Korea with the Royal Warwickshire Regiment as some of his school friends had done. But during a Warwickshire club and ground fixture at RAF Innsworth in Gloucestershire their officer in charge of cricket asked the Warwickshire coach if he had any good cricketers coming up for service, and he recommended Cartwright. But later, the secretary of the Warwickshire County Club received a phone call from Colonel Garthwaite of the Royal Artillery base at Shoeburyness in Essex, where another Warwickshire player was already stationed. How would young Cartwright like to join them? They had a fine ground, a competitive fixture list against good club sides and he could also represent the Royal Artillery. So he was posted to the 63rd Heavy Anti-Aircraft Regiment, at Shoeburyness. He would eventually also play for the Army and the Combined Services, both teams staffed with young professionals like himself, but captained by the colonel.[16]

Brian Close was allowed to suspend his period of national service for seven months in order to tour Australia and New Zealand with the MCC team during the winter of 1950–1, and Fred Trueman had no difficulty in obtaining the permission of the RAF to spend the summer of 1952 playing in all four test matches against India. One reason was probably the attitude of the British sporting press who were desperate to put the Cold War in perspective and produce a cricket team that could beat Australia. As one writer demanded, 'If the answer to England's fast bowling problems was in the forces then arrangements must be made for his release.'[17] Trueman was the leading wicket taker in the series. Close, on the other hand, was not a success in Australia. *Wisden* pronounced that his bowling suffered from a lack of accuracy

---

[16] S. Chalke, *Tom Cartwright: The Flame Still Burns* (Bath: Fairfield Books, 2007), pp. 53–6. The Royal Artillery were still playing an annual two-day match with the Royal Engineers at Lord's in the 1950s. Cartwright remembered the dinner at the Tavern at which each of the players sat between two high-ranking officers who called them by their Christian names for the night. Officers' cricket teams occasionally recruited sons of toil from the other ranks to bowl for them. When RAOC Chigwell played Forest Harlequins in 1952 their main bowlers were Privates Thomas and Wells. *RAOC Gazette* 34 (1952), 57.

[17] Quoted in Fred Trueman, *Ball of Fire: An Autobiography* (St Albans: Mayflower, 1977), p. 39.

and his batting from a want of discretion but that he ought to 'escape harsh criticism' due to his 'extreme youth'.[18]

If military hierarchies were keen to benefit from recruiting accomplished sportsmen, the military service in the 1950s offered facilities for playing a range of sports that were probably better than most available to civilians at that time. Many civilian sports grounds, athletic and cycle tracks had been commandeered for war service and were slow to be returned to their former use. Others succumbed to the postwar need for more factories and housing. Sports ground refurbishment was often delayed and indoor training facilities quite uncommon. These facts were noted by the Wolfenden Report in 1960. Established by the Central Council of Physical Recreation, the committee, under the chairmanship of John Wolfenden, was the first time that a body of responsible men and women had sat down to examine the relationship between sport and the wider welfare of society.[19] The Committee took evidence from representatives of all three service sports boards who were cautiously satisfied with their facilities. The Army Sport Control Board, for example, was probably choosing its words carefully when it concluded that its sports grounds and maintenance operations were slightly better than those in 'normal civilian life'. But the fact was that only some employers, especially the bigger ones such as the London banks, Shell, ICI or Imperial Tobacco, had better ones.[20] The Honorary Secretary of the Army Athletics Association was also eager to inform the 'National Service man' that, so far as track and field was concerned, the army had a 'thoroughly up-to-date, going-concern organisation for promoting and managing athletics and we welcome the young soldier be he athlete or tyro'.[21] That there were opportunities for athletes with different levels of attainment and in many sports was persuasively illustrated by the programme for the Inter-Wing Athletic Championships at RAF Watton in Norfolk on 21 May 1958 which listed thirteen different sports which were regularly played by the airmen there.[22] It seems

---

[18] See *Wisden Cricketers' Almanac* (1952), p. 791. The Ministry of Labour and National Service refused to allow the Yorkshire batsman, Gerald Smithson, to interrupt his national service in the coal mines to go on the MCC's tour to the West Indies in 1948. It changed its mind after the decision was criticised in the newspapers. A. Bradbury, 'Miner and Cricketer', *Wisden Cricket Monthly*, April 1985, 45.

[19] Their report, *Sport in the Community* (CCPR, 1960), is available online at www.sportdevelopment.org.uk/html/wolfenden.html.

[20] See the questionnaire which the ASCB completed for Wolfenden. Wolfenden Committee Records, Sport England, London.

[21] Major J. Biddulph on the army in 'Athletics in the Services', *The Athlete* (Summer 1950), 81. See also Squadron Leader K. R. Cooper, 'Athletics in the Royal Air Force', *The Athlete* (Winter 1950–1), 178–80.

[22] In Amateur Athletic Association records, BULSC.

clear that many young sportsmen found that their period of conscription provided facilities and opportunities to practise and train which had not always been present in their civilian worlds. Sportsmen and musicians often escaped the square holes in which, it was occasionally said, the military placed round national service pegs. Three examples from athletics will emphasise the point.

Derek Ibbotson was beginning to make an athletic reputation before he was called up to the RAF in December 1954.[23] Born and brought up in West Yorkshire, he had joined his local club, the Lockwood Harriers, at the age of sixteen. He won the Yorkshire mile three years in succession and in 1952, aged twenty-one, he was fifth in the Inter-Counties three miles at the White City, all this while working as an electrician for the National Coal Board. But it was his RAF service which gave him the chance to become more serious about running. Ibbotson did his basic training at Hednesford, Staffordshire, where, with woodland close to the camp, he found a flourishing group of cross-county runners whom he was encouraged by a corporal physical training instructor to join. Ibbotson even remained an extra week after the completion of the eight weeks of basic training in order to represent the unit in the RAF Cross Country Championships. It was probably athletes he met at the championships who suggested that he contact a Squadron Leader Davis at RAF Yatesbury. Davis was a former half-mile champion of Wales, a qualified coach for the AAA and an education officer at a training camp which specialised in courses on electronics and radar where Ibbotson soon joined him. Ibbotson became one of a group of active runners who benefited from the patronage of Davis and the fact that the commanding officer at Yatesbury was also a keen supporter of athletics. Once work was finished for the day, the Davis runners were allowed to go to training immediately and eat later rather than go to the early-evening meal in the canteen with the rest of the camp. Davis also introduced Ibbotson to the then new ideas about interval training, and in this atmosphere it is perhaps not surprising that 1955 was the young airman's best year so far, both in the country and on the track. Ibbotson finished third in the Yorkshire Cross Country Championship, fourth in the RAF Championship and eighth in the Northern race. These performances led to an invitation from Manchester University Athletic Club to take part in a special invitation event in which, on 21 May 1955, he finished second to the much more celebrated Gordon Pirie. A letter from Air-Vice Marshal V. L. F. Fuller-Good followed, congratulating

---

[23] This paragraph is drawn from T. O'Connor, *The Four Minute Mile: The Derek Ibbotson Story* (London: Stanley Paul, 1960), pp. 44–50.

him on 'one of the finest performances by an RAF athlete', which had brought fame for himself and credit to the RAF. Ibbotson won the RAF Cross County Championship in 1956. After demobilisation Ibbotson developed a reputation for being unafraid to speak his mind but he had nothing but praise for his period of national service. He later wrote that he owed 'most of his success in athletics' to the help he received in the RAF. He thought them 'fitness mad' and began to train properly for the first time. It was there that he also became accustomed to regular competition, which, though not all of the highest class, broke the monotony of training as well as providing opportunities for tactical experiments.

Gordon Pirie had done his own national service earlier, also in the RAF and he too found it benefited his athletics. After basic training at Padgate he had been posted to RAF Cranwell for a five-week training course to turn him into a wireless mechanic. Cranwell was better known as the RAF's officer training school, and it was not surprising that among its facilities was one of the best athletic tracks in the country in 1950. An experienced runner, Warrant Officer Harrison, from RAF Swinderby just down the road, kept an eye on Pirie, and even after a posting to Watchet, Somerset, he was able to get almost as much athletics as this insatiable athlete wanted. Looking back at his period in the service Pirie listed what he saw as the obvious benefits for the serious athlete like himself. He did not have to think much about the basic necessities of life: work, food, clothes or shelter. The RAF placed few obstacles to the increase in his training load. Duties were light, there were few chores, fatigues or drill and senior officers were supportive. In the summer of 1950 he was able to combine regular training with competitive running for the RAF, South London Harriers and the bank for whom he had worked in Civvy Street. Pirie made such good use of his national service that he thought of retraining as a physical training instructor and becoming a regular airman but significantly decided against it because the job seemed to require him to become more of a sporting all-rounder.[24]

Brian Hewson, later to compete in both the 800 metres and 1500 metres for Great Britain in both the European Championships and the Olympic Games, actually *did* sign on for three years because he felt that the military provided a better environment in which to develop his athletics. He was already a double AAA junior champion when he was posted to the 67th Training Regiment of the Royal Artillery at Oswestry, Shropshire. He found there a commanding officer who

---

[24] D. Booth, *The Impossible Hero: A Biography of Gordon Pirie* (London: Corsica Press, 1999), pp. 44–52.

was enthusiastic about athletics and who had already had Christopher Chataway in his unit. Partly as a result of the athletics reputation that the young Chataway was constructing, Lieutenant Colonel Burnaby had built a modern athletics track using the muscle and sweat of a few score of conscripts to do the work. After Oswestry Hewson was posted to Woolwich, where he discovered another CO who favoured sport and was keen to keep him on the strength. He was given a job as a pay clerk in a small outfit which had only fifteen permanent staff, six of whom were runners. In the event, he spent the remainder of his three years there and, as Woolwich was close to the home of his parents, Hewson was soon in possession of an army living-out allowance and living at home. Apart from the probably considerable benefit of his mother's cooking he was encouraged to train and race as much as he needed to. As a regular soldier he was granted more leave than the national serviceman, thirty days a year, and this allowed ample opportunity to test himself in international events in countries such as Germany and Sweden. Hewson's second and third years in the army, 1953 and 1954, were his breakthrough period as an international athlete in which he also won his first AAA half-mile championship and kept his army supporters happy by winning the Army 880 yards title. He was a key member of the four-man unit team which won the NAAFI Medley relay at Mitcham three years in a row.[25] Roy Fowler, from Stone, Staffordshire, was another promising long-distance runner who was posted to the 67th Regiment of the Royal Artillery at Oswestry. Whilst there he began to consolidate his ability as an athlete benefiting from both the order imposed by army discipline and the opportunities to enhance and refocus his training. When the camp was scheduled for closure Fowler was allowed to remain as part of the care and maintenance unit. He also learned the rudiments of physiotherapy and would look back on his national service as a time when he learnt how to 'restrain his headstrong qualities' and as a period crucial to his future.[26]

Not all sportsmen were as enthusiastic about national service. Some professional footballers, in particular, felt that their postings, many difficult miles away from the clubs for which they had signed, involved a serious interruption in what was looked upon as a relatively short career. Brian Clough, on an RAF camp at Watchet in Somerset, found that he could rarely make it home to Middlesbrough to play for his hometown team. Ronnie Clayton too, with the 55th Training

[25] B. Hewson, *Flying Feet* (London: Stanley Paul, 1962), pp. 43–7. The medley distances were 880, 440, 220 and 120 yards.
[26] J. Bale and M. Henson, *A Fighter Second to None: Roy Fowler of Leek and his World of Running* (Stoke-on-Trent: North Staffordshire Press, 2006), pp. 30–5.

Regiment Royal Artillery stationed on the west coast of North Wales at Tonfanau, found himself playing for his unit in the Mid-Wales League on a Saturday rather than for his club, Blackburn Rovers. Moreover when he did receive a weekend pass home he was not regularly chosen to play. There was a feeling among the managers of many clubs that national service was inhibiting the development of their players. Not only were they playing too much football but they were picking up bad habits in the hurly-burly, kick-and-rush atmosphere which, it was thought, prevailed in service football. The players had another grievance, which was that, if they could play for their clubs on Saturdays, which many did, of course, they were paid £6, a much larger sum than they were getting in wages from the state. No play meant no pay. John Sydenham had just broken into the Southampton first team and had also been chosen for the England Under-23s when he was called up in 1960. His resentment was further fuelled by the fact that it was clear by then that national service was coming to an end. He was rather depressed about it, but found that he played so much football in the army that it relieved his desperation to get out. As he told Tom Hickman, 'Football saved me … But if it hadn't been for that I really think I would have gone over the wall.'[27]

Reflecting half a century later on his service as a PTI with the King's Own Royal Regiment, Jimmy Armfield was much more positive about the experience while emphasising that it was not always easy to combine serving football with serving the Queen. Between 1954 and 1956 he played a lot of army football and turned out regularly on Saturdays for Blackpool, then one of the leading English clubs. It helped that he was stationed at nearby Preston:

I met up with the team on a Saturday, played the match and went back to camp the next day. Everyone assumed I would be able to take time off each weekend but it was never easy. Once I was on guard duty all Friday night and still played on the Saturday. I was on duty till eight in the morning, went back to barracks, collected my boots and caught the bus to Blackpool from the bottom of the

---

[27] Hickman, *The Call-Up*, p. 236. For Clayton, see R. Clayton, *A Slave to Soccer* (London: Stanley Paul, 1960), pp. 39–44. Tonfanau won the championship of the Welsh League (North) in 1954, were Mid-Wales League champions every year from 1952 to 1958 except 1955, and with a team including several professionals, deemed to be amateurs while in the services, won the Welsh Amateur Cup in 1958. We are indebted to Ian Garland for these details. There are many accounts underlining the large number of games played by young professionals during their national service. Duncan Edwards, of Manchester United and England, famously claimed that while he was in the army 'I had a pair [of football boots] which lasted two years – and during that time I played 180 matches'. Duncan Edwards, *Tackle Soccer This Way* (London: Stanley Paul, 1958), p. 28.

road. I arrived at 11.30, walked home and had a lie-down for an hour. Then I had a bite to eat, walked down to the ground and played 90 minutes.[28]

Sport went through a period of almost unprecedented popularity in Britain after the Second World War, both in the austerity-burdened civilian world and in the military. There seems little doubt that the continuation of conscription in the form of national service provided a fresh impetus and lustre to sport in the navy, army and Air Force. Not only was it something on which many of the under-employed young men in uniform could enjoy playing or watching in its variety of forms; it also contributed to the development of those qualities of teamwork and *esprit de corps* so prized and frequently publicly praised by most military leaders. It helped raise sporting standards in all three services as nearly all of the most accomplished young sportsmen in the country were put into uniform for two years. It further strengthened the links between the civilian and military worlds that had been boosted by the war and was accompanied by a much enhanced attention from the civilian media.

Of course it was the six biggest sports, athletics, boxing, cricket, football, rugby and swimming, which benefited most. In boxing, for example, both the Army and inter-service championships could fill London's Albert Hall in the 1950s. Even the individual championships of a large corps, such as the RAOC, in which it was important to encourage participation to keep the tournament as open as possible, could attract the crowds. No current champions, either at national, inter-service or army level, were allowed to compete. One of the aims was to deter the elite group from boxing too much, but the policy was also designed to encourage the others. Even with the stars removed, these championships could still fill the Craven Hill Theatre at Bicester.[29] Other much lesser-known sports also flourished in the decade of conscription. Tug of war had been an AAA championship event since 1910 and had been traditionally dominated by teams put out by the police, fire or armed services. In the 1950s few could pull down the RAOC unit at Feltham, Middlesex. The Feltham team won the 100 stone title three years in succession from 1952 and the Catchweight title for four successive years between 1952 and 1955. Tug of war was a summer sport, and the Feltham team were welcomed by the organisers of sports days, both civilian and military, throughout the south of England. Between May

---

[28] J. Armfield, *Right Back to the Beginning: The Autobiography* (London: Headline, 2004), p. 50.
[29] *RAOC Gazette* 34 (1953), 359.

and August 1952, for example, the Feltham teams went to over twenty such meetings and were only pulled over the line once.[30]

Sport was even used to commemorate the spirit and comradeship of the airmen of various nationalities who had fought in the Battle of Britain. The Britannia Shield provided another competition in which national servicemen could take part. It was open to amateurs serving in the armed services of all the Allied nations and was essentially a team event whose members competed in four sports: boxing, fencing, shooting and swimming. It was organised by the Royal Air Force Sports Board and by the late 1950s took a week to complete, usually in October, when Battle of Britain Week was held. The RAF usually won it but teams from Czechoslovakia, France, the Netherlands and the United States Forces in Europe also had their names inscribed on the trophy.[31]

Not surprisingly this sporting action was accompanied by a much-enhanced attention from the media. As we have already noted, the importance of maintaining good relations with newspapers had long been recognised by service chiefs. Brigadier A.R. Aslett, director of the Army Sport Control Board, probably summed up their views in his answer to a question from the Wolfenden Committee in 1958. In spite of those journalists and their papers which thrived on 'controversy and quarrels', in general newspapers 'did a useful job' and provided 'a lot of free "advertisement"'.[32] There seems to have been a gradual increase in the sophistication with which service sports authorities managed the press, which can be illustrated by two examples from the annual football match between the British and French Armies. In March 1947, when the game was played in Paris, it was only 'certain members' of the national press who were invited to accompany the team. Compare this with 1958, when the French team visited London. The Army Football Association advertised the match in the programme of all the London professional clubs and sent a handout to all the capital's leading sports journalists. The AFA also tried to arrange interviews with leading players from both sides on television and it was well-publicised that the team

---

[30] Thirty-two teams entered the 1952 Watford Town Sports tug of war, the largest ever such event in England. At the Feltham unit's annual tug of war dinner in 1953, the brigadier referred to the defeat which the team had suffered in the Army championships, the first for some time in that event, and speculated that it might be a good thing as it didn't do to think oneself 'invulnerable'. See Lovesey, *Official Centenary*, pp. 116, 193. *RAOC Gazette* 34 (1952–3), 34, 89, 359; 35 (1953–4), 99.

[31] *The Britannia Shield Competition Handbook* (1958); Minutes RAF Sports Board, 24 October 1947, RAFSB. In 1954 the boxing was held at Wembley.

[32] See his response to the questionnaire from the Wolfenden Committee, 29 September 1958, Wolfenden Committee Records, Sport England.

was to have a training session at Aldershot with Walter Winterbottom, the manager of the England football team.[33]

Given all the notice being taken of service sport especially on what were then the back pages of the national press it was perhaps not surprising that a few, admittedly rather tentative, attempts were made by the army at least to link sporting opportunities with recruiting. The Army Cup was one of the stars of an exhibition set up by the Lancashire Division of the Territorial Army in February 1950 with the hope that it would persuade young men in the north-west to join either the 'Terriers' or the regulars.[34] Later the same year, following some criticism within the Army FA that service football could become too much of a good thing and asking whether representative games at Command level were really necessary, the Northern Command member of the executive claimed that such matches, when played against civilian clubs, were not simply 'money spinners' but also aids to recruiting.[35] The revival of the officers-only team, the Army Crusaders, was partly justified by the claim that its visits to grammar and public schools, especially soccer-playing, officer-producing ones such as Malvern and Shrewsbury, were helping to maintain the supply of the right type.[36] By 1958, with the end of national service clearly in sight, the Ministry of Defence appears to have become more interested in the possibilities of linking sport in general and football in particular with recruitment. A member of the AFA executive, Lieutenant Colonel A.J. (James) Wilson was asked to prepare a paper on the subject, which he did, but which does not appear to have survived.[37] Obviously why men joined the services is a complex issue but it may well be that the opportunities for sport, like those for travel and adventure, played a part in the decision of some young men to sign on.

---

[33] Army FA Mins, 27 January 1947, 17 January 1958, AFA. That these sporting events had their social and strategic side is reflected in the invitation issued to all the members of the Army Council to watch the match and dine afterwards at the Café Royal. It is to be hoped the occasion was not spoiled by the result, a 2–0 victory for the French Army.

[34] Army FA EC Mins, 17 January 1950, AFA.

[35] Army FA Gen. Com. Mins, 22 May 1950, AFA.

[36] Army FA EC Mins, 22 April 1952, AFA.

[37] AFA EC Mins, 17 January, 14 March 1958, AFA. Wilson (who retired as Lieutenant-General Sir James Wilson, KBE, MC) (1921–2004) was not only a very active member of the Army FA Executive, but also a regular football reporter for the *Sunday Times* from 1957 to 1990. See his *Unusual Undertakings: A Military Memoir* (London: Leo Cooper, 2002), esp. pp. 218–19. The Northern Command representative on the Army FA was still optimistic that a match between the Command and Newcastle United would help recruitment.

That the reputation and visibility of service sport was enhanced by national service can hardly be denied. This was particularly true of the Army and the RAF in which the great majority of conscripts served their time. But the benefits did not arrive entirely unencumbered by costs. One of the problems faced by the sports authorities of the military was how to ensure that both the national servicemen and the regular airmen, sailors and soldiers were given a similar sporting chance. As some jobs in the services were reserved for men who had signed a regular engagement, such as meteorology in the RAF, for example, so there was some anxiety about the tendency of the national serviceman to take up more than his fair share of sporting facilities and opportunity. This issue was complicated in both the Army and the RAF by the related one of whether anything should be done to curb the playing strengths of the big training units as opposed to the non-training ones. Training units in the Army and in Technical Training Command in the RAF were much bigger than non-training units, which appeared to provide them with a significant advantage when it came to sporting competition. This difficulty overlapped with an older one about the place of the paid player in the peacetime armed forces. The relationship between amateur and professional, so controversial in civilian sport, caused problems for service sport too, especially in football and rugby, the sports in which most young professionals were located.

If we look first at the training unit question it came up in both the army and the RAF in 1950. At a meeting of the General Committee of the Army FA, for example, it was suggested that in order to make the Army Cup competition fairer, it should be divided into two with the Basic Training units and Training Regiments in one part and the units of normal strength, about 600 men, in the other. According to the RAF Sports Board all the major sports, identified as cricket, hockey, rugby and soccer, had already divided their competitions into senior and junior sections in order to give the smaller stations the chance to compete on more equal terms.[38] The Army, while recognising the problem, did not like the proposed solution. However, another way of restricting the sporting advantage of the training units was thought by some to be by prescribing the number of professionals who could take part.

According to the Census of 1951 there were about 8,000 males who made their living from playing sport of which number slightly under half were professional footballers in the English League.[39] This number

[38] Army FA Mins Gen. Com., 22 May 1950, AFA; RAF Sports Board Mins, 31 March 1950, RAFSB.
[39] There were about 350 in the Scottish League. Most of the remainder were boxers, cricketers, jockeys, Rugby league players, and those semi-professionals who worked

did not decrease much during the 1950s, and it is probable that there may have been as many as 1,000 registered professionals doing their national service and available for selection for unit teams during the decade. And as they were often pretty good players unit teams would find it difficult not to select them. The question facing the organisers of army football was what to do about it? As early as 1947 the football representative of 57th Training Regiment, Royal Armoured Corps, proposed that the Army Cup should be for amateur teams only and suggested a separate competition for the professional players. For him, it was not just a matter of giving the regular soldier a better chance to play for his regimental team, but it would foster what he called the 'old Army spirit'. We will return to the more ideological issues which may have been at work here later.[40] The chairman of the Army FA, Major General A. M. Cameron, pointed out that conditions were different to those pre-war in that professional footballers were now members of the armed forces. Although not unsympathetic he thought it would be a 'great mistake to limit the Army Cup to amateur players only. The competition was organised for soldiers and professional footballers in the Army were soldiers'. Discussion of the question was resumed at the Annual General Meeting in July 1947, but no changes to the rules were made.

But it was an issue that kept returning. A slightly more subtle approach was the argument that young service professional footballers were able to play regularly with their civilian clubs and tended only to play in the most important unit games like the Army Cup. On such occasions they inevitably took the places of either good amateur conscripts or the regular soldier. No one wanted to ban the professional entirely, this argument continued, but limiting their numbers in the more prestigious fixtures might be a fair compromise.[41] In May 1950 the General Committee of the Army FA was faced with several proposals to limit the number of professional players who could be fielded by units in the Army Cup. 1/Queen's Own Royal West Kent Regiment had suggested that only five professionals should be allowed to play, the School of Artillery suggested four and the 14th/20th Hussars two. The Committee recommended five to the AGM and listed four main benefits: first, it would lessen the temptation for units to pack a team

at other jobs but received an additional wage for playing football for clubs outside the Football League. See R. Holt and T. Mason, *Sport in Britain 1945–2000* (Oxford: Blackwell, 2000), p. 65.

[40] AFA Gen. Com. Mins, 4 July 1947, AFA. It is worth remembering that in 1947 national service was still only a one-year commitment.

[41] Army FA AGM Mins, 3 June 1949, AFA.

with professionals; second it might improve the standard of other teams who had few if any professionals on the establishment; third, it would have the very desirable object of bringing more amateurs and regular soldiers into unit teams; and finally, it was unlikely to restrict many, if any, professionals from playing in the Army Cup because very few units had more than five anyway.[42]

But although most of those powerful in army football seemed pleased with the outcome only three seasons went by before it was decided to undertake a thorough re-examination of the question after a proposal by 2/Durham Light Infantry to reduce further the number of professionals in Army Cup ties from five to three. The Executive Committee circulated a questionnaire to all units who had competed in the Army Cup or who were members of the Army FA in the season 1953–4. It was beginning to look as though the Adjutant General might have to be consulted, but in the end a vote on what was after all only a simple rule change was sufficient. 213 votes were recorded, 149 in favour of the proposal and 64 against, which was sufficient for the two-thirds majority necessary. From 1954–5, only three registered professional players would be permitted to turn out for their units in the Army Cup.[43] The success of the Durham Light Infantry's resolution on the numbers of professionals seems to have encouraged their football supremo to make other suggestions for improving the purpose and structure of army football, in particular that a committee should be formed by the Army FA to visit units with the object of ensuring that military service came before sport. The Committee would report to a higher authority if they found evidence that full-time training, the provision of special meals and sleeping quarters and the excusing of military duties for sportsmen was going on. The secretary was requested to reply that this was outside the province of the Army Football Association.[44]

Almost the next thing that happened was that 2/Durham Light Infantry won the Army Cup, a competition for which they had only entered fourteen times (although they had reached the final three times and won it once, in 1912–13). The achievement was made more surprising by the fact that the Battalion had been disbanded in 1948 and only reformed in 1952. In a period in which the larger training

---

[42] Army FA AGM Mins, 8 June 1950, AFA.
[43] Army FA AGM Mins, 22 June 1953, 20 August 1954, AFA. Interestingly it was decided at the same time to appoint a team manager for the full Army team. RSM C.F. Blackman, Royal Artillery, was given the job for the season. The Scottish Command had a competition for minor units which allowed a maximum two professionals per team. Army FA EC Mins, 17 February 1956, AFA.
[44] Army FA EC Mins, 9 September 1954, AFA.

regiments had come to dominate the competition, the victory of the men from the north was the first by an infantry regiment since 1934, and the first by a team stationed in BAOR. It is worth considering this sporting achievement for the light it throws on sport in the armed services generally and on regimental sport in the era of conscription.[45] The 2nd Battalion had reformed and spent two and a half years in Germany. They had little money to spend on sports equipment, and it was the enthusiasm and keenness of the games-playing Major Gibson, obviously encouraged by his CO, which built up a sports store and began to produce men and teams in a number of sports: cross-country running, basketball, swimming and track and field athletics as well as football. The regimental journal stressed that the success of battalion teams in the various sports had not been achieved at the expense of ordinary company games and that every soldier who wanted a game of whatever sport had been able to get one. But it was the footballers who had the most success and captured the imagination of the regiment. It had reached the semi-final of the BAOR Cup in the previous season, 1953–4, and was to win it in 1954–5, a unique double. About fifteen or sixteen players were involved in the team during these two seasons, two or three of whom missed the ultimate triumph having been demobilised, and all of them were national servicemen save one. This, together with the fact that most of them seem to have been local lads from County Durham, must have helped the growth of a wider regimental interest in a team whose Army Cup final eleven comprised eight privates, one bugler, one lance-corporal and a corporal, was managed by Regimental Sergeant-Major Rafferty and trained by Company Sergeant-Major Dalgetty. That there was more general support for the team is indicated by the fact that over 300 supporters went by bus to Minden for the final of the BAOR Cup on a very cold day in March 1955. During the game the supporters of the Durham team sang 'Blaydon Races', an unofficial but popular anthem of the northeast; at the end they chaired the players off the ground, a typical civilian response to sporting victory. The semi-final of the Army Cup was also played in Germany at a stadium in Wuppertal against the RAOC Depot from Feltham. Again large numbers of the garrison gave their support and saw their team pull off a surprising victory.

So to the final at Aldershot in April. Many supporters of the regiment (including former members) travelled considerable distances to see the match. A large contingent travelled south from the Barnard Castle

---

[45] What follows is based on the *Durham Light Infantry Regimental Journal* (1955), *Daily Telegraph*, 28 April 1955, and *Northern Echo*, 3 November 2006.

The national service years 235

Figure 17. Soldiers of the 2nd Battalion, The Durham Light Infantry, with the victorious battalion football team, Aldershot Military Stadium, 27 April 1955.

Depot, and about 100 came over from Germany, most of whom flew over for the day in two specially chartered aircraft. The 1st Battalion gave a grant to help support the cost of all this travel and the *Regimental Journal* emphasised that seventy-six soldiers below the rank of sergeant paid their own way from Germany for the match.[46] After the victory, by one goal to nil against the Royal Army Pay Corps Training Centre (Devizes) team, who apparently played the more composed football, the regiment claimed that they had received many telegrams of congratulation. 'It would appear that the morale and hopes of ordinary regimental football teams have been raised considerably' – clearly a reference to the fact that the team contained only two professionals, although another

---

[46] The 1st Training Battalion RASC played hosts to the team during their stay in Aldershot. The regimental journal also underlined the fact that in spite of all this interest, training and regular duties continued, including a divisional signals exercise to which the battalion was allowed to send out only those who were not going to the match. Those who were taking part in the exercise were allowed to listen to the broadcast of the match 'over the wireless' on the British Forces Network.

two had played good-class amateur football in Durham for Bishop Auckland and Willington.

One attitude which was probably being reflected by these paternalistic references to 'ordinary regimental footballers' was that support for the perceived underdog which is supposed to be a key element in the British sporting sub-culture. If there was anything better than the triumph of the rank outsider it was defeat for the overwhelming favourite which, in sport, if not in life, usually accompanied it. Surely this concern explains the Army FA's keenness to mark and praise such moments with examples scattered through its records. There are several from the national service years including the success of the 7th Armoured Division Workshops, REME, also from BAOR, whose team reached the semi-final of the Army Cup although it represented a unit with fewer than 300 men. Pleasure was also expressed in 1951 when the 4th Training Battalion, REME, won the cup with a team composed almost entirely of regular soldiers. The lesson to be drawn from this was a comforting one: that enthusiasm, fitness and a well-balanced team could still succeed against those bolstered by the inclusion of national service professionals.[47]

The ideology of amateurism was still the most powerful one in British sport in the 1950s. Fair play, mutual respect for the opposition and participation for enjoyment were the ideals which still ruled a world which was also the epitome of the voluntary principle in action with the unpaid enthusiast the key to keeping alive many clubs and associations in many sports. But the pursuit of excellence and the growth of international competition meant that the gap between the ordinary player and the potential champion was widening in many sports. Changes in the nature of work and the educational pressures involved in the emergence of a meritocracy meant that in many sports individuals could not hope to participate at the highest levels without some sort of material support or reward. We see now the harbingers of change which were scattered about the 1950s. The MCC appointed a professional to captain the England cricket team, and several athletes began to speak out in favour of a looser form of amateurism which would fall somewhere between what had become the norm in Britain and the more open and organised college and state-sponsored

---

[47] See the Annual Report of the Army FA, 1949–50 for the first example and the Annual Report 1950–1 for the second. Similarly when the 9th Battalion RAOC (Donington) won the Army Cup in 1954 their regimental journal described it as an 'outstanding success for a team with no special privileges'. Fitness, unselfishness and fighting spirit had upheld the finest tradition of sport in the army. *RAOC Gazette* 35 (1954), 417–18.

systems of the United States and the Soviet Block.[48] How were these pressures reflected in military sport during the decade of national service?

Amateurism was not only a way of separating the social classes. But the military were conscious that officers not only required superior styles of uniform, accommodation and messing but also their own sports clubs. Of course officers had always dominated equestrian events, the modern pentathlon and individual sports such as fencing, golf, racquets and tennis, but there might also be a need to provide sporting and social opportunities in those sports where competition from other ranks was strongest. The Milocarian Athletic Club was an interesting example of an attempt to meet this need, more particularly as it aimed to recruit its membership from all three services. It had been founded in 1930 to encourage and raise the standard of athletics and cross-country running amongst officers but also to play a part in bringing the three services in closer touch with each other. It entered teams for the AAA relay championships (winning the 4 x 400 yards in 1932 and 1934) and other meetings, and several of Britain's leading athletes of the 1930s were members. In 1946 it presented the Milocarian trophy to the AAA for competition among schools as a memorial to those members of the club who had been killed in the Second World War. In its first full track season after the war, five of its members represented Great Britain in the 1948 Olympic Games.[49]

The Army FA also revived their officers-only team, the Army Crusaders. Periodic complaints that not enough officers were prepared either to play or to administer the game at unit level continued throughout the 1950s, and the Crusaders were thought to offer part of a solution. The club was given a small grant by the Army FA, but participating players were expected to contribute something towards the expenses of each match. By the early 1950s the Crusaders were playing about twenty matches a season mainly against public and grammar schools and mainly in the south of England. Interestingly it proved difficult to find a volunteer to organise the Crusaders in North Britain. In 1952–3 a northern tour was organised which included the first visit to Manchester Grammar and Bolton Schools. It was repeated

---

[48] Probably the most important reflection of these changes was the Wolfenden Enquiry into Sport and the Community discussed above. See also Holt and Mason (eds.), *Sport in Britain*, ch. 3.

[49] The club believed strongly that 'the cause of joint Service co-operation is helped greatly, on the lowest officer levels, by members of the three Services competing together'. Training for war and fighting was 'more than ever a joint service affair'. *RAOC Gazette* 35 (1953), 135. See also Lovesey, *Official Centenary History*, p. 191.

the following season.[50] Most matches against schools were won, but the Crusaders rarely beat adult civilian clubs, in part because the idea was to give as many members a game as possible – sixty-five officers turned out in 1953–4 when the season was described as not so successful against club sides but 'most enjoyable'.[51] Perhaps an even clearer picture of the Crusaders comes from their entry into the Argonaut Trophy, the semi-final of which was reached in 1952. This was a cup presented by the *Tatler* magazine 'for amateur sides who would not normally consider entering competitive football because of team uncertainty, and it was accepted by all concerned that the results were not as important as twenty-two enthusiasts meeting on and off the field'.[52]

The aim to widen opportunity to represent the Service as opposed to the unit was a noble one and was given a further nudge from an unexpected source in 1952 when the popular football magazine, *Charles Buchan's Football Monthly*, published an article arguing that it was wrong for the army and the RAF to select professional players for their representative teams. The writer suggested that selection for these teams ought to be reserved for the amateur footballer who had entered the service as a career. The presence of so many young professional footballers meant that the regular soldier or airman had little chance of appearing either in the Inter-Services tournament or in the Kentish Cup matches against the Belgian and French army teams.[53] The navy, in the meantime, continued with its policy of selecting only amateur players to represent it, and it must have been particularly satisfying to all who sailed in the Royal Navy FA when its team actually won the Inter-Services championship in 1948–9.[54] But even among the young professionals few could actually be chosen to play for the service, and there is some evidence that good amateur players conscripted in the army and RAF also thought that they should be given more chance to

---

[50] Army FA Annual Reports 1950–1, 1951–2 and 1952–3. Army FA EC Mins, 4 July 1947, 23 June 1950, AFA.

[51] Army FA Annual Report, 1953–4. As we have seen it was thought a worthwhile recruiting exercise.

[52] *Tatler and Bystander*, 26 March 1952, 631. Shades of the early days of the Amateur Football Association (see chapter 5 above). When the British Army team recovered from a 3–1 deficit to draw 3–3 with the French Army in Paris in 1955, the Army FA's annual report thought that the 'game was noteworthy for the inclusion of an officer in our team', the first to appear in one of these matches for some years. It was 2nd Lieutenant P. Woosnam of the Royal Artillery, who would later have a successful professional career with Leyton Orient, West Ham and Aston Villa.

[53] *Charles Buchan's Football Monthly*, March 1952, p. 41.

[54] It was a feat the navy was unable to repeat in the national service period. Three of those who played went on to win amateur international honours. Ackland, 'The Forces', p. 384.

play representative football.⁵⁵ This was the context in which the Army FA decided to select an all-amateur army team drawn from the other ranks which, it was hoped, would eventually challenge the best amateur teams in the country and further extend the scope of football in the army by giving more players a chance to represent the service. In 1954 the Army fielded an eleven composed entirely of amateurs for the first time since the war, against the United Hospitals.⁵⁶

Support for civilian amateur sport not only meant subscribing to the moral code of sportsmanship and fair play which underpinned it but also accepting those sometimes quirky decisions designed to uphold traditional notions of amateurism which could threaten to undermine military sporting autonomy. John Charles had already built a reputation for himself as a footballer with Leeds United when he was called up to join the 12th Royal Lancers in 1950. At school he had been a promising boxer, and the army encouraged him to fight as a heavyweight. He responded by knocking out his first eleven opponents. Here was a potential champion – except that the rules of the Amateur Boxing Association, which applied to all member associations including the services, stated that anyone who made money from any sport could not box under ABA rules.⁵⁷ The Rugby Football Union was among the high priests of a more traditional amateurism and had probably been taking a dim view of professional Rugby League players turning out for military union clubs. The Royal Signals at Catterick had built a particularly strong side in the early 1950s including such Rugby League stars as Billy Boston, Brian Gabbitas and Phil Jackson. The Signals won the Yorkshire Cup twice in three years before the Yorkshire Rugby Union banned Rugby League-playing national servicemen from the competition.⁵⁸

On the other hand, the hierarchical structure of military life did not always go down well in civilian sporting circles. Jack Crump, Secretary of the British Amateur Athletics Board, wrote in his autobiography that Donald Finlay was the outstanding choice to captain the English team at the 1950 British Empire and Commonwealth Games. Finlay had been a very successful high hurdler who had won a bronze medal in the

---

[55] See the notes in the *RAOC Gazette* 35 (1954). Picking up a story from civilian newspapers it noted that 'more and more young National Service soldiers were complaining that pro' footballers like Quixall, Blunstone and Gunter grabbed too much of the limelight in Army soccer'.
[56] Army FA Annual Report 1953–4. It does not appear to have been an entirely successful venture on the field.
[57] M. Risoli, *John Charles: Gentle Giant* (Edinburgh: Mainstream, 2003), p. 48.
[58] T. Collins, *Rugby League in Twentieth Century Britain: A Social and Cultural History* (London: Routledge, 2006), p. 137.

1932 Olympics but his rank of group captain in the RAF was thought to have made him 'somewhat remote' to some members of the team who had served in the ranks and who told Crump that they would feel uncomfortable if Finlay was made captain.[59]

But despite these difficulties and uncertainties about what sport was for and who could take part against whom there were some signs, within the military at least, that a clearer sense was emerging of the role sport could play in modern service life. This is indicated by the published reflections in regimental journals of two senior army officers, Colonel John Sheffield of the RAOC and General Sir George Erskine, who had commanded the British campaign against the Mau Mau insurgency in Kenya. Both agreed that as many men as possible in a unit should take part in as many different sports as possible.[60] Both stressed the importance of organised sports on a platoon basis. It was also deemed essential to encourage individuals to take part in both civilian and military competitions, although it was felt that such activities could not expect the same official support as team events. The production of a good unit team was an obvious requirement which paid rich dividends in terms of morale. There was the warning that not all units could 'win all along the line all the time; it is however highly desirable to win occasionally even if it is only the District Novices or the Small Units shield. Nor should some degree of specialisation be deplored.' None of these views was surprising and would almost certainly have been commonplace among many serving officers in the previous half century. What was more modern perhaps was an acceptance of the value of the 'skilled performer'. Don't disparage the gladiator, a word usually used to describe any other rank who played any sport to an above-average level of skill (no officer was ever stigmatised by the term gladiator). If standards were to be raised it was largely the efforts of the skilled players both on and off the field that would be responsible. 'To encourage him, give him special training facilities and send him to the championships. This is not professionalism but common sense. No Commanding Officer should feel he is doing anything wrong in giving concessions to assist those who are chosen to represent the Regiment, District, Command or Army.'[61]

---

[59] John Archer was appointed instead. Crump, *Running Round the World*, pp. 108–9.
[60] The only sport that appears to have been reserved exclusively for the regular, territorial and reserve personnel of all three services in the years of national service was skiing. See 'Winter Sports for the Services', *RAOC Gazette* 34 (1952), 161.
[61] Colonel John Sheffield in *RAOC Gazette* 38 (8 January 1957), 320–1, and General Sir George Erskine, *Army Medical Services Magazine* 8 (1956), 48. Erskine also wrote that it was 'quite wrong that any soldier should avoid his fair share of overseas service because he is required to "pack" a team'.

Do these views reflect the growth of a view of sport more in line with the modern civilian sporting world? In one sense military sport remained what it had always been, not compulsory, not a parade but a voluntary activity that participants chose. But it was during the national service period that there were moments when some of the leading players appeared to be operating within a context that was closer to that of the state-sponsored athletes of Eastern Europe than the voluntary amateurism of the west. When Roy Fowler became a member of the cross-country squad while serving in the 67th Regiment of the Royal Artillery at Oswestry he was in receipt of a set of Regimental Orders which informed squad members that 'intensive training' would start forthwith for the Army Cross Country Championships to be run on 1 March 1957 and that 'they will parade at the guardroom daily at 1500 hours from 8 February 1957'. Moreover the training 'would take priority over all other normal activities. If permission is required to excuse a man from attending on any particular day, application will be made to the Adjutant by noon that day'. So much for sport not being a parade.[62]

There are other examples. RAF Benson, a Bomber Command station in Oxfordshire, became not only an important centre for RAF rowing but one of the most determined and up-to-date rowing clubs in Britain during the 1950s. A former wing commander and rowing enthusiast, Jack Hay, worked on the base as a civilian but used his service contacts to ensure that prominent rowers were posted to Benson. It was not only a matter of facilities, although the Thames was nearby and the airmen rowers shared the use of a Nissen hut-cum-boathouse with the civilian Wallingford Rowing Club. It was the time spent on practice and physical training which made RAF Benson something of a unique experiment in British rowing. The main features were long distances rowed at high rates of stroke, six days a week, winter and summer, morning and evening, before and after work. Road running and circuit training were also part of a fitness programme that seems not too far removed from some of the schemes east of the Iron Curtain. Only two of the team were officers but, it is alleged, all were billeted together and shared a regime of no smoking nor drinking, no late nights and no leave during the summer regatta period. Before rowing at Henley the crew were flown to RAF Tangmere on the south coast for a weekend's special preparation. It seems to have worked because at Henley, in 1953, the RAF four won the Wyfold Cup and the eight won the Thames. The RAF four, representing Great Britain, went on to win the bronze medal

---

[62] We owe this reference to John Bale who interviewed Roy Fowler in 2006.

at the European Championships in Copenhagen, while five of the eight which had won the Thames Cup became Head of the River in 1954. In the 1956 Olympic Games in Melbourne, three of the rowing team were serving airmen and several of the others had been.[63]

Of course not all military sporting experiences had such happy landings. A national serviceman with the Royal Corps of Signals in Korea in 1954 complained that he had had ten days' pay stopped because he refused to play outside right in a football match. In a letter to his mother he explained that he had been chosen to play inside right and when told by an officer to play at outside right he refused as he did not like the position. His MP threatened to raise the matter in parliament if the sentence of loss of pay was not quashed. Fortunately, perhaps, he was only three months away from demobilisation.[64]

Tolstoy famously wrote that 'the chief attraction of military service' was that it consisted of 'compulsory and irreproachable idleness'. As there seems little doubt that most of the conscripts, for at least some of their time, were under-employed and that all had recognised periods when they were free of military duties, it should surprise no one that the military provided a range of opportunities to fill non-work time, opportunities which ranged from amateur dramatics, camp radio stations, education classes and music groups to the cinema, NAAFI and sport. All of these could bring pleasure to those who took part and sport had the additional advantage of being more visible to the wider world by its exposure in the civilian sporting press. Sport could provide prestige which few other non-military activities could match. As we have seen this was particularly true of the 'people's game'. All those young professionals who joined up meant that both the RAF and especially the army could offer serious competition to most of the leading professional clubs in England and Scotland during the 1950s. Service teams were supposed to be listed in the papers with name, rank and unit, but when *The Times* reported the RAF–Army match in March 1953 all twenty-two players were given only the name of their professional club. The RAF team contained seven future internationals and the Army five.[65]

---

[63] We owe some of these references to Chris Dodd of the National Rowing Museum. See also C. Porter, *A Very Public Servant* (Bassendean: Access Press, 2004), pp. 15–17, and the RAF Sports Board Mins, 20 September 1956, RAFSB.

[64] *Times*, 14 October 1954. It seems a clear case of a young soldier thinking that he was still a civilian really. The paper's military correspondent pointed out that, although games in the army should be played in a voluntary spirit, a soldier was expected to obey the orders of his superiors in all circumstances. It is noteworthy that even in Korea there were unit football leagues, weather and fighting permitting. The Education Corps section of the Commonwealth Division also produced a newsletter for the troops which included UK football results (Hickman, *The Call-Up*, p. 83).

[65] *Times*, 26 March 1953. The RAF won this match 6–0!

The Army had two famous victories over Glasgow Rangers at Ibrox Park, the 1954 match attracting a crowd of over 20,000 with receipts of over £1,000.[66] It went on profitable and successful tours to entertain the troops, most notably in BAOR. On the 1956 tour it lost only once in seven games against some of the leading clubs from West Germany and Holland. An army team also played and beat the local Aldershot team in a match to mark the centenary of the presence of the army in Aldershot, which was both played under floodlights and televised.[67] Sport undoubtedly continued to bring publicity and prestige to the three services. In the Melbourne Olympics of 1956, for example, the RAF had a total of twenty-one serving members participating and one third of the British team were or had been in the RAF.[68]

What did National Service do for the generation who experienced it? There were some contemporary anxieties that national service men themselves thought it a waste of time, and some commentators believed that many of the returnees had lost the capacity for work. A report undertaken by King George's Jubilee Trust in 1954 suggested that most young men at least benefited from enhanced physical fitness and also character development. The War Office commissioned an inquiry of its own in 1956, under the scrutiny of that most experienced of chairmen, John Wolfenden, to examine the employment of national servicemen in the United Kingdom. After interviewing 'many hundreds' of national servicemen, the overwhelming impression was that a large majority regarded their two years' period of service as 'an infliction to be undergone rather than a duty to the nation'.[69]

Some historians were sorry to see the infliction cured. Corelli Barnett, for example, thought that by 1957 National Service had become an accepted institution, part of the pattern of British life. National servicemen, especially if they were officers or NCOs – which the vast majority were not, of course – 'brought all the talents and diversity of the nation into the forces'. Barnett thought that it was a 'misfortune' that it ended and Britain became once more the 'only European nation without a

---

[66] Army FA Mins AGM, 24 May 1955, AFA.
[67] Army FA EC Mins, 25 June 1956, AFA. In general, though, the military seemed cautious about television. When the ABC Company wanted to show the football match between the British Army and the French Army the issue was deferred until after consultations with an equally conservative FA.
[68] RAF Sport Board Mins, 29 March 1957, RAFSB.
[69] *Report of the Committee on the Employment of National Service Men in the United Kingdom* [Cmnd. 35] 1956–7, p. 19. The King's Jubilee Trust investigation, *Citizens of Tomorrow: A Study of the Influences Affecting the Upbringing of Young People* (London: Odhams Press, 1955) included National Service as part of a wider study of 'the influences affecting the upbringing of young people' (see pp. 15–133).

citizen army'.[70] Peter Clarke seems to agree, although he was probably thinking more about the impact of the ending of National Service on civil society than on the military when he wrote that it had given two generations 'a taste of military discipline and an insight into what was meant by the term military efficiency, a common culture of reference which, for better or worse, a later generation growing up from the 1960s missed'.[71]

What has been forgotten here, perhaps, is that the national serviceman was a civilian in uniform. There can be little doubt that most young conscripts wanted to do their best whether in navy, army or Air Force. They wanted to make the most of the experience, and sport was one of the things which helped them to do this. But the majority of national servicemen also looked forward to the day when they would be once more released into civil society where real life could restart. Few of them appear to have joined the old comrades' associations appropriate to their regiments and units, which again underlines the essentially temporary nature of their military loyalties. There is also an even more interesting contemporary illustration of this essential point. The two reports on national service to which we have already referred, that of the King George's Jubilee Trust in 1954 and the War Office's own inquiry conducted during 1956–7, did not always share the same views about its impact and purpose but on one thing they did agree: national servicemen spent too many weekends at home. (It was for this reason that much service sport was played during the working week.) The report of the Trust was convinced that 'self-reliance' and what they called 'a broader outlook' were more likely to be encouraged by serving abroad. Going home at the weekends meant that the national serviceman continued to 'rely on his parents rather than learn to stand upon his own feet and integrate himself more closely with his service and his unit'. It was active service which developed self-confidence and team work and improved morale.[72] The War Office committee, reporting on the employment of National Servicemen, understood that the five-day week had become an accepted part of industrial and social life but doubted the wisdom of allowing its benefits to the conscript.

> We regard it as unsettling and ... not conducive to the happiness of the individual National Service man. It encourages him to live a 'double life', putting up with his week's duties in the Army in the expectation of returning to his civilian environment at the week-end; and it therefore discourages him from

---

[70] C. Barnett, *Britain and Her Army 1509–1970* (London: Allen Lane, 1970), p. 487.
[71] P. Clarke, *Hope and Glory: Britain 1900–1990* (London: Allen Lane, 1996), p. 232.
[72] See *Citizens of Tomorrow*, p. 131.

developing the attitude of being committed to the community of his camp or unit.[73]

This was a route down which the Army Council did not want to travel. A ban on weekend leave for home-based conscripts 'when there are no reasons of duty to keep men with their units' would, they felt, 'lead to irritation and dissatisfaction' and outweigh any advantages which might be gained.[74]

Sport probably helped to commit many ordinary National Servicemen to their camp or unit, but even sport couldn't compete with the family, dating and all the comforts, physical and psychological, subsumed in that seductive four-letter word, home, and certainly not at weekends.[75] And sometimes the services had to allow leading sportsmen to return to civilian sport at the expense of the military variety, taking what satisfaction they could from the comments in the newspapers praising their sagacity, as when Close and Trueman were released to play test cricket for England. Perhaps less well known but equally to the point was the example from 1958 when the army allowed Lance-Corporal Bobby Charlton (17th Co. RAOC) and Private Peter Dobing (East Lancashire Regiment) to play for their respective civilian clubs, Manchester United and Blackburn Rovers, in the FA Cup semi-final on a day when they had been selected to represent the Army against the Navy.[76] The reasons advanced were that Manchester United only had a limited number of players available after the Munich air disaster and the need for equity between both clubs.

If National Service was one major innovation of the post-war armed forces, another was the retention of the women's services on a permanent basis. The first women's service had been formed in early 1917,

---

[73] Cmnd. 35, p. 17.
[74] *Ibid.* 35, p. 26. In 1949 the Army Council decreed that, to foster *esprit de corps*, all soldiers should remain in barracks on one weekend every month; sport was a major feature of these 'Regimental Weekends'. One CO suggested playing rugby against civilian clubs, for example, because their hospitality was usually very good and when 'combined with a mild "pub-crawl" and sing song on the way home, can be a not unattractive alternative to week-end leave'. French, *Military Identities*, p. 312; *RAOC Gazette* 38 (1957), 320.
[75] The strength of this commitment should not be exaggerated but nor should it be doubted. Eddie Firmani and his wife cut short their honeymoon in 1955 so that he could play for his station team in the final of the RAF Cup. Firmani was born in South Africa but had come to England to play professional football with Charlton Athletic. Of his period of national service he wrote: 'I shall always be grateful to the RAF; after those two years I never again felt a stranger in England. *I now felt as English as the next man* [sic].' E. Firmani, *Football with the Millionaires* (London: Sportsman's Bookclub, 1960), pp. 30–1.
[76] Army FA EC Mins, 14 March 1958, AFA.

the Women's Auxiliary Army Corps (renamed Queen Mary's Army Auxiliary Corps in April 1918). Later the same year the Women's Royal Naval Service was set up, and in 1918, at the same time that the RAF was established, the Women's Royal Air Force. A total of almost 90,000 women enlisted, most (some 57,000) in the WAAC, serving as mechanics and drivers as well as in domestic and clerical jobs. A substantial number of women served behind the lines in France and Flanders, and some in Germany immediately after the Armistice. The early women's services faced considerable antagonism from those opposed to women in uniform, and despite lobbying to be retained as a peacetime reserve they were disbanded shortly after the war. In the late 1930s they were re-established, the Auxiliary Territorial Service in 1938, the Women's Royal Naval Service in May 1939, and the Women's Auxiliary Air Force (formed from RAF companies of the ATS) in July 1939. Wartime figures peaked at 214,420 for the ATS, 180,000 for the WAAF and almost 75,000 for the WRNS. Although women were again concentrated in domestic and clerical areas, their roles gradually expanded. In the RAF women came to replace men on a one-to-one basis in eighty-three trades, the ATS worked alongside men on anti-aircraft batteries, and WRNS worked as cipher and signal officers, served in the Naval Control Service organising merchant shipping and ran the naval launches in major ports. By the end of the war the success of the women's services was admitted even by sceptics. In 1946 it was announced that they were to be maintained on a permanent voluntary basis 'in order to lessen the needs of the services for men'. In 1949 their permanent status was confirmed, the ATS being renamed the Women's Royal Army Corps and the WAAF the Women's Royal Air Force.[77] The permanent women's services were small, however, declining from a total strength of 30,700 in 1949 and 21,900 in 1950 to a low of 11,700 in 1958; across the 1950s they comprised around 2 per cent of the armed forces as a whole.[78]

From an early stage the women's services had encouraged sport. The growth of women's athletics was accelerated by the First World War when, as Jeremy Crump has commented, women's work in the

---

[77] For the women's services see L. Noakes, *Women in the British Army: War and the Gentle Sex, 1907–1948* (London: Routledge, 2006); T. Stone, 'Creating a (Gendered?) Military Identity: The Women's Auxiliary Air Force in Great Britain in the Second World War', *Women's History Review* 8:4 (1999), 605–24; Squadron Leader B.E. Escott, *Women in Air Force Blue* (Wellingborough: Patrick Stephens Ltd, 1989); U. S. Mason, *The Wrens 1917–77: A History of the Women's Royal Naval Service* (Reading: Educational Explorers, 1977); S. Bidwell, *The Women's Royal Army Corps* (London: Leo Cooper, 1977).

[78] Figures from the *Annual Abstract of Statistics*.

services 'provided a context in which their participation in athletics became possible'. The WRAF seems particularly to have encouraged it. The WRAF serving on the Rhine after the Armistice played a good deal of sport. The 1919 Cologne RAF sports included a WRAF 100 yards race, and the 1919 RAF sports at Stamford Bridge a 440 yards WRAF relay race which was won by the South-Western Area team. Both the 1918 United States and Empire Sports and the Inter-Services Championships held in September 1919 at Stamford Bridge included women's services relay races – both won easily by the WRAF.[79] By the Second World War it was expected that servicewomen should take part in sport. The 1942 report on the amenities and welfare of the women's services found facilities for games adequate or better at the larger stations. 'Hockey and tennis are popular, sometimes swimming is available.' For smaller and more remote sites it recommended that 'local goodwill should be mobilised to secure tennis, hockey and cycling for personnel'. The committee noted that they were 'not satisfied that those employed in sedentary duties take enough active recreation or that physical training is carried out regularly'.[80] Towards the end of the war both the ATS and the WAAF formed Central Sports Committees and were granted funds from their respective Sports Boards to administer their own sports and games.[81] The reminiscences of individual servicewomen provide snapshots of their sporting experiences in the wartime forces. Mary Churchill, a corporal at the WAAF Recruiting Depot at Innsworth, took part in an Inter-Service Athletics Meeting involving the WAAF and the local RAF stations organised in the summer of 1941 to 'relieve boredom'. After winning six events she was promoted to sergeant and sent on an officers' course in PTI and Administration.[82] Elizabeth Lister, a signaller in the ATS, recalled that she was 'a sports woman. I swam, did the long jump and played tennis.'[83] Doris Poore, as an ATS pay clerk at Reading, enjoyed 'hockey matches with other battalions of ATS; it was a chance to visit

---

[79] *The WRAF on the Rhine* 2 (August 1919), 12–16, 3 (September 1919), 4–5; J. Crump, 'Athletics', in T. Mason (ed.), *Sport in Britain: A Social History* (Cambridge University Press, 1989), 44–77, at 62; *Times*, 9 September 1918, 22 August, 5 September 1919; Escott, *Women in Air Force Blue*, pp. 52–5. See also F. A. M. Webster, *Athletics of Today for Women* (London: Frederick Warne & Co., 1930), pp. 10, 13–14.
[80] *Report of the Committee on Amenities and Welfare Conditions in the Three Women's Services* [Cmd. 6384] 1941–2, para 171.
[81] Minutes of the RAF Sports Board, 9 February 1944, RAFSB.
[82] 'Mary Churchill – WAAF', at www.bbc.co.uk/ww2peopleswar/stories/65/a6015665.shtml, accessed 26 August 2008. (Not to be confused with Winston Churchill's daughter of the same name who served in the ATS.)
[83] Elizabeth Lister, 'ATS – Training, Work and Camaraderie', at www.bbc.co.uk/ww2peopleswar/stories/18/a7320818.shtml, accessed 26 August 2008.

248 Sport and the Military

Figure 18. 'WAF Girl Triumphs' – the women's services relay race at the 1919 Inter-Service Games at Stamford Bridge.

neighbouring towns on a Saturday'.[84] Servicewomen overseas also played sport. A WRNS cricket team led by Betty Archdale, who had captained the 1934–5 women's tour of Australia, frequently played on the Colombo ground in 1942, on one occasion playing and beating a Ceylonese team (Archdale 75 not out).[85]

Both physical training and sport in the women's services were clearly gendered. The inter-war years had seen both a great expansion of women's sport and the participation of thousands of women in physical recreation through the 'Keep Fit' movement and the Women's League of Health and Beauty. But these developments had been accompanied by renewed attacks on female athletics, which were accused of producing 'sexless' and 'sterile' women.[86] The potentially 'defeminising'

[84] Doris Poore, 'Rookies in the ATS Pay Corps', at www.bbc.co.uk/ww2peopleswar/stories/46/a2995446.shtml, accessed 26 August 2008.
[85] D. Macpherson, *The Suffragette's Daughter: Betty Archdale* (Dural Delivery Centre, NSW: Rosenberg, 2002), pp. 141–2.
[86] J. Hargreaves, *Sporting Females* (London: Routledge, 1994), ch. 6; S. Fletcher, *Women First: The Female Tradition in English Physical Education 1880–1980* (London: Athlone Press, 1984), pp. 74–6.

effects of physical training therefore caused some concern to the women's services, always anxious to stress the essential 'femininity' of their members. The wartime ATS and WAAF emphasised that 'great care has been taken to avoid all undue strain on the abdominal muscles, and so on the generative organs, since if the muscles, from over-exercise, lack elasticity, the dangers of childbirth are increased'. The WAAF presented physical training as a route to sex appeal. 'Figure, health, teeth, complexion and even charm depend on physical excellence and physical training rightly undertaken is a sure road to beauty'.[87] Servicewomen's sport was confined to games considered 'suitable' for women: cricket, hockey, netball, badminton, squash, tennis and swimming plus, in recognition of their military standing, fencing and rifle-shooting. For athletics in the 1950s they were restricted to the 100 and 220 yards, 80 metres hurdles, long jump, high jump and javelin; the WRAF also included 440 yards and discus but 'not in competition'. Before the 1990s women in the military who wanted to play football had to play for civilian teams and within the army were subject to sexual taunts, 'that thing about women football players being lesbians' as one servicewoman put it.[88]

The ideology of service sport, however, was apparently transferred wholesale from the men's services to the women's (always excepting the social control aspect of avoiding drunkenness and brothels). In the 1950s Brigadier Barclay of the Army Physical Training Corps listed among the benefits of physical and recreational training for women health, morale, contentment, physical efficiency, team spirit and 'the psychological outlook'. He also claimed that 'women who have no aptitude for sport are unsuitable as Leaders'. Inter-service competition and prestige were clearly important. Barclay declared himself 'horrified' by the army women's performance at the 1955 inter-service athletic meetings. Sport was seen as an aid to recruitment, especially important in the later 1950s as enlistment in the women's services fell sharply. In 1954 the WRAC turned down a suggestion to introduce inter-service competition in squash on the grounds that 'it would not necessarily

---

[87] *ATS Physical Training Tables* (London: HMSO, 1939); *WAAF Physical Training Tables and Recreational Handbook* (London: HMSO, 1941), pp. 3–4; *The Book of the WAAF* (London: Amalgamated Press, 1942), pp. 18, 21–2, 35–7; Stone, 'Creating a (Gendered?) Military Identity', 617. Physical training was compulsory in the WAAF except for women over thirty-five and – theoretically though not always in practice – in the ATS from 1942.

[88] J. Williams, *A Game for Rough Girls? A History of Women's Football in Britain* (London: Routledge, 2002), p. 59. The inclusion of rifle-shooting as a sport for women was curious, since it was only in 1980 that army women were allowed to train with small arms for self-defence (Noakes, *Women in the British Army*, pp. 150–2).

provide an inducement to recruiting'. In 1957 it triumphantly reported the results of WRAC participation in a cricket week at Colwell:

> thanks to the calculated and enthusiastic chatter of our Army players ... Service life was well advertised to many potential recruits among their fellow players. At least one of these civilian players has since applied to enlist, and no doubt there will be others from among the 150 Colwell cricketers.

(Here the WRAC had a star player: Myrtle Maclagan, one of England's top women cricketers, who had rejoined the WRAC in 1951 after serving in the wartime ATS and became Inspector of Physical Training in 1963.) The 1958 Advisory Committee on Recruiting emphasised the 'excellent opportunities for sport and recreation' as part of the 'fine life that the Women's Services can offer a girl today'. Some of the same problems beset the women's services as the men's. Rapid turnover of personnel, the inevitable result of national service, was also a problem in the women's services though for different reasons (particularly marriage). The average length of service was three years in the WRNS and WRAF, less in the WRAC, so that sports teams differed markedly in quality from year to year. Participation rates, again, were always a problem. Even in the WRAF, which heavily promoted sport, many servicewomen were 'less keen'. In 1947 the Director of the WRNS expressed concern that unless sports organisation was improved, since most girls had had few opportunities of playing games during the war, recruits would take no exercise 'except ballroom dancing'. Colonel Macfie of the WRAC suggested in 1955 that 'the present day "just-grown-up" young woman did NOT WANT to play games'.[89]

In the post-war years the women's inter-service sporting competitions were dominated by the WRAF. This probably reflected the much greater integration of women into the Air Force compared to the other two services. While the ATS/WRAC operated as a parallel organisation to the army (and the WRNS were technically civilians), WAAF/WRAF 'was *not* a separate service ... but instead came almost entirely under the auspices of RAF organisation and administration'.[90] This had considerable benefits in terms of sport and physical training. The WAAF/WRAF emerged from the war with their PT school 'an integral part of the magnificently equipped RAF School of Physical Training at

---

[89] Minutes of the Army (Women's) Central Sport Committee, 14 June 1954, 26 July 1955, 1997-10-144, NAM; *Report of the Advisory Committee on Recruiting* [Cmnd. 545] 1958–9, pp. 4–5, 49; *Lioness* 30:1 (1957), 17; C. Salmon, 'Maclagan, Myrtle Ethel (1911–1993)', *Oxford Dictionary of National Biography* (Oxford: Oxford University Press, 2004); Escott, *Women in Air Force Blue*, p. 283; 'Physical Training and Sport in the Women's Royal Naval Service, 1947–8, 1950–1', ADM 1/20822, TNA.

[90] Stone, 'Creating a (Gendered?) Military Identity', 606.

Cosford'. As a result WRAF athletes were 'extremely well-trained'. In contrast the WRNS, which during the war had used any PT experts who happened to enlist to train recruits and 'organise such sport as it was possible to have', as a permanent service initially had no provision at all for physical or recreational training. The ATS were left with a small ATS Physical Training Wing at Aldershot, separate from the main Army School of Physical Training. In 1947 it was reported to be 'fighting a hopeless battle to keep up compulsory P.T. against indifference or even hostility on the part of Commanding Officers, complete lack of qualified instructors and absence of facilities'.[91] In 1955 Brigadier Barclay, Inspector of Physical Training for the army, remarked revealingly that it had 'come as a great surprise' to him to find that his responsibilities included the physical training of servicewomen. The previous year the WRAC journal *The Lioness*, deploring the WRAF's superiority at athletics, had exclaimed hopelessly 'Can nothing persuade the Army that keen and fit women are infinitely more useful ...?'[92] The WRAC's sporting stars tended to be trained by civilian sportswomen or by men. Audrey Williamson, silver medallist in the 200 metres at the 1948 London Olympics (behind Fanny Blankers-Koen), certainly developed her skills in the ATS. Williamson had had no athletic training before joining up aged eighteen in September 1944, but her abilities soon became obvious, and she rose rapidly through the ranks on the physical training side. By 1948 she was a junior commander based at Chester as Supervising Officer Physical Training/ATS for Western Command and held the army women's record for 100 yards (later setting records for the 220 yards and long jump). But after nomination as an Olympic possible she was transferred to Aldershot for training by Captain Harbin of the Royal Hampshire Regiment at the Army School of Physical Training: it was he who decided she should run the 200 metres instead of the 100 metres for which she had been nominated.[93]

Was the period between 1945 and 1960 the summit for service sport? In some respects it could be argued that it was. There were better

[91] 'Physical Training and Sport in the Women's Royal Naval Service, 1947–8, 1950–1', ADM 1/20822, TNA; Minutes of the Army (Women's) Central Sport Committee, 26 July 1955, 1997–10–144, NAM. For a slightly more optimistic report on the post-war ATS, see Senior Commander J. K. Clark, 'Physical and Recreational Training in the ATS', *Mind, Body and Spirit* 27 (1947), 16.
[92] Minutes of the Army (Women's) Central Sport Committee, 26 July 1955, 1997–10–144, NAM; *Lioness*, 27:4 (1954), 68.
[93] 'ATS Olympic Athlete', *Mind, Body and Spirit* 29 (1948), 54–5; Mike Rowbottom, 'Only the "Athlete of the Century" beat Williamson to Gold', *Independent*, 31 January 2004. See also *Gloucestershire Echo*, 5, 6 August 1948. This was the first time the women's 200 metres had been run at the Olympics and some still thought it 'too gruelling for women'.

facilities and more opportunity for more servicemen to enjoy them (though it seems clear that sporting opportunities for service*women* have taken longer to develop). The relationship between service and civilian sport had probably never been stronger, as the release of Charlton and Dobing for the 1958 FA Cup semi-final illustrates. The presence of so many of the nation's leading young performers in a wide range of sports almost certainly helped to raise standards among the rest and also provided some overwhelmingly good publicity in a media which gave sport an increasing amount of time and space. But as we have seen there were also anxieties that airmen and soldiers on regular engagements were rarely able to represent the service as a whole. Moreover although two years might have seemed a long time out of the lives of many national servicemen it looked a short period to some of those who were responsible for running service sport. A member of the RAF Athletics Association's executive committee thought that team spirit was difficult to foster among athletes who were not staying around for very long but was both more attainable and more important in a team made up of relatively long-term regulars.[94] Finally Norman Ackland, a strong supporter of service football, thought that the post-war reorganisation of the army had robbed the Army Cup of much of its glamour. 'We knew where we were in the old days when the Black Watch beat the Scots Guards or the Sherwoods defeated the Durhams, but in modern days teams called say 999 Field Regt. RA or T.T. Wing Training Centre R.E. can hardly mean the same to the general public, though they may to the parent unit'. Of course, he was a civilian.[95]

---

[94] John De'Ath's reminiscences at www.raf.mod.uk/rafathletics/Administration/the-sirandrewhumphreytrophy.cfn, accessed 30 September 2008. The RAF team won nineteen consecutive Inter-Service Championships between 1965 and 1983.
[95] Ackland, 'The Forces', p. 380.

Conclusion

> Nowhere in civil life does sport play such an important part as in the Army.
>
> *The Army; the Finest Job in the World* (recruiting pamphlet c. 1936)

One of the major conclusions of our work must be simply to emphasise the sheer quantity of sport in the British military between the 1880s and 1960 – a much greater quantity than any previous authors have acknowledged. Consider the career of Eric Harrison of the Royal Artillery. At Woolwich, which he entered in 1912, Harrison was a notable athlete, captained the college rugby team and played rugby for the Army, Blackheath and Kent. In his last term he was promoted above his contemporaries because of 'our Padre's preaching of the Rugger Gospel and its influence on the Commandant towards the Captain of the XV'. His sporting ability having unexpectedly failed to override his poor marks to get him into the mounted Royal Field Artillery, in early 1914 he joined the Royal Garrison Artillery at Shoeburyness. Here he played a lot of army football 'and Southend, then in the Second Division [of the Southern League], asked whether I would consider playing centre forward for the season 1914–15'. His team won the Eastern Command Athletics Championships, and he was asked to run for England against Scotland and Ireland in the 120 yards hurdles. The Great War restricted his sporting activities, but when he was moved to a staff job at Beauquesne he was able to go riding in the afternoons 'usually with the intent of riding down partridges or hares'. After the war Harrison played for the Mother Country in the Imperial Inter-Services Rugby Tournament. He was selected for the 1920 Olympics team for the 440 yards hurdles, only to be diagnosed with heart trouble and forbidden to run; in 1924, his doctors having allowed him to run sprints, he reached the semi-finals of the 110 yards hurdles at the Paris Olympics. As the Captain of a Mountain Battery on Salisbury Plain his main energies were devoted to hunting (he became master of the RA Harriers), shooting, fishing and point-to-point racing. At the Staff

College in the mid-1920s he ran the College Drag and played hockey for England. Posted to Meerut, he took up pig-sticking, ran the Lahore Hounds (which hunted bagged jackals but tried to keep this quiet) and did a good deal of big-game shooting. Back in England before the war his career choices seem to have been governed largely by the opportunities for hunting in any post offered him. He had had, he reflected in old age, 'a very lucky life'.[1]

Lucky perhaps and certainly impressive in its scope, but Harrison's sporting career as a serving officer was not particularly remarkable. Indeed, it usefully highlights many of the themes we have considered here: the availability of sporting opportunities in the armed services and the determination of many servicemen to make the most of them even in the least encouraging circumstances; the tendency of the military to reward sporting excellence with promotion or professional perks; the interaction with civilian sporting organisations; the prestige that high-class sportsmen brought to the military. We have attempted in this book to demonstrate the ways in which sport contributed to British military life between the late nineteenth century and the abolition of conscription in 1960. There are four particular issues which deserve reconsideration here: the role of sport in encouraging *esprit de corps* and morale; the use of sport to promote recruiting; the part it played in the relations between the military and civil society; and the perhaps larger issue of how far and in what respects it was considered to be, and actually was, a preparation for war. As this latter is the most complicated issue it will be dealt with first.

The question of what relationship – if any – exists between sport and war is a difficult one and subject to a wide range of interpretation. George Orwell's well-known denunciation of sport as 'mimic warfare' and 'war minus the shooting', partly prompted by the visit of Moscow Dynamo football team to Britain in late 1945, refers in fact to the partisan passions it could produce in the spectators especially in a context of strong nationalist feeling.[2] Concrete evidence on the *military* value of sport is limited and ambiguous. A study of US servicemen during the Second World War suggested that previous participation in sports, especially 'bodily contact' sports like football, made soldiers more likely to adjust easily to army life. But sport was only one factor among many. And the finding was complicated by a strong correlation between sports participation and higher levels of education – which in turn tended to

---

[1] Harrison, *Gunners, Game and Gardens*.
[2] G. Orwell, 'The Sporting Spirit', in *The Penguin Essays of George Orwell* (London: Penguin, 1984), pp. 327–30 (first published in *Tribune*, 14 December 1945).

correlate with other 'better adjustment' factors such as a stable home life and good childhood health.[3] Perhaps more useful, though more speculative, is Konrad Lorenz's discussion of the relationship between sport and aggression. Unlike Orwell, Lorenz saw international sporting contests as a 'safety valve' for 'militant enthusiasm'. But he also saw sport as originating from 'highly ritualised, but still serious' forms of fighting. Sport, he suggested, taught men 'a conscious and responsible control of [their] own fighting behaviour'. Moreover, and in words strikingly reminiscent of those of the headmaster of Harrow in 1906,[4] Lorenz argued that sporting team spirit allows the reproduction of 'truly valuable patterns of human behaviour', rooted, he suggested, in tribal warfare:

readiness to sacrifice himself in the service of a common cause, disciplined submission to the rank order of the group, mutual aid in the face of deadly danger, and, above all, a superlatively strong bond of friendship between men.[5]

Our study suggests that sport's military utility in the British armed forces was less a matter of promoting aggression on the front line than in its contribution to physical fitness, relieving boredom, and in strengthening those ties that bind men together.

The 1932 edition of *Infantry Training* emphasised the practical values of sport to the soldier.

Fitness of body and contentment of mind come more readily in the free atmosphere of games. The platoon commander should organise in the afternoon football, cricket, boxing, and cross country running, especially in competition with other platoons, and take part in them himself. The men will respond wholeheartedly, and will carry the spirit of their games into their work. A platoon which plays football, runs, and boxes, will be qualified to meet and overcome the stress and strain of battle and of long marches.[6]

Joanna Bourke suggests that during both world wars 'combat effectiveness seemed to be inscribed on the body itself'. This went well beyond a simple appreciation of the need for physical fitness and reasonable physical strength. Bourke quotes the statement of the British medical officer Robert William MacKenna during the First World War that 'a definite parallelism exists between a man's physical state and the courage he exhibits. Bravery, unless a man be a poltroon, is more naturally expected of a man in splendid physical condition than a weakling; for

---

[3] S.A. Stouffer *et al.*, *The American Soldier: Adjustment During Army Life*, 2 vols. (Princeton University Press, 1949), vol. I, pp. 142–6.
[4] See Introduction.
[5] K. Lorenz, *On Aggression* (London: Methuen, 1972 (1st edn 1963)), pp. 241–3.
[6] Quoted in French, *Military Identities*, pp. 115–16.

the relation and interaction between soul and body is an intimate one'. Similarly in the Second World War recruits were assessed for combat effectiveness on the basis of 'a brief inspection of the body build to determine characteristics of masculinity' (an angular, muscular body indicating a 'strong masculine component').[7] If military masculinity was written on the body, however, it is by no means clear how far sport contributed to this. While a sportsman might well be expected to pass such a test with flying colours, in civil society military drill rather than sport was presented as the answer to a physically efficient nation. In the army too compulsory physical training filled this role.[8] As a voluntary activity, sport could only build on physical training, never replace it. Moreover, service sport was never only about participation, though some thought it should be: the spectacular was always a significant aspect of the military sporting experience.

Officers had always been encouraged to engage in those equestrian and blood sports which entailed a real physical element of risk such as hunting, polo, racing horses over jumps and shooting. Injuries were frequent and death not unknown. As David French has reminded us, taking part in such activities on a frequent and regular basis helped 'to teach soldiers that violence was a natural part of life'. Military men 'needed to cultivate a certain amount of ferocity'.[9] It should not, perhaps, come as a surprise that officers had a tendency to use the same language to describe games, field sports and war. This loose use of language did not go unchallenged within the officer corps. In the anonymous *Handbook of the Boer War* published in 1910 and written by an officer who had served twenty-six months in South Africa, the notion that war was a branch of sport was severely criticised. The author suggested that the idea had arisen from Britain's long immunity from invasion combined with the isolation of the army from civil life and 'the growing national passion for sport'. It had led to the refusal to take war seriously, to the degrading use of sporting metaphor in army orders, and to a situation where young officers knew more about cricket than about their profession (and were likely to be promoted for it). He acknowledged that 'in so far as Athletics and Sport tend to manliness, self-reliance, good comradeship, endurance of bodily hardship, and contempt of danger, they are an excellent preparatory school for war', but decried the belief that 'a good sportsman is necessarily a good soldier'.[10]

---

[7] J. Bourke, *An Intimate History of Killing* (London: Granta Books, 1999), pp. 109–11.
[8] Bourke, *Dismembering the Male*), p. 176.
[9] French, *Military Identities*, p. 117.
[10] *A Handbook of the Boer War* (Aldershot: Gale & Polden, 1910), pp. 26–34. The author has been identified as Captain Wyndham Frederick Tufnell, 3/The Buffs (East Kent

The idea that war was simply a more exciting form of sport was not entirely exploded by the Great War. The successful behind-the-lines sports programme in the British forces was organised by men who were largely committed to the sport–war analogy and who acted as its propagandists in the immediate post-war period. In the same way the war acted to confirm, rather than undermine, the connection between sport and war in the minds of some rugby union enthusiasts in the 1920s. In the American forces, Wanda Wakefield found the language of sport and war still in common – though not unquestioned – use as late as the Second World War.[11] This was not the case in the British services. A war that involved both the serious risk of invasion and the mass bombings of civilians on both sides was clearly in no sense 'sporting'. Moreover, the generation of officers who had been brought up by the Victorian and Edwardian public schools to see war as the 'greater game' was rapidly being replaced by one whose childhood and youth had taken place against the background of the slaughter on the Western Front. In these men the analogy between sport and war had been replaced by a soberer sense of the concrete benefits sport could bring to the armed forces, in war as well as peace.

One of them was *esprit de corps*, that spirit of disciplined confidence so crucial in creating and maintaining the corporate interests of a body of men. As this book has emphasised, sport was one of the ways in which regimental identities were created and reinforced in the late nineteenth-century British army. Sporting victories provided occasions for elaborate, almost ritualised, celebrations which themselves became part of a regiment's history and identity. Sport provided an accessible and instantly comprehensible source of unit pride and distinction in all three services. It was probably more effective in this respect than either the regimental journals or the unit histories which were largely created and used for the same ends. As one infantry officer of the Great War put it, *esprit de corps* was built on 'enthusiasm for the team you belong to whether it's the Leeds United [sic] or whatever it is'.[12] For the civilian sailors, soldiers and airmen of the two world wars, unit athletics, boxing and especially football provided a recognisable locus for the formation and expression of group identity. At an individual level sport served a role as a shared interest between men, a starter of conversations, something to bring servicemen together, however temporarily, bridging divides of generation and class – a role perhaps especially

---

Regiment). It seems likely that this was the 'W.T.' whose 1916 letter to the *Times* heads chapter 2.
[11] Collins, 'English Rugby Union'; Wakefield, *Playing to Win*, pp. 100–6.
[12] French, *Military Identities*, p. 282.

important to the 'civilians in uniform' in wartime and the national service years. During the Second World War Alan Ross, an ex-public schoolboy and a budding poet, served in the navy on escort duties with North Sea convoys. One of his shipmates was a builders' labourer from the Seven Sisters Road in North London. What they had in common was Tottenham Hotspur, and both had seen Willie Hall and George Hunt in their 1930s heyday. As Ross later wrote, 'you could scarcely have a closer bond'.[13]

Closely related to *esprit de corps* is morale. That sport had the capacity to improve morale, both in peace and war, seems certain. A.C. Grayling, writing recently about dancing, described one of its effects as being a 'temporary and agreeable self-abandonment when one leaves aside all thoughts and avocations, all anxieties and pre-occupations, and dwells ... in an extended present moment, which is like a place apart, away from the troublesome world'.[14] Sport has a similar ability to transport those who play or watch. It must have improved the lot of many servicemen through the years covered by this study. All three services considered that sport had made a substantial contribution to morale in the First World War, an understanding that was reflected in the setting up of the sport control boards and the expansion of funding for service sports between the wars. After the Second World War, Lieutenant-Colonel John Sleeman, 5th Battalion Royal Tank Regiment, explicitly linked the regiment's success in battle to its emphasis on sport. First he stressed physical fitness and team work because in the latter there was 'no honour for the individual, only honour for the Regiment'. There had never been a concentration on officer sports to the detriment of team games in which all ranks competed, nor was there any concentration on one particular sport (though he did give some credit to the 'Ironsides', an officers' club formed in the early 1930s which organised regimental teams in a range of sports including rugby, hockey, squash, tennis, golf, cricket and yachting). Secondly he underlined the way in which sport helped to establish a competitive spirit which was a major factor in 'our success in active operations'. Above all, Sleeman suggested that the Tanks' ability in the Second World War 'to fight with inferior equipment, to sustain heavy losses and yet keep on winning' was due not only to good leadership and sound training but also to morale 'high enough to overcome all obstacles'. The 'biggest factor' in developing such morale, he argued,

---

[13] A. Ross, *Blindfold Games* (London: Collins Harvill, 1988), p. 207.
[14] *Daily Telegraph*, 23 December 2006.

was the 'regimental policy on man-management', which included 'the encouragement of participation in games and sports by all ranks'.[15]

Supporters of military sport frequently claimed that it provided an incentive to recruiting, and the services have attempted to use it as such since at least the 1920s. How far it was successful remains unclear. For other ranks in particular the decision to join the armed forces normally depended on a complex of issues including the state of the economy, unemployment levels, the desire for escape and to 'see the world', and family or community links with the services or with one regiment in particular. Sport – together with wider improvements in service life in terms of food and housing, relaxation of petty discipline and pay – may certainly have helped to make enlistment a more attractive option, but further than this it is hard to go. Perhaps the case is stronger for officers, especially before 1939. John Vaughan was hardly alone when he declared that 'sport was the greatest consideration throughout my Army career'.[16] Henry Anthony Lascelles appeared to be set for an academic career. Educated at Winchester and Oriel College, Oxford, he read medieval history and art and was a lover of music and choral singing. His father was a historian of the eighteenth century. It was Lascelles' love of sport which drew him into the army where, in spite of poor eyesight, he represented England at squash, the Army at tennis and was a formidable middle- and long-distance runner on the track and across country.[17] A regiment known for its sporting enthusiasm, or for success at some particular sport, was likely to be attractive to officers. Vaughan was delighted to transfer to the 10th Hussars because the regiment had 'a very good sporting reputation'; Nigel Poett chose the Durham Light Infantry despite family connections with another regiment because of its success at polo.[18] The availability – almost unlimited at some times and places and especially in British India – of sports such as polo, pig-sticking and big-game shooting, at a price that made them accessible even to poorer officers, was certainly a major part of the appeal of military life before the Second World War. In 1958 the Advisory Committee on Recruiting had to accept that the interest of service life had been 'appreciably diminished for those who are attracted by adventure, travel and sport in its more arduous and dangerous forms'.[19]

---

[15] Lieutenant-Colonel John Sleeman, 'Morale – Games and Sports', in 'Papers relating to Sporting Records of the Royal Tank Regiment, 1933–1954', LIDDELL 9/28/92, Liddell Hart Centre, London.
[16] Vaughan, *Cavalry and Sporting Memories*, p. 111.
[17] *Times*, 21 July 2000.
[18] Vaughan, *Cavalry and Sporting Memories*, p. 111; French, *Military Identities*, p. 51.
[19] *Report of the Advisory Committee on Recruiting* [Cmnd. 545] 1958–9, p. 7.

Sport's main contribution to recruitment, however, may well have been less direct. It is clear that sport has played an important role in increasing the visibility of the armed forces in the wider society. Sport provided a useful bridge between civilian life and the life of the serviceman, a rare example of an interest common to both worlds. As regimental sport developed in the later nineteenth century, regimental sportsmen began to play regularly with their civilian neighbours and to compete in civilian contests. Soldiers and sailors made a significant contribution to the development of modern sport in important military centres such as Aldershot, Portsmouth and Plymouth. When service football teams were admitted to the Devon County Football Association in 1891 they proceeded to dominate the County Cup for the next nine seasons.[20] Sport helped to build links between the regular army and the Territorials. In India, and elsewhere in the British Empire, sport provided rare opportunities for contact with civilians. For the military authorities, sporting success was a source of prestige and an important means through which to advertise the services and project a positive image of service life. It is no surprise to find the Adjutant General persuading the Treasury that other ranks chosen to represent the United Kingdom in the Melbourne Olympics of 1956 should be granted paid leave for intensive training as well as for competing in the games themselves on the grounds that there was 'an obvious morale and publicity value in members of the Services participating in the Olympic games'.[21]

This is not to say that the adoption of sport by the armed forces was unproblematic. At times physical training and sport were asked to do too much. The inter-war navy's conviction that sport, discipline and morale were inextricably linked was so deeply held that in 1920 Admiral Beatty, 'believing that healthy minds went hand in hand with healthy bodies', proposed to give responsibility for welfare to the Physical Training Department. By the time of the 1931 Invergordon Mutiny, the Naval Personnel Committee, which dealt with welfare requests from the lower deck, had been downgraded to become merely 'an adjunct of the Admiralty's Department of Physical Training and Sports'.[22]

As a voluntary activity taking place in a highly disciplined community, as an activity which potentially breaches the barriers of rank in a strongly hierarchical organisation, sport as it has evolved in the British services contains inherent tensions. Nor are these confined to the

---

[20] See www.devonfa.com/historyofdevonfa.htm.
[21] DEFE7/1220/PPo/P(55)5, TNA, quoted in French, *Military Identities*, p. 305.
[22] Carew, *The Lower Deck of the Royal Navy*, pp. 240 fn. 120, 199.

period studied here. In 1985 the *Times* Diary reported that the head of the Army Sport Control Board had 'ordered that christian names must not be used between officers and other ranks "on the field of play". At the moment, he says, even nick-names are being used "to the detriment of acceptable standards".'[23] The very enthusiasm with which services embraced sport brought its own problems. From Victorian India to post-war Germany there were occasions when sporting preoccupations were allowed to override military imperatives. Both officers and other ranks were sometimes promoted more for their sporting abilities than for their professional ones. As inter-unit and inter-service sporting structures became established the importance attached to them tempted some officials to allow regimental sportsmen concessions such as time off for training, special food and other privileges in defiance of both military laws and the amateur spirit. In both world wars, as we have seen, sporting stars might be kept out of the line because of their contribution to unit morale. In the Second World War leading professional sportsmen were not only often channelled into the physical training units but were routinely used to provide sporting spectacles for the troops, occasionally being recalled from active service to do so. In this they resembled the actors and entertainers that made up ENSA but the sight of fit, highly trained young men engaged in a strenuous but apparently frivolous activity behind the lines made them liable to adverse comment, not least from some of their fellow servicemen. But by the 1940s it had become clear both that there were always more men outside the battle than within it, and that high-quality sporting spectacle provided a valuable boost to the morale of resting, training and non-combatant troops.

British sport took on its modern shape in the 1880s. It was widely considered to be one of the wonders of the age. It is not easy to see how the armed forces could have escaped its influence given that most of their officers were drawn from the sport-infested public schools and that many of the young working-class males who made up the other ranks were increasingly attracted by this pervasive example of popular culture. There was also a more gradual and tentative realisation that physical training and sport were effectively complementary, especially from the physical trainers themselves. The expansion of sport in the services was largely due to the initiatives of junior officers and NCOs and as in the civilian world was essentially a voluntary activity. But its growth first in the army and more gradually in the navy meant that it could not be too long before it was taken under more central control,

---

[23] *Times*, 3 December 1985.

Figure 19. Sport as spectacle in wartime: RAF personnel watch the 1943 Tripoli Cup final.

signs of which process were visible before 1914 although it was not completed until after the First World War.

During the two decades after 1919 the leaders of service sport emphasised their commitment to the ideology of amateurism, although there was a persistent admiration for the champion performer. In many respects service sportsmen had opportunities to train and practise denied to young men of similar income and background in civil society. In the quintessential amateur sports of athletics, fencing, hockey, rugby and squash, as well as most equestrian events, the services provided the facilities for sportsmen to reach higher standards while avoiding the social stigma of professionalism. There was something of a paradox here in that, while all three services were strong supporters of traditional amateur values, they were also contributing to their eventual decline by providing opportunities for athletes to practise and train which they would not have had either the time or money to do in the civilian world. In this respect the experience of service sportsmen is clearly a staging post on the road to the professional who devotes all his time to his sport.

Conclusion

The Second World War saw the return of the civilians to all three arms including small but significant numbers of professional sportsmen. That the wartime force was largely conscripted also propelled issues of morale and welfare towards the top of military agendas. Both participatory and spectacular sport had a part to play in this process. Conscription persisted for a decade and a half after 1945, years in which service sport reached levels of achievement not seen since before 1914 as the leading players in many sports brought success and prestige particularly to the army and Royal Air Force and probably helped to raise sporting standards overall by their advice and example. But there is some evidence of a recognition that what had been a halcyon period for military sport could not be expected to continue after the end of national service. In the spring of 1961 the British Army football team accepted an invitation to play the Greek Army in Salonica. A very successful occasion prompted a discussion of whether there should be a return match in order to repay the hospitality of the Greeks. It was underlined that, if the Greek Army team was to be invited, the match should take place before the end of 1961, 'since the standard of services football would then drop and would be no match for that of the Greek team'.[24] In the event neither army, Combined Services nor the Treasury could find the money to bring the Greek Army team to Britain. It seems that in future there would have to be very good reasons, probably political ones, before the government would support military teams on tours abroad. The British also refused to take part in the track and field championship of the Conseil International du Sport Militaire in 1962.[25] Lieutenant-General James Wilson looked back with nostalgia to the time in the late 1950s when he was involved in the management of an Army team which contained the 'cream of the country's young footballers, Scots, Welsh and Irish, as well as English. It was a privilege to be involved in the management of such talent.'[26] Such times would never quite return to military sport.

---

[24] DEFE 7/1220/PPo/23/61, TNA (13 June 1961). The match in Salonica was drawn 2–2, watched by a crowd of 50,000 with a further 20,000 unable to get in. The Greek Army team contained six internationals. The Greek Deputy Minister for National Defence in a letter dated 8 June 1961 wrote that 'thousands of sportsmen of the Macedonian Capital approved of and enthusiastically applauded the representatives of our old and faithful ally' and 'admired the excellent behaviour, the sportsmanship and the technical ability of the British team'.

[25] DEFE 7/1220/PPo, TNA.

[26] J. Wilson, *Unusual Undertakings: Military Memoirs* (Barnsley: Leo Cooper, 2002), p. 219.

Select bibliography

UNPUBLISHED PAPERS

THE NATIONAL ARCHIVES

ADM 1/7796: Adoption of Ju-Jitsu by the Navy, 1906
ADM 1/8549/16: Physical and Recreational Training of the Royal Navy (1919)
ADM 1/8566/237: Games and Sport in the Royal Navy. Proposal to form Central Committee, 1919
ADM 1/8619/24: The Financing of the Physical Training and Sports Branch
ADM 1/18968: Encouragement of Team Games in HM Ships, 1945
ADM 1/20882: Physical Training and Sport in the Women's Royal Naval Service, 1947–8, 1950–1
AIR 2/71 File 8465: RAF Sports Board and RAF Officers' Sports Fund
AIR 2/71 File 6510: Boxing: Gifts of Cups etc. by Sir Charles Wakefield
AIR 2/95: Formation and Administration of RAF Officers' Sports Fund, 1917–19
AIR 2/129: RAF Polo c. 1919–20
AIR 2/162: Formation of a Central Sports Fund, RAF, c. 1920–21
DEFE 7/1220: Sport and Recreation: General, 1947–63
FO371/55626: Foreign Office correspondence over Army football in occupied zones, 1946
WO32/5492: Army Athletic Association – proposed formation, 1913–14
WO32/5493: Army Athletic Association, 1914
WO95/55: War Diary: Deputy Inspector of Physical & Bayonet Training, 1917–19
WO163/4B–WO163/20: Proceedings of the War Office Council / Army Council
WO170/7469: Physical Training and Sports Centre, Central Mediterranean Forces, June–Dec. 1945
WO 203/1248: Welfare: Inter-Services Sports Exhibition Control Committee minutes, Nov. 1944–Feb. 1945
WO204/2044: Allied Forces: Welfare and Recreation, Mediterranean Theatre, 1943–5
WO374/64933: Starr, Lieut. F.J. (1916–21)

Select bibliography

LIDDELL HART CENTRE FOR MILITARY ARCHIVES

KIRKE 5/5: Speeches given by General Sir Walter Kirke at TA Dinners, 1937–39
KIRKE 5/6: Speeches given by General Sir Walter Kirke relating to the work of the Territorial Army Sport Board, 1938–9
LIDDELL 9/28/56: 'Achievements in sport of the Royal Tank Regiment in 1959'
LIDDELL 9/28/92: Papers relating to Sporting Records of the Royal Tank Regiment, 1933–1954
LIDDELL 15/3/58: Papers relating to Military Education, 1929–39

NATIONAL ARMY MUSEUM

Colonel G. W. W. Hill, 'Fifty Years of Sport in the Royal Irish Fusiliers', unpublished typescript, 7707–45
David Morgan, 'Stick and Ball Games', unpublished typescript, 9205–276
Papers of Field Marshal Lord Roberts
Minutes of the Army (Women's) Central Sports Committee

IMPERIAL WAR MUSEUM

War Diary of Commander John Dover
War Diary of Alex East
War Diary of E. N. Foinette
War Diary of W. J. Grant
War Diary of M. A. Hawarden
War Diary of John Jenkins
War Diary of A. G. Parker
War Diary of Brig. W. Carden Roe
War Diary of W. A. Quinney

OTHER

Amateur Athletic Association Minutes, University of Birmingham Special Collections
Army Football Association records, Army Football Association, Aldershot
Army Physical Training Corps records, Army Physical Training Corps Museum, Aldershot
Army Sport Control Board records, Army Sport Control Board, Aldershot
Football Association archives, London
Hampshire Football Association records, Southampton
Albert Hill, unpublished MS autobiography, copy in the possession of Tony Mason
William Pickford Papers, Hampshire Football Association, Southampton
Royal Air Force Sport Control Board records, RAF Halton
Royal Leicestershire Regiment records, Record Office for Leicestershire, Leicester and Rutland, Leicester

Royal Navy and Army Boxing Association and Imperial Services Boxing Association records, Royal Navy School of Physical Training, Portsmouth.
Royal Navy Football Association records, Royal Navy School of Physical Training, Portsmouth
United Services (Football) League Committee (Portsmouth), Royal Navy School of Physical Training, Portsmouth
Donald Weir Papers, Record Office for Leicestershire, Leicester and Rutland, Leicester
Wolfenden Committee Records, Sport England, London.

ONLINE SOURCES

Bedfordshire Regiment, War Diaries (1914–19), Bedfordshire and Luton Archives and Records Service online at http://blars.adlibsoft.com/ and at www.bedfordregiment.org.uk/
4th County of London Yeomanry, War Diaries (1939–44) at www.warlinks.com/armour/
11th Hussars (Prince Albert's Own), War Diaries (1939–1945) at www.warlinks.com/armour/
Diary of Steve Lonsdale, 1940–5 at www.wartimememories.co.uk/africa.html#lonsdale
Diary of Arthur Ward, 1939–45 at www.bbc.co.uk/ww2peopleswar/
Gooch papers, at http://www.lib.byu.edu/estu/wwi/1914m/gooch/1–12.htm

UNPUBLISHED THESES

Campbell, J. D., 'The Army Isn't All Work: Physical Culture in the Evolution of the British Army, 1860–1920', unpublished PhD thesis, University of Maine (2003)
Diaper, A., 'Kicking Football to the Front. An Investigation into the Role of English Football during the Great War 1914–1918', unpublished MA thesis, University of Central Lancashire (1997)
Fox, N., 'The Royal Navy Physical Training Branch: A Study of Innovation', unpublished PhD thesis, University of Liverpool (1982)
Hunt, T., 'The Development of Sport in County Westmeath, 1850–1905', unpublished PhD thesis, De Montfort University (2005)
Walton, O., 'A Social History of the Royal Navy, 1856–1900: Corporation and Community', unpublished PhD thesis, University of Exeter (2004).

PUBLISHED PRIMARY SOURCES

PARLIAMENTARY PAPERS

Report of the Royal Commission on the Sanitary State of the Army in India [C. 3184] 1863
Report of the Committee Appointed to Consider the Education and Training of Officers of the Army [Cd. 982] 1902

Report of the Committee Appointed by the Secretary of State for War to Enquire into the Nature of the Expenses Incurred by Officers of the Army, and to Suggest Measures for Bringing Commissions Within Reach of Men of Moderate Means [Cd. 1421] 1903

Minutes of Evidence Taken before the Committee Appointed to Consider the Existing Conditions under which Canteens and Regimental Institutes Are Conducted [Cd. 1494] 1903

Report of the War Office Committee of Enquiry into 'Shell-Shock' [Cmd. 1734] 1922

Report of the Committee on Amenities and Welfare Conditions in the Three Women's Services [Cmd. 6384] 1941–2

Report of the Committee on the Employment of National Service Men in the United Kingdom [Cmnd. 35] 1956–57

Report of the Advisory Committee on Recruiting [Cmnd. 545] 1958–9

TRAINING MANUALS ETC.

Manual of Physical Training, 1908
Cavalry Training, 1912
S.S. 137 *Recreational Training*, October 1917
S.S. 143 *Instructions for the Training of Platoons for Offensive Action*, 1917
S.S. 143 *The Training and Employment of Platoons*, 1918
Handbook of Physical and Recreational Training for the Use of the Royal Navy 1920 Volume II Recreational Training, 1922
ATS Physical Training Tables, 1939
WAAF Physical Training Tables and Recreational Handbook, 1941
The Soldier's Welfare: Notes for Officers, issued by the War Office, 1941

REGIMENTAL AND TROOP JOURNALS

Aldershot Command News
BEF Sports Journal
Black Watch Chronicle
Border Regiment Regimental Association News Sheet
Borderers Chronicle
Brigade of Guards Magazine
Bugle
Cavalry Journal
Durham Light Infantry Regimental Journal
Faugh-a-Ballagh
5th Glo'ster Gazette
Green Howards Gazette
Green Tiger
The Gunner
Household Brigade Magazine
XI Hussar Journal
Journal of the Royal Artillery

The Lioness
London Scottish Regimental Gazette
Mind, Body and Spirit
Oak Tree
Open Exhaust
RAOC Gazette
Red Hackle
Rifle Brigade Chronicle
Royal Engineers Journal
Sherwood Foresters Regimental Annual
Sport and Spuds
The WRAF on the Rhine

OTHER PERIODICALS

Army Quarterly
Athletic News
Baily's Magazine
Bell's Life
Broad Arrow
Chums
The Country Gentleman
Country Life
Field
Fighting Forces
Journal of the Royal United Service Institution
Lloyd's Weekly News
Navy and Army Illustrated
Picture Post
Portsmouth Football Mail and News
Prisoner of War
RAF Quarterly
Sporting Life
Times
Union Jack
United Service Magazine
Wisden Cricket Monthly

CONTEMPORARY BOOKS, ARTICLES AND MEMOIRS

Aflalo, F. G. (ed.), *The Sportsman's Book for India*, London: H. Marshall & Son, 1904
Alderson, Lieutenant-Colonel E. A. H., *Pink and Scarlet or Hunting as a School for Soldiering*, London: Heinemann, 1900
Anon., *A Handbook of the Boer War*, Aldershot: Gale & Polden, 1910
 A Soldier's Diary of the Great War, London: Faber & Gwyer, 1929
Ansell, Colonel Sir M., *Soldier On*, London: Peter Davies Ltd 1973

Select bibliography

Arlott, J., Wooller, W., and Edelston, M., *Wickets, Tries and Goals*, London: Sampson Low, Marston & Co., 1949

Armfield, J., *Right Back to the Beginning: The Autobiography*, London: Headline, 2004

The ASCB Handbook India 1936–7

'ATS Olympic Athlete', *Mind, Body and Spirit* 29 (1948), 54–55

Baden-Powell, R. S., *Pigsticking; or, Hoghunting: A Complete Account for Sportsmen, and Others*, London: Harrison & Sons, 1889

Baden-Powell, Major-General R. S. S., *Sport in War*, London: Heinemann, 1900

Baden-Powell, Lieutenant-General Sir Robert, *Indian Memories*, London: Herbert Jenkins, 1915

Baden-Powell, Sir Robert, *Pig-Sticking or Hog-Hunting: A Complete Account for Sportmen and Others* London: Herbert Jenkins, 1924

Banning, Lieutenant-Colonel S. T., *Administration, Organisation and Support Made Easy*, Aldershot: Gale & Polden, 1908

Blacker, General Sir C., *Soldier in the Saddle*, London: Burke, 1963

Blood, Sir B., *Four Score Years and Ten*, London, G. Bell & Sons, 1933

Bohun Lynch, J. G., *The Complete Amateur Boxer*, London: Methuen, 1913

The Book of the WAAF, London: Amalgamated Press, 1942

Brackenbury, H., 'Military Reform', Part I, *Fraser's Magazine* 74 (1866), 692

The Britannia Shield Competition Handbook, 1958

British Sports and Sportsmen Past and Present 13 vols., London, 1908–

Burgess, R., *Football: My Life*, London: Souvenir Press, 1952

Burton, Lieutenant-Colonel F. N., *The War Diary (1914–1918) of the 10th (Service) Battalion Royal Welsh Fusiliers*, Plymouth: William Brendon, 1926

Buxton, A., *Sport in Peace and War*, London: Arthur L. Humphreys, 1920

[Cairns, W. E.], *Social Life in the British Army*, London: J. Long, 1900

Churchill, W., *My Early Life*, London: Thornton Butterworth Ltd, 1930

Clark, J. K., 'Physical and Recreational Training in the ATS', *Mind, Body and Spirit* 27 (1947), 16

Clark, N., *All in the Game*, London: Methuen, 1935

Clayton, R., *A Slave to Soccer*, London: Stanley Paul, 1960

Cooper, H., *An Autobiography*, London: Coronet, 1972

Crocker, V. A., *There's a Soldier at the Gate: Second World War Memoirs of a Tenth Royal Hussar*, Victoria, BC: Trafford, 2005

Crump, J., *Running Round the World*, London: Hale, 1966

Cullis, S., *All For the Wolves*, London: Rupert Hart-Davis, 1960

Dale, T. F., 'Polo and Politics', *Blackwood's Magazine* 165 (1899), 1032–6

Polo Past and Present, London: Country Life, 1905

Davies, W. J. A., *Rugby Football and How to Play It*, London: Webster's, 1923

Dawson, Captain L., *Sport in War*, London: Collins, 1936

De Lisle, H. de B., *Polo in India*, 2nd edn, Bombay: Thacker, 1913

The Rules of Polo in India, 1907, Bombay: Thacker, 1907

De Lisle, General Sir Beauvoir, *Reminiscences of Sport and War*, London: Eyre & Spottiswoode, 1939

Select bibliography

Tournament Polo, London: Eyre & Spottiswoode, 1938
Dixon, A., *Tinned Soldier*, London: Jonathan Cape, 1941
Douglas, K., *Alamein to Zem Zem*, London: Faber and Faber, 1992 (1st edn 1946)
Drybrough, T. B., *Polo*, London: Longmans, 2nd edn, 1906
Edwards, D., *Tackle Soccer This Way*, London: Stanley Paul, 1958
Ellis, A. E., *Refereeing Round the World*, London: Sportsman's Book Club, 1956
'Ex-Non-Com', 'The Soldier in Relation to Regimental Sport', *United Service Magazine* 40 (1909–10), 32–6
Fairfax-Blakeborough, J., 'Nature and Sport at the Back of the Front', *Baily's Magazine* 107 (May 1917), 196–9
Feilding, R., *War Letters to a Wife: France and Flanders, 1915–1919*, London: Medici Society, 1930
Finney, T., *Football Round the World*, London: Sportsman's Book Club, 1955
Fox, Colonel Sir M., 'Army and Navy Boxing', *Household Brigade Magazine* 16 (1913), 111–12
Fraser, J., *Sixty Years in Uniform*, London: Stanley, Paul & Co., 1939
Games and Sports in the Army, London: Army Sport Control Board, 1931–60
Gannon, Brigadier J., *Before the Colours Fade: Polo, Pig, India, Pakistan and Some Memories*, London: J. A. Allen, 1976
Gibson, A., and Pickford, W., *Association Football and the Men Who Made It*, 4 vols., London: Caxton, 1906
Goold Walker, G. (ed.), *The Honourable Artillery Company in the Great War*, London: Seeley & Co., 1930
Gough, General Sir H., *Soldiering On*, London: Arthur Barker, 1954
Harington, General Sir C., *Tim Harington Looks Back*, London: Murray, 1940
Harrison, E., *Gunners, Game and Gardens*, London: Leo Cooper, 1978
'Ian Hay' (John Hay Beith), *Carrying on After the First Hundred Thousand*, Edinburgh: Blackwood, 1917
Hayes, Captain, *Indian Racing Reminiscences*, London: W. Thacker, 1883
Henniker, M. C. A., *Memoirs of a Junior Officer*, Edinburgh: Blackwood, 1951
Hewson, B., *Flying Feet*, London: Stanley Paul, 1962
Hills, Captain J. D., *The Fifth Leicestershire: A Record of the 1/5th Battalion the Leicestershire Regiment, TF during the War 1914–1919*, Loughborough: Echo Press, 1919
Horrocks, Lieutenant-General Sir B., *A Full Life*, London: Collins, 1960
Jellicoe, Admiral Viscount, *The Grand Fleet 1914–1916*, London: Cassell, 1919
Joy, B., *Forward, Arsenal!*, London: Phoenix House, 1952
C. E. K. (Captain Kinahan), 'The Need of Games in the Army', *Faugh-a-Ballagh* 4 (January 1907), 11–13
Kee, R., *A Crowd Is Not Company*, London: Eyre & Spottiswoode, 1947
Kentish, Brigadier-General R. J. 'Army Association Football', *BEF Sports Journal* 1 (8 February 1919), 1

Select bibliography

King George's Jubilee Trust, *Citizens of Tomorrow: A Study of the Influences Affecting the Upbringing of Young People*, London: Odhams Press, 1955

Kipling, R., 'The Maltese Cat', in *The Day's Work*, London: Macmillan, 1898

LC, 'Modern Developments in Physical Training', *Journal of the Royal United Services Institution* 67 (1922), 67–81

Lathbury, Lieutenant G. W., 'Wasted Time in Regimental Soldiering', *Journal of the Royal United Service Institution* 81 (1936) 826–30

Lindsell, Colonel W. G. *Military Organisation and Administration*, Aldershot: Gale & Polden, 1932

Lyons, J., 'Sport and Territorials: How to Popularise the Force', *National Defence* 3 (August 1909), 137–9

McLaren, B., *The Voice of Rugby: An Autobiography*, London: Bantam Books, 2005

McKibbin, M. N., *Barbed Wire: Memories of Stalag 383*, London: Staples Press, 1947

Marling, P., *Rifleman and Hussar*, London: John Murray, 1931

Martel, G., *An Outspoken Soldier*, London: Sifton, Praed & Co., 1949

Mays, S., *Fall out the Officers*, London: Eyre & Spottiswoode, 1969

Miller, Lieutenant-Colonel E. D., *Modern Polo*, London, 4th edn: Hurst & Blackett, 1922

Fifty Years of Sport, London: Hurst & Blackett, 1925

Moberley, Major R. B., *Campaign in N.W. Europe, June 6th 1944–May 7th, 1945: Second Battalion the Middlesex Regiment (DCO)*, Cairo: R. Schindler, 1946

Mockler-Ferryman, Major A. F., *Annals of Sandhurst*, London: Heinemann, 1900

Moray Brown, J., 'Polo', in R. Weir, *The Badminton Library: Riding and Polo*, London: Longmans, 1895

'The Training of Polo Ponies', *Blackwood's Magazine* 149 (1891), 645–51

Morgan, Sir F., *Peace and War*, London: Hodder & Stoughton, 1961

Neame, Lieutenant-General Sir P., *Playing with Strife*, London: Harrap, 1947

Newton, Captain P. I., 'Sport: its Uses and Abuses as an adjunct to the Training of the Soldier', *Journal of the Royal Artillery* 48 (1921–2), 250–7

Orwell, G., 'The Sporting Spirit', in *The Penguin Essays of George Orwell*, London: Penguin, 1984

Pawson, T., *Indelible Memories: Playingfields and Battlefields*, privately printed, n.d.

Pennington, Lieutenant-Colonel R. L. A., 'Army Reform from a Battalion Point of View', *Fortnightly Review* 69 (1901), 312–29

Porter, C., *A Very Public Servant*, Bassendean: Access Press, 2004

Powell, A. *The Valley of Bones*, London: Flamingo, 1983 (1st edn 1964)

Richards, A., *Carwyn: A Personal Memoir*, London: Michael Joseph, 1984

Richards, Captain D. J. R., 'Sport', *Journal of the Royal Artillery* 47 (1921–2), 409–17

Richards, F., *Old-Soldier Sahib*, London: Faber and Faber, 1936

'*The Robin Hoods*'. *1/7th, 2/7th & 3/7th Battns. Sherwood Foresters 1914–1918. Written by Officers of the Battalions*, Nottingham: J. & H. Bell, 1921
Ross, A., *Blindfold Games*, London: Collins Harvill, 1988
Royal Naval Football Association Handbook
Royal Navy and Royal Marines Sports Handbook
Rous, S., *Football Worlds: A Lifetime in Sport*, London: Faber, 1978
St Quintin, T. A., *Chances of Sports of Sorts*, Edinburgh: Blackwood, 1912
Sassoon, S., *Memoirs of a Foxhunting Man*, London, 1971
Scarfe, N., *Assault Division: A History of the 3rd Division from the Invasion of Normandy to the Surrender of Germany*, Staplehurst: Spellmount, 2004 (1st edn 1947)
Sheffield, G., and Bourne, J. (eds.), *Douglas Haig: War Diaries and Letters 1914–1918*, London: Weidenfeld & Nicolson, 2005
Sport and the Community: The Report of the Wolfenden Committee on Sport, 1960
Stein, C., 'Soldiering and Sport', *Baily's Magazine* 74 (1900), 235–40
Stouffer, S. A., et al., *The American Soldier: Adjustment During Army Life*, 2 vols., Princeton University Press, 1949
Swinton, Major-General Sir E. (ed.), *Twenty Years After: The Battlefields of 1914–18 Then and Now*, Supplementary Volume, London: Newnes, n.d.
Talbar, A., 'Sports in the Jewish Brigade', in G. Eisen, H. Kaufman and M. Lammer (eds.), *Sport and Physical Education in Jewish History*, Netanya: Wingate Institute, 2003
Temple Clarke, Captain A. O., *Transport and Sport in the Great War Period*, London: Garden City Press, 1938
Terraine, J. (ed.), *General Jack's Diary*, London: Eyre & Spottiswoode, 1964
Thorne, T., *Brasso, Blanco and Bull*, London: Robinson, 2000
Trueman, F., *Ball of Fire: An Autobiography*, St Albans: Mayflower, 1977
Vaughan, Major-General J., *Cavalry and Sporting Memories*, Bala: Bala Press, 1954
Vibart, Colonel H. M., *Addiscombe: Its Heroes and Men of Note*, London: Constable & Co., 1894
Wakefield, W. W. and Marshall, H. P., *Rugger*, London: Longmans, Green, & Co., 1927
Wardrop, A. E., *Modern Pig-Sticking*, London: Macmillan, 1914
Warner, P., *Imperial Cricket*, London: London and Counties Press Association, 1912
Webster, F. A. M., *Athletics of Today for Women*, London: Frederick Warne & Co., 1930
Wilfrid Blunt's Egyptian Garden: Fox Hunting in Cairo, London: The Stationery Office, 1999
Wilson, Lieutenant-Colonel Sir J., *Unusual Undertakings: A Military Memoir*, Barnsley: Leo Cooper, 2002
Wood, General Sir E., *From Midshipman to Field Marshal*, London: Methuen, 1912.
Wyndham, H., *The Queen's Service*, London: Heinemann, 1899
Wythe, Major G. et al., *The Inter-Allied Games, Paris 22nd June to 6th July 1919*, Paris: The Games Committee, 1920

'You Have Been Warned', 'The Army, the Officer, and the Horse', *Journal of the Royal Artillery* 64 (1937–8), 323–39

Younghusband, Captain G. J., *Polo in India*, London: W. H. Allen & Co., 1890

SECONDARY SOURCES

Ackland, N., 'The Forces', in A. H. Fabian and G. Green (eds.), *Association Football*, 4 vols., London: Caxton, 1960, vol. I

Addison, P. and Calder, A., eds., *Time to Kill: The Soldier's Experience of War in the West, 1939–1945*, London: Pimlico, 1997

Agnew, P., *Finney: A Football Legend*, Preston: Carnegie Press, 1989

Alexander, J., *McCrae's Battalion: The Story of the 16th Royal Scots*, Edinburgh: Mainstream, 2003

Allen, C., *Plain Tales from the Raj*, Newton Abbot: Readers Union, 1976

Allen, D., 'Bats and Bayonets: Cricket and the Anglo-Boer War, 1899–1902', *Sport in History* 25 (2005), 17–40

Anglesey, Marquess of, *A History of the British Cavalry 1816 to 1919, IV: 1899 to 1913*, London: Leo Cooper, 1986

Arthur, Sir G., *Life of Lord Kitchener*, 3 vols., London: Macmillan, 1920

Ashworth, T., *Trench Warfare 1914–1918: The Live and Let Live System*, London: Macmillan, 1980

Badsey, S., 'Cavalry and the Development of Breakthrough Doctrine', in P. Griffith (ed.), *British Fighting Methods in the Great War*, London: F. Cass, 1996

  Doctrine and Reform in the British Cavalry 1800–1918, Aldershot: Ashgate, 2008

Baker, N., 'A More Even Playing Field? Sport During and After the War', in N. Hayes and J. Hill (eds.), *Millions Like Us? British Culture in the Second World War*, Liverpool University Press, 1999

Baker Brown, Brigadier-General W., *History of the Corps of Royal Engineers* vol. IV, Chatham: The Institution of Royal Engineers, 1993, 1st printed 1952

Bale, J., and Hewson, M., *A Fighter Second to None: Roy Fowler of Leek and His World of Running*, Stoke-On-Trent: North Staffordshire Press, 2006

Ball, S. J., 'A Rejected Strategy: The Army and National Service 1946–63', in H. Strachan (ed.), *The British Army, Manpower and Society into the Twenty-First Century*, London: Frank Cass, 2000

Barnett, C., *Britain and Her Army 1509–1970*, London: Allen Lane, 1970

Barton, B., *Servowarm History of the FA Amateur Cup*, Newcastle: Barton, 1984

Baynham, H., *Before the Mast: Naval Ratings of the Nineteenth Century*, London: Hutchinson, 1971

  Men from the Dreadnoughts, London: Hutchinson, 1976

Best, G., 'Militarism and the Victorian Public School', in B. Simon and I. Bradley (eds.), *The Victorian Public School*, Dublin: Gill & Macmillan, 1975

Bidwell, S., *The Women's Royal Army Corps*, London: Leo Cooper, 1977
Bidwell, S., and Graham, D., *Fire-Power: British Army Weapons and Theories of War 1904–1945*, London: George Allen & Unwin, 1982
Birley, D., 'Sportsmen and the Deadly Game', *British Journal of Sports History* 3 (1986), 288–310
Birtley, J., *Freddie Mills, His Life and Death*, London: New English Library, 1978
Blair, D.J., 'The Greater Game: Australian Football and the Army in Melbourne and on the Front during World War I', *Sporting Traditions* 11 (1995), 91–102
Bond, B., *British Military Policy Between the Two World Wars*, Oxford: Clarendon Press, 1980
  'Doctrine and Training in the British Cavalry 1870–1914', in M. Howard (ed.), *The Theory and Practice of War: Essays Presented to Captain B. H. Liddell Hart*, London: Cassell, 1965
Booth, D., *The Impossible Hero: A Biography of Gordon Pirie*, London: Corsica Press, 1999
Borsay, P., *A History of Leisure: The British Experience since 1500*, London: Palgrave, 2006
Bourke, J., *Dismembering the Male: Men's Bodies, Britain and the Great War*, London: Reaktion Books, 1996
  An Intimate History of Killing, London : Granta Books, 1999
  'The British Working Man in Arms', in H. Cecil and P. Liddle (eds.),
Bourne, J., *Facing Armageddon: The First World War Experienced*, London: Leo Cooper, 1996
Bourne, J.M., 'The East India Company's Military Seminary, Addiscombe 1809–1858', *Journal of the Society for Army Historical Research* 57 (1979), 206–22
Brereton, J.M., *The British Soldier. A Social History from 1661 to the Present Day*, London: The Bodley Head, 1986
Bristow, N., *Making Men Moral: Social Engineering During the Great War*, New York: New York University Press, 1996
Campbell, J.D., '"Training for Sport Is Training for War": Sport and the Transformation of the British Army, 1860–1914', *International Journal of the History of Sport* 17 (December 2000), 21–58
Carew, A., *The Lower Deck of the Royal Navy: 1900–1939: The Invergordon Mutiny in Perspective*, Manchester: Manchester University Press, 1981
Carter, Wing Commander P., 'Who Needs Officer Qualities?', *Journal of the Royal Air Force College, Cranwell* (March 2002), 14
Chalke, S., *Tom Cartwright: The Flame Still Burns*, Bath: Fairfield Books, 2007
Charlston, J., 'Disorganised and Quasi-official but Eventually Successful: Sport in the US Military, 1814–1914', *International Journal of the History of Sport* 19 (2002), 70–87
Churchill, R.S., *Winston S. Churchill*, vol. I *Youth: 1874–1900*, London: Heinemann, 1966

Winston S. Churchill, vol. II Companion Part 1: *1901–1907*, London: Heinemann, 1967
Clarke, P., *Hope and Glory: Britain 1900–1990*, London: Allen Lane, 1996
Clayton, A., 'Sport and African Soldiers: The Military Defusion of Western Sport throughout Sub-Saharan Africa', in W. J. Baker and J. A. Mangan (eds.), *Sport in Africa: Essays in Social History*, London: Frank Cass, 1987
  The British Officer: Leading the Army from 1660 to the Present, London: Longman, 2005
Collingham, E. M. *Imperial Bodies: The Physical Experience of the Raj c.1800–1947*, Cambridge: Polity, 2001
Collins, T., 'English Rugby Union and the First World War', *Historical Journal* 45 (2002), 797–817
  Rugby League in Twentieth Century Britain: A Social and Cultural History, London: Routledge, 2006
  A Social History of English Rugby Union, London: Routledge, 2009
Crang, J., *The British Army and the People's War 1939–45*, Manchester: Manchester University Press, 2000
  'The British Army as a Social Institution, 1939–1945', in H. Strachan (ed.), *The British Army, Manpower and Society into the Twenty-First Century*, London: Cass, 2000
  'The British Soldier on the Home Front: Army Morale Reports, 1940–45', in P. Addison and A. Calder (eds.), *Time to Kill: The Soldier's Experience of War in the West, 1939–1945*, London: Pimlico, 1997
Crump, J., 'Athletics', in T. Mason (ed.), *Sport in Britain: A Social History*, Cambridge University Press, 1989
Cunningham, H., *The Volunteer Force*, London: Croom Helm, 1975
Deghy, G., *Noble and Manly: The History of the National Sporting Club*, London: Hutchinson, 1956
DeGroot, G., 'Educated Soldier or Cavalry Officer? Contradictions in the Pre-1914 Career of Douglas Haig', *War and Society* 4 (1986), 51–69
Dennis, P., *The Territorial Army 1906–40*, London: Royal Historical Society, 1987
Dimeo, P., 'Football and Politics in Bengal: Colonialism, Nationalism, Communalism', *Soccer and Society* 2 (2001), 57–74
Eksteins, M., *Rites of Spring: The Great War and the Birth of the Modern Age*, London: Papermac, 2000
Ellis, J., *The Sharp End of War: The Fighting Man in World War II*, Newton Abbot: David & Charles, 1980
Escott, B. E., *Women in Air Force Blue*, Wellingborough: Patrick Stephens Ltd, 1989
Farwell, B., *Mr Kipling's Army*, New York: Norton, 1981
Ferguson, B., *The Black Watch and the King's Enemies*, London: Collins, 1950
Fitzpatrick, D., 'Unofficial Emissaries: British Army Boxers in the Irish Free State, 1926', *Irish Historical Studies* 30 (1996), 206–32

Fletcher, S. *Women First: the Female Tradition in English Physical Education 1880–1980*, London: Athlone Press, 1984

French, C. F., 'The Fashioning of Esprit de Corps in the 51st Highland Division from St Valery to El Alamein', *Journal of the Society for Army Historical Research* 77 (1999), 275–92

French, D., *Military Identities: The Regimental System, the British Army, and the British People, c.1870–2000*, Oxford University Press, 2005

'The Mechanization of the British Cavalry between the World Wars', *War in History* 10 (2003), 296–320

'Officer Education and Training in the British Regular Army, 1919–39', in G. C. Kennedy and K. Neilson (eds.), *Military Education: Past, Present and Future*, Westport, Conn.: Praeger, 2002

Raising Churchill's Army: The British Army and the War against Germany, 1919–1945, Oxford University Press, 2000.

'Tommy Is No Soldier: The Morale of the Second British Army in Normandy, June–August 1944', *Journal of Strategic Studies* 19 (1996), 154–78

Fuller, J. G., *Troop Morale and Popular Culture in the British and Dominion Armies 1914–1918*, Oxford University Press, 1990

Genders, R., *League Cricket in England*, London: Werner Laurie, 1952

Gannon, J., 'Polo: The Indian Inter-Regimental Tournament', *Royal Armoured Corps Journal* 2 (1948), 130–7, 207–20

Garnham, N., *Association Football and Society in Pre-Partition Ireland*, Belfast: Ulster Historical Foundation, 2004

'"The Only Thing British That Everybody Likes": Military–Civilian Relations in Late Victorian Ulster', *Eire-Ireland* 41 (2006), 59–79

Gibson, C., 'The British Army, French Farmers and the War on the Western Front 1914–1918', *Past and Present* 180 (2003), 175–239

Gray, J. G., *Prophet in Plimsoles: An Account of the Life of Colonel Ronald B. Campbell*, Edinburgh: Edina Press, 1978

Greenland, W., *The History of the Amateur Football Alliance*, Harwich: Amateur Football Alliance, 1965

Griffith, P., *Battle Tactics on the Western Front: The British Army's Art of Attack, 1916–18*, London: F. Cass, 1994

(ed.), *British Fighting Methods in the Great War*, London: F. Cass, 1996

Guha, R., *A Corner of a Foreign Field: The Indian History of a British Sport*, London: Picador, 2002

Haley, B., *The Healthy Body in Victorian Culture*, Cambridge, Mass.: Harvard University Press, 1978

Halpern, P. G (ed.), *The Keyes Papers*, 3 vols., London: Navy Records Society, 1979–81

Hapgood, E., *Football Ambassadors*, London: Sporting Handbooks, 1945

Harding, J., *Lonsdale's Belt. The Story of Boxing's Greatest Prize*, London: Robson Books, 1994

Hargreaves, J., *Sporting Females*, London: Routledge, 1994

Hargreaves, R., 'Divertissement', *Cavalry Journal* 31 (1941), 204–25

Harries-Jenkins, G., *The Army in Victorian Society*, London: Routledge and Kegan Paul, 1977

Harrison, M., *Medicine and Victory: British Military Medicine in the Second World War*, Oxford: Oxford University Press, 2004
Hearl, T., 'Fighting Fit: Some Military Initiatives in Physical Education in Britain, 1800–1860', in *The Fitness of the Nation: Physical and Health Education in the Nineteenth and Twentieth Centuries: Proceedings of the 1982 Annual Conference of the History of Education Society of Great Britain* (History of Education Society, 1983)
Hess, R., 'A Healing Hegemony: Florence Nightingale, the British Army in India and 'a want of … exercise', *International Journal of the History of Sport* 15 (1998), 1–17
Hickman, T., *The Call-Up: A History of National Service*, London: Headline, 2004
Higham, R., *Armed Forces in Peacetime. Britain 1918–1940: A Case Study*, London: G. T. Foulis & Co., 1962
Holmes, R., *Firing Line*, London: Penguin, 1987
  Sahib: The British Soldier in India 1750–1914, London: HarperCollins, 2005
  Tommy: The British Soldier on the Western Front, London: HarperCollins, 2004
Holt, R., *Sport and the British: A Modern History*, Oxford University Press, 1989
Holt, R., and Mason, T., *Sport in Britain 1945–2000*, Oxford: Blackwell, 2000
Holton, J., *Stan Cullis: The Iron Manager*, Derby: Breedon, 2000
Jackson, L., 'Patriotism or Pleasure? The Nineteenth Century Volunteer Force as a Vehicle for Rural Working-Class Male Sport', *Sports Historian* 19 (1999), 125–39
James, D., *Lord Roberts*, London: Hollis & Carter, 1954
James, G., *The Authorised Biography of Joe Mercer OBE*, Leicester: ACL & Polar, 1993
Johnson, B. S. (ed.), *All Bull: The National Servicemen*, London: Quartet, 1973
Kemp, Colonel J. C., *The History of the Royal Scots Fusiliers 1919–1959*, Glasgow: Robert Maclehose & Co., 1963
Kemp, P., *The British Sailor: A Social History of the Lower Deck*, London: Dent, 1970
Kentish, B., *This Foul Thing Called War*, Lewes: Book Guild, 1997
Lanfranchi, P., et al., *100 Years of Football. The FIFA Centennial Book*, London: Weidenfeld and Nicolson, 2004
Lanfranchi, P., and Taylor, M., 'Professional Football in World War Two Britain', in P. Kirkham and D. Thoms (eds.), *War Culture: Social Change and Changing Experience in World War Two Britain*, London: Lawrence and Wishart, 1995, pp. 187–97
Liddle, P. H., and Richardson, M. J., 'Voices from the Past: An Evaluation of Oral History as a Source for Research into the Western Front Experience of the British Soldier, 1914–18', *Journal of Contemporary History* 31 (1996), 651–74
Liddle, P., and Whitehouse, I., 'Not the Image but Reality: British POW Experience in Italian and German Camps', *Everybody's War: The Journal of the Second World War Experience Centre* 8 (2003), 14–25

Liddell Hart, B., *The Tanks*, vol. I, London: Cassell, 1959
Lonsdale, J., *The Army's Grace: The Life of Brigadier-General R.M. Poore*, Tunbridge Wells: Spellmount, 1992
Lorenz, K., *On Aggression*, London: Methuen, 1972 (1st edn 1963)
Lovesey, P., *The Official Centenary History of the Amateur Athletic Association*, Enfield: Guinness Superlatives, 1980
Lowerson, J., *Sport and the English Middle Classes 1870–1914*, Manchester University Press, 1993
McCarthy, T., *War Games: The Story of Sport in World War Two*, London: Macdonald, Queen Anne Press, 1989
McDevitt, P.F., *May the Best Man Win: Sport, Masculinity and Nationalism in Great Britain and the Empire 1880–1935*, New York: Palgrave Macmillan, 2004
Mackay, R., *Half the Battle: Civilian Morale in Britain during the Second World War*, Manchester University Press, 2002
McKee, C., *Sober Men and True: Sailor Lives in the Royal Navy 1900–1945*, Cambridge, Mass.: Harvard University Press, 2002
MacKenzie, J.M., *The Empire of Nature*, Manchester University Press, 1988
MacKenzie, S.P., 'British Prisoners of War in Nazi Germany', *Archives*, 28 (2003), 183–7
 The Colditz Myth: British and Commonwealth Prisoners of War in Nazi Germany, Oxford University Press, 2004
 'The Treatment of Prisoners of War in World War Two', *Journal of Modern History* 66 (1994), 487–520
McKinstry, L., *Sir Alf: A Major Reappraisal of the Life and Times of England's Greatest Football Manager*, London: HarperSport, 2006
McLaren, J., *The History of Army Rugby*, Aldershot: Army Rugby Union, 1986
Macpherson, D., *The Suffragette's Daughter: Betty Archdale*, Dural Delivery Centre, NSW: Rosenberg, 2002
McVay, D., and Smith, A., *The Complete Centre Forward: The Authorised Biography of Tommy Lawton*, Worcester: Sports Books, 2000
Mace, J., *The History of the Royal Air Force Rugby 1919–1999*, Oxon: RAF Rugby Union, 2000
Magnus, P., *Kitchener: Portrait of an Imperialist*, London: John Murray, 1958
Majumdar, B., 'From Recreation to Competition: Early History of Indian Football', *Soccer and Society* 6, 2005
Mangan, J.A., *Athleticism in the Victorian and Edwardian Public School*, Cambridge University Press, 1981
Mangan, J.A., and McKenzie, C., '"Pig Sticking is the Greatest Fun". Military Conditioning on the "Hunting Fields" of Empire', in J.A. Mangan (ed.), *Militarism, Sport, Europe*, London: Frank Cass, 2003
Mansfield, N., 'Foxhunting and the Yeomanry: County Identity and Military Culture', in R.W. Hoyle (ed.), *Our Hunting Fathers: Field Sports in England after 1850*, Lancaster: Carnegie, 2007
Mason, T., *Association Football and English Society 1863–1915*, Brighton: Harvester, 1980
 'Football on the Maidan: Cultural Imperialism in Calcutta', *International Journal of the History of Sport* 7 (1990), 85–96.

Mason, T. (ed.), *Sport in Britain. A Social History*, Cambridge University Press, 1989

Mason, U.S., *The Wrens 1917–77: A History of the Women's Royal Naval Service*, Reading: Educational Explorers, 1977

Miles, W., *The Life of a Regiment, vol. V: The Gordon Highlanders 1919–1945*, Aberdeen University Press, 1961

Moore, B., and Fedorowich, K. (eds.), *Prisoners of War and Their Captors in World War II*, Oxford: Berg, 1996

Murray, W., 'Armored Warfare: the British, French and German Experiences', in W. Murray and A.R. Millett (eds.), *Military Innovation in the Interwar Period*, Cambridge University Press, 1996

Nannestad, I., 'British Services Football in India 1944 to 1946', *Soccer History* 15 (2007), 3–9

Navias, M.S., 'Terminating Conscription? The British National Service Controversy 1955–56', *Journal of Contemporary History* 24 (1989), 195–208

Noakes, L., *Women in the British Army: War and the Gentle Sex, 1907–1948*, London: Routledge, 2006

O'Connor, T., *The Four Minute Mile: The Derek Ibbotson Story*, London: Stanley Paul, 1960

Oldfield, E.A.L., *History of the Army Physical Training Corps*, Aldershot: Gale and Polden, 1955

Osborne, J.M., 'Sports, Soldiers and the Great War', *Proceedings of the Eighth Annual Meeting of the British Society of Sports History* (1991), 17–34

Otley, C.B., 'The Social Origins of British Army Officers', *Sociological Review* 18 (1970), 213–39

Parker, P., *The Old Lie: The Great War and the Public School Ethos*, London: Constable, 1987

Phillips, B., 'Is Sergeant Jack Hart Britain's Unrecognised Sprinting Star?', *Track Stats* 39 (2001), 25–31

Phillips, G., 'Douglas Haig and the Development of Twentieth-Century Cavalry', *Archives* 28 (2003), 142–62

Phillips, M.G., 'Sport, War and Gender Images: The Australian Sportsmen's Battalions and the First World War', *International Journal of the History of Sport* 14 (1997), 78–96

Polley, M., '"No Business of Ours"? The Foreign Office and the Olympic Games, 1896–1914', *International Journal of the History of Sport*, 13 (1996), 96–113

Pope, S.W., 'An Army of Athletes: Playing Fields, Battlefields, and the American Military Sporting Experience, 1890–1920', *Journal of Military History* 59 (1995), 435–56

Porter, D., 'Revenge of the Crouch End Vampires: The AFA, the FA and English Football's "Great Split" 1907–14', *Sport in History*, 26 (2006), 406–28

Procida, M.A., 'Good Sports and Right Sorts: Guns, Gender, and Imperialism in British India', *Journal of British Studies* 40 (2001), 454–88

Purcell, T., and Gething, M., *Wartime Wanderers: Bolton Wanderers – A Football Team at War*, Edinburgh: Mainstream, 2001

Rasor, E. L., *Reform in the Royal Navy: A Social History of the Lower Deck 1850–1880*, Hamden, Conn.: Archon Books, 1976

Raugh, H. E., 'Training Ground for a Future Field Marshal: Wavell in the Boer War and Edwardian India, 1901–1908', *Journal of the Society for Army Historical Research* 72 (1994), 8–18

Razzell, P. E., 'Social Origins of Officers in the Indian and British Home Army: 1758–1962', *British Journal of Sociology* 14 (1963), 248–60

Reader, W. J., *'At Duty's Call': A Study in Obsolete Patriotism*, Manchester University Press, 1988

Riedi, E., 'Brains or Polo? Equestrian Sport, Army Reform and the Gentlemanly Officer Tradition, 1900–1914', *Journal of the Society for Army Historical Research*, 84 (2006), 236–53

Riedi, E., and Mason, T., '"Leather" and the Fighting Spirit: Sport in the British Army in World War I', *Canadian Journal of History* 41 (2006), 485–516

Rippon, A., *Gas Masks for Goal Posts: Football in Britain during the Second World War*, Stroud: Sutton, 2005

Risoli, M., *John Charles: Gentle Giant*, Edinburgh: Mainstream, 2003

Roberts, J., '"The Best Football Team, The Best Platoon": The Role of Football in the Proletarianization of the British Expeditionary Force, 1914–18', *Sport in History* 26 (2006), 26–46

Rollin, J., *Soccer at War 1939–45*, London: Collins, 1985

Royle, T., *The Best Years of Their Lives: The National Service Experience 1945–63*, London: Coronet, 1988

Ruck, R. M., 'R.E. Football in the Early Seventies', *Royal Engineers Journal* n.s. 42 (1928)

Salmon, C., 'Maclagan, Myrtle Ethel (1911–1993)', *Oxford Dictionary of National Biography*, Oxford: Oxford University Press, 2004

Sandrock, M., *Running with the Legends*, Leeds: Human Kinetics, 1996

Sheffield, G., *Leadership in the Trenches*, Basingstoke: Macmillan, 2000

Sheffield, G., and Todman, D. (eds.), *Command and Control on the Western Front: The British Army's Experience 1914–18*, Staplehurst: Spellmount, 2004

Shepperd, A., *Sandhurst: The Royal Military Academy Sandhurst and Its Predecessors*, London: Country Life Books, 1980

Shipley, S., *Bombardier Billy Wells: The Life and Times of a Boxing Hero*, Whitley Bay: Bewick Press, 1993

Showalter, D. E., 'Army and Society in Imperial Germany: The Pains of Modernization', *Journal of Contemporary History* 18 (1983), 583–61

Sinha, M., *Colonial Masculinity: The 'Manly Englishman' and the 'Effeminate Bengali' in the Late Nineteenth Century*, Manchester University Press, 1995

Skelley, A. R., *The Victorian Army at Home: The Recruitment and Terms and Conditions of the British Regular 1859–1989*, London: Croom Helm, 1977

Smith, D., and Williams, G., *Fields of Praise. The Official History of the Welsh Rugby Union*, Cardiff: University of Wales Press, 1980

Smith, K., *Glory Gunners: The History of Royal Artillery (Portsmouth) FC*, Bognor Regis: K.S. Publications, 1999

Smyth, Brigadier Sir J., *Sandhurst: A History of the Royal Military Academy, Woolwich, the Royal Military College, Sandhurst and the Royal Military Academy Sandhurst 1741–1961*, London: Weidenfeld and Nicolson, 1961

Spiers, E., *The Army and Society 1815–1914*, London: Longman, 1980

'The British Cavalry, 1902–1914', *Journal of the Society for Army Historical Research* 57 (1979), 71–9

The Late Victorian Army 1868–1902, Manchester University Press, 1992

The Scottish Soldier and Empire, 1854–1902, Edinburgh: Edinburgh University Press, 2006

Stone, T., 'Creating a (Gendered?) Military Identity: The Women's Auxiliary Air Force in Great Britain in the Second World War', *Women's History Review* 8 (1999), 605–24

Strachan, H., *Wellington's Legacy: The Reform of the British Army 1830–54*, Manchester University Press, 1984

Taylor, M., 'Leisure and Entertainment', in P. Liddle et al. (eds), *The Great World War 1914–45 Volume 2*, London: HarperCollins, 2002

Todman, D., *The First World War: Myth and Memory*, London: Hambledon and London, 2005

Tossell, D., *Bertie Mee: Arsenal's Officer and Gentleman*, Edinburgh: Mainstream, 2005

Tranter, N., *Sport, Economy and Society in Britain 1750–1914*, Cambridge University Press, 1998

Travers, T., 'The Hidden Army: Structural Problems in the British Officer Corps, 1900–1918', *Journal of Contemporary History* 17 (1982), 523–44

How the War Was Won, London: Routledge, 1992

Vamplew, W., *Pay Up and Play the Game: Professional Sports in Britain, 1875–1914*, Cambridge University Press, 1988

Van der Merwe, F. J. G., 'Sport and games in Boer Prisoner-of-war Camps during the Anglo-Boer War, 1899–1902', *International Journal of the History of Sport* 9 (1992), 439–540

Veitch, C., 'Play Up! Play Up! And Win the War! Football, the Nation and the First World War 1914–15', *Journal of Contemporary History* 20 (1985), 363–78

Vourkoutiotis, V., 'What the Angels Saw: Red Cross and Protecting Power Visits to Anglo-American POWs, 1939–45', *Journal of Contemporary History*, 40 (2005), 689–706

Wakefield, W., *Playing to Win: Sports and the American Military 1898–1945*, Albany, N.Y.: SUNY, 1997

Walker, R. F., 'The Boer War Diaries of Lt. Col. F. C. Meyrick', *Journal of the Society for Army Historical Research* 73 (1995), 155–80

Walvin, J., *The People's Game*, Edinburgh: Mainstream, 1994

Ward, A., *Armed with a Football: A Memoir of Tim Ward, Footballer and Father*, Oxford: Crowberry, 1994

Williams, G., *The Code War*, Harefield: Yore Publications, 1994

Williams, J., *A Game for Rough Girls? A History of Women's Football in Britain*, London: Routledge, 2002

Williamson, D. G., *The British in Germany 1918–1930: The Reluctant Occupiers*, Oxford: Berg, 1991

Wilson, J. M., *Siegfried Sassoon: The Making of a War Poet*, London: Duckworth, 1998

Wolff, L., *In Flanders Fields*, London: Longmans Green, 1959

Young, N., 'A Splendid Response? Cricket and the First World War', *Imperial War Museum Review* 12 (1999), 36–47

Index

Addiscombe Military College, 5
Akers-Douglas Committee. *See* Committee on the Education and Training of Officers (1902)
Aldershot, 8, 9, 22, 25, 26, 52, 53, 151, 189, 243
Aldershot Athletic Ground, 26
Alderson, Lieutenant-Colonel E.A., 43, 68
Amateur Athletic Association, 18, 157–9, 169, 177, 188, 221
Amateur Football Association, 159–62, 176
Amateurism, 47–8, 108, 118–19, 120, 182
Ansell, Colonel Sir Mike, 131, 132
Applegarth, Willie, 101
Armfield, Jimmy, 227
Army Football Association, 21, 26, 46–7, 49, 155, 190
  relationship with FA, 155–6, 160–2
  supports football in public schools, 1919, 162
Army Gymnastic Staff. *See* Army Physical Training Corps
Army Physical Training Corps, 8, 16, 20, 25, 49, 83, 102, 111, 135, 183–5, 197, 201, 204
Army Physical Training Staff. *See* Army Physical Training Corps
Army School of Physical Training, 8, 184, 197
Army Sport Control Board, 107, 112, 113–15, 118–19, 127, 129, 182, 199, 223, 229, 261
Army Sport Control Board India, 135
Athletic News, 19, 84, 85, 93, 103, 162, 171
Athletics, 16–18, 25, 47, 84, 88, 101, 136, 137, 146, 157–9, 171, 175, 188–9, 204, 207, 220, 221, 223, 224–6, 237, 239, 246, 251, 253
  Army Athletic Meeting, 16–18, 83, 136

Baden-Powell, Lieutenant-General Sir Robert, 57, 68–9, 71–3, 90
Benfield, Lance-Corporal Tommy, 156
Big-game hunting, 54, 71, 135
Blunt, Wilfred, 55
Boer War, 32, 37, 50, 256
  and army reform, 60–6
Bonney, Sergeant Richard, 28, 166–8
Boxing, 7, 18–20, 28, 43, 47–8, 96, 108, 118, 121, 122, 126, 137, 153, 221, 228, 239
  amateurism in, 120
  Army Boxing Association, 120
  in the First World War, 87, 89–90, 91, 103–6, 108–9
  Imperial Services Boxing Association, 121, 187
  in India, 34, 136
  in the navy, 121
  in the RAF, 120, 122
  Royal Navy and Army Boxing Association, 48
  in the Second World War, 187–8, 192, 195, 197
Britannia Shield, 229
British army
  battalions
    1/7th (Robin Hood) Battalion Sherwood Foresters, 86, 94, 97
    17th (1st Football) Battalion, Middlesex Regiment, 84, 87
    2/7th (Robin Hood) Battalion Sherwood Foresters, 101
    2nd Middlesex Regiment, 179, 205–6
    4th Royal Army Ordnance Corps, 221
    5th (Territorial) Battalion Bedfordshire Regiment, 108
    5th Battalion Royal Tank Regiment, 258

283

284 Index

British army (cont.)
  6th Royal Tank Regiment, 220–1
  McCrae's Battalion (16th Royal Scots), 86
  Divisions
    1st Armoured Division, 202–3
    7th Armoured Division, 132, 203
    48th (South Midland) Division, 93–4
    51st Highland Division, 179
  Regiments and corps
    4th Hussars, 52, 53, 59, 60, 74
    10th Hussars, 57, 69, 77, 78, 259
    11th Hussars, 55, 203–4, 205, 206
    5th Royal Inniskilling Dragoon Guards, 131
    Army Service Corps (Grove Park), 85
    Black Watch, 17, 29, 35, 139, 155, 180
    Brigade of Guards, 18, 46
    Durham Light Infantry, 28, 34, 37, 46, 70, 233–6, 259
    East Surrey Regiment, 220
    East Yorkshire Regiment, 147
    Grenadier Guards, 7, 9, 52, 146, 172
    Hampshire Regiment, 25, 180
    Highland Light Infantry, 44, 110
    King's Royal Rifle Corps, 7
    Lancashire Fusiliers, 39
    Leicestershire Regiment, 19, 22, 23, 27, 34, 39, 40–1, 43, 87, 92, 100, 106, 135, 138–9, 153, 156, 174
    Northumberland Fusiliers, 34
    Queen's Own (Royal West Kent Regiment), 22
    Rifle Brigade, 28
    Royal Artillery, 112, 130, 140
    Royal Irish Fusiliers, 17, 25, 27, 130, 144, 148, 158, 170, 171
    Royal Munster Fusiliers, 25, 125
    Royal Welch Fusiliers, 32, 35, 44
    Sherwood Foresters, 33, 35, 42, 149
    Somerset Light Infantry, 149
    Welch Regiment, 23, 34, 39
    Women's Royal Army Corps, 245–51
British Expeditionary Force Sport Board, 107–8
British Olympic Association, 169, 170, 175
Brodrick, St John, 74–5
Burgess, Ron, 178, 185, 190
Busby, Matt, 185, 192

Cairns, W. E., 36, 41, 53, 67
Campbell, Lieutenant-Colonel R. B., 25, 48, 90, 102, 103, 104–6, 115, 174
Carden Roe, Brigadier W., 130
Cartwright, Tom, 222

Cavalry, 42, 61–8, 75–9, 130–3
  attempted reform of after Boer War, 75–6
  mechanisation of, 131–3
Charity matches, 151, 186–7
Charles, John, 239
Churchill, Winston, 53, 56, 59, 69, 74
Civilian–military relations, 144–77, 221, 260
Clayton, Ronnie, 226
Close, Brian, 222
Clough, Brian, 226
Colchester, 27, 149
Committee on the Education and Training of Officers (1902), 63–5
Committee on the Expenses of Officers (1903), 65–6, 75
Compton, Denis, 195
Coote, Commander B. T., 104, 115, 116, 174
Corinthians, 22, 153, 160
Couper, Colonel V. A., 25, 49, 161
Cricket, 24, 29, 31–2, 86, 122, 136, 189, 222–3, 250
Cross-country running, 25, 43, 84, 224–5, 241
Cullis, Stan, 180, 185
Curtis, Captain E. G., 15, 35, 37

De Lisle, General Sir Henry de Beauvoir, 70, 74–5
Devonport, 23, 130, 152
Douglas, Admiral Sir Archibald, 44
Douglas, Keith, 182
Douglas, Major-General C. W. H., 76, 77

Edgeworth-Johnstone, Captain Walter, 8, 18
Egypt, 55, 86, 108, 132, 182, 191, 201
Exeter, Marquis of, 175

FA Amateur Cup, 40, 147, 164–7
FA Cup, 10–12
Ferris, Sergeant Sam, 175
Finlay, Group Captain Donald, 175, 239
Finney, Tom, 186, 192
First World War, 3, 80–92, 158, 180, 181, 246, 255, 257
  boxing in, 87, 89–90, 91, 103–6, 108–9
  equestrian sport in, 78, 94, 253
  football in, 80, 84–7, 88, 92–4, 98–101, 102, 107, 110
  Physical and Bayonet Training Staff, 102–6
  rugby in, 85, 97, 100, 108
  sport at Scapa Flow, 91

Index

Fisher, Admiral Lord, 26
Football, 8–12, 15, 16, 21–3, 40, 44–7, 49, 123–4, 146–56, 159–68, 226–8, 229–30, 231–6, 237–9, 242–3, 253, 260, 263
  Army Cup, 22, 44, 46, 47, 83, 147, 152, 155, 163–6, 190, 231–6, 252
  in the First World War, 80, 84–7, 88, 92–4, 98–101, 102, 107, 110
  in India, 32, 34–5, 138
  in the navy, 29–31, 238
  in the Second World War, 180, 184–6, 189–97, 200–7
  Navy Cup, 30–1
  United Services League (Portsmouth), 27, 30, 147, 151
Football Association, 155–6, 159–62, 167–8, 183–4
Football teams
  Army Crusaders, 230, 237–8
  Bolton Wanderers, 182, 183, 185
  Mohun Bagan, 35, 138, 139, 195
  Plymouth Argyle, 151, 152, 166
  Royal Artillery (Portsmouth), 27, 163–8
  Royal Engineers, 9–12
  Royal Marine Light Infantry (Gosport), 147–8
Fowler, Roy, 226, 241
Fox, Colonel Malcolm, 18, 173
Fraser, Sergeant Major John, 33, 37, 69
French, Field Marshal Sir John, 48, 62, 76, 145
French army, 100, 108, 123–4, 191
Fuller, Major-General J.F.C., 139
Funding, 28–9, 127–30

Gambling, 7, 47, 53, 55, 94, 112, 214
German army, 43, 68, 69, 215
German navy, 43, 116
Goslin, Harry, 182, 183
Gosport, 147–8
Gough, General Sir Hubert, 55, 57, 102
Greig, Captain J.G., 24
Grenfell, Lieutenant-Commander F.H., 173

Haig, Field Marshal Sir Douglas, 62, 75, 76, 77, 86, 105, 106, 131, 169
Haldane, Lord, 77
Hammersley, Major Frederick, 8
Hampshire Football Association, 149–51
Harington, General Sir Charles, 27, 80, 94, 114, 115, 127, 169
Harrison, Eric, 253–4
Hart, Sergeant Jack, 136
Hartley, Colonel B. C., 115

Hawarden, Sergeant Andrew, 209–14
Henniker, Brigadier Sir Mark, 130, 135, 139, 141
Hewson, Brian, 225–6
Hill, Albert, 101
Hockey, 32, 34, 137, 138, 247
Horrocks, Lieutenant-General Sir Brian, 170
Humphries, Ernest, 33, 36
Hunting, 52–3, 67–8, 77–8, 79, 131, 132, 133, 142, 253
  in Egypt, 55
  in India, 54, 254

Ibbotson, Derek, 224–5
India, 7, 32–6, 37, 40, 54, 134–9, 141, 194–5, 259, 260
Indian Army, 35–6, 136–8, 140
Indian–British relations, 35–6, 71, 136–9
Inter-Allied Games, Paris (1919), 109
Inter-Theatre of War Championships (1919), 108, 109, 119
Iraq, 122, 180
Ireland, 25, 34, 40, 139, 149, 191

Jack, Brigadier-General J. L., 85
Jackson, Major V.A., 113–15
Jellicoe, Admiral Sir John, 91

Kentish, Brigadier General Reginald, 25, 26, 27, 46, 49, 107, 113, 144, 161, 170
Kentish Cup, 123–4, 229–30
Keyes, Admiral Sir Roger, 134
Kinahan, Captain C.E., 27
Kipling, Rudyard, 59
Kirke, General Sir Walter, 182
Kitchener, Field Marshal Lord, 38
Knight-Bruce, J. H. W., 18, 28, 43, 96
Korea, 242

Lansdowne, Lord, 62–3
Lascelles, Lieutenant-Colonel Anthony, 220, 259
Lawton, Tommy, 185, 190
Liddell Hart, Sir Basil, 131, 132, 142
Lloyd's Weekly News, 172–3
Lonsdale, Steve, 201
Lorenz, Konrad, 255

Malta, 7, 26, 116, 130, 177
Marindin, Major Francis, 10, 22
Marling, Percival, 52
Martel, General Sir Giffard Le Quesne, 48, 121–2
Masculinity, 72–3, 90, 121, 256

Mass Observation, 199–200
Mays, Spike, 136, 139
McCalmont, Major R., 160–2
McLaren, Bill, 216
Media interest in military sport, 171–3, 229–30
Mercer, Joe, 184, 185
Merriman, Captain William, 10
Military sport
  benefits of, 17, 67–70, 91, 140
    esprit de corps, 39–40, 49, 68, 98–9, 179–80, 257–8
    health and fitness, 17, 33, 37–8, 41–2, 89, 255
    morale, 40–1, 91–6, 115, 182, 186, 199, 258–9
    training for war, 42–3, 67–8, 77, 89–90
  criticism of, 43–4, 60–6, 76, 139, 140–3
  official attitudes to, 38, 48, 102, 107, 110, 114, 145, 169, 263
  problems with, 44–7, 182, 220–1, 260–1
    discipline, 44, 46–7, 260–1
    favouritism, 45–6, 101, 136, 140, 184–6, 222, 261
    professionalism, 167–8, 262
Miller, Lieutenant-Colonel E.D., 68, 69
Mills, Freddie, 187, 195
Milocarian Athletic Club, 237
Modern pentathlon, 169
Money prizes, 18, 19, 20, 47, 104–6, 113, 114, 119, 121, 157–9, 187
Montgomery, Field Marshal Bernard, 194, 207

National service, 217–45
National Sporting Club, 7, 19, 153
Navy and Army Illustrated, 29, 38, 171–2
Neame, Lieutenant-General Sir Philip, 135
Nightingale, Florence, 33
Non-commissioned officers, 27

O'Conor, Captain Rory, 117
Officer–men relations, 18, 41, 44–5, 96–8, 115, 136
Officers, 26–7, 50–79, 139, 256
  education, 63–5, 140–3
  recruitment, 51–2, 259
  selection, 6, 96, 142, 179
Olympic Games, 13, 17, 136, 158, 168–70, 174, 175, 237, 240, 242, 243, 251, 253, 260
Orwell, George, 254
Otway, Charles, 83–4

Participation rates, 19, 29, 41, 250

Pawson, Tony, 179
Physical training, 41–2, 102–4, 111, 115, 127
  in schools, 173
Pickford, William, 30, 144, 149, 150, 166
Pig-sticking, 56–7, 67–73, 78, 134
  Kadir Cup, 56–7
Pirie, Gordon, 225
Poland, 194
Polo, 50, 57–78, 130–1, 132, 139, 259
  criticism of by army reformers, 60–6, 76
  fatalities, 73
  in India, 58–60, 134–5
  in the navy, 134
  in the RAF, 133–4
Poore, Major Robert, 24, 32
Portsmouth, 27, 30, 147–8, 149, 163–8
Prince, Lieutenant-Colonel Herbert, 175
Prisoners of war, 207–14
Purchase of discharge, 154–6

Racing, 53–4, 94
  in India, 55–6
Recruiting, 1, 6, 15, 38–9, 84, 125, 177, 183, 230, 249, 259–60
Red Cross, 187, 208, 210, 213, 214
Richards, Frank, 32, 41
Roberts, Engineer Commander E.W., 31, 128
Roberts, Field Marshal Lord, 60–2, 74–6, 77
Rous, Sir Stanley, 183, 186, 193, 207
Rowing, 241–2
Royal Air Force, 91, 117–18, 128–9, 130, 184, 187, 189, 198, 221, 223–5, 241–2
  athletics in, 175
  boxing in, 118, 120, 122
  equestrian sport in, 133–4
  football in, 185, 190–1, 193
  rugby in, 118, 122, 153, 186
  Uxbridge stadium, 118
  Women's Royal Air Force, 246–51
Royal Air Force College, Cranwell, 133, 148, 162, 225
Royal Air Force Sports Board, 117, 130, 159
Royal Commission on the Sanitary State of the Army in India (1863), 33
Royal Flying Corps, 48, 101
Royal Military Academy, Woolwich, 5–6, 130, 142, 253

Index

Royal Military College, Sandhurst, 5–6, 60, 142–3
Royal Naval Engineering College, Keyham, 31
Royal Navy, 2, 6, 15–16, 29–31, 41, 91, 115–17, 127–8, 130, 134, 171, 197, 260
  boxing in, 121
  football in, 29–31, 238
  Mediterranean Fleet, 26, 29–30, 116, 176
  Naval School of Physical Training, 104, 115
  Physical Training and Sports Branch, 127–8
  rugby in, 31, 130
  sport at sea, 29
  Women's Royal Naval Service, 246–8, 250–1
Royal Navy Football Association, 30, 150, 153
Royal Navy Physical Training Branch, 41
Royal Navy Sports Control Board, 116, 128, 130
Royds, Admiral Sir Percy, 48
Rugby Football Union, 23, 85, 153, 239
Rugby league, 23, 85, 187, 239
Rugby union, 24, 121–2, 124, 143, 153, 162, 176, 239, 253
  and the Territorial Army, 183
  Army Cup, 23, 39, 40, 122
  Army Rugby Union, 23
  Imperial Inter-Services Tournament (1919), 108, 253
  in the First World War, 85, 97, 100, 108
  in India, 28, 34, 40
  in the navy, 31, 130
  in the RAF, 118, 122, 153, 186
  in the Second World War, 182, 186–7, 205, 207, 216

Scapa Flow, 91
School of Military Engineering, Chatham, 10–12
Second World War, 178–216, 257, 258
  athletics in, 188–9
  boxing in, 187–8
  cricket in, 189
  football in, 180, 184–6, 189–97, 200–7
  participatory sport in, 196–207, 215–16
  prisoner of war camps, 207–14
  professional footballers in, 183–6, 191–5
  rugby in, 186–7
  spectacular sport (Home Front), 186–91, 214–15

  sport against German teams (1945–6), 207
  theatres of war
    Far East, 194–5
    Italy, 180, 185, 186, 191–2, 196, 198, 204
    North Africa, 180, 182, 186, 191, 196, 198, 200–4
    North-west Europe, 194, 204–7
  touring teams, 191–5
  troopships, sport on, 197
Shell shock, 180
Ships
  HMS *Anson*, 30
  HMS *Ark Royal*, 180
  HMS *Empress of India*, 29
  HMS *Hood*, 117
  HMS *Penelope*, 116–17
  HMT *Mooltan*, 197
Show-jumping, 131, 169
Simpson, Captain William, 44, 46
Sleeman, Lieutenant-Colonel John, 258
Smith-Dorrien, General Sir Horace, 26, 44, 55
South Africa, 31–2, 37, 54, 122
Southern League, 165–8
Sport and war, 3–4, 43, 254–7
Sporting Life, 83, 84, 171
Sports grounds, facilities and equipment, 6, 8, 26, 27, 129–30, 152, 197–8, 205, 223
Sportsmanship, 46–7, 107, 119–20
Squash, 130, 177
Stalag 383, 209–14
Stanley Committee. *See* Committee on the Expenses of Officers (1903)
Starr, Frank, 19, 38, 48, 83, 84, 98, 103, 106, 107, 109, 120
Strachey, R.J., 38, 145
Sydenham, John, 227

Tanks Central Schools, Bovington, 113
Temple Clarke, Captain A., 87
Tennis, 137, 140, 177, 200, 201, 204, 247
Territorial Army, 39, 125–7, 182–3, 230
Territorial Army Sport Board, 125–7, 183
The Field, 17, 57, 80, 88, 167, 171
Thorne, Tony, 217, 220
Trenchard, Air Marshal Lord, 118
Tripoli, 198
Trueman, Fred, 222
Tug of war, 228–9

Index

United States Army, 3, 90, 109, 257

Vaughan, Major General John, 77, 91, 259

Wakefield, W.W., 109, 118, 153
Wallis, Lieutenant Colonel Clive, 220
Wand-Tetley, Brigadier T.H., 158, 192, 204
Ward, Arthur, 196, 200, 202–3, 204
Ward, Sir Edward, 38, 145
Ward, Tim, 190
Wardrop, Major A.E., 56–7, 71–3
Wellington, Duke of, 13
Wells, 'Bombardier' Billy, 20, 34, 103
Williams, Bleddyn, 182
Williamson, Audrey, 251
Wilson, Lieutenant General Sir James, 230, 263
Wilson, Lieutenant W.C., 23, 153
Windrum, Sergeant Major Frederick, 28, 166–8
Winterbottom, Sir Walter, 184, 230
Wolfenden Committee, 223, 229
Wolseley, Field Marshal Lord, 18, 62, 63
Women's services, 245–51
Wood, Field Marshal Sir Evelyn, 18, 52, 62, 63, 66
Wooderson, Sydney, 188
Wynyard, Captain Edward, 24